Anne Clifford's autobiographical writing, 1590–1676

Anne Clifford's autobiographical writing, 1590–1676

❧

EDITED AND ANNOTATED BY

Jessica L. Malay

Manchester University Press

Selection and editorial copyright © Manchester University Press 2018
All other matter © as acknowledged

The right of Jessica L. Malay to be identified as the editor of this work has been asserted by her in accordance with the Copyright, Designs and Patents Act 1988.

Published by Manchester University Press
Altrincham Street, Manchester M1 7JA

www.manchesteruniversitypress.co.uk

British Library Cataloguing-in-Publication Data
A catalogue record for this book is available from the British Library

ISBN 978 1 5261 1787 8 hardback
ISBN 978 1 5261 1788 5 paperback

First published 2018

The publisher has no responsibility for the persistence or accuracy of URLs for any external or third-party internet websites referred to in this book, and does not guarantee that any content on such websites is, or will remain, accurate or appropriate.

Typeset in Minion Pro by
by Servis Filmsetting Ltd, Stockport, Cheshire
Printed in Great Britain
by CPI Group (UK) Ltd, Croydon CR0 4YY

Dedicated to

David A. McNulty

CONTENTS

List of Illustrations	*page* viii
Acknowledgements	ix
List of Abbreviations	x
Introduction	1
The Lady Anne Clifford's Memoir, 1603	15
Countess of Dorset's Diary, 1616, 1617 and 1619	26
The Life of Me the Lady Anne Clifford, 1589–1649	95
The Lady of the North, Yearly Memoirs, 1650–1675	117
Countess of Pembroke's Daybook, 1676	226
Appendix: Genealogical Table	265
Glossary of Persons	268
Bibliography	301
Index	307

ILLUSTRATIONS

1 Page from Anne Clifford's Daybook of 1676, private collection — *page* 13
2 Margaret Russell, by unknown artist (1585) © National Portrait Gallery, London — 16
3 Anne Clifford, by William Larkin (1618) © National Portrait Gallery, London — 73
4 Anne Clifford, Countess of Pembroke, by John Bracken (1670), from *The Great Picture Triptych* (1646), attributed to Jan van Belcamp, © Abbot Hall Gallery, Kendal — 118
5 Skipton Castle, by Thomas D. Whitaker (1878) from *The History and Antiquities of the Deanery of Craven in the County of York*, editor's collection — 120
6 Appleby Castle, from Samuel and Nathanial Buck, *A Collection of Engravings of Castles, and Abbeys in England* (1726–1739), editor's collection — 122
7 Brougham Castle, from Samuel and Nathanial Buck, *A Collection of Engravings of Castles, and Abbeys in England* (1726–1739), editor's collection — 125
8 Brough Castle, from Samuel and Nathanial Buck, *A Collection of Engravings of Castles, and Abbeys in England* (1726–1739), editor's collection. — 153
9 Pendragon Castle, from Samuel and Nathanial Buck, *A Collection of Engravings of Castles, and Abbeys in England* (1726–1739), editor's collection. — 161
10 The Countess Pillar, Brougham, Westmorland (now Cumbria), photograph by editor — 210
11 Anne Clifford's Monument, St Lawrence's church, Appleby, Westmorland (now Cumbria), photograph by editor — 264

ACKNOWLEDGEMENTS

Many of the discoveries and much of the research for this edition emerged from work on Anne Clifford's *Great Books of Record* and therefore thanks need to go to the Leverhulme Trust for their generous support of the Great Books Project. The Modern Humanities Research Association funded a Research Associate to aid in the completion of this project. Dr Mary Chadwick came on board through this funding. She was tireless in transcribing accounts and letters which brought to light additional information that has been used in the notes of this edition. She also assisted in proofreading stages. She was a cheerful companion throughout this work and was happy to talk about all things Anne Clifford when everyone else had heard quite enough.

My colleagues at the University of Huddersfield have been supportive throughout this journey. The university has provided much additional financial support to bring this project to completion. I also received much encouragement from my colleagues around the world, whose work has so much enhanced our knowledge of early modern women writers and their lives.

The staff at archives throughout the UK have been particularly supportive. They have constantly facilitated access to their collections in a helpful and friendly manner. Most especially I appreciated the welcome and assistance of the staff at the Cumbria Archives in Kendal and Carlisle. I would like to thank Chatsworth House, Longleat House, Dalemain House and Skipton Castle for permission to access their private collections. And most especially I would like to thank the Right Hon. Lord Hothfield for allowing generous access to the Hothfield collection. Much of what we know about Anne Clifford comes from this carefully preserved collection.

Finally, I would like to thank David McNulty, who has listened patiently to hours of conversation about Anne Clifford and accompanied me on many a journey to 'Anne Clifford' country.

ABBREVIATIONS

BL   British Library, London, UK
CAS   Cumbria Archives Service, various locations in UK.
H1   WDHOTH/10, Great Books of Record (Skipton Castle set),
H2   WDHOTH/10, Great Books of Record (Hothfield set)
KHLC   Kent History and Library Centre, Maidstone, UK
LJC   *Letters of John Chamberlain*, ed. Norman Egbert McClure (1939)
NA   National Archives, Kew, UK
NAS   Northamptonshire Archive Service, Northampton, UK
NPJ   Nichols, *Progress of James I*, ed. John Nichols (1828)
WD   WDCAT/16, Great Books of Record
YAS   Yorkshire Archaeological Society, University of Leeds, Special Collections, Leeds.

Introduction

The Lady Anne Clifford was Countess of Pembroke, Dorset and Montgomery by marriage,[1] and by birth Baroness Clifford, Westmorland, and Vesey, Lady of the Honour of Skipton in Craven and the High Sheriffess of Westmorland. She was a descendant of the ancient Clifford family founded in the twelfth century by Margaret de Toeni, heiress of Clifford Castle in Herefordshire. Her mother, Margaret Russell, was a member of the powerful Russell family, Earls of Bedford, which included Anne Russell, Countess of Warwick, gentlewoman of Elizabeth I's privy chamber and one of the Queen's closest intimates. Her father was George, 3rd Earl of Cumberland, renowned for his daring sea voyages and as champion to Queen Elizabeth. He was later a member of James I's privy council. Anne began her life with the expectation that she would live the typical and prescribed life of a seventeenth-century aristocratic woman – marrying into an important family and working behind the scenes to advance the interests of that family (and her own). Instead with the death of her brother Robert in 1591, the one-year-old Anne became sole heir of the vast Clifford hereditary estates in Westmorland and north-west Yorkshire. However, her status as heir was soon compromised by her father, who began legal manoeuvres to place his own brother Francis as heir.[2] This and George Clifford's infidelities led to great strains in his marriage to Margaret Russell, which Anne describes in detail in the 1603 Memoir. In this early part of Anne's life she lived as a fledgling courtier, often sleeping near Queen Elizabeth in her aunt Anne Russell's chamber. From this vantage point she witnessed the exercise of political power that would inform her own practices and decisions later in life.

George Clifford died in 1605 and by his will left the Clifford hereditary estates of the North[3] to his brother Francis Clifford, 4th Earl of Cumberland, with the stipulation that, should his brother leave no direct male heirs, his daughter

---

1 She married first Richard Sackville, 3rd Earl of Dorset, in 1609; and second Philip Herbert, 1st Earl of Montgomery and 4th Earl of Pembroke, in 1630.
2 Anne Clifford, *Great Books of Record*, ed. Jessica L. Malay (2015), pp. 660–668.
3 These included much of Westmorland, including the castles of Brougham, Brough, Pendragon and Appleby, as well as the manor and castle of Skipton and other properties in the region of Craven, in North Yorkshire.

Anne would inherit these estates.[4] He pleaded with his wife Margaret and to Anne to accept his will, writing in his last letter to her: 'I beg of thee thou wilt take as I have meant in kindness the course I have set down for disposing of my estate'.[5] Anne was to receive £15,000 upon her marriage according to the will, but only on the condition that the will was not contested. Anne's mother, Margaret, was scornful of this settlement, complaining that it was 'a portion that many merchant's daughters have had' and telling Anne that 'your ancient inheritance from your forefathers from a long descent of ancestors is richly worth a hundred thousand pounds'.[6] Margaret Russell refused to accept the will and this ignited an inheritance dispute that would last for decades, with repercussions that rumbled on for over a century.

Anne's mother led the battle to regain her daughter's inheritance in the early years of the lawsuit. She designed the legal and political strategies that achieved early success.[7] Margaret Russell was able to secure documentary evidence that proved the Clifford hereditary lands continued under a Crown entail because they had been given to the Cliffords by the Crown through a letter patent.[8] This meant the land returned to the Crown should the direct heirs (the male or female children of the holder of the land) die. Having proved the Crown interest in the Clifford hereditary lands, Margaret was incredulous that James I did not side with Anne in this case. She wrote to Edward Bruce, Lord Kinloss, that 'Baronies, Honours, Dignities of Office I have found and laid at his Majesty's feet'.[9] This may be why after considering a number of possible marriages for Anne, she finally settled on Richard Sackville, 3rd Earl of Dorset. There was a long-standing affection between the two, and by 1609 Richard was a favourite of Prince Henry. Margaret hoped that the prince would use his influence with his father to allow the Clifford hereditary lands to descend to Anne, which would have left the Crown entail intact.[10] Unfortunately Prince Henry died in 1612 and the court case between Anne and her uncle Francis continued for another five years until the King's Award settled the matter in 1617.

---

4 NA, PROB/11/108, 'Will of George Clifford' written 1605, proved 1606.
5 CAS Kendal, HOTH Box 44, 'letter from George Clifford to Margaret Russell, the "Last Letter"', October 1605.
6 Portland MS 23, Letter, 1615, p. 77; Letter, 1615, p. 69.
7 Richard Spence, *The Lady Anne Clifford* (1997), pp. 48–56. *Great Books*, ed. Malay, pp. 739–758.
8 See *Great Books*, ed. Malay, pp. 697–706.
9 Portland MS 23, Letter, 1606, p. 40. James I seemed completely uninterested in maintaining this entail and in 1608 attempted to gift the Clifford hereditary lands in Westmorland and Skipton in Yorkshire to Francis Clifford. See *Great Books*, ed. Malay, pp. 734–738.
10 See Malay, 'The Marrying of Anne Clifford: Marriage Strategy in the Clifford Inheritance Dispute', *Northern History* 159.2 (2012), pp. 251–264.

During this early period of her life Anne entered into the Court life of Queen Anne of Denmark and her daughter the princess Elizabeth, and maintained a large circle of aristocratic friends and acquaintances. She attended plays and danced in masques designed by Inigo Jones and written by Ben Jonson, Samuel Daniel (her early tutor) and others. She became the mistress of Knole House (Kent) and Little Dorset House (London). She was a patron of writers and scholars, and she herself became a scholar and writer. And yet, all of her activities as wife, courtier, aristocrat, scholar and writer were dominated by her efforts to secure the Clifford hereditary lands. The death of her mother in 1616 was the final blow to these efforts and led to the King's Award of 1617, which awarded Anne's uncle Francis the Clifford hereditary estates. This is the subject of many of her entries in her diary of 1616, 1617 and 1619. Despite this setback, Anne continued to believe she would inherit these lands eventually. The King's Award followed George Clifford's will for the most part. It awarded Richard Sackville £20,000 as Anne's marriage portion.[11] It also placed Anne and her children (male or female) as heir to the Clifford hereditary lands should Francis's direct line of male heirs fail. In 1617, Anne's cousin Henry (son of Francis and later 5th Earl of Cumberland) had no living male children and so there was a reasonable possibility that Anne could inherit her father's estates, and she clung to this possibility.

After the death of her husband Richard in 1624 Anne, now the mother of Margaret and Isabella (her three sons having died in infancy), sought to secure her position as the likely heir of the Clifford hereditary lands. Her cousin Henry's last son, Henry, died as an infant in 1622 and it looked at this point incredibly unlikely that her cousin would have a male heir.[12] Still, Anne was concerned that Henry would somehow manage to circumvent the King's Award, and this, along with problems Anne was experiencing with her brother-in-law Edward, 4th Earl of Dorset, over her jointure and her daughters' inheritance, led to her marriage to Philip Herbert, Earl of Pembroke and Montgomery. This marriage was not particularly happy, but it served its purpose, with Philip always supporting

---

11 The tenants of Westmorland also paid a heavy price for this award as James allowed Francis to raise rents and fees above their customary levels in order to pay Richard the £20,000. A number of tenants fell into poverty, some were imprisoned when they could not pay and some died because of the privation caused by the King's Award. This is one of the reasons they were so resistant to Anne Clifford's attempts to reinstate her rights as landlord in Westmorland after 1643 as discussed in the 'Yearly Memoirs: 1650–1675' below. See John Breay, *Light in the Dales*, vols 2 and 3 (1996), pp. 117–126.
12 Henry Clifford's last child, a daughter, Frances, was born in 1626 but did not live into adulthood. This left Henry with only one daughter, Elizabeth, later Countess of Cork, as his heir. Spence, *Lady Anne Clifford*, p. 80.

Anne in matters pertaining to the Clifford hereditary lands. In 1643, at the age of fifty-three, after the death of her cousin Henry, Anne Clifford inherited these lands in the North after decades of legal battles, political manoeuvring and personal grief as told in great detail in the autobiographies[13] that follow. Because of the civil wars of the 1640s she was not able to travel to her lands immediately, but in 1649 she finally arrived in the North and quickly began a rebuilding and restructuring campaign that is still visible in the landscape today.

Anne Clifford lived during the reigns of four monarchs and two heads of state in her long life of eighty-six years. She experienced exile and isolation as well as great political power. She is best known to us as the writer of a number of autobiographies in different forms and styles that cover most periods of her life. These originally circulated in manuscript, but print extracts began to appear in the eighteenth century. For the modern reader it was Vita Sackville-West's 1923 edition of the 1603 memoir and 1616, 1617 and 1619 diary that brought Anne Clifford to the attention of a modern audience. Her autobiographies provide a vivid picture of her life as moves between moments of domestic joy, conflict, contentment and misery to the great political events of her time. She describes the death of kings and queens, civil wars, the Great Plague and the Great Fire of London. Through her writing we are shown the inner workings of great houses, great estates and great people, and we also get a glimpse of those individuals who lived more modest lives. We experience Anne's triumphs and also those moments of despair, when she sought solace in her religious faith. Anne Clifford was an avid autobiographical writer who believed it was important to record and reconsider (daily) the events, actions and people that added up to a life. And though only a small fraction of her autobiographical writing remains, as discussed below, the texts we have provide a rich view of the culture of early modern England and the life of this remarkable woman.

The title of this edition, *Anne Clifford's autobiographical writing, 1590–1676*, is intended to challenge twentieth-century assumptions about autobiography that have relied too heavily on Philippe Lejeune's 1973 definition of 'autobiography' as 'a retrospective prose narrative produced by a real person concerning his own existence, focusing on his individual life, in particular on the development

---

13 I use this as a collective term for the life-writing texts included in this edition. My intention here is to challenge Philippe Lejeune's 1973 definition of autobiography as a strictly crafted narrative of a person's life. Instead through the use of the plural I suggest that Anne Clifford wrote a number of narratives about her life, each with a particular purpose and a style designed for that purpose. Together these narrative come together to reveal Anne's own story from a variety of perspectives. For a detailed discussion of scholarship in early modern autobiography relevant to this edition, see below.

of his personality'.[14] This approach privileged a strictly crafted narrative form that has been anachronistically applied to the early modern individual, generally male, resulting in the undervaluing, or indeed the inability to recognize, the autobiographical that exists in many types of texts from the period.[15] Instead Felicity Nussbaum suggests that we should avoid too much reliance on previous scholarship that privileged the 'humanist tendency to model discourse [of the self] as cogent, univocal, gathered and controlled'.[16] This approach has opened up possibilities for recognizing the creativity present in the way in which early modern individuals like Anne Clifford described their lives. Meredith Anne Skura believes that a fruitful engagement with autobiographical material of the period can come from a consideration of 'how and why people talked about themselves before "the modern autobiography" or "self" was culturally encoded', noting that 'a writer's way of telling a story can be at least as revealing as direct statements about herself'.[17] Philippa Kelly and Ronald Bedford agree, insisting that self-representation in early modern England sought to 'creatively construct the meaning of a life' that was motivated by the 'evaluation' or 'sum' of one's actions.[18] Adam Smyth suggests that early modern discourse of self-representation constructed a sense of self through 'a process of identifying, even overlapping with other figures, narratives and events, and by looking out into the world, rather than within'.[19] Anne Clifford's autobiographies are generally, but not always, coherent. They can be fragmentary. They can be so finely focused as to identify the hair on her head and the fingernails of her hand,

---

14 Philippe Lejeune, *On Autobiography*, trans. Katherine Leary (orig. 1973; 1989). See also Meredith Anne Skura, *Tudor Autobiography: Listening for Inwardness* (2008), p. 2. Earlier, in 1969, Peter Delaney suggested that the way forward in approaching early modern autobiography was to 'frame a definition [of autobiography] which excludes the bulk of random or incidental self-revelation scattered through seventeenth-century literature' and prioritizes texts that were '*primarily* written to give a coherent account of the author's life'. Delaney, *British Autobiography in the Seventeenth Century* (1969), p. 1

15 Elizabeth Jane Bellamy, 'Afterward: Intention Redux: Early Modern Life Writing and Its Discontents'. *Textual Practice* 23.2 (2009), 307–309. See also essays by Molly Murray, Kathleen Lynch, Suzanne Trill and Adam Smyth in *A History of English Autobiography*, ed., Adam Smyth (2016), pp. 41–100.

16 Felicity Nussbaum, *The Autobiographical Subject: Gender and Ideology in Eighteenth Century England* (1989), p. 22. See also Ronald Bedford and Philippa Kelly, *Early Modern English Lives: Autobiography and Self-Representation 1500–1660* (2007), pp. 1–9.

17 Skura, pp. 3, 8.

18 Bedford and Kelly, p. 2.

19 Adam Smyth, *Autobiography in Early Modern England* (2010), p. 11. Kevin Sharpe and Steven N. Zwicker also invite scholars of early modern self-representation to eschew inherited models of autobiography that privileged 'coherence and explanation' in *Writing Lives: Biography and Textuality, Identity and Representations in Early Modern England* (2008), p. 25.

while at other times Anne collapses years into a few sentences. There is often a repetition which creates a cadence marking the reader's movement through a text. Her texts at times ignore a strict chronology, as she takes her reader from her chamber in Brougham, to a walk through Hardwick Hall decades earlier. More than 1100 people appear in her autobiographies – from the young Arthur Swindin, once her fisher boy, to the princes and princesses of Europe, and all manner of local folk. There is no easy way to characterize these fragments of a life knitted together in a variety of ways, in different autobiographical forms, as she recorded her experience of her life. And while this book claims to be the first complete edition of Anne Clifford's autobiographical writing, many other texts she produced also have a claim to being autobiographical, including her account books, her books of heraldry, her carefully preserved collection of letters and her *Great Books of Record*.[20]

Anne Clifford's surviving autobiographical writing reveals her deep commitment to maintaining a record or account of her life. In this she was not unlike many early modern men and women who saw their existence as not simply a walk across a stage, with its entrance and exits, but as a life imbedded within a rich community of the past that was also leading into an unknowable future existence. The autobiographical texts early modern writers produced reveal the ways in which they attempted to understand their lives in this larger context, charged by both religious expectations and their worldly hopes for their descendants.

The Texts

The 1603 memoir and the 1616, 1617 and 1619 diary[21] almost always appear together in the surviving manuscripts. The use of the term memoir and diary in reference to these two texts follows the practice of scholars and previous editors, and these are useful and appropriate terms. Joseph Brooker describes a memoir as 'a piece of writing about oneself which evades the demands of comprehensiveness: giving itself licence, for instance, to focus on certain chosen periods while leaving others undiscussed' and sheds 'light not only on the writer, but

---

20   This edition makes some use of these texts, and includes information in the notes that more fully develops subject matter mentioned in the diaries.
21   There is no room here to enter into a lengthy discussion of the wider definition of these two terms. The use of the word memoir is appropriate to the narrative structure here which is temporally sequential, but does not record the minutiae of daily life. The use of the term diary in relation to the autobiography of the years 1616, 1617, 1619 is appropriate given the labelled day-by-day recording of events that is reproduced in this autobiography.

on his or her surroundings, or on some specific aspect of one's life'.[22] This is the case in the 1603 memoir where Anne focuses on the events surrounding the death of Queen Elizabeth and the early months of King James's reign. The term 'diary' in relation to the autobiography of the years 1616, 1617 and 1619 generally fits given the labelled day-by-day recording of events that is reproduced in this text.

This memoir and the diary have the most complex textual history of Anne Clifford's autobiographical writing. The earliest reference to these in print is in Thomas Pennant's *A Tour in Scotland and Voyage to the Hebrides, 1772* (1776). William Seward's *Anecdotes of Some Distinguished Persons* (1795) includes an extract from the memoir of 1603. Several manuscript copies containing extracts from the memoir and diary were also circulating in the late eighteenth century.[23] Margaret Cavendish Bentinck, Duchess of Portland (1715–1785), produced the earliest and most complete transcription of the memoir and diary we possess to date. Her manuscript copy was produced some time between 1770 and 1780.[24] The source for her copy was the original manuscript produced by Anne Clifford, the Gower manuscript (now lost), that was in the possession of Admiral Hon. John Leveson-Gower (d. 1792).[25] Leveson-Gower was the son of Mary Tufton, Anne Clifford's great-granddaughter. The 1603 memoir is a summary of events for a particular year and bears a close resemblance to the yearly memoirs Anne produced after 1649. The 1616, 1617 and 1619 diary appears closer in structure to the Daybook of 1676, with its daily entries and greater detail. Without the Gower manuscript it is impossible to know if Anne Clifford prepared this work as a single manuscript containing the memoir and diary, or if it was part of a larger manuscript book. However, the subject matter suggests Clifford saw the years 1603 and 1616, 1617 and 1619 as key periods in her early life. The 1603 memoir contains evidence of her relationship with Queen Elizabeth and the heady days in the first year of James I's reign. The 1616, 1617 and 1619 diary records the story of her struggles against King James, her husband and the most important men of the realm, as Anne sought desperately to retain her claim to the hereditary Clifford lands in the North.

---

22 'Around 2000: Memoir as Literature', in *A History of English Autobiography*, ed. Adam Smyth (2016), pp. 374–387 (375).
23 Including BL, Add. MS 75384, 1603 Memoir, transcribed by Rachel Lloyd and BL, Add. MS 34105, extracts by William Horword.
24 Longleat Archives, Wiltshire, Portland MS 23. This manuscript has been called the Portland MS and this term will be used to identify it here.
25 See BL, Add. MS 34105, where William Horword relates that in 1780 he took his extracts from the 1616, 1617, 1619 diary out of 'a manuscript copy in the possession of the Duchess Dowager of Portland in 1780, from the original in possession of Lord Gower', fol. 62.

Internal evidence suggests that the Gower manuscript is also the source for three nineteenth-century manuscript copies of the memoir and diary.[26] The earliest of these was produced about 1807 (according to the watermark) by Sarah Bazett Capel, Countess of Essex (d. 1838), wife to George Capel-Coningsby, 5th Earl of Essex. Sarah Capel was a gifted artist who specialised in producing watercolour copies of sixteenth-century portraits.[27] The manuscript where the memoir and diary appear also includes transcriptions of other historical documents relating to women.[28] The next manuscript of the memoir and diary is often called the Knole diary. It was produced by Elizabeth (and probably her sister Mary) Sackville of Knole House in Kent in about 1826 according to watermark evidence.[29] Elizabeth was heir to her father John Frederick Sackville, 3rd Duke of Dorset. She married in 1813 George West, 5th Earl De La Warr, who assumed the name and arms of Sackville, becoming George Sackville West. The diary remained in the hands of their descendants. The Knole Diary served as the base text for the first print edition of the memoir and diary in 1923, edited by Vita Sackville-West, great-granddaughter to Elizabeth Sackville. It was also the source text for D.J.H. Clifford's 1990 edition of Anne Clifford's autobiographies.[30] The third nineteenth-century manuscript of the memoir and diary was produced by the Countess Catherine Vorontsov who also became the Countess of Pembroke upon her marriage with George Herbert, 11th Earl of Pembroke, in 1808. She completed her copy of the memoir and diary on 7 February 1828, dating the final page of the manuscript.[31]

Both the Bodleian MS and the Clanwilliam MS are attractively presented in bound covers. The Bodleian MS is bound in dark blue leather. The title, *Curious*

---

26 These are noted in the text as they occur.
27 More than a hundred of these were printed in Lucy Aikins, *Memoirs of the Court of Queen Elizabeth* (1818).
28 Bodleian Library, Oxford, MS Eng. misc. d. 133. Capel's manuscript was purchased by the Bodleian Library, in the early twentieth century. This manuscript will be referred to as the Bodleian MS in this edition.
29 Unfortunately this manuscript, held at the Kent History and Library Centre, Maidstone (MS U269/3/3/5), has disappeared and I have had to rely on a microfilm copy. Katherine O. Acheson was able to examine the actual manuscript, and the watermark evidence is taken from the introduction to her edition of *The Diary of Anne Clifford: 1616–1619*, New York: Garland, 1995, p. 18. Acheson also provides in this work a detailed comparison of the Knole diary with Portland MS, and a discussion of the contributions of Elizabeth and Mary Sackville to the Knole diary manuscript.
30 Vita Sackville-West, *The Diary of the Lady Anne Clifford* (1923); D.J.H. Clifford, *The Diaries of Lady Anne Clifford* (1990). This manuscript will be referred to as the Knole diary in this edition.
31 Belfast, Northern Ireland, PRONI, D3044/G/5. This manuscript is now in the Clanwilliam/ Meade Papers in the Public Records office of Northern Ireland, and will be referred to as the Clanwilliam MS in this edition.

Manuscripts, is stamped in gold on the spine, and above it is the monogram of Sarah Capel, Countess of Essex. The memoir and diary are found on fols 57–185. It is a fair copy – in a neat nineteenth-century hand. The Clanwilliam MS is bound in red leather. The title, *The Diary of Anne Countess of Dorset Pembroke & Montgomery Daughter & Heiress to George Clifford Earl of Cumberland*, is embossed in gold on the front cover. Underneath the title is the monogram of Catherine, Countess of Pembroke. Again the manuscript is in fair copy in a neat hand. The Knole diary has the least finish, and is found in three hand-stitched paperbooks. The handwriting is much less legible and has more of an amateur or draft quality about it. It also contains many transcription errors and is the least complete. It leaves out twenty-two of the entries that appear in the margins of the Portland MS. The Clanwilliam MS leaves out seventeen and the Bodleian MS has fifteen fewer marginal entries than the Portland MS.[32]

The textual and transmission history of Anne Clifford's later autobiographies is less complex. Anne included her 'Life of Me the Lady Anne Clifford' (1589–1649) and her yearly memoirs (1650–1675) in her *Great Books of Record*.[33] The *Great Books* recount the story of Anne's ancestors – the Veteriponts and Cliffords of the North. The Clifford hereditary lands that eventually came to Anne descended from these two families. This story of Anne's ancestors is told through legal documents initially collected for the great lawsuit, and later documents discovered by Anne Clifford and her antiquarian associates.[34] And while the *Great Books* are certainly a historical narrative, they are also very much Anne's story of herself – of where she came from and who she saw herself to be. Thus it was perfectly logical for her to end the *Great Books*, with its stories of her ancestors, with her own story – her own autobiography. And she does this in three different ways. She includes the important legal and administrative documents relating to her life in her section of the *Great Books* – these are mainly the legal records of the lawsuit over the Clifford lands. She follows the records of her life with a longer memoir, her 'Life of Me'.[35] And one might expect that

---

32 This suggests that Sarah Capel and to a lesser extent Catherine Vorontsov and the Sackville sisters made choices concerning what to copy, what words and grammatical constructions to change and what to omit.

33 The *Great Books of Record* which Anne Clifford designed and produced between 1648 and 1653 is an imposing work of just over 635,300 words, written on double or elephant folio sheets (approximately 26 by 17 inches) bound in three large volumes. Four sets were produced, while a planned set in vellum was never completed. Three sets remain survive, see CAS, Kendal, WDCAT/16; WDHOTH/10 (two sets).

34 These included Roger Dodsworth, Charles Fairfax, William Dugdale, Simonds D'Ewes and others.

35 In the *Great Books* Anne included short biographies of all her ancestors and longer ones for her parents after the records of each individual.

this is where the *Great Books* would end, with Anne Clifford's depiction of her triumphant tour through the lands of her inheritance in 1649 that ends the 'Life of Me'. However, she continued to add yearly memoirs to the *Great Books*, summarizing and putting into context the events and details of each year.[36] She constructed these yearly memoirs from her daybooks, letters, accounts, news reports and her own memories.

Anne Clifford's accounts provide useful details about the way the yearly memoirs of 1650–1675 were managed, and the importance of this autobiographical project to Anne. Each year the first part of the yearly summary would be composed in the autumn and then copied into the third volume of each set of the *Great Books* by one of Anne Clifford's secretaries, generally Thomas Strickland. The final entries for the year would be copied into the *Great Books* at the end of December or in early January. If extra paper was needed it was inserted in the autumn. The three sets are remarkably similar in the entries for each year until 1663 when one set was sent to her daughter, Margaret Sackville, in the Southeast of England. In this set[37] Anne Clifford's usual headings for each year, in her own hand, are not found after 1663. This set also lacks the biblical references that appear in the other two sets that were inserted by Anne.[38] The yearly entries in this set are often shorter and it is missing material that is in the other two sets. The pages are not paginated, and there is a section appearing between the 1668 and 1669 entries which is a retrospective of the visits Margaret Sackville made to Anne Clifford. These were taken from previous entries covering 1653–1669. In Anne Clifford's accounts she pays Allan Strickland and William Watkinson to make copies of the yearly memoirs. These were likely commissioned and sent to London to be added to the set that Anne's daughter had in the south.[39] The two surviving sets that remained in the North during Anne's lifetime[40] are nearly identical, with notes and additional material in Anne Clifford's hand continuing to appear throughout. Anne Clifford's accounts show she dedicated significant resources to the production and updating of her yearly autobiographical memoirs. She clearly saw these as part of the larger story of the Clifford dynasty in the North. The last yearly memoir is for the year 1675 and is followed by an elegy written by her grandson, Thomas Tufton. Fortunately the survival of

36 In this edition the yearly memoirs are collected together under the title 'The Lady of the North, Yearly Memoirs, 1650–1675'.
37 WDHOTH/10, Hothfield set.
38 This set is also likely the source for Fisher's copy of Anne Clifford's autobiography, BL, Harley 6177, which was the source text for D.J.H. Clifford's edition of Anne Clifford's autobiographies.
39 See CAS, Kendal, JAC 495–497, Anne Clifford's accounts, 1669–1675.
40 WDHOTH/10, Skipton set; WDCAT/16.

Anne's daybook for the last three months of her life, the Daybook of 1676, fills in with stunning detail the last days of Anne Clifford's life.

We know that Anne habitually for many years kept daybooks, where she carefully recorded or dictated the details of each day. One of her principal gentlemen, George Sedgewick, wrote in his own autobiography, 'she kept in a large folio paperbook a diary or journal, wherein she caused to be entered the occurrences of the day, and all the strangers [visitors] that came to her house, whether upon visits or business'.[41] George Williamson, Anne's early twentieth-century biographer, believed the 1616, 1617 and 1619 diary may have been an early form of her daybooks.[42] We know that at her death many of her daybooks survived. Anne's secretary, Edward Hasell, wrote at the end of the Daybook of 1676:

> Thus far of this book and a great many more of the same kind, answerable to as many several years last past successively as containing a continued thankful commemoration (as my Honourable Lady hath often said), of God's great mercies and blessings to her and hers, were written altogether by her Ladyship or [by] her directions.[43]

Unfortunately, there is no evidence that any other daybook survives. Williamson believes these were destroyed by Thomas Tufton in the early seventeenth century, but he makes this assumption on the basis of Thomas Whitaker's report, written in 1805, that 'among the evidences of Skipton are several memoranda of large parcels of papers sent away by order of Thomas, Earl of Thanet'.[44] However, Whitaker also states the belief that these manuscripts had been taken to Hothfield, in Kent, the home of the Earls of Thanet, Anne Clifford's descendants, not that they were destroyed.[45] Still, the survival rate of manuscripts related to Anne Clifford is quite high, so it is unusual that, except for the Daybook of 1676, no other volume of what must have been several volumes of daybooks has come to light. It may be then that the other daybooks were destroyed.

The Daybook of 1676 survives because Edward Hasell had it in his possession when Anne died and the final entry is made by him. He never returned it to Anne's family. The manuscript was preserved by his descendants and is now in

---

41 CAS, Carlisle, DLONS/L/12/2/16, 'George Sedgewick, A Summarie or Memorial of my owne Life', p. 77. For a printed version see Joseph Nicholson and Richard Burn, *The History and Antiquities of the Counties of Westmorland and Cumberland*, vol. 1 (1777), p. 303.
42 George Williamson, *Lady Anne Clifford* (1922), p. 83.
43 See p. 263.
44 Williamson, *Lady Anne Clifford*, p. 361.
45 Whitaker, *History of Craven* (1878), p. 390.

a private collection. It is written in Hasell's hand[46] and shows that he prepared in advance the pages to be written upon each day. Each page was laid out in two columns and some text was pre-entered. It appears that entries were made throughout the day and all spaces on the page, including the left hand margin, could be used if the events of the day required, with writing generally horizontal on the page, but at times vertical (see Figure 1). Two nineteenth-century publications printed extracts from this manuscript: Robert Southey in his *Southey's Commonplace Books* and William Jackson in his *Papers and Pedigrees*.[47] In 1922 Williamson printed a much larger portion of it,[48] which was followed by D.J.H. Clifford's edition in 1990 which is extensive but does not include all material found in the manuscript, and thus the first complete edition of this manuscript is printed in this edition.

Editorial Principles and Practices

The purpose here is to provide an edition of the autobiographies that is useful for scholarship, while at the same time providing an accessible text for the modern reader. The spelling has been modernized throughout, though archaic forms and uses of words have not been modernized. Punctuation has been regularized, but aims to maintain the structure and flow of the original texts. The base text for the 1603 memoir and the 1616, 1617 and 1619 diary is the Portland MS. Significant variations between this manuscript and each of the nineteenth-century manuscripts are identified in the notes. Material which appears as marginal notes in the four manuscripts of the memoir and diary is integrated into the text, with a footnote indicating this. I have included marginal material in the text in order to maintain the narrative flow, as did Anne Clifford in her later autobiographical writing. In the 'Life of Me' and the 1650–1676 memoirs she inserts commentary and additional information directly into the main text. Thus the inclusion of the marginal notes in the main text in the earlier memoir and diary is consistent with Anne Clifford's later practice. It is also likely that marginal notes in the 1603 memoir and 1616, 1617, and 1619 diary retain echoes of their original layout in Anne Clifford's daybooks (see Figure 1), where the page was divided into different sections, and material placed in the left-hand

---

46 Only three insertions are in Anne Clifford's unique hand – the date headings for each month.
47 Robert Southey, *Southey's Commonplace Books: Analytical Readings*, 3rd Series, ed. John Wood Warter (1859), pp. 502–504; William Jackson, *Papers and Pedigrees Mainly Relating to Cumberland and Westmorland* (1892), pp. 54–58.
48 Williamson, *Lady Anne Clifford*, pp. 265–280.

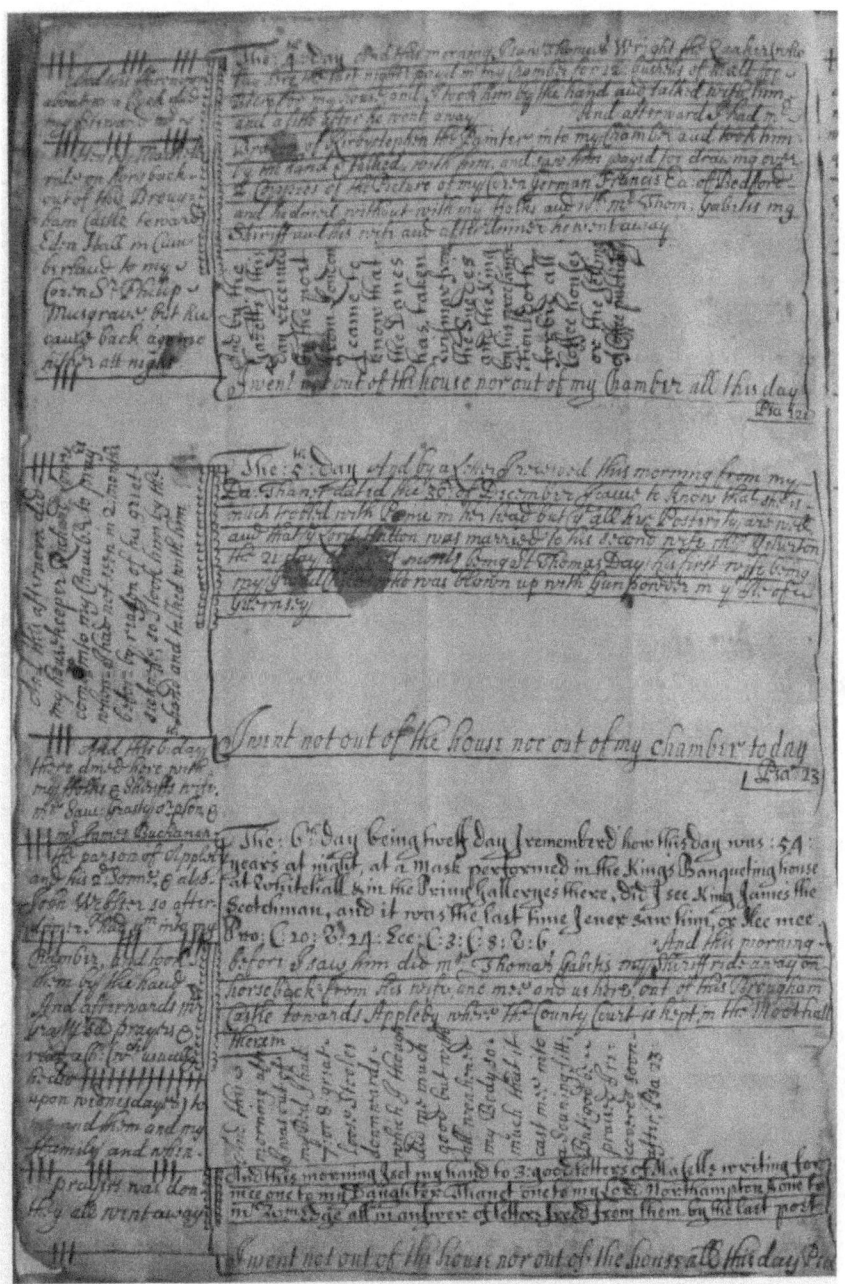

1 Page from Anne Clifford's Daybook of 1676

column throughout the day. Thus many marginal notes may have been material written the left-hand column of the original text, though many are clearly later insertions. All marginal notes are indicated in the footnotes, with additional information concerning their source and use in the manuscripts more fully explained when necessary.

The manuscript used as the base text for the 'Life of Me' and the 'Yearly Memoirs, 1650–1675' is the CAS, Kendal, WDCAT/16 set of the *Great Books of Record*, volume 3.[49] Generally there is great consistency between the three extant sets of the *Great Books*. Unique material from each set is included in the text with the source identified in the notes.[50] The Daybook of 1676 exists in only one manuscript – the original manuscript in the scribal hand of Edward Hasell (with monthly headings in Anne Clifford's hand). The page layout for this manuscript is idiosyncratic (see Figure 1) and is printed here as one continuous text, with no attempt made to reproduce the layout of the original manuscript. This at times leads to some degree of repetition, but also accurately reproduces the text in its entirety.

A glossary of persons has been included following the autobiographies, with useful information included for identifying the over 1100 people mentioned in this edition. Every attempt has been made to provide at least some information on even the most humble individuals. When an individual is identified only by his or her title in the text or if an individual needs further explanation to allow identification, a note provides the full name and other relevant information in order to facilitate the use of the glossary. Children who died in infancy are generally not included. It is not possible to provide even short biographies of each individual mentioned in this edition. The principle used both in the notes and the glossary is to show how the individual is related to the events, places, and actions recorded in the autobiographies.

---

49 In the notes the three sets are indicated as follows: WDCAT/16 as WD; WDHOTH/10, the Skipton set, as H1; WDHOTH/10, the Hothfield set, as H2.
50 For a detailed discussion of the manuscripts of the *Great Books of Record*, see Malay, 'Constructing Narrative of Time and Place: Anne Clifford's *Great Books of Record*', *Review of English Studies* 66.277 (2015), 859–875. For an original-spelling edition of these autobiographies with extensive collation notes, see Malay, ed., *Great Books*, pp. 795–906.

The Lady Anne Clifford's Memoir, 1603

In Christmas I used to go much to the Court, and sometimes did I lie in my aunt of Warwick's[1] chamber on a pallet, to whom I was much bound for her continual care and love of me, in so much as if Queen Elizabeth had lived, she intended to have preferred me to be of the Privy Chamber. For at that time there was as much hope and expectation of me both for my person and my fortunes as of any other young lady whatsoever. A little after the Queen removed to Richmond she began to grow sickly. My Lady[2] used to go often thither and carried me with her in the coach, and using to wait in the coffer chamber,[3] and many times came home very late. About the 21st or 22nd of March my aunt of Warwick sent my mother word about six of the clock at night, she living then at Clerkenwell, that she should remove to Austin Friars[4] her house, for fear of some commotion, though God in his mercy did deliver us from it.

Upon the 24th Mr Flocknell, my aunt of Warwick's man, brought us word from his Lady that the Queen died about two [or] three of the clock in the morning. This message was delivered to my mother and me in the same chamber where afterwards I was married.[5] About ten of the clock King James was proclaimed in Cheapside by all the Council[6] with great joy and triumph, which triumph I went to see and hear. This peaceable coming in of the King was unexpected of all sorts of people.

I was at Queen Elizabeth's death 13 years and two months old. And this

---

1 Anne Russell, Countess of Warwick.
2 Her mother Margaret Russell, Countess of Cumberland.
3 A dormitory-like room that was part of Elizabeth's private chambers where ladies serving the queen slept.
4 North-east of the city of London within the city walls. Clerkenwell sat outside the city walls to the west and was vulnerable if rioting or armed conflict broke out.
5 Anne married on 25 February 1609. The marriage was hastened because Richard Sackville's father, Robert, 2nd Earl of Dorset, was on his deathbed (he died three days after the marriage). The validity of the marriage was questioned by Richard Sackville's siblings (BL, MS Stowe 558) but was validated later that year by the Archbishop of Canterbury (KHLC, U269/Q18). This statement places the composition of the 1603 memoir after 1609.
6 The Privy Council, a permanent council made up of elite men who advised the monarch. This council wielded great power, as seen here in the transfer of the crown from Elizabeth to James.

2 Margaret Russell, by unknown artist (1585)

day Mr Richard Sackville was 14 years, he being then at Dorset House with his grandfather[7] and that great family. At the death of this worthy Queen my mother and I lay at Austin Friars in the same chamber where afterwards I was married.[8]

The first time that King sent to the lords in England he gave command that

7 Thomas Sackville, 1ˢᵗ Earl of Dorset, Lord Treasurer of England.
8 \I was at … married/

the Earls of Northumberland and Cumberland,[9] the Lord Thomas Howard and the Lord Mountjoy[10] should be added to the Council.[11]

Within two or three days we returned to Clerkenwell again. A little after this Queen Elizabeth's corpse came by night in a barge from Richmond to Whitehall, my mother and a great company of ladies attending it, where it continued a good while standing in the drawing chamber, where it was watched all night by several lords and ladies, my mother sitting up with it two or three nights, but my Lady would not give me leave to watch by reason I was held too young. At this time we used to go very much to Whitehall and walked much in the garden which was much frequented with lords and ladies, being all full of several hopes, every man expecting mountains and finding molehills, excepting Sir Robert Cecil and the house of the Howards, who hated my mother and did not much love my aunt of Warwick.[12] About this time my Lord of Southampton[13] was enlarged of his imprisonment out of the Tower.

When the corpse of Queen Elizabeth had continued at Whitehall as long as the Council had thought fit, it was carried from thence with great solemnity to Westminster, the lords and ladies going on foot to attend it, my mother and my aunt of Warwick being mourners.[14] But I was not allowed to be one, because I was not high enough, which did much trouble me then, but yet I stood in the church at Westminster to see the solemnity performed.

Queen Elizabeth's funeral was on the 28th day of April being Thursday.[15]

A little after this my Lady and a great deal of other company as Mistress Elizabeth Brydges, my Lady Newton[16] and her daughter, my Lady Finch[17] went down with my aunt of Warwick to North Hall, and from thence we all went to Theobalds to see the King, who used my mother and my aunt very graciously, but we all saw a great change between the fashion of the Court as it is now, and of that in the Queen's time, for we were all lousy by sitting in Sir Thomas Erskine's chamber.

As the King came out of Scotland, when he lay at York, there was a strife

---

9 Henry Percy, 9th Earl of Northumberland, and George Clifford, 3rd Earl of Cumberland.
10 Charles Blount.
11 \The first time ... Council/
12 The Russells and Howards competed for favour in Elizabeth's reign. The Russells were staunch Protestants, while the Howards were sympathetic to Catholicism.
13 Henry Wriothesley, 3rd Earl of Southampton.
14 Two colour illustrations of this funeral procession exist: BL, Add. MS 5408 and Add. MS 35324.
15 \Queen Elizabeth's ... Thursday/
16 Catherine Paston, a lady of Elizabeth's Privy Chamber.
17 Elizabeth Heneage, 1st Countess of Winchilsea in her own right.

between my father and my Lord Burghley,[18] who was then President, who should carry the sword, but it was adjudged on my father's side, because it was his office by inheritance, and so is lineally descended on me.[19] From Theobalds the King went to Charterhouse where my Lord Thomas Howard was created Earl of Suffolk and my Lord Mountjoy Earl of Devonshire and restored my Lord of Southampton and Essex[20] who stood attainted.[21] Likewise he created many Barons, amongst which my uncle Russell was made Lord Russell of Thornhaugh and for knights they were innumerable.

All this spring I had my health very well not having so much as a taste of the green sickness.[22] My father used to come sometimes to us at Clerkenwell, but not often, for he had at this time as it were wholly left my mother, yet the house was kept still at his charge.[23]

About this time my aunt of Bath and her Lord[24] came to London and brought with them my Lord Fitzwarren[25] and my cousin Frances Bourchier whom I met at Bagshot, where I lay all night with my cousin Frances Bourchier and Mistress Mary Cary, which was the first beginning of the greatness between us. About five miles from London there met them my mother, my Lord of Bedford and his Lady,[26] my uncle Russell[27] and much other company, so that we were in number about 300, which did all accompany them to Bath House, where they continued most of that summer, whither I went daily and visited them and grew more inward with my cousin Frances and Mistress Cary.

About this time my aunt of Warwick went to meet the Queen, having Mrs Brydges with her and my cousin Anne Vavasour. My mother and I should have gone with them, but that her horses, which she borrowed of Mr Elmes[28] and old

---

18　William Cecil, 1st Earl of Essex.
19　A marginal note reiterates the episode: 'A dispute between George, Earl of Cumberland, and the Lord Burghley about the carrying of the sword before the King at York adjudged in favour of the said Earl'. Anne was always keen to defend her inheritable honours and rights, insisting these descended to her as lineal heir of her father.
20　Robert Devereux, 3rd Earl of Essex.
21　This refers to the seizure of their property by the Crown in consequence of their involvement (or in Robert Devereux, 3rd Earl of Essex's case, his father's involvement) in 'Essex's Rebellion' led by Robert Devereux, 2nd Earl of Essex, against Queen Elizabeth in 1601. James I is here releasing their property back to them.
22　Hypochromic anaemia caused by a lack of iron in the blood.
23　During the late 1590s George Clifford became estranged from his wife, Margaret Russell, because of his affair with a woman Anne would later term 'a lady of quality'.
24　Elizabeth Russell, Anne's aunt, and her husband William Bourchier, 3rd Earl of Bath.
25　Richard Bourchier, Anne's first cousin.
26　Edward Russell, Anne's first cousin, and his wife Lucy Harington, who was first cousin to Mary and Philip Sidney.
27　William Russell, 1st Baron Russell of Thornhaugh, Anne's uncle.
28　Either John or Thomas Elmes.

Mr Hickling[29] were not ready. Yet I went the same night and overtook my aunt at Tittenhanger, my Lady Blount's[30] house, where my mother came the next day to me about noon, my aunt being gone before.

Then my mother and I went on our journey to overtake her, and killed three horses that day with extreme of heat and came to Wrest, my Lord of Kent's,[31] where we found the doors shut and none in the house but one servant who only had the keys of the hall, so that we were enforced to lie in the hall all night, till towards morning at which time came a man and let us into the higher rooms, where we slept three or four hours.[32] This morning we hasted away betimes and came that night to Rockingham Castle where we overtook my aunt of Warwick and her company, where we continued a day or two with old Sir Edward Watson and his Lady,[33] then we went to my Lady Needham's[34] who once served my aunt of Warwick, and from thence to a sister of hers whose name I have forgotten.[35] Thither came my Lady of Bedford,[36] who was then so great a woman with the Queen as every body much respected her, she having attended the Queen from out of Scotland. The next day we went to Mr Griffin of Dingley,[37] which was the first time I ever saw the Queen and Prince Henry,[38] where she kissed us all and used us kindly. Thither came my Lady of Suffolk,[39] my young Lady Derby[40] and my Lady Walsingham,[41] which three ladies were the great favourites of Sir Robert Cecil. That night we went along with the Queen's train, there being an infinite number of coaches, and as I take it my aunt and my mother and I lay at Sir Richard Knightley's,[42] where my Lady Elizabeth Knightley made exceedingly much of us. The same night my mother and I and my cousin Anne

29 William Hickling.
30 Frances Pigott.
31 Henry Grey, 8th Earl of Kent.
32 See Thomas Carew's poem 'To My Friend G.N. from Wrest' (1639) for a description of the house where Anne and her mother spent this uncomfortable night. In Carew's poem he describes the hall as thronged with 'living men … where, at large tables fill'd with wholesome meats, / The servant, tenant and kind neighbour eats'. On this occasion it was not so welcoming.
33 Sir Edward Watson and his wife Anne Digby.
34 Elizabeth Watson. She appears in Anne Russell's will under her married name of Needham (NA, PROB 11/103/291, Will of Anne Russell, 1604).
35 Either Temperance married to Thomas Dolman, Catherine married to Thomas Palmer, or Mary married to Anthony Mayney.
36 Lucy Harington, wife of Anne's cousin Edward Russell, 3rd Earl of Bedford.
37 Dingley Hall, the home of Sir Edward Griffin.
38 Henry Stuart. Anne's first husband, Richard Sackville, was a favourite of this prince.
39 Catherine Knyvet, Countess of Suffolk.
40 Elizabeth De Vere, Countess of Derby.
41 Ethelreda 'Audrey' Shelton.
42 Sir Richard Knightley of Fawsley Hall, Northamptonshire, and his wife Elizabeth Seymour.

Vavasour rid on horseback through Coventry and went to a gentleman's house where the Lady Elizabeth her Grace lay,[43] which was the first time I ever saw her, my Lady Kildare and the Lady Harington[44] being her governesses. The same night we returned to Sir Richard Knightley's. The next day, as I take it, we went along with the Queen to Althorp, my Lord Spencer's house,[45] where my mother and I saw my cousin Henry Clifford, my uncle's son, which was the first time we ever saw him.

The Queen and the Prince came to Althorp the 25th of June being Saturday but as I remember my aunt of Warwick, my mother and I came not thither till the next day, [the] 26th which Sunday was kept with great solemnity, there being an infinite number of lords and ladies. Here we saw my cousin Clifford first,[46] then we saw the Queen's favour to my Lady Hatton[47] and my Lady Cecil,[48] for she showed no favour to the elderly ladies but to my Lady Rich[49] and such-like company.[50]

From thence the 27th being Monday the Queen went to [Sir] Hatton Fermor's,[51] where the King met her, where there were an infinite company of lords and ladies and other people that the county could scarce lodge them. From thence the Court removed and was banqueted with great royalty by my father at Grafton[52] where the King and Queen were entertained with speeches and delicate presents, at which time my Lord and the Alexanders[53] did run a course at the field, where he hurt Henry Alexander very dangerously. Where the Court lay this night I am uncertain. At this time of the King's being at Grafton,

---

43 Elizabeth Stuart, daughter to James I and later the Queen of Bohemia.
44 Frances Howard, Countess of Kildare and Anne Kelway.
45 Robert Spencer, 1st Baron Spencer of Wormleighton.
46 Henry Clifford, later 5th Earl of Cumberland. He was Anne's cousin and he inherited her father's northern lands. She inherited these lands after his death in 1643 according to the stipulations of the King's Award.
47 Elizabeth Cecil, Lady Hatton (later Lady Coke).
48 Elizabeth Drury, Countess of Exeter.
49 Penelope Devereux, sister to Robert Devereux, 2nd Earl of Essex.
50 \The Queen and the Prince ... company/
51 Easton Neston House, the home of Sir Hatton Fermor. All manuscripts have only the word 'Hatton'. In the Portland MS there is a space after Hatton which suggests that there was a word that could not be transcribed in the source manuscript. In Seward's print text it appears as 'Hatton Fermers' (p. 222), without any indication that this refers to a person rather than a place.
52 George Clifford was granted the keepership of Grafton Regis in 1602. See Richard Spence, *The Privateering Earl: George Clifford, 3rd Earl of Cumberland 1558–1605* (1995), p. 181.
53 Sir William Alexander is listed as a Gentleman Extraordinary of the Privy Chamber of Prince Henry (NPJ, p. 607), while a Walter Alexander is listed as a Principal Gentleman Usher to Prince Henry. See Roy Strong, *Henry Prince of Wales* (1986), p. 28. This Henry Alexander may be connected with them.

my mother was there, but not held as mistress of the house, by reason of the difference between my Lord and her, which was grown to a great height.

The night after my aunt of Warwick, my mother and I, as I take it, lay at Doctor Challoner's,[54] where my aunt of Bath and my uncle Russell met us, which house my grandfather of Bedford used to lie much at, being in Amersham. The next day the Queen went to a gentleman's house, whose name I cannot remember, where there met her many great ladies to kiss her hand, as the Marquess of Winchester,[55] my Lady of Northumberland,[56] my Lady of Southampton,[57] etc. From thence the Court removed to Windsor where the feast of St George was solemnized, though it should have been done before.[58] There I stood with my Lady Elizabeth's Grace in the shrine in the Great Hall at Windsor to see the King and all the knights sit at dinner. Thither came the Archduke's ambassador,[59] who was received by the King and Queen in the Great Hall where there was such an infinite company of lords and ladies and so great a Court as I think I shall never see the like again.

At Windsor there was such infinite number of ladies sworn of the Queen's Privy Chamber as made the place of no esteem or credit. Once I spoke to my Lady of Bedford to be one, but had the good fortune to miss it.[60]

From Windsor the Court removed to Hampton Court, where my mother and I lay at Hampton Court in one of the round towers, round about which were tents, where they died two or three in a day of the plague.

At Hampton Court my mother, myself and the other ladies dined in the presence as they used in Queen Elizabeth's time, but that custom lasted not long. [61]

About this time my Lady of Hertford[62] began to grow great with the Queen and the Queen wore her picture.[63]

There I fell extremely sick of a fever so as my mother was in some doubt it might turn to the plague but within two or three days I grew reasonable well,

---

54 Dr Robert Chaloner, of Church House, Amersham. The rectory was under the patronage of the Russells, Earls of Bedford.
55 William Paulet, 4th Marquess of Winchester.
56 Dorothy Devereux, sister to Penelope and Robert Devereux, 2nd Earl of Essex.
57 Elizabeth Vernon, Countess of Southampton and maid of honour to Queen Elizabeth.
58 This feast is traditionally held on 23 April. Dudley Carleton also describes this event, noting that it was held with 'much solemnity' with Prince Henry; Ludovic Stuart, 2nd Duke of Lennox; and the earls of Southampton, Mar and Pembroke invested into the Order of the Garter, the highest order of chivalry in England. See Maurice Lee, ed., *Dudley Carleton to John Chamberlain 1603-1624* (1972), p. 35.
59 Charles de Ligne, 2nd Prince of Arenberg.
60 \At Windsor ... miss it/
61 \At Hampton Court ... long/
62 Frances Howard, Countess of Hertford and later Duchess of Lennox.
63 \About this time ... picture/

and was sent away to my cousin Stidolph's at Norbury,[64] Mrs Carniston going with me, for Mrs Taylor[65] was newly put away from me, her husband dying of the plague shortly after. A little afore this time my mother and my aunt of Bath and my cousin Frances went to North Hall, my mother being extreme[ly] angry with me for riding before with Mr Menerell, where my mother in her anger commanded that I should lie in a chamber alone, which I could not endure, but my cousin Frances got the key of my chamber and lay with me which was the first time I loved her so very well. The next day Mr Menerell as he went abroad fell down suddenly and died, so as most thought it was of the plague, which was then very rife. It put us all in great fear and amazement for my aunt had then a suit to follow in Court and my mother to attend the King about the business between my father and her.[66] My aunt of Warwick sent us medicine from a little house near Hampton Court where she then lay with Sir Moyle Finch and his Lady. Now was the Master of Orkney[67] and the Lord Tullibardine[68] much in love with Mrs Cary and came thither to see us with George Murray in their company who was one of the King's bedchamber. Within nine or ten days we were allowed to come to the Court again, which was before I went to my cousin Stidolph's.

Upon the 25th of July the King and Queen were crowned at Westminster, my father and my mother both attending them in their robes, my aunt of Bath and my uncle Russell, which solemn sight my mother would not let me see because the plague was so hot in London. Therefore I continued at Norbury where my cousin did feed me with breakfasts and pear pies and such things as shortly after I fell into the green sickness.

My cousin Frances Bourchier stood to see the coronation though she had no robes and went not amongst the company.[69]

After the coronation, the Court returned to Hampton Court, where my mother fetched me from Norbury, and so we lay at a little house near Hampton Court about a fortnight and my aunt of Bath lay in Hogan's lodgings,[70] where my cousin Frances and I and Mary Cary did use to walk much about the gardens and house when the King and Queen were gone.

64 Sir Francis Stidolph of Norbury.
65 Anne Taylor, Anne's governess and distant relation, portrayed in Anne's Great Picture.
66 Margaret Russell sought the King's help in forcing George Clifford to provide financial support for Margaret and Anne. For drafts of her petitions to James I see CAS, Kendal, WDHOTH/44.
67 Patrick Stewart, 2nd Earl of Orkney, one of the Scottish lords who came to Court with James I. He was married at this time, but had a number of mistresses and illegitimate children throughout his life.
68 William Murray, Lord Tullibardine, another Scottish lord who came to Court with James I.
69 \My cousin ... company/
70 William Hogan or Huggins, Keeper of the Gardens, Hampton Court.

About this time my cousin Anne Vavasour was married to Sir Richard Warburton. From Hampton Court, my mother, my aunt of Bath, myself and all our company went to Lancelevy[71] Lord Francis Palmes his house, where we continued as long as the Court lay at Basingstoke and I went often to the Queen and my Lady Arbella.[72]

Between Lancelevy and Mr Duton's[73] we lay at one Sir Edmund Fettiplace's called Bessels Leigh, where we had great entertainment. Then we lay a night or two at Wantage[74] at Gregory Webb's, a tenant of my Lord of Bath's and from his house to Mr Duton's.[75]

Now was my Lady Rich[76] grown great with the Queen insomuch as my Lady of Bedford was something out with her and when she came to Hampton Court was entertained but even indifferently, and yet continued to be of the bedchamber. One day the Queen went from Basingstoke and dined at Sir Henry Wallop's[77] where my Lady, my aunt and I had lain two or three nights before, and did help to entertain her. As we rid from my Lady Wallop's[78] to Lancelevy, riding late by reason of our stay at Basingstoke, we saw a strange comet in the night like a canopy in the air, which was a thing observed all over England.

From Lancelevy we went to Mr Duton's where we continued about a week and had great entertainment and at that time kept a fast by reason of the plague which was then generally observed all over England. From Mr Duton's we went to Barton to one Mrs Dormer's[79] where Mrs Humphrey her mother[80] and she entertained us with great kindness. From thence we went often to the Court at Woodstock where my aunt of Bath followed her suit to the King, and my mother wrote letters to the King, and her means was by my Lord Fenton and to the Queen by my Lady of Bedford. My father at this time followed his suit to the King about the border lands, so that sometimes my mother and he did meet by chance, where their countenance did show the dislike they had of one another, yet he would speak to me in a slight fashion, and give me his blessing. While we lay here we rid through Oxford once or twice, but whither we went I

---

71 Lancelevy, Hampshire.
72 Arbella Stuart, granddaughter to Bess of Hardwick and an heir to the English and Scottish thrones.
73 Henry Duton, a Member of Parliament.
74 In Oxfordshire.
75 \Between Lancelevy ... Duton's/. Henry Duton. In the Portland MS the name appears as Dulon, but is Duton in the nineteenth-century manuscripts.
76 Penelope Devereux.
77 Farnleigh Wallop, Hampshire.
78 Elizabeth Corbet.
79 Justina Humfrey, a distant relation of Anne's, through the St Johns.
80 Joan Inkforbie, a distant relation of Anne's, through the St Johns.

remember not. There we saw the Spanish ambassador[81] who was then new come into England about the peace.

Not long before Michaelmas[82] myself, my cousin Frances Bourchier, Mrs Goodwin and Mrs Hawkridge waiting on us, went in to my mother's coach from Barton to Cookham,[83] where my uncle Russell, his wife and son then lay.[84] From thence the next day we went to Nonsuch where Prince Henry and her Grace lay where I stayed about a week and left my cousin Frances there who was proposed to continue with her Grace, but I came back by Cookham and came to Barton[85] before my aunt of Bath came in to the country.[86]

While we lay at Barton I kept so ill a diet with Mrs Mary Cary and Mrs Harrison in eating fruit so as I fell shortly after into the green sickness. From this place my aunt of Bath having little hope of her suit took her leave of my mother and returned into the West Country. While they lay at Barton my mother and my aunt paid for the charge of the house equally. Some week or fortnight after my aunt was gone, which was about Michaelmas,[87] my Lady went from Barton to Green's Norton and lay one night at my cousin Thomas Sellinger's where we saw old Mr Hickling, where he and his daughter[88] preferred William Pond to serve my Lady. To this place we came about ten o' the clock in the night and I was so weary as I could not tell whether I should sleep or eat first. The next day we went to North Hall where we found my aunt of Warwick something ill and melancholy. She herself had not been there passing a month but lay at Sir Moyle Finch's in Kent by reason of the great plague, which was then much about North Hall.

Not long after Michaelmas my uncle Russell, my aunt Russell his wife, their son, my Lord of Bedford, my mother and I gave all allowance to Mr Chambers my aunt's steward,[89] in which sort the house was kept during our being there. I used to wear my hair-coloured velvet gown every day, and learned to sing and play on the bass viol of Jack Jenkins, my aunt's boy. Before Christmas my cousin

---

81 Juan de Tassis, 2nd Count of Villamediana.
82 29 September, the Feast of Saint Michael and All Angels.
83 Aemilia Lanyer's country house poem 'A Description of Cookham' describes her period serving as a waiting gentlewoman to Anne and her mother, likely in 1604. See Malay, 'Positioning Patronage' (2013).
84 William Russell, 1st Baron Russell of Thornhaugh, his wife Elizabeth Long and their son Francis Russell, later 4th Earl of Bedford.
85 Barton Court.
86 \Not long before … county/
87 29 September.
88 William Hickling and his daughter Christian who was married to Anne's relative Thomas Elmes.
89 Simon Chambers is mentioned in Anne Russell's will.

Frances was sent for from Nonsuch to North Hall by reason that her Grace was to go from thence to be brought up with Lady Harington in the country. All this time we were merry at North Hall, my cousin Frances Bourchier, my cousin Francis Russell and I did use to walk much in the garden and were great with each other. At this time I fell directly in to the green sickness.

Now there was much talk of a masque which the Queen had at Winchester and how all the ladies about the Court had gotten such ill-names that it was grown a scandalous place, and the Queen herself much fallen from her former greatness and reputation she had in the world.[90]

---

90 This masque, *Henry's Welcome to Winchester*, was performed between 11 and 17 October 1603. It is unclear what Anne found objectionable. It may be that she disapproved of the Court ladies and the Queen performing in the masque. If so, she would later revise her opinion as she performed in the Queen's later Court masques.

Countess of Dorset's Diary, 1616, 1617 and 1619

January 1616

Upon New Year's Day I kept my chamber all the day, my Lady Rich[1] and my sister Sackville[2] dining with me, but my Lord[3] and all the company at Dorset House went to see the masque at the Court.[4]

The first day Sir George Villiers[5] was made Master of the Horse and my Lord of Worcester[6] Lord Privy Seal.[7]

Upon the 3rd died my Lady Thomas Howard's[8] son.

Upon the 4th I went to see my Lady of Effingham[9] at my Lady Lumley's[10] and went to sup at my Lady Shrewsbury's[11] where there was a great company and a play after supper.

Upon the 5th being Twelfth Eve, my Lord played at dice in the Court and won nine hundred twenty shilling pieces and gave me but twenty.[12]

Upon the 6th being Twelfth Day,[13] I supped with my Lady of Arundel[14] and sat with her in her Ladyship's box to see the masque, which was the second time it was presented before the King and Queen.[15]

---

1 Frances Hatton, after March 1619 Countess of Warwick.
2 Mary Curzon was Anne's sister-in-law, married to Edward Sackville, later 4th Earl of Dorset.
3 Anne's husband, Richard Sackville, 3rd Earl of Dorset.
4 *The Golden Age Restored* by Ben Jonson, performed in the Palace of Whitehall's banqueting house with a stage design by Inigo Jones.
5 George Villiers, Duke of Buckingham and favourite of James I.
6 Edward Somerset, 4th Earl of Worcester.
7 \The first day … Seal/
8 Elizabeth Cecil, later Countess of Berkshire.
9 Anne St John, related to Anne.
10 Elizabeth Darcy, Lady Lumley.
11 Mary Cavendish. Shrewsbury House was a mansion on Cheyne Walk, adjoining the gardens of Winchester Palace. It reportedly had a room 120 feet in length where this performance was likely held.
12 \Upon the 5th … twenty/
13 6 December and the feast of Epiphany. This was the end of the twelve days of Christmas and a final day of celebration.
14 Alethea Talbot, Countess of Arundel. This event occurred at Arundel House, a palace on the Strand near St Clement Danes.
15 *The Golden Age Restored* by Ben Jonson. It was also performed on New Year's Day in 1616.

This Twelfth Day at night my Lady of Arundel made a great supper to the Florentine Ambassador[16] where I was and carried my sister Sackville[17] along with me so she sat with me in the box to see the masque. This night the Queen wore a gown with a long train which my Lady Bedford bore up.[18]

Upon the 8th I went to see Lady Raleigh at the Tower.[19]

Upon the 14th my Lord supped at the Globe.[20]

Upon the 21st being Sunday, my Lord and I went to church at Sevenoaks to grace the Bishop of St Davids's prayers.[21]

February 1616

All the time I stayed in the country.[22] I was sometimes merry and sometimes sad as I heard news from London.

Upon Thursday the 8th of February I came to London, my Lord Bishop of St David's riding with me in the coach and Mary Neville. This time I was sent up for by my Lord about the composition with my uncle of Cumberland.[23]

Upon Monday the 12th my Lord Ros[24] was married to Mrs Anne Lake, the Secretary's daughter.[25]

Upon Thursday the 15th my Lord and I went to see my young Lady Arundel[26]

---

16 Amerigo Salvetti, whose wife, Frances Colbrand, was distantly related to Anne.
17 Mary Curzon, Anne's sister-in-law, married to Edward Sackville, later 4th Earl of Dorset.
18 \This Twelfth Day ... bore up/
19 Elizabeth Throckmorton, wife of Sir Walter Raleigh. She was often with him during his imprisonment in the Tower of London.
20 \Upon the 14th ... Globe/. The Globe Theatre, in Southwark.
21 Richard Milbourne, Rector of Sevenoaks, Kent, from 1591 to 1616. He was elevated to the bishopric of St David's in 1615 and consecrated in Lambeth in July 1615, but remained at Sevenoaks until 1616.
22 At Knole House, Kent.
23 This concerns Anne's lawsuit for the hereditary Clifford lands in Westmorland and Skipton in Yorkshire. In the summer of 1615 the Justices of the Court of Common Pleas arbitrated an agreement, the Judges' Award (and referred to in this diary variously as the agreement, the composition, the award etc.) in which these lands were to be awarded to Anne's uncle, Francis Clifford, 4th Earl of Cumberland, in exchange for a cash settlement. For a discussion of this lawsuit see Spence, *Anne Clifford*, pp. 40–58. For documents related to the lawsuit see Anne Clifford, *Great Books*, ed. Malay (2015), pp. 734–775. A letter from Anne's mother Margaret Russell to Richard Sackville reveals the extent of Anne's emotional distress as she asked him to 'press her not farther to torture her noble heart dried with grief or her eyes and face so much changed with weeping, and we her friends not in such hope of her having children again, as there was likelyhood of' (Portland MS 23, Letter, December 1615, pp. 66–67).
24 William Cecil, Lord de Ros. In 1606 Anne's mother attempted to arrange a match between William and Anne. See Malay, 'Marrying of Anne Clifford' (2012).
25 Thomas Lake, Secretary of State.
26 Alethea Talbot.

and in the afternoon my Lady Willoughby[27] came to see me. My Lady Grey[28] brought my Lady Carr[29] to play at glecko[30] with me when I lost fifteen pounds to them, they two and my Lady Grantham[31] and Sir George Manners supping here with me.

Upon the 16th my Lady Grantham and Mrs Newton[32] came to see me. My Lady Grantham told me the Archbishop of Canterbury[33] would come to me the next day and she persuaded me very earnestly to agree to this business which I took as a great argument of her love. Also my cousin Russell[34] came to see me the same day and chid me and told me of all my faults and errors in this business and he made me weep bitterly. Then I spoke a prayer and went to see my Lady Wotton[35] at Whitehall where we walked five or six turns but spoke nothing of this business though her heart and mine were both full of it.

From hence I went to the Abbey at Westminster where I saw the Queen of Scots her tomb and all the other tombs[36] and came home by water where I took an extreme cold.

Upon the 17th being Saturday, my Lord Archbishop of Canterbury, my Lord William Howard, my Lord Ros, my cousin Russell,[37] my brother Sackville[38] and a great company of men of note were all in the gallery at Dorset House where the Archbishop of Canterbury took me aside and talked with me privately one hour and a half and persuaded me both by divine and human means to set my hand to these agreements but my answer to his Lordship was that I would do nothing till my Lady[39] and I had conferred together. Much persuasion was used

27 Elizabeth Montagu, Lady Willoughby and later Countess of Lindsey.
28 Elizabeth Talbot, Countess of Kent. As a widow she may have married the antiquarian John Selden, Anne's good friend. He was certainly in her household in 1649, see BL, MS Harley 7001, fol. 212.
29 Frances Howard, Countess of Somerset. She was involved in one of the most spectacular scandals of the period. She confessed to being involved in the murder of Thomas Overbury, who criticized her divorce of Robert Devereux, 3rd Earl of Essex.
30 The English card game of Gleek for three players using forty-four cards.
31 Frances Puckering, Lady Grantham.
32 Katherine Puckering, Lady Newton, youngest sister of Frances above.
33 George Abbot, Archbishop of Canterbury from 1611 to 1633.
34 Francis Russell, 4th Earl of Bedford.
35 Margaret Wharton, Anne's first cousin.
36 Anne's first cousin, Elizabeth 'Bess' Russell and her uncle John Russell both had tombs in the chapel of St Edmunds in the Abbey, devised by John Russell's wife Elizabeth Cooke. Anne commissioned several tombs for friends, family and herself, see White, 'Lady Anne Clifford's Church Monuments' (2009).
37 Francis Russell, 4th Earl of Bedford.
38 Anne's brother-in-law Edward Sackville, later 4th Earl of Dorset.
39 Anne's mother, Margaret Russell, who was in Brougham Castle, Westmorland. All of the hereditary Clifford lands in Westmorland were under Margaret's management as part of her jointure (support provided during widowhood). The partnership of mother and

by him and all the company, sometimes terrifying me and sometimes flattering me, but at length it was concluded that I should have leave to go to my mother and send an answer by the 22nd of March next whether I will agree to this business or not and to this prayer my Lord of Canterbury and the rest of the lords have set their hands.

After it was concluded I should go into the North to my mother then my uncle Cumberland and my cousin Clifford[40] came down into the gallery, for they had all this while been in some other chamber with lawyers and others of their party.[41]

Next day was a marvellous day to me through the mercy of God for it was generally thought that I must either have sealed to the agreement or else to have parted with my Lord.

Upon the 19th I sent Tobias and Thomas Beddings[42] to most of the ladies in the town of my acquaintance to let them know of my journey into the North.

Upon the 20th came my Lord Russell and my cousin Gorges.[43] In all this time of my troubles my cousin Russell was exceeding careful and kind to me.

Upon the 21st my Lord and I began our journey northward. The same day my Lord Willoughby[44] came and broke his fast with my Lord. We had two coaches in our company with four horses apiece and about six and twenty horsemen, I having no women to attend me but Willoughby and Judith,[45] Thomas Glemham[46] going with my Lord.

At this meeting my Lord's footman Acton[47] won the race from the northern man, and my Lord won both at [blank] and stayed there a fortnight with my Lord of Essex and my Lord Willoughby. Before they came to London they heard that three of Lord Abergavenny's[48] sons were drowned between Gravesend and

---

daughter in the quest for the Clifford hereditary lands can be seen in their letters found in Portland MS 23 and CAS, Kendal, WDHOTH/44.
40 Francis and Henry Clifford.
41 \After it was ... party/
42 Thomas Billingsley: he would remain in Anne's service and would later accompany Anne's grandsons to Europe.
43 Sir Edward Gorges. Gorges was related to Anne through both the Russells and the Cliffords.
44 Robert Bertie, 14th Baron Willoughby and later 1st Earl of Lindsey.
45 Mistress Willoughby and Judith Simpton, Anne's waiting gentlewomen. Willoughby may have been related to the Berties. This family had close ties to the Cliffords.
46 Richard Sackville's cousin, and a member of the inner circle of Anne and Richard's household, he appears regularly in this diary.
47 Acton Curvett, chief footman.
48 Edward Neville. These drowned sons were brothers-in-law to Mary Sackville, Richard's aunt. John Chamberlain in his correspondence with Dudley Carleton gives an account of their death, claiming: 'They were lost by their own negligence and wilfulness' (LJC, vol. 1, p. 616). Chamberlain and Anne Clifford shared a number of acquaintances. Chamberlain

London and about this time the marriage between Sir Robert Sidney and my Lady Dorothy Percy[49] was openly known.[50]

Upon the 26th we went from Lichfield to Croxall, and about a mile from Croxall my Lord and I parted, he returning to Lichfield and I going on to Derby. I came to my lodging with a heavy heart considering how things stood between my Lord and I. I had in my company ten persons and thirteen horses.

March 1616

Upon the 1st we went from the parson's house over the dangerous moors being eight miles, and afterwards the ways being so dangerous that the horses were fain to be taken out of the coach and the coach to be lifted down the hills. This day Rivers's[51] horse fell from a bridge into the river. We came to Manchester about ten o'clock at night. Upon the 20th in the morning my Lord William Howard with his son my cousin William Howard[52] and Mr John Dudley[53] came hither to take the answer of my mother and my self, which was a direct denial to stand to the Judges' Award. The same day came Sir Timothy Whittington hither who did do all he could to mitigate the anger between my Lord William Howard and my mother, so as at the last we parted all good friends and it was agreed upon that my men and horses should stay, and we should go up to London together after Easter.

Upon the 22nd my Lady and I went in a coach together to Whinfell[54] and rid about the park and saw all the woods.

Upon the 24th my Lady Somerset[55] was sent from Blackfriars by water as prisoner to the Tower.

Upon the 27th my cousin William Howard sent me a dapple grey nag for my own saddle.

---

was a close friend of Sir Henry Wotton whose brother was married to Anne's first cousin, Margaret Wharton. Chamberlain's letters are a rich resource for information about the period and are referred to throughout the notes when relevant.

49 It was a private marriage, probably with the blessing of Sidney's parents and Dorothy's mother.
50 \At this meeting … known/
51 George Rivers, a close friend of Sackville family and the executor of Richard Sackville's will.
52 Anne and William shared the same great-grandfather, William Dacre, 2nd Baron Graystoke.
53 Likely the illegitimate son of Edward Sutton, 5th Baron Dudley, with Elizabeth Tomlinson. Anne will later call him her cousin. They were related through the Stanleys and Howards.
54 Whinfell forest, near Brougham in Westmorland.
55 Frances Howard, Countess of Somerset.

Upon the 31st being Easter Day, I received[56] with my Lady in the chapel at Brougham.

This Lent I kept very strictly and did eat nothing that had butter in it.[57]

April 1616

Upon the first came my cousin Charles Howard and Mr John Dudley, with letters to show that it was my Lord's pleasure that the men and horses should come away without me and after much falling out betwixt my Lady and them, all my folks went away, there being a paper drawn to show that their going was by my Lord's direction and contrary to my will. At night I sent two messengers to my folks to entreat them to stay. For some two nights my mother and I lay together and had much talk about this business.

Upon the 2nd I went after my folks in my Lady's coach, she bringing me a quarter of a mile in the way where she and I had a heavy and grievous parting.[58] Most part of the way I did ride on horseback behind Mr Hodgson.[59]

As I came away I heard that John Digby who was late ambassador in Spain was made Vice Chamberlain to the King and swore one of the Privy Council.

Not long after this my cousin Sir Oliver St John was made Lord Deputy of Ireland in the place of Sir Arthur Chichester.[60]

Upon the 10th we went from Ware to Tottenham where my Lord's coach with his men and horses met me and came to London to Lesser Dorset House.

Upon the 11th I came from London to Knole where I had but a cold welcome from my Lord. My Lady Margaret[61] met me at the outermost gate and my Lord came to me in the drawing chamber.

Upon the 12th I told my Lord how I had left those writings which the judges and my Lord would have me sign and seal behind with my mother.[62]

Upon the 13th my Lord and Thomas Glemham went up to London.

Upon the 17th came Tom Woodgate from London but brought no news of my going up which I daily look for.

---

56 She received communion this Easter.
57 \This Lent ... in it/. Here she refers to the practice of abstaining from forms of pleasure as a spiritual discipline during the forty days of Lent.
58 This was the last time Anne would see her mother. In 1656 she erected a monument, the Countess Pillar, on this spot to commemorate this parting. It remains in place today.
59 The Hodgson family were tenants on the Clifford estates in Westmorland. This Mr Hodgson was likely a servant of Margaret Russell.
60 \Not long ... Chichester/
61 This is her daughter Margaret whom she also calls the 'Child', born in 1614.
62 This was a strategy to gain more time and to allow Anne to return to her mother.

Upon the 17th my mother sickened as she came from prayers being taken with a cold dullness in the manner of an ague, which afterwards turned to great heats and pains in her side so as when she was opened it was plainly perceived to be an impostume.[63]

Upon the 18th Basket[64] came hither and brought me a letter from my Lord to let me know this was the last time of asking me whether I would set my hand to this award of the judges.

Upon the 19th being Friday, I returned my answer to my Lord that I would not stand to this award of the judges what misery soever it brought me to. This morning the Bishop of St David's[65] and my little child were brought to speak to me.

About this time I used to rise early in the morning and go to the standing[66] in the garden and taking my prayer book with me and beseech God to be merciful towards me and to help me in this as He hath always done.

May 1616

Upon the 1st Rivers came from London in the afternoon, and brought me word that I should neither live at Knole nor Bolebroke.[67]

About this time I heard my sister Beauchamp[68] was with child.[69]

Upon the 3rd came Basket down from London and brought me a letter from my Lord by which I might see that it was his pleasure that the Child should go the next day to London which at the first was somewhat grievous to me but when I considered that it would both make my Lord more angry with me and be worse for the Child, I resolved to let her go after I had sent for Mr Legg and talked with him about that and other matters and wept bitterly.[70]

Upon the 4th being Saturday between ten and eleven o'clock the Child went into the litter to go to London, Mrs Bathurst and her two maids with Mr Legg

---

63 \Upon the 17th ... impostume/. An impostume is an abscess. The ague was a form of malaria.
64 Peter Basket, a servant in the Knole household.
65 Richard Milbourne.
66 The Standing, now known as the Duchess's Seat, provides a good view of the south-eastern side of Knole house and is a secluded part of the garden.
67 Sackville was within his rights to 'place' his wife where he chose, so long as it was reasonable accommodation (see E. Foyster, 'At the Limits of Liberty', pp. 42–43). This was part of Sackville's strategy to force her to sign the Judges' Award.
68 This pregnancy was either not successful, or the infant died before 1618.
69 \About this time ... child/
70 This separation from her daughter was another tactic Sackville employed to pressure Anne to sign the Judges' Award.

and a good company of the servants going with her. In the afternoon came a man called Hilton born in Craven[71] from my Lady Willoughby to see me which I took as a great argument of her love being in the midst of all my misery.

My Lady Margaret lay in the great house at Dorset House for now my Lord and his whole company were removed from the little house where I lay when I was first married.[72]

Upon the 8th I dispatched a letter to my mother. About this time died my Lord of Shrewsbury[73] at his house in Broad Street.[74]

Upon the 9th I received a letter from Mr Bellasis[75] how extreme ill my mother had been and in the afternoon came Humphrey Golding's son with letters that my mother was exceeding ill, and as they thought in some danger of death so as I sent Rivers presently to London with letters to be sent to her and certain cordials and conserves. At night was brought me a letter from my Lord to let me know that his determination was the Child should go live at Horsley[76] and not come hither any more, so this was a grievous and sorrowful day to me.

Upon the 10th Rivers came from London and brought me word from Lord William[77] that she was not in such danger as I feared.

Upon the 10th early in the morning I writ a very earnest letter to my Lord to beseech him that I might not go to the little house which was appointed for me, but that I might go to Horsley and sojourn there with my child and to the same effect I wrote to my sister Beauchamp.[78]

The same day came the stewards from London whom I expected would have given warning to many of the servants to go away because the audit was newly come up.[79]

Upon the 11th being Sunday before Mr Legg went away I talked with him an hour or two about all the business and matters between me and my Lord, so as I gave him better satisfaction made him conceive a better opinion of me than

---

71 Craven in North Yorkshire, the area where the Clifford castle of Skipton stood. It was one of the disputed properties in the lawsuit. Anne and her mother lobbied the local tenants to support Anne's claims throughout the lawsuit and beyond.
72 \My Lady Margaret ... married/
73 Gilbert Talbot, 7th Earl of Shrewsbury.
74 \About this time ... Street/
75 Likely James Bellasis of Hallrigg, one of Anne's distant relations.
76 Richard Sackville inherited the lease to a house in West Horsley, near Guildford in Surrey.
77 William Howard of Naworth.
78 \Upon the 10th ... sister Beauchamp/
79 Richard Sackville was experiencing financial difficulties during this period, and Anne believed he would limit the size of the household at Knole, perhaps in anticipation of carrying out his threats to remove her from the house.

ever he did. A little before dinner came Matthew[80] down from London, my Lord sending me by him the wedding ring that my Lord Treasurer and my Old Lady[81] were married withal, and a message that my Lord would be here the next week, and that the Child would not go down to Horsley, and I sent my Lord the wedding ring that my Lord and I was married with. The same day came Mr Marsh[82] from London and persuaded me much to consent to this agreement.

The 12th at night Grosvenor came hither and told me my Lord had won two hundred pounds at cocking, and that my Lord of Essex[83] and my Lord Willoughby who were on my Lord's side won a great deal, and how there were some unkind words passed between my Lord and his side and Sir William Herbert and his side. This day my Lady Grantham sent me a letter about these businesses between my uncle Cumberland and me and I returned her an answer.

All this time my Lord was at London where he had infinite and great resort coming to him. He went much abroad cocking, to bowling alleys, to plays and horse races and was commended by all the world. I stayed in the country having many times a sorrowful and heavy heart, and being condemned by most folks because I would not consent to the agreements, so as I may truly say I am like an owl in the desert.[84] Upon the 13th being Monday my Lady's footman Thomas Petty brought me letters out of Westmorland by which I perceived how very sick and full of grievous pain my dear mother was so as she was not able to write herself to me, and most of her people about her feared she would hardly recover this sickness. At night I went out and prayed to God my only helper that she might not die in this pitiful case.

The 14th Richard Jones came from London to see me and brought a letter with him from Matthew[85] the effect whereof was to persuade me to yield to my Lord's desire in this business at this time or else I was undone for ever.

---

80 Matthew Caldicott, Sackville's gentleman servant. Anne had a difficult relationship with Matthew, who opposed her in order to secure his own position with Sackville. This type of manoeuvring was not unusual in large households where favoured servants vied with a wife for position and authority in a household.
81 Cecily Baker, wife to Thomas Sackville.
82 Christopher Marsh served Anne until his death in 1656, and was also her close friend.
83 Robert Devereux, the first husband of Frances Howard, Countess of Somerset. This marriage was annulled.
84 Here Anne refers to Psalm 102.6 from the Coverdale psalter (published in several editions and set as the companion to the Book of Common Prayer): 'I am become like a pelican in the wilderness: and like an owl *that is in the desert*'. It is clear this is her source for this psalm. In the Geneva Bible of 1599 the verse is slightly different: 'I am like a pelican of the wilderness: I am like an owl *of the deserts*'. The 1611 King James Version reads: 'I am like an owl *of the desert*' (my italics). Anne often used biblical verses as a type of shorthand to express her emotions.
85 Matthew Caldicott.

Upon the 15th my Lord and my cousin Cecily Neville came down from London, my Lord lying in Leicester chamber and I in my own.

Upon the 17th my Lord and I after supper had talk about these businesses, Matthew[86] being in the room, where we all fell out, and so we parted for the night.

Upon the 18th being Saturday in the morning my Lord and I having much talk about these businesses we agreed that Mr Marsh should go presently down to my mother and that by him I should write a letter to persuade her to give over her jointure presently to my Lord and that he would give her yearly as much as it was worth.[87] This day my Lord went from Knole to London.

Upon the 20th went my child with Mary Neville and Mrs Bathurst to West Horsley from London. Mary Hutchins went with her for still she lay in bed with Lady Margaret.

Upon the 20th being Monday, I dispatched Mr Marsh with letters to my mother about the business aforesaid. I sent them unsealed because my Lord might see them.[88]

My brother Compton and his wife[89] kept house at West Horsley and my brother Beauchamp and my sister his wife sojourned with them, so as the Child was with both her aunts.

Upon the 22nd Mr Davis came down from London and brought me word that my mother was very well recovered of her dangerous sickness. By him I writ a letter to my Lord that Mr Amherst[90] and Mr Davis might confer together about my jointure,[91] to free it from the payment of debts and all other encumbrances.

Upon the 24th being Friday, between the hours of six and seven at night died my dear mother at Brougham[92] in the same chamber where my father was born, thirteen years and two months after the death of Queen Elizabeth and ten years and four months after the death of my father, I being then

---

86 His presence shows his high status in the household.
87 This would mean that Sackville would have control of the Westmorland estates that made up Margaret's jointure.
88 So Richard could read them if he wished.
89 Henry Compton and Cecily Sackville.
90 Richard Amherst, steward to the Earls of Dorset.
91 A jointure was a legal agreement that detailed what a wife would receive for her maintenance and the maintenance of her children should her husband predecease her. Jointures were often a point of conflict in marriages. Anne's jointure was finalized in 1623, see KHLC, U269/T70/10, Settlement of the Jointure of Anne, Countess of Dorset.
92 This was a huge emotional blow to Anne and disaster for her hopes to gain the Clifford hereditary lands. Her mother was the architect of their legal strategies from the beginning in 1605 and had also covered most of the legal costs.

twenty-six years old and four months and the Child two years old wanting a month.[93]

My Lord was at London when my mother died, but he went to Lewes before he heard the news of her death.[94] At this great meeting at Lewes, my Lord Compton, my Lord Mordaunt, Tom Neville, John Herbert and all that crew with Walter Raleigh, Jack Lewis[95] and a multitude of such company were there. There was bowling, bull-baiting, cards and dice with such sports to entertain the time.[96]

Upon the 24th my Lady Somerset[97] was arraigned and condemned at Westminster Hall where she confessed her fault[98] and asked the King's mercy and was much pitied of all the beholders.

Upon the 25th my Lord of Somerset[99] was arraigned and condemned in the same place and stood much upon his innocency.

Upon the 27th being Monday, my Lord came down to Buckhurst. My Lord Vaux[100] and his uncle Sir Henry Neville[101] and diverse others came with him, but the lords that promised to go with him stayed behind agreeing to meet him the next day at Lewes.

Upon the 28th my Lady Selby[102] came hither to see me and told me that she had heard some folks say that I have done well in not consenting to the Composition.[103]

Upon the 29th Kendal came and brought me the heavy news of my mother's death, which I held as the greatest and most lamentable cross that could befall me. Also he brought her will along with him, wherein she appointed her body should be buried in the parish church of Alnwick,[104] which was a double grief to

---

93 \Upon the 24th ... month/
94 \My Lord was ... death/
95 John Mordaunt, William Compton, Thomas Neville, 'Wat' Raleigh, son of the explorer and courtier Sir Walter Raleigh, Jack (John) Lewis or Lewes.
96 \At this great ... time/
97 Frances Howard, Countess of Somerset.
98 She confessed her part in the murder of Sir Thomas Overbury.
99 Robert Carr, Earl of Somerset, was found guilty for his part in the same murder. In January 1609 Chamberlain wrote that Carr was in negotiations to marry Anne (LJC, vol. 1, p. 280).
100 Edward Vaux, 4th Baron of Harrowden.
101 Sir Henry Neville is both Richard Sackville's and Edward Vaux's uncle-in-law, having married first Richard's aunt Mary Sackville (d. 1613), and second Edward's aunt Catherine.
102 Dorothy Bonham who lived at Ightham Mote, about five miles from Knole.
103 The Judges' Award.
104 St Michael's church, Alnwick, Northumberland. Margaret Russell's favourite brother Francis spent most of his adult life on the borders and married Julianna Foster of Alnwick. He was murdered during a meeting between his father-in-law John Foster and a Scottish delegation.

me when I considered her body should be carried away, and not be interred at Skipton, so I took that as a sign that I should be disinherited of the inheritance of my forefathers. The same night I sent Hammon[105] away with the will to my Lord who was then at Lewes.

Upon the 30th the Bishop of St David's came to me in the morning to comfort me in these my afflictions, and in the afternoon I sent for Sir William Selby to speak to him about the conveyance of my dear mother's body into Northumberland and about the building of a little chapel wherein I intended she should be buried. And on the 30th at night or the 31st my Lord was told the news of my mother's death, he being then at Lewes with all this company.[106]

Upon the 31st came Mr Amherst from my Lord to me and brought me word that my Lord would be here on Saturday. The same day Mr Jones brought me a letter from Mr Woolrich[107] wherein it seemed that it was my mother's pleasure her body should be conveyed to what place I appointed and which was some contentment to my aggrieved soul.[108]

June 1616

Upon the 1st being Saturday my Lord left all the company at Buckhurst and came hither about seven o'clock in the morning and so went to bed and slept till twelve, when I made Rivers write my letter to Sir Christopher Pickering,[109] Mr Woolrich, Mr Domville[110] and Ralph Conniston[111] wherein I told them that my Lord had determined to keep possession for my right, and to desire that the body might be wrapped in lead[112] till they heard from me. About four of the clock my Lord went to London.

About this time came my Lady Cavendish,[113] Sir Robert Yaxley and Mr

---

105 Possibly Thomas Harmon, listed in the Knole catalogue, See D.J.H. Clifford, *The Diaries of Anne Clifford* (1990), pp. 274–276.
106 \And on the 30th ... company/
107 Possibly William Woolrich, husband to Anne Wharton. His brother-in-law Philip, 3rd Lord Wharton, was married to Anne's aunt Frances Clifford.
108 This was a deathbed change to the will.
109 Margaret Russell called Pickering her faithful friend. George Clifford appointed him as one of the constables of the forest near the border with Scotland. He was also distantly related to the Cliffords.
110 This may be the clergyman Robert Domville, mentioned below.
111 Margaret Russell calls Ralph Conniston her trusted servant, and she made him one of the executors of her will.
112 Sealing the dead body in a lead coffin facilitated the elaborate rituals and burial practices of the elite that often took some time.
113 Christiana Bruce. Her brother, Edward Bruce, 2nd Lord Kinloss, was killed in a duel with

Watson[114] to see me and comfort me after the loss of my mother, and persuaded me much to consent to the agreement.[115]

Upon the 4th Mr Marsh and Rivers came down from London and gave me to understand how my Lord by the knowledge and consent of Lord William Howard and the advice of his learned council[116] had sent a letter down into Westmorland to my Lady's servants and tenants to keep possession for him and me, which was a thing I little expected but gave me much contentment for I thought my Lord of Cumberland had taken possession of her jointure quietly.[117]

Upon the 8th being Saturday, Rivers and Mr Burridge were sent down into Westmorland with letters from the Council[118] for the restoring of the possession of Appleby Castle as it was at my Lady's decease.

At this time my Lord desired to have me pass my right of the lands in Westmorland to him and my Child and to this end he brought my Lord William Howard to persuade me,[119] and then my Lord told me I should go presently to Knole and so I was sent away upon half an hour's warning leaving my cousin Cecily Neville and Willoughby behind me at London and so went down alone with Katherine Burton[120] about eight o'clock at night so as it was twelve before we came to Knole.

Upon the 15th came the steward[121] to Knole with whom I had much talk. At this time I wrought very hard and made an end of one of my cushions of Irish stitch work.[122]

Upon the 17th came down Dr Layfield,[123] Ralph Conniston and Basket, Dr

Edward Sackville in 1613 which may have been over Sackville's attempted seduction of Christiana. See LJC, vol. 1, p. 450, p. 474.
114 Likely Sir Thomas Watson, knighted 1618.
115 \About this time ... agreement/
116 His lawyer.
117 The Clifford lands of Westmorland which Margaret Russell possessed in her widowhood as part of her jointure. With the lawsuit at a standstill and the Judges' Award still unsigned, Sackville here attempts to secure the Clifford inheritance in Westmorland for Anne.
118 The Council of the North was an administrative and judicial body that administered the King's laws in the North. In 1616 the President was Edmund Sheffield, 3rd Baron Sheffield (later 1st Earl of Musgrave).
119 Sackville sought to ensure that if Anne died in possession of Westmorland the land would pass to Margaret first and then, if she died without heirs, to himself.
120 Anne dismisses this gentlewoman servant in October 1619 over a disagreement in August 1619.
121 Richard Amherst, a lawyer and steward for Richard Sackville.
122 A series of straight stitches that produces a geometric pattern often used in place of tent or cross stitch as it took less time.
123 John Layfield, Doctor of Divinity. Layfield was a close personal friend and spiritual adviser to Margaret Russell. He accompanied George Clifford as his chaplain on his expedition to the West Indies in 1598 and wrote an account of it that was printed in *Purchas's Pilgrims* (1625). The manuscript copy is BL, MS Sloane 3289.

Layfield bringing with him the conveyance which Mr Walter[124] had drawn and persuaded me to go up and set my hand to it, which I refused, because my Lord had sent me down so suddenly two days before.[125]

Upon the 19th my Lord came down for me and Doctor Layfield with him, when my Lord persuaded me to consent to his business, and assured me how good and kind a husband he would be to me.

Upon the 20th my Lord and I, Doctor Layfield and Katherine Burton went up to London and the same day as I take it I passed (by fine before my Lord Hobart)[126] the inheritance of Westmorland to my Lord if I had no heirs of my own body.[127]

This summer the King of Spain's eldest daughter called Anna Maria[128] came into France and was married to the French King[129] and the French King's eldest sister[130] went into Spain and was married to the King of Spain's eldest son.[131]

Upon the 21st being Friday, my Lord wrote his letters to my Lord William Howard and gave directions to Mr Marsh to go with them and that the possession of Brougham Castle should be very carefully looked to. The same day he went down to Horsley to see the Child at his sister's.[132]

Upon Sunday the 23rd my Lord and I went in the morning to St Bride's church[133] and heard a sermon.[134]

Upon the 24th my Lord and my Lord [blank] and my cousin Cecily Neville went by barge to Greenwich and waited on the King and Queen to chapel and dined at my Lady Bedford's[135] where I met my Lady Home[136] my old acquaintance. After dinner we went up to the gallery where the Queen used me exceeding well. About this time I went into the Tiltyard[137] to see my Lady

---

124 John Walter, a lawyer and later Chief Baron of the Exchequer.
125 The document that would make Richard Anne's heir to the Westmorland estates after their daughter.
126 Henry Hobart, one of the judges who crafted the Judges' Award.
127 Here she indicates she has signed the document making Richard her heir if they have no surviving children.
128 Anna Maria of Austria.
129 Louis XIII of France.
130 Elisabeth of France, Queen consort of Spain and Portugal.
131 \This summer ... son/, later Phillip IV of Spain.
132 Cecily Sackville.
133 Fleet Street, London. The minister was James Palmer (b. 1585) a reformist preacher, educated at Magdalene College, Cambridge. He was appointed vicar of St Bride's church in 1637.
134 \Upon Sunday ... sermon/.
135 Lucy Harington, Bedford House on the Strand.
136 Mary Sutton, Countess of Home.
137 Northampton House, also called Suffolk House. At this time it was owned by Thomas Howard, Earl of Suffolk.

Knollys[138] where I saw my Lady Somerset's little child[139] being the first time I ever saw it.[140]

Upon the 28th came Kendal with letters from my Lord William[141] so as my Lord determined I should go presently into the North.

Upon the 30th being Sunday, presently after dinner my Lady Robert Rich, my cousin Cecily Neville and I went down by barge to Greenwich where in the gallery there passed some unkind words between my Lady Knollys and me. I took my leave of the Queen and all my friends there. About this time it was agreed between my Lord and me that Mrs Bathurst should go away from the Child and that Willoughby should have the charge of her till I should appoint it otherwise. He gave me his faithful promise that he would come after me into the North as soon as he could, and that the Child should come out of hand so that my Lord and I were never greater friends than at this time.

About this time [end of June, beginning of July] Acton my Lord's footman lost his race to my Lord Salisbury's[142] Irish footman and my Lord lost 200 twenty shilling pieces by betting on his side.[143]

July 1616

Upon the 1st my Lord Hobart came to Dorset House where I acknowledged a fine to him of a great part of my thirds in my Lord's land but my Lord gave me his faithful word and promise that in Michaelmas term next he would make me a jointure of the full thirds of his living.[144]

About one o'clock I set forward on my journey.[145] My Lord brought me down to the coach side where we had a loving and kind parting.

Upon the 11th Ralph[146] brought me word that it[147] could not be buried at

---

138 Elizabeth Howard, Lady Knollys and later Countess of Banbury.
139 Anne Carr. She was born in the Tower of London where her parents were imprisoned for the murder of Thomas Overbury. She later married Anne's cousin, William Russell, 1st Duke of Bedford. Lady Knollys was her aunt.
140 \About this time … saw it/
141 Sir William Howard of Naworth.
142 William Cecil, 2nd Earl of Salisbury. He was the brother-in-law of Anne's first cousin Henry Clifford.
143 \About this time … side/
144 Anne has just signed away her rights to one-third of the profits of Richard Sackville's freehold property during her widowhood. Women often signed away the right to their 'thirds' as part of a jointure agreement. The use of the word 'term' refers to the legal year made up of four terms: Hilary, Easter, Trinity and Michaelmas.
145 To Brougham Castle in Westmorland.
146 Ralph Conniston, gentleman servant to Margaret Russell in Westmorland.
147 The body of her mother, Margaret Russell.

Appleby so I sent Rivers away presently who got their consents. About five o'clock came my cousin William Howard and about five or six of his [men]. About eight we set forward, the body going in my Lady's own coach with my four horses and my self following it in my own coach with two horses and most of the men and women on horseback, so as there was about 40 in the company and we came to Appleby about half an hour after eleven o'clock and about twelve the body was put into the grave. About three o'clock in the morning we came home where I showed my cousin Howard my letter that I writ to my Lord.

Upon the 17th I rid into Whinfell Park and there I willed the tenants that were carrying off hay at Julian Bower that they should keep the money in their own hands till it were known who had a right to it.[148]

Upon the 25th I signed a warrant for the killing of a stag in Stainsmore being the first warrant I ever had signed of that kind.[149]

Upon the 29th I sent my folks into the park to make hay when they being interrupted by my uncle Cumberland's people. Two of my uncle's people were hurt by Mr Kidd the one in the leg, the other in the foot, whereupon complaint was presently made to the judges at Carlisle and a warrant sent forth for the apprehending of all my folks that were in the field at that time to put in surety to appear at Kendal at the assizes.[150]

August 1616

Upon the 1st day came Baron Bromley[151] and Judge Nicholls[152] to see me as they came from Carlisle and ended the matter about the hurting of my uncle Cumberland's men and have released my folks that were bound to appear at the assizes.

Upon the 4th my cousin John Dudley supped here and told me that I had given very good satisfaction to the judges[153] and all the company that was with

---

148 This would both influence the tenants to support Anne's cause in the inheritance dispute and diminish the funds her uncle Francis and cousin Henry Clifford could use in legal actions against her.
149 This is the action of the rightful owner of the manor. With this act Anne was attempting to create a precedent that she could later use to forward her claims to the Clifford hereditary lands in Westmorland.
150 Anne is attempting to assert her claim to the Westmorland estates by putting her people 'on the ground'. Actions of this nature could easily descend into violence as dependants tried to prove their value and loyalty to their lords.
151 Sir Edward Bromley, a Baron of the Exchequer.
152 Augustine Nicholls, judge and later Keeper of the Great Seal for Prince Charles.
153 Bromley and Nicholls.

them. About this time my Lady of Exeter was brought to bed of a daughter[154] and my Lady Montgomery of a son[155] being her first son.[156]

Upon the 11th came Mr Marsh and brought a letter of the King's hand to it that I should not be molested in Brougham Castle and withal how all things went well and that my Lord would be here very shortly.

Upon the 22nd I met my Lord at Appleby towns-end where he came with a great company of horse, Lord William Howard, he and I riding in the coach together and so we came that night to Brougham. There came with him Thomas Glemham, Coventry, Grosvenor,[157] Grey Dick etc. The same night Prudence, Bess, Penelope and some of the men came hither but the stuff was not yet come so as they were fain to lie three or four in a bed.

Upon the 24th in the afternoon I dressed the chamber[158] where my Lady died and set up the green velvet bed where the same night we went to lie there. Upon Saturday and Sunday [24th and 25th] my Lord showed me his will whereby he gave all his land[159] to the Child saving three thousand five hundred pound a year to my brother Sackville and fifteen hundred pounds a year which is appointed for the payment of his debts, and my jointure excepted, which was a matter I little expected.[160]

Upon the 26th came my cousin Clifford[161] to Appleby, but with far less train than my Lord.

Upon the 27th our folks being all at [Penrith] there passed some ill words between Matthew, one of the [Clifford] keepers and William Dunn whereupon they fell to blows and Grosvenor, Grey Dick, Thomas Todd and Edward's[162] swords made a great uproar in the town and three or four were hurt and the man who went to ring the bell fell from a ladder and was sore hurt.

Upon the 28th we made an end of dressing the house in the forenoon and in the afternoon I wrought Irish stitch and my Lord sat and read by me.

---

154 This daughter died in infancy.
155 Susan De Vere, Countess of Montgomery. Her husband, Philip Herbert, would become Anne's second husband. This infant son died a little over a year later.
156 \About this time ... son/
157 Thomas Coventry, 1st Baron Coventry, also a gifted lawyer; Richard Grosvenor, 1st Baron Grosvenor.
158 She brought in furnishings and made the bed. This was also the room where her father was born.
159 All his disposable land, but not the Sackville inheritance including Knole, which was entailed on the male and would pass to his brother.
160 \Upon Saturday ... expected/
161 Henry Clifford. He arrived with less pomp than Richard Sackville.
162 Evan Edwards. Anne described him as a man with a 'wise and well-tempered mind'. See Flintshire Archives, letter 1657, D/HE/477.

September 1616[163]

October 1616

Upon the 11th Mrs Samford[164] went to London by whom I sent a very earnest letter to my Lord that I might come up to London.

The 17th was the first day that I put on my black silk grogram gown.

Upon the 18th being Friday, died my Lady Margaret's old beagle.[165]

Upon the 22nd came Rivers down to Brougham and brought me word that I could not go to London all this winter.

Upon the 31st I rid into Whinfell in the afternoon. This month I spent in working and reading. Mr Domville[166] read a great part of the History of the Netherlands.[167]

November 1616

Upon the 1st I rose betimes in the morning and went up to the Pagan Tower[168] to my prayers and saw the sun rise.

Upon the 4th Prince Charles was created Prince of Wales in the Great Hall at Whitehall where he had been created Duke of York about 13 years before. There was barriers and running at the ring[169] but it was not half so great pomp as was at the creation of Prince Henry.[170] Not long after this Lord Chancellor was created Viscount Brackley[171] and my Lord Knollys Viscount Wallingford,[172] my

---

163 There are no entries for this month in this diary. She and Richard spent four days at Naworth Castle, the home of Lord William Howard as described in the Daybook of 1676. With tensions running high, they went on to York to meet with Edmund Sheffield, 3rd Baron Sheffield, President of the Council of the North, in an attempt to mediate an agreement with Francis Clifford. For a detailed discussion of Anne's strategies at this time see Spence, *Anne Clifford*, pp. 55–57.
164 This is likely a Mrs Sandford, from the large gentry family of Sandfords, many of whom were connected with the Clifford family in Westmorland.
165 \Upon the 18th ... beagle/
166 Robert Domville, a clergyman.
167 Jean François Le Petit, *A Generall Historie of the Netherlands*, trans. Edward Grimston (1608).
168 The Pagan Tower is the large square keep at Brougham Castle. It is the earliest part of the castle, built at the end of the twelfth century. From the top it provides spectacular views of the surrounding countryside.
169 Tilting competitions. The barriers were the fence that separated the competitors as they ran at each other.
170 Richard Sackville was a favourite of Prince Henry (d. 1612).
171 Thomas Egerton. His third wife was Alice Spencer, widow of Anne's cousin Ferdinando Stanley, 5th Earl of Derby.
172 William Knollys, later 1st Earl of Banbury.

Lord Coke[173] was displaced and Montagu was made Lord Chief Justice in his place. [And] upon the 4th I sat in the drawing chamber all the day at my work.[174]

Upon the 9th I sat at my work[175] and heard Rivers and Marsh read Montaigne's *Essays*,[176] which book they have read almost this fortnight.

Upon the 12th I made an end of the long cushion of Irish stitch which my cousin Cecily Neville began when she went with me to the bath, it being my chief help to pass away the time to work.[177]

Upon the 19th William Dunn came down from London with letters from my Lord, whereby I perceived there had passed a challenge between him and my cousin Clifford which my Lord sent him by my cousin Cheyney.[178] The Lords of the Council sent for them both and the King made them friends, giving my Lord marvellous good words and willed him to send for me, because he meant to make an agreement himself between us. This going up to London of mine I little expected at this time. By him I also heard that my sister Sackville was dead.[179]

Upon the 20th I spent most of the day in playing at tables. All this time since my Lord went away I wore my black taffeta night gown[180] and a yellow taffeta waistcoat and used to rise betimes in the morning and walk upon the leads[181] and afterwards to hear reading.

Upon the 22nd I did string the pearls and diamonds my mother left me into a necklace.

Upon the 23rd I went to Mr Blinke's house in Cumberland[182] where I stayed an hour or two and heard music and saw all the house and gardens. [And] upon the 23rd Baker, Hookfield, Harry the Caterer,[183] and Tom Fool[184] went from hence towards London.[185]

173 Edward Coke, the famed legal scholar, also Attorney General and Chief Justice of the King's Bench.
174 Henry Montagu. \Upon the 4th Prince ... place/
175 Needlework.
176 Michel de Montaigne, *The Essayes or Morall, ... of Lord Michaell de Montaigne*, trans. John Florio (1603).
177 Bath, Somerset.
178 The Cheyney family of Kent was closely associated with the Russells, Earls of Bedford, through Sir Thomas Cheyney. A Mr Cheyney is listed as a gentleman servant in the Knole catalogue, and Anne calls him cousin. This duel never took place (see LJC, vol. 2, p. 35).
179 It is unclear to whom this refers. Mary Curzon, wife of Edward Sackville, was alive and well, as were Richard Sackville's married sisters. He had no unmarried sisters at this time. This may be a false rumour.
180 Evening attire, not bed wear.
181 Anne is walking on the roof of Pagan Tower.
182 Probably refers to Thomas Blenkinsop of Helbeck, Margaret Russell's ward.
183 One who provisions the household.
184 This would be a household fool whose antics (real or performed) entertained the family.
185 \upon the 23rd Baker ... London/

Upon the 24th Baker[186] set out from London to Brougham Castle to fetch me up.

Upon the 26th Thomas Hilton[187] came hither and told me of some quarrels that would be between some gentlemen that took my Lord's part and my cousin Clifford which did much trouble me.

Upon the 29th I bought of Mr Cliborne who came to see me a cloak and a saveguard[188] of cloth laced with black lace to keep me warm in my journey.

December 1616

Upon the 4th came Basket with all the horses to carry me to London but he left the coach behind him at Roos.

Upon the 9th I set out from Brougham Castle towards London. About three o'clock in the afternoon we came to Roos. All this day I rode on horseback on Rivers his mare 29 miles that day.[189]

Upon the 11th I went to York. Three of Lord Sheffield's daughters[190] and Mrs Matthew the Bishop's wife[191] came to see me this night. Mrs Matthew lay with me. About this time died Mr Marshall my Lord's Auditor and Surveyor and left me a purse of ten Angels[192] as a remembrance of his love.

Upon the 12th William Dunn overtook us at Wentbridge, having found the diamond ring at Roos which I was very glad of.[193]

The 15th day was Mr John Tufton just eight years old, being he that was after married to my first child in the church at St Bartholomew's.[194]

Upon the 18th I alighted at Islington where my Lord was, who came in my Lady Withypole's[195] coach which he had borrowed. My Lady Effingham the widow,[196] my sister Beauchamp and a great many more came to meet me so that

---

186 This is likely a different servant from the Baker in the previous entry.
187 Either Thomas Hilton the elder (d. 1631) or the younger (d. 1645). Both were gentleman tenants of the Cliffords in Westmorland.
188 This is an outer skirt or petticoat worn to protect a woman's clothing, or in this case for warmth especially when riding, bought in preparation for her journey south.
189 Roos, near Kendal, in Westmorland (now Cumbria).
190 Edmund Sheffield had as many as nine daughters by 1616.
191 Agnes Wellesbourne and Tobias Matthew.
192 An angel coin, called this because it bore the image of the Archangel St Michael slaying a dragon. It was worth 11 shillings in 1612.
193 \Upon the 12th ... glad of/
194 \The 15th day ... Bartholomew's/ This insertion was made some time after the marriage of Margaret Sackville and John Tufton on 21 April 1629.
195 Frances Cornwallis, Richard Sackville's cousin.
196 Anne St John. Her husband William Howard, 3rd Baron Howard of Effingham, died in 1615.

we were in all ten or eleven coaches and so I came to Dorset House where the Child met me in the gallery. The house was well dressed up against I came. The Child was brought down to me in the gallery which was the first time I had seen her after my mother died.[197]

Upon the 23rd my Lady Manners[198] came in the morning to dress my head. I had a new black wrought taffeta gown which my Lady St John's[199] tailor made. She used often to come to me and I to her and was very kind one to another. About five o'clock in the evening my Lord and I and the Child went in the great coach to Northampton House, where my Lord Treasurer[200] and all the company commended her and she went down into my Lady Walden's chamber.[201] My cousin Clifford[202] saw her and kissed her but I stayed with my Lady Suffolk.[203] All this time of me being at London I was much sent to and visited by many, being unexpected that ever matters should have gone so well with me and my Lord, everybody persuading me to hear and to make an end since the King had taken the matter in hand, so as now I had a new part to play upon the stage of this world.

Upon the 26th I dressed myself in my green satin night gown.

Upon the 27th I dined at my Lady Elizabeth Grey's lodgings in Somerset House where I met my Lady Compton[204] and my Lady Fielding[205] and spoke to them about my coming to the King. Presently after dinner came my Lord thither and we went together to my Lady Arundel's where I saw all the pictures in the gallery and the statues in the lower rooms.[206]

Upon the 28th I dined above in my chamber and wore my night gown because I was not very well which day and yesterday I forgot that it was fish day and eat flesh at both dinners. In the afternoon I played at glecko with my Lady Grey and lost 27 pounds and odd money.

Upon the 31st this night I sent Thomas Woodgate with a sweet bag to the Queen for a New Year's gift, and a standish to Mrs Hanno, both which cost me about 16 or 17 pounds.[207]

197 \The child ... died/
198 Frances Carey, Lady Manners, later Countess of Rutland.
199 Joan Roydon.
200 Thomas Howard, 1st Earl of Suffolk. who owned Northampton House.
201 Elizabeth Home.
202 Henry Clifford.
203 Catherine Knyvet, Countess of Suffolk.
204 Elizabeth Spencer married to William, 2nd Baron Compton.
205 Susan Villiers, sister of George Villiers, Duke of Buckingham and James I's favourite.
206 Arundel House was adjacent to Somerset House and housed a magnificent collection of European art collected by Alethea Talbot, Countess of Arundel during her travels with Inigo Jones in Italy 1613–1614.
207 New Year's gifts were part of the culture of gift exchange in the period. A standish was an inkstand or pot.

January 1617

Upon New Year's Day presently after dinner I went to the Savoy to my Lord Carey's.[208] From thence he and I went to Somerset House to the Queen where I met Lady Derby, my Lady Bedford, and my Lady Montgomery[209] and a great deal of other company that came along with the King and the Prince.

As the King passed by he kissed me. Afterwards the Queen came out into the drawing chamber where she kissed me and used me very kindly. This was the first time I either saw the King, Queen or Prince since my coming out of the North.[210]

My Lord Arundel[211] had much talk with me about the business and persuaded me to yield to the King in all things. From Somerset House we went to Essex House to see my Lady of Northumberland. This was the last time I ever saw my Lady of Northumberland.[212] From thence I went to see my Lady Rich[213] and so came home. After supper I went to see my sister Beauchamp and stayed with her an hour or two for my Lord was at the play at Whitehall that night.

Upon the 2nd I went to the Tower to see my Lady Somerset and my Lord. This was the first time I saw them since their arraignment.[214]

Upon the 5th I went into the Court. We went up into the King's Presence Chamber where my Lord Villiers was created Earl of Buckingham,[215] my Lord, my Lord of Montgomery[216] and diverse other Earls bringing him up to the King. I supped with my Lord of Arundel and my Lady and after supper I saw the play of the mad lover in the hall.[217]

Upon the 6th being Twelfth Day I went about four o'clock to the Court with my Lord. I went up with my Lady Arundel and ate a scrambling supper with

---

208 Robert Carey, later 1st Earl of Monmouth. Savoy Palace was adjacent to Somerset House.
209 Elizabeth De Vere, Lucy Harington and Susan De Vere.
210 \As the King ... North/
211 Thomas Howard, Earl of Arundel.
212 \This was the ... Northumberland/. This marginal note was a later addition reflecting upon the death of Dorothy Devereux, who died 3 August 1619.
213 Frances Hatton or Frances Wray who married Richard Rich in December 1616, becoming the mother-in-law of Frances Hatton, Lady Rich. Frances Wray would become the Countess of Warwick in 1618, and the dowager Countess of Warwick in 1619.
214 Frances Howard and Robert Carr were at this time imprisoned in the Tower for the murder of Sir Thomas Overbury.
215 George Villiers, Duke of Buckingham and James I's favourite.
216 Richard Sackville and Philip Herbert, who would become Anne's second husband.
217 *The Mad Lover*, by John Fletcher, performed by the King's Men.

her and my Lady Pembroke at my Lord Duke's lodging.[218] We stood to see the masque[219] in the box with my Lady Ruthven.[220]

Upon the 8th we came down from London to Knole. This night my Lord and I had a falling out about the land.

Upon the 9th I went up to see the things in the closet[221] and began to have Mr Sandys his book read to me about the government of the Turks,[222] my Lord sitting the most part of the day reading in his closet.

Upon the 10th my Lord went up to London upon the sudden, we not knowing it till the afternoon.

Upon the 16th I received a letter from my Lord that I should come up to London the next day because I was to go before the King on Monday next.

Upon the 17th when I came up my Lord told me I must resolve to go to the King the next day.

Upon the 18th being Saturday I went presently after dinner to the Queen to the drawing chamber, where my Lady Derby told the Queen how my business stood and that I was to go to the King, so she promised me she would do all the good in it she could. The Queen gave me warning to take heed of putting my matters absolutely to the King lest he should deceive me.[223] When I had stayed but a little while there, I was sent for out, my Lord and I going through my Lord Buckingham's chamber who brought us into the King being in the drawing chamber. He put out all that were there and my Lord and I kneeled by his chair side when he persuaded us both to peace and to put the matter wholly into his hands, which my Lord consented to, but I beseeched His Majesty to pardon me for that I would never part with Westmorland while I lived upon any condition whatsoever. Sometimes he used fair means and persuasions, and sometimes foul means but I was resolved before so as nothing would move me. From the King we went to the Queen's side[224] and brought my Lady St John to her lodging and so went home. At this time I was much bound to my Lord for he was far kinder to me in all these businesses than I expected, and was very unwilling that the King should do me any public disgrace.

218 Lodovic Stuart, at the Palace of Whitehall.
219 *Christmas, His Mask*, by Ben Jonson. Chamberlain also gives an account of this evening (LJC, vol. 2, p. 49).
220 Barbara Ruthven.
221 A small room, often off a bedchamber, used for private study and to store valuables.
222 George Sandys, *A Relation of a Journey ... Containing a description of the Turkish Empire* (1615). Sandys was George Clifford's godson.
223 \The Queen ... deceive me/. The wording in this marginal insertion is changed slightly in the three nineteenth-century manuscript copies, and is instead: 'The Queen gave me warning not to trust my matters absolutely to the King lest he should deceive me.'
224 The Queen's rooms in the palace.

Upon the 19th my Lord and I went to the Court in the morning thinking the Queen would have gone to the Chapel, but she did not, so my Lady Ruthven and I and many others stood in the closet to hear the sermon.[225] I dined with my Lady Ruthven. Presently after dinner she and I went up to the drawing chamber, where my Lord Duke, my Lady Montgomery, my Lady Burghley[226] persuaded me to refer these businesses to the King. About six o'clock my Lord came for me so he and I and Lady St John went home in her coach. This night the masque was danced at the Court but I would not stay to see it because I had seen it already.[227]

Upon the 20th I and my Lord went presently after dinner to the Court. He went up to the King's side about his business. I went up to my Lady Bedford in her lodgings where I stayed in Lady Ruthven's chamber till towards three o'clock about which time I was sent for up to the King into his drawing chamber when the door was locked and nobody suffered to stay there but my Lord and I, my uncle Cumberland, my cousin Clifford, my Lord of Arundel, my Lord of Pembroke,[228] my Lord of Montgomery and Sir John Digby. Four lawyers there were my Lord Chief Justice Montagu[229] and Hobart, Yelverton[230] the King's solicitor, Sir Ranulphe Crew that was to speak for my Lord of Cumberland and Mr Ireland that was to speak for my Lord and me. The King asked us all whether we would submit to his judgement in this case, to which my uncle of Cumberland, my cousin Clifford and my Lord answered they would, but I would never agree to it without Westmorland at which the King grew into a great chaff,[231] my Lord of Pembroke and the King's solicitor speaking much against me. At last, when they saw there was no remedy, my Lord, fearing the King would do me some public disgrace, desired Sir John Digby to open the door, who went out with me and persuaded me much to yield to the King. My Lord Hay[232] came out to me to whom I told in brief how this business stood. Presently after my lord came from the King where it was resolved that if I would not come to an agreement, there should be an agreement made without me.[233]

---

225 The Chapel Royal at the palace of Whitehall was a separate building and was for the use of the wider household and visitors to the palace. The Queen would also have a smaller private chapel, referred to here as her closet.
226 Elizabeth Drury, Lady Burghley and later Countess of Exeter.
227 *Christmas, His Mask* also performed 6 January above.
228 William Herbert, 3rd Earl of Pembroke.
229 Henry Montagu, 1st Earl Montague.
230 Sir Henry Yelverton, a lawyer.
231 Generally the term means light-hearted banter or ridicule but clearly Anne uses the term here to mean anger.
232 James Hay, 1st Earl of Carlisle and a favourite of James I.
233 Chamberlain records the details of this day and the award (LJC, vol. 2, p. 63).

We went down, Sir Robert Douglas and Sir George Chaworth bringing us to the coach. By the way my Lord and I went in at Worcester House to see my Lord and my Lady,[234] and so came home. This day I may say I was led miraculously by God's providence and next to that I must attribute all my good to the worth and nobleness of my Lord's disposition for neither I nor anybody else thought that I should have passed over this day so well as I thank God I have done.[235]

Upon the 22nd the Child had the sixth fit of her ague.[236] In the morning Mr Smith[237] went up in the coach to London to my Lord to whom I wrote a letter to let him know in what case the Child was, and to give him humble thanks for his noble usage towards me at London. The same day my Lord came down to Knole to see the Child.

Upon the 23rd my Lord went up betimes to London again. The same day the Child put on her red baize coat.

Upon the 25th I spent most of the time in working and going up and down to see the Child. About five or six o'clock her fits took her which lasted six or seven hours.

Upon the 28th at this time I wore a green plain flannel gown that William Dunn made me and my yellow taffeta waistcoat. Rivers used to read to me in Montaigne's *Essays* and Moll Neville[238] in the *Fairie Queene*.[239]

Upon the 30th Mr Amherst the preacher came hither to see me with whom I had much talk. He told me that now they began to think at London that I had done well in not referring this business to the King and that everybody said God had a hand in it.

February 1617

Upon the 4th should have been the Child's fit, but she missed it. Acton came presently after dinner with a letter to Tom the groom to meet my Lord at Hampton Court with his hunting horses. At night Thomas Woodgate came from London and brought a squirrel to the Child. My Lord wrote me a letter by

---

234 Edward Somerset, 4th Earl of Worcester, and his wife Elizabeth Hastings.
235 Anne's courage here should not be underestimated. More than fifty-nine years later she would record memories of this day (see her Daybook of 1676 in this edition).
236 An acute or high fever, often returning periodically. Anne remembers this day in the Daybook of 1676.
237 William Smith, a gentleman servant at Knole.
238 Anne's cousin Mary 'Moll' Neville who is also a waiting gentlewoman in her household.
239 Mary Neville reads Edmund Spenser's *Faerie Queene*. A volume entitled 'All Edmond Spencer's Workes' appears on Anne's Great Picture now in Abbot Hall Gallery, Kendal. She would also erect a monument to him in Poets' Corner, Westminster Abbey, in 1620.

which I perceived my Lord was clean out with me and how my enemies have wrought much against me.

All the time of my being in the country there was much ado at London about my business insomuch that my Lord, my uncle of Cumberland, my cousin Clifford, both the Chief Justices and the counsel of both sides were diverse times with the King about it and that the King hearing it go so directly for me he said there was no law in England to keep me from the land.[240] There was during this time much cockfighting at the Court, where my Lord's cocks did fight against the King's, although this business was somewhat chargeable to my Lord, yet it brought him into great grace and favour with the King, so as he useth him very kindly and speaketh very often to him and better of him than any other man. My Lord grew very great with my Lord of Arundel.[241]

Upon the 6th the Child had a kind of grudging of her ague again. At night Mr Osberton came from London and told me that the Baron de Joiners[242] came out of France and had great entertainment both of the King and Queen and was lodged at Salisbury House.

Upon the 7th presently after dinner Mr Osberton and I had a great deal of talk, he telling me how much I was condemned in the world and what strange censures most folks made of my courses, so as I kneeled down to my prayers and desired God to send a good end to these troublesome businesses, my trust being wholly in him that always helped me.

Upon the 8th the Child had a great fit of her ague again insomuch I was very fearful of her that I could hardly sleep all night, so I beseech God Almighty to be merciful to me and spare her life.

Upon the 12th the Child had a little grudging of her ague. Rivers came down presently from London and told me that the judges had been with the King diverse times about my business but as yet the award is not yet published, but it is thought it will be much according to the award formerly set down by the judges. He told me that he had been with Lord William,[243] who as he thought did not very well like of the agreement considering how he had heretofore showed himself in this business. My Lord did nothing so often come to my Lord William as he did heretofore for the friendship between them grew cold, my Lord beginning to harbour some ill opinion of him.[244] After supper the Child's

---

240 See introduction.
241 \All the time ... Arundel/
242 Baron de la Tour. James Hay commissioned a masque from Ben Jonson, *Lovers Made Men*, to entertain the new ambassador.
243 Lord William Howard of Naworth.
244 \My Lord ... of him/

nose fell a-bleeding which as I think was the chief cause she was rid of her ague.

Upon the 13th the King made a speech in the Star Chamber about duels and combats my Lord standing by his chair where he talked with him all the while, he being in extraordinary grace and favour with the King.[245] My sister Compton and her husband were now on terms of parting so as they left Horsley, she lying in London. It was agreed that she should have a 100 pounds a year and he to take the children from her.[246]

Upon the 14th I sent Mr Edwards' man to London with a letter to my Lord, to desire him to come down hither. All this day I spent with Marsh who did write the Chronicles of the year 1607[247] who went in afterwards to my prayers desiring God to send me some end of my troubles, that my enemies might not still have the upper hand of me.

Upon the 16th my Lord came hither from London before dinner and told me how the whole state of my business went and how things went at Court. He told me the Earl of Buckingham was sworn a Privy Councillor and that my Lord Willoughby's brother, Mr Henry Bertie, was put into the Inquisition at Ancona.[248]

Upon the 17th about eight o'clock in the morning my Lord returned to London.

At night Mr Askew came and brought me a letter from my Lady Grantham and told me a great deal of news from London. I signed a bill to give him seven pounds at his return from Jerusalem. This day I gave the Child's old clothes to Legg for his wife.

About this time there was much ado between my Lord of Hertford[249] and my

---

245 In a report of the event, the King stated that 'for as the King was to his people as a shepherd to his flock' he was determined to end the disruption caused by duelling. See NA, SP 14/90, fol. 117.
246 \My sister Compton ... from her/. Anne helped reconcile the two in January 1619. Cecily died in 1624 and Compton went on to remarry.
247 This appears to be a summary of the events of 1607 similar in composition to those that appear in the *Great Books* for 1650–1676 below. This and later entries concerning her chronicles suggests that making yearly summaries from her daybooks was a practice she began very early in her life. These summaries before 1650 have not survived.
248 \He told me ... Ancona/. Sir Henry Wotton, wrote to Thomas Lake the Secretary of State on 3 February about the imprisonment of Henry Bertie. Wotton believed Bertie was betrayed by his servant for possessing a book translated by John Pory critical of Cardinal Peron. However, Bertie relates in a letter to his brother, Lord Willoughby, that he believed his imprisonment was because he refusal to sell a horse (Lincolnshire Archives, Lincoln, 8ANC8/16). In the Daybook of 1676 Anne recalls hearing this news which she says 'did much trouble me'. He was related to her through his grandmother, who was a Brandon.
249 Edward Seymour, 1st Earl of Hertford (d. 1621).

Lord Beauchamp[250] about the assurances of lands to Mr William Seymour,[251] but my sister Beauchamp[252] grew great with my Lord of Hertford and so got the upper hand.[253]

Upon the 21st the Child had an extreme fit of her ague and the doctor sat by her all the afternoon and gave her a salt powder to put in her beer.[254]

Upon the 22nd Basket went up with the great horses to my Lord because my Lord intended to ride a day with the Prince.[255] Legg came down and brought me word how that the King would make a composition and take a course to put me from my rights to the lands, so as if I did not consider of it speedily it would be too late and how bitter the King stood against me. My sister Compton sent to borrow twelve pounds so I sent her ten twenty shilling pieces.

Upon the 24th, 26th [and] 27th I spent my time in working and hearing Mr Rand read the Bible and walking abroad. My Lord writ me word that the King had referred the drawing and perfecting of the business to the solicitor.

My soul was much troubled and afflicted to see how things go, but my trust is still in God and compare things past with things present and read over the Chronicles.

March 1617

Upon the 1st after supper mother Dorset[256] came hither to see me and the Child. About this time the curtain in the Child's chamber window was let up to let in the light which had been close shut up for three weeks or a month before.[257]

Upon the third Petley and Tom[258] went to Buckhurst with my Lord's horses and hounds to meet my Lord there by whom I wrote a letter to my Lord to beseech him that he would take Knole in his way as he goes to London. About this time the King and my Lord Chancellor[259] delivered the seals to Sir Francis Bacon and he was Lord Keeper.[260]

---

250 Edward Seymour, Lord Beauchamp (d. 1618), husband to Richard Sackville's sister, Anne.
251 Brother of Edward Seymour, Lord Beauchamp.
252 Anne, sister to Richard Sackville.
253 \About this time ... upper hand/
254 Children were regularly given 'small beer' with low alcohol content as part of their daily meals.
255 Prince Charles, later Charles I.
256 Anne Spencer, Dowager Countess of Dorset.
257 \About this time ... curtain/. It was common to darken a room for a child with fever.
258 Most likely Thomas and William Petley, servants listed in the Knole catalogue.
259 Thomas Egerton, 1st Viscount Brackley. His third wife Alice Spencer was the widow of Anne's cousin Ferdinando Stanley, 5th Earl of Derby.
260 \About this time ... Keeper/

Upon the 6th Coach puppied in the morning.²⁶¹

Upon the 8th I made an end of Exodus with Mr Rands.²⁶² After supper I played at glecko with the steward,²⁶³ as I often do after dinner and supper.

Upon the 9th Mr Rands said service in the chapel but made no sermon in the afternoon. I went abroad in the garden, and said my prayers in the standing. I was not well at night so I ate a posset and I went to bed.

Upon the 11th we perceived that the Child had two great teeth come out, so as now she had in all 18. I went in the afternoon and said my prayers in the standing in the garden and spent my time in reading and working as I used to. The time grew tedious so as I used to go to bed about eight o'clock and lie abed till eight the next morning.

Upon the 12th I wrote to my Lord, to Sir Walter Raleigh, to Marsh etc.

Upon the 13th I made an end of Leviticus with Mr Rands. I sent by Willoughby a little jewel of opal to my Lady Trenchard's girl.²⁶⁴

Upon the 14th I made an end of my Irish stitch cushion. This afternoon Basket came from London and told me that my Lord and my uncle of Cumberland were agreed and that the writings were sealed. The 14th being Friday, my uncle of Cumberland and my cousin Clifford came to Dorset House to my Lord where he and they signed and sealed the writings and made a final conclusion of my business and did what they could to cut me off from my right, but I referred my cause to God.²⁶⁵

The King set forward this day on his journey to Scotland, the Queen and the Prince going with him to Theobalds.²⁶⁶

Upon the 15th my Lord came down to Buckhurst and was so ill by the way he was fain to alight once or twice and go into a house. All the household were sent down from London to Knole.

Upon this Friday or Saturday died my Lord Chancellor Egerton²⁶⁷ my Lady Derby's husband.²⁶⁸

---

261 Anne kept dogs as pets throughout her life.
262 Richard Rands, who was the Rector of St Mary the Virgin, Hartfield, East Sussex, in 1622. This living was in the gift of the Sackvilles.
263 Richard Amherst.
264 The daughter of Elizabeth Morgan.
265 \The 14th being ... God/
266 This progress lasted six months, with the King returning to London on 16 September.
267 Thomas Egerton, 1st Viscount Brackley. He died on Wednesday 15 March 1617. He was the second husband of Alice Spencer, Countess of Derby. Her first husband was Ferdinando Stanley, 5th Earl of Derby, Anne's first cousin. Alice retained the higher status of title Countess of Derby despite her second marriage as was common practice in the period, thus Anne refers to her as Lady Derby.
268 \Upon this ... husband/

The 16th my Lord sent for John Cook to make broths for him and Josiah to wait in his Chamber by whom I wrote a letter to entreat him that if he were not well I might come down to Buckhurst to him. This day I spent walking in the Park with Judith and carrying my Bible with me thinking on my present fortunes and what troubles I have passed through. This day I put on my grogram mourning gown[269] and intend to wear it till my mourning time come out because I was found fault with all for wearing such ill clothes.[270]

Upon the 17th the women made an end of the sheet of my Lady Sussex[271] her work that is for the palace which was begun in April, presently after I came out of the North from my mother.[272]

Upon the 19th Willoughby brought me very kind messages from my sister Compton, my sister Beauchamp and the rest of the ladies I sent her to. About this time my Lord Hay was sworn a Privy Councillor. About this time my Lord took Adam[273] a new barber to wait on him in his chamber.[274]

Upon the 20th I spent most of the time in walking abroad and playing at cards with the steward and Basket and had such ill luck that I resolved not to play in three months. After supper I wrote a letter to my Lord to entreat him that he would come and see me and the Child as soon as he could.

The 21st Ned footman came from Buckhurst and told me that my Lord was reasonable well and that he had missed his fit which did much comfort me.

The 22nd my cook Hortelius came down from London to me by Dr Layfield. And the steward came from Buckhurst and told me my Lord had not been well so as his going to London had been put off till the next week and that he had lent out his house to my Lord Keeper[275] for two terms until my Lady Derby was gone out of York House[276] and my brother Sackville had written to my Lord to lend him the litter to bring up my sister Sackville[277] to London who was thirteen

---

269 Grogram was a coarse fabric of silk, or a mixture of mohair or wool and silk.
270 \This day ... clothes/. Anne would later also be criticized during her second marriage for not dressing appropriately for her station. In her funeral sermon given by Bishop Edward Rainbow, he turned her modest dress into a virtue, commenting: 'that although she clothed her self in humble and mean attire, yet like the wise and virtuous woman ... her gifts were so bountiful and so frequent' ('A Sermon', 1676, p. 30).
271 Bridget Morison. The sheet is a piece likely from a pattern designed by the Bridget or at least given to Anne by her. It was common for women in the period to exchange patterns.
272 \Upon the 17th ... mother/
273 Adam Bradford, the barber at Knole.
274 \About this time my Lord Hay ... chamber/
275 Sir Francis Bacon, later 1st Viscount St Alban, the famed philosopher and scientist.
276 York House was leased to the Keepers of the Great Seal and thus Alice Spencer, Lady Derby was expected to move after the death of her husband, the previous Keeper.
277 Mary Curzon, wife to Edward Sackville and Anne's sister-in-law.

weeks gone with child. This day I began a new Irish stitch cushion not one of those for Lady Rich but finer canvas.

Upon the 24th we made rosemary cakes.

Upon the 26th my Lord came hither with Thomas Glemham from Buckhurst. He was troubled with a cough and was fain to lie in Leicester Chamber.[278]

Upon the 27th my Lord told me that he had acknowledged no statutes on his lands and that the matter was not so fully finished but there was a place left for me to come in.[279] My Lord found me reading with Mr Rands and told me that it would hinder his study very much so as I must leave off reading the Old Testament until I can get somebody to read it with me. This day I made an end of reading Deuteronomy.

Upon the 28th I walked with my Lord abroad in the Park in the garden, where he spake to me very much of this business with my uncle Cumberland. I wrought very much within doors and strived to set as merry a face as I could upon a discontented heart, for I might easily perceive that Matthew and Lindsey[280] had got a great hand of my Lord and were both of them against me, yet by this means they put my Lord William[281] clean out of all grace and trust with my Lord which I hope may be the better hereafter for me and my child knowing that God often brings things to pass by contrary means.

Upon the 29th the possession of Brougham Castle was delivered by my Lord's warrant to Thomas Taylor etc. of my uncle Cumberland's servants, most of the gentlemen and justices being there present.[282] Upon the 29th my Lord went to London, I bringing him down in his coach. I found this time that he was nothing so much discontented with this agreement as I thought he would have been and that he was more pleased and contented with all the passages at London than I imagined he would have been.

Upon the 30th I spent in walking and sitting in the Park having my mind much more contented than it was before my Lord came from Buckhurst.

---

278 A named chamber at Knole. Robert Dudley, the Earl of Leicester, leased Knole in the mid-16th century.
279 Richard Sackville was required by the King's Award to specify land as a guarantee that neither he nor Anne would undertake further legal action regarding the Clifford hereditary lands. This was required because Anne refused to sign the agreement. This meant Richard could not sell this land should his financial situation worsen.
280 Edward Lindsey, receiver general of Richard Sackville's revenue.
281 William Howard of Naworth.
282 \Upon the 29th ... present/. This marginal insertion is not included in the nineteenth-century manuscript copies.

April 1617

Upon the 2nd my Lord came down from London with Tom Glemham with him. My Lord told me how the King was gone with so few company as he had but one Lord went with him through Northamptonshire. About this time the Marquis of D'Ancre was slain in France which bred great alterations abroad.[283]

Upon the 4th my Lord told me that he had as yet passed no fines and recoveries[284] of my land but that my uncle Cumberland had acknowledged statutes for the payment of the money, and that all writings were left with my Lord Keeper and my Lord Hobart till the next term, at which time they were fully to be concluded on. This was strange news to me, for I thought all matters had been finished. This day we began to leave the little room and dine and sup in the great chamber.

Upon the 5th my Lord went up to my closet and saw how little money I had left, contrary to all that they had told him. Sometimes I had fair words from him and sometimes foul but I took all patiently and did strive to give him as much content and assurance of my love as I could possibly, yet I always told him that I would never part with Westmorland upon any condition whatsoever.[285] About this time Lady Robert Rich was brought to bed of her third son which was her fifth child called Henry.[286]

Upon the 6th after supper because my Lord was sullen and not willing to go into the nursery I made Mary bring the Child to him into my chamber which was the first time she stirred abroad since she was sick. Upon the 7th my Lord lay in my chamber.[287]

Upon the 8th I sat by my Lord and my brother Sackville in the drawing chamber and heard much talk about many businesses and did perceive that he was

---

283 \About this time ... alterations abroad/. Cocino, Marechall d'Ancre, was murdered with the consent of Louis XIII of France.
284 Forms of property conveyance, through which Sackville would give up any claims on the Clifford hereditary lands beyond what was stipulated in the King's Award.
285 The King's Award effectively took Westmorland away from Anne, securing it to the male heirs of her uncle Francis. Here she insists she will not sign the award and accept the agreement. In this way she was able to leave open the possibility that she could renew legal action, in which case Richard Sackville's lands offered as guarantee against this would be forfeit. In October of this year (1617) he wrote to her: 'I love and hold [you] a sober woman, your lands only excepted which transports you beyond yourself and makes you devoid of all reason'. CAS, Kendal, WDHOTH/44, letter, 6 October 1617.
286 \About this time ... Henry/. Frances Hatton, Lady Rich. This child did not survive.
287 This is significant because it established they were having conjugal relations. This type of evidence was often used to support a wife if a husband wished to sue for a legal separation (the right to live apart) from her. It also established a timeline if Anne became pregnant.

entered into a business between my Lady of Exeter and my Lord Ros[288] of which he will not easily quit himself.

Captain Mainwaring and these folks told me that for certain the match with Spain and our Prince would go forward.[289] The King of Spain was grown so gracious to English folks that he had written his letter in behalf of Lord Willoughby's brother to get him out of the inquisition.[290]

Upon the 11th my Lord was very ill this day and could not sleep so that I lay on a pallet. Upon the 12th Mrs Watson came hither with whom I had much talk of my Lord's being made a Knight of the Garter.[291] This night I went into Judith's chamber where I mean to continue until my Lord be better.

Upon the 13th my Lord sat where the gentlewomen used to sit. He dined abroad in the great chamber and supped privately with me in the drawing chamber and had much discourse of the humours of the folks at Court.

Upon the 14th I was so ill with lying in Judith's chamber that I had a plain fit of a fever.

Upon the 15th I was so sick and my face so swelled that my Lord and Tom Glemham were fain to keep the table in the drawing chamber as I sat within. Marsh came in the afternoon to whom I gave directions to go to Mr Davis and Mr Walter about the drawing of letters to the tenants in Westmorland, because I intend to send him thither. This night I left Judith's chamber and came to lie in the chamber where I lay when my Lord was in France[292] in the green cloth of gold bed where the Child was born.

Upon the 16th my Lord and I had much talk about these businesses, he urging me still to go to London and to sign and seal but I told him that my promise was so far passed to my mother and to all the world that I would never do it whatsoever became of me and mine. Yet still I strived as much as I could to settle a good opinion in him towards me.

Upon the 17th in the morning my Lord told me he was resolved never to move me more in these businesses because he saw how fully I was bent.

---

288 This suggests that William Cecil, Lord Ros, and Frances Brydges may have been having an affair.
289 Mainwaring was captain of the *Prince Royal* that would in 1623 bring the Prince home after his escapade to secure the Spanish Princess for his bride. That marriage never took place.
290 \Captain Mainwaring … Inquisition/. Refers to Henry Bertie mentioned previously.
291 The Most Noble Order of the Garter was founded in 1348 and is the highest order of chivalry in England. Richard Sackville was never awarded this honour.
292 As part of the agreement made upon their marriage, Richard Sackville was allowed to spend a year in Europe. He left in the spring of 1611 and returned on 8 April 1612.

Upon the 18th being Good Friday I spent most of the day in hearing Kate Burton read the Bible and a book of Preparation to the Sacrament.[293]

Upon the 19th I signed 33 letters with my own hand which I sent by him to the tenants in Westmorland.[294] The same night after supper my Lord and I had much talk and [he] persuaded me to yield to these businesses, but I would not, and yet I told him I was in perfect charity with the world. All this Lent I ate flesh and observed no day but Good Friday.[295]

About the 20th being Easter Day my Lord and I and Tom Glemham and most of the folks received the communion by Mr Rands yet in the afternoon my Lord and I had a great falling out, Matthew continuing still to do me all the ill offices he could to my Lord. All this time I wore my white satin gown and my white waistcoat.

Upon the 22nd this night we played at barley break upon the bowling green.[296] This day we came to dine abroad in the great chamber.[297]

Upon the 23rd my Lord Clanricarde[298] came hither. After they were gone my Lord and I and Tom Glemham went to Mr Lane's[299] house to see the fine flowers that is in the garden. This night my Lord should have lain with me in my chamber, but he and I fell out about Matthew.

Upon the 24th my Lord went to Sevenoaks again. After supper we played at barley break upon the green. This night my Lord came to lie in my chamber.

Upon the 25th being Friday I began to keep my fish days which I intend to keep all the year long. After dinner I had a great deal of talk with Richard Dawson that served my Lady,[300] he telling me all the manner how the possession of Brougham Castle was delivered to my uncle of Cumberland's folks, and how Mr Worleigh and all my people are gone from home except John Raivy who kept all the stuff in the Baron's chamber, the plate being already sent to Lord William Howard's.

---

293 William Bradshaw, *A Direction for the Weaker sort of Christians … Receiving of the Sacrament* (London, 1615). This was dedicated to Anne's cousin Grace Rokeby, wife of Conyers Darcy, 1st Earl of Holderness.
294 While Anne could not mount legal action to reclaim the northern estates of her father, she would continue to protect her interests in Westmorland through other means, such as these letters to the tenants.
295 It was customary to eat fish during Lent.
296 A game played by three couples. One couple is placed in the middle called 'hell' and has to catch the others who are allowed to 'break' or change partners if it looks as if they may be caught. When caught the couple has to take their turn as catchers. It could be quite a lively and high-spirited game.
297 \This day … Chamber/, This is a marginal insertion in the Portland MS, but is placed in the text in the nineteenth-century manuscript copies.
298 Richard Burke, 4th Earl of Clanricarde.
299 Edward Lane.
300 Anne's mother, Margaret Russell.

Upon the 26th I spent the evening in working and going down to my Lord's closet where I sat and read much in the Turkish History and Chaucer.[301]

Upon the 28th was the first time the Child put on a pair of whalebone bodice.[302] My Lord went a-hunting the fox and the hare. I sent William Dunn to Greenwich to see my Lady Roxburgh[303] and remember my service to the Queen.

About this time my Lord made the steward alter most of the rooms in the house and dress them up as fine as he could and determined to make all his old clothes in purple stuff for the gallery and drawing chamber.[304]

May 1617

Upon the 1st I cut the Child's strings[305] off from her coats and made her use to go about so as she had two or three falls at first but had no hurt from them.

Upon the 2nd the Child put on her first coat that was laced with lace being of red baize. Upon the 3rd my Lord went from Buckhurst to London and rid it in four hours, he riding very hard and hunting all the while. He was at Buckhurst and had his health exceeding well.

The 7th my Lord Keeper[306] rode from Dorset House to Westminster in great pomp and state. All of the Lords going with him amongst which my Lord was one.

Upon the 8th I spent the day in working the time being very tedious unto me as having neither comfort nor company only the Child.

Upon the 12th I began to dress my head with a roule[307] without a wire. I wrote not to my Lord because he wrote not to me since he went away. After supper I went with the Child who rode on the piebald nag that came out of Westmorland with Mrs [blank]. Mr Ryder came hither and told me Lord Sheffield's wife[308] was lately dead since the King went from York.[309]

---

301 This is probably the 1602 edition of Chaucer's works edited by Thomas Speght. Anne includes a volume entitled 'All Jeffrey Chawcers workes' in her Great Picture. She wrote to the Countess of Kent in January 1650 from Appleby Castle asking her to thank the antiquarian John Selden for sending a copy of Chaucer to her, commenting, 'If I had not excellent Chaucer's book here to comfort me, I were a pitiful case' (BL, MS Harley 7001, fol. 212).
302 Children of the period were dressed as adults. A picture of Margaret Sackville by Paul van Somer, 1618 (still at Knole), is a good example of this.
303 Jane Drummond, Countess of Roxburgh, Mistress of the Robes to Queen Anne.
304 This refers to the decorating of the rooms not clothing for personal wear.
305 Strings of fabric sewn on to the back of children's clothing to help guide them when learning to walk. A good example of this is the picture *A Child in Leading Strings* by Pantoja de la Cruz (1551–1609) now at Boughton House, Northamptonshire.
306 Francis Bacon.
307 A cushion or pad of hair or other material used in dressing the hair.
308 The wife of Edmund Sheffield, Ursula Tyrwhitt.

Upon the 13th[310] the Child came to lie with me which was the first time that ever she lay all night in a bed with me ever since she was born.

Upon the 14th[311] the Child put on her white coats and left off many things from her head, the weather growing extreme hot.

Upon the 17th the steward came from London and told me that my Lord was much discontented with me for not doing this business because he must be fain to tie land for the payment of the money which will much encumber his estate.

Upon the 18th Mr Woolrich came hither to serve me, he bringing me news that all in Westmorland was surrendered to my uncle of Cumberland.

Upon the 19th came my cousin Sir Edward Gorges who brought me a token from my Lady Somerset.

Upon the 24th we set up a great many of the books that came out of the North[312] in my closet this being a sad day with me thinking of the troubles I have passed. I used to spend much time in talking with Mr Woolrich about my dear mother and other businesses in the North. This term my Lord's mother-in-law did first of all sue out of her thirds which was an increase of trouble and discontent to my Lord.[313]

Upon the 26th my Lady St John's tailor came hither to me to take measure of me and to make me a new gown. In the afternoon my cousin Russell[314] wrote me a letter to let me know how my Lord had cancelled my jointure[315] he had made upon me last June when I went into the North and by these proceedings I may see how much my Lord is offended with me and that my enemies have the upper hand of me but I am resolved to take all patiently casting all my care upon God. This footman told me that my cousin Russell and my Lady Bedford were agreed, and my Lord Herbert and his Lady[316] and that next week they were to seal the writings and the agreement which I little expected.[317]

---

309 \Mr Ryder ... York/ This is a marginal insertion in the Portland MS, but placed in the text in the nineteenth-century manuscript copies.
310 The 14th in the nineteenth-century manuscript copies.
311 The 15th in the nineteenth-century manuscript copies.
312 These were her mother's books. Margaret Russell was a patron of a number of writers of the period, including Samuel Daniel, Robert Greene, Richard Greenham, Thomas Lodge, Henry Lok and William Perkins. These would also include manuscript copies of works like Boetius's *De Consolatione Philosophia* (*The Philosophical Comfort*) which also found its way into the Great Picture and survives today: see Leeds University Special Collections, Leeds, YAS, Boetius, DD 121 Bundle 118, #12.
313 \This Term ... Lord/. This is a marginal insertion in the Portland MS, but placed in the text in the nineteenth-century manuscript copies.
314 Edward Russell, 3rd Earl of Bedford.
315 This would be seen as a severe act outside of expected norms.
316 Henry Somerset and Anne Russell, Anne's first cousin.
317 This concerned properties owned by Francis Russell, 2nd Earl of Bedford, and a dispute

Upon the 27th I wrote a letter to my Lord to let him know how ill I took his cancelling of my jointure but yet told him I was content to bear it with patience whatsoever he thought fit.

Upon the 29th I wrote a letter to my sister Beauchamp and sent her a lock of the Child's hair. I wrote a letter to my sister Compton and my aunt Glemham,[318] I being desirous to win the love of my Lord's kindred by all the fair means I could.

The 31st Mr Hodgson told me how my cousin Clifford went in at Brougham Castle and saw the house but did not lie there and that all the tenants were very well effected towards me and very ill towards them.

June 1617

Upon the 3rd Mr Herdson[319] came hither in the morning and told me that as many did condemn me for standing out so in this business, so on the other side many did commend me in regard that I have done that which is both just and honourable. This night I went into a bath.

Upon the 6th after supper we went in the coach to Goodwife Sisley's[320] and ate so much cheese there that it made me very sick.

Upon the 8th being Whitsunday we all went to church but my eyes were so blubbered with weeping that I could scarce look up and in the afternoon we fell out about Matthew. After supper we played at barley break upon the bowling green.

Upon the 9th I wrote a letter to the Bishop of London[321] against Matthew. The same day Mr Hodgson came home who had been with my cousin Russell at Chiswick[322] and what a deal of care he had of me and my cousin Russell and my cousin Gorges sent me word that all my businesses would go well [and] that they could not find that the agreement was fully concluded in regard there was nothing had passed the great seal.

Upon the 13th I essayed[323] on my sea water green satin gown and my damask

---

over what property should have descended to Anne Russell through her father John Russell, Baron Russell.
318 Anne Sackville, Lady Glemham, Richard Sackville's aunt.
319 This could be John Herdson of Brome Park, Kent, who died in 1622.
320 Jane Sisley, a nursery maid at Knole.
321 John King, the Bishop of London. Anne's problems with Matthew Caldicott would be considered a spiritual matter because he was interfering between husband and wife.
322 Francis Russell, later 4th Earl of Bedford. He inherited property in Chiswick from his father, Sir William Russell of Thornhaugh.
323 Tried on.

embroidered with gold, both which gowns the tailor which was sent down from London made fit for me to wear with open ruffs after the French fashion.

Upon the 16th Mr Woolrich came home and brought me a very favourable message from the Court.

Upon the 19th I wrote a letter to the Queen of thankfulness for the favours she had done me and enclosed it to Lady Ruthven desiring her to deliver it. Ever since the King's going in to Scotland the Queen lay at Greenwich, the Prince being often with her till about this time she removed to Oatlands.[324]

Upon the 20th I received a letter from my cousin Gorges which advised me of many proceedings and showed me the care my cousin Russell had of all my business and within it a letter from my Lady Somerset. I returned a present answer to both these letters and sent my cousin Gorges half a buck which my Lord had sent me half an hour before with an indifferent kind letter.

Upon the 21st I spent the time as I did many wearisome days besides, in working and walking. After supper I walked in the garden and gathered cherries and talked with Josiah who told me he thought all of the men in the house loved me exceedingly well, except Matthew and two or three of his consorts.

Upon the 23rd my Lord sent Adam to trim the Child's hair and sent the doucets of two deer,[325] and wrote me a letter between kindness and unkindness.

Upon the 25th my Lord went up to London to christen Sir Thomas Howard's child[326] with the Prince, my Lord being exceeding great with all them, and so with my brother Sackville, he hoping by their means to do me and my child a great deal of hurt.

Upon the 30th still working and being extremely melancholy and sad to see things go so ill with me, and fearing my Lord would give all his land away from the Child.

July 1617

Upon the 1st still working and sad.

Upon the 2nd I received a letter from Sir George Rivers who sent me word that my Lord was settling his land upon his brother and that the value of the fines I released to my Lord by all likelihood was very great which did much perplex me.

Upon the 3rd I rode on horseback to Withyham to see my Lord Treasurer's

---

324 \Ever since ... Oatlands/
325 The testicles of a deer, a delicacy of the period, referred to in Ben Jonson's *Sad Shepherd*.
326 Thomas Howard, later 1st Earl of Berkshire.

tomb³²⁷ and went down into the vault and came home again, I weeping the most part of the day seeing my enemies had the upper hand of me.

My Lady Rich sent a man hither with a letter of kindness by whom I sent a letter to my Lord desiring him to come hither because I found myself very ill.

Upon the 7th and 8th still I kept in, complaining of my side which I took to be the spleen.

Upon the 9th Marsh brought me the King's Award.

Upon the 10th [and] 11th I spent the time in perusing that and other writings, the award being as ill for me as possible.

Upon the 12th Mr Davis came hither to whom I showed him [the] award, desiring him to make an abstract of it to send down to the tenants.³²⁸ Presently after my Lord came down hither, he being somewhat kinder to me than he was, out of pity, in regard he saw me so much troubled.

About this time there was a great stir about my Lady Hatton's daughter, my brother Sackville undertaking to carry her away with men and horses,³²⁹ and he had another squabble about a man that was arrested in Fleet Street. After this he went to the Spa and left my sister Sackville to keep my sister Beauchamp company.³³⁰

Upon the 15th at night Mrs Arundell's³³¹ man brought me a dapple grey horse which she had long promised me. About this time my Lord Keeper and all his company went away from Dorset House.³³²

Upon the 16th my Lady Wotton came hither on horseback, she and my Lord having lain that night at Sir Percival Hart's, and so hunted a deer as far as Otford. She stayed not above an hour in regard she saw I was so resolutely determined not to part with Westmorland. About this time my Lord Ros went

---

327 The church of St Michael and All Angels, Withyham, Sussex, contained the Sackville chapel where Thomas Sackville, 1st Earl of Dorset, was interred.
328 This abstract survives, see KHLC, 'The Substance of his Majesties Award', U269/E67. Another copy, from Davis's abstract by Edmund Langley is CAS, Carlisle, DLons L13/1/3. A copy of this abstract is also present in all three extant manuscripts of the *Great Books* and contains marginal notes from Anne and later readers. See *Great Books*, ed. Malay, pp. 772–775. Anne retained some rights in relation to the Clifford hereditary estates because she was the heir after the male heirs of Francis Clifford.
329 Sir Edward Coke arranged a marriage between Frances Coke and John Villiers, which was opposed by Frances's mother Elizabeth Cecil, Lady Hatton. Edward Sackville joined with Sir John Holles and Sir Robert Rich to kidnap Frances from her father at the request of Lady Hatton.
330 \About this time ... Beauchamp company/. Edward Sackville went to the continent to avoid any repercussions.
331 This is likely Anne's cousin Mary Cary mentioned often in the 1603 memoir. She married John Arundell of Trerice in Cornwall.
332 \About this time ... house/

over beyond the sea, there being a great discontentment between him and his wife.³³³

Upon the 26th I sent letters into Westmorland and sent to Hugh Hartley's wife a bored angel³³⁴ and to Lady Lower³³⁵ a pair of Willoughby's gloves.³³⁶ The same night Dr Donne came hither. About this time Lord Zouche³³⁷ went by sea into Scotland to the King and Sir John Digby set out on his long-expected journey to Spain.³³⁸

The 27th being Sunday I went to church forenoon and afternoon Dr Donne preaching and he and the other strangers dining with me in the great chamber.³³⁹

Upon the 31st I sat still thinking the time to be very tedious.

August 1617

Upon the 1st I rode on horseback with Moll Neville, Kate Burton and as many horses as I could get. I alighted at Sir Percival Hart's and afterwards went to Lady Wroth,³⁴⁰ whither my Lady Rich came from London to see me. She told me that Mr Henry Bertie was out of the Inquisition house and was turned papist and that Sir Henry Goodyear was turned papist.³⁴¹

Upon the 2nd my brother Compton came hither. Before supper my Lord came from London, this time of his being here he lying in my chamber.

Upon the 3rd in the afternoon we had much falling out about the keeping of the house which my Lord would have me undertake which I refused, in regard things went so ill with me.³⁴² This night the Child lay all night with my Lord and me, this being the first night she did so.

Upon the 4th in the morning my Lord went to Penshurst but would not

---

333 \About this time … wife/. Anne will describe this growing scandal in the following months. In 1607 Anne's mother had hoped to arrange a marriage between Anne and William Cecil, Lord Ros. See Malay, 'The Marrying of Anne Clifford', pp. 255–256.
334 A coin with a hole bored through it to show it was all gold.
335 Penelope Perrot, married to William Lower.
336 A pair of gloves made by Mistress Willoughby, Anne's gentlewoman servant.
337 Edward la Zouche, 11th Baron Zouche.
338 \About this time … Spain/
339 The poet John Donne was the Rector of St Nicholas, Sevenoaks, near Knole from 1616 to 1631. The strangers Anne refers to here are people she knows but who are not from her household.
340 Sir Percival's home was Lullingstone Castle about ten miles from Knole. Mary Sidney (Wroth's) home was Penshurst Place, about twenty miles from Lullingstone.
341 \She told me … papist/. This is a marginal insertion in the Portland MS, but placed in the text in the nineteenth-century manuscript copies.
342 Aristocratic women were often placed in charge of large households. Sackville's continued financial difficulties may explain Anne's reluctance to take it on.

suffer me to go with him, although my Lord and my Lady L'Isle[343] sent a man on purpose to desire me to come. He hunted and lay there all night there being my Lord Montgomery, my Lord Hay, my Lady Lucy[344] and a great deal of other company yet my Lord and I parted reasonable good friends, he leaving with me his grandmother's wedding ring.

Upon the 4th being Wednesday the King came to Brougham and upon the 7th hunted all day in Whinfell and upon the 8th he went from Brougham.[345] Both my uncle of Cumberland and my cousin Clifford was there and gave him great entertainment and there was music and many other devices.[346]

Upon the 8th I kept my chamber all day.

At night Mr Rands came and persuaded me to be friends with Matthew, but I told him that I had received so many injuries from him that I could hardly forget them.

Upon the 10th being Sunday I kept my chamber being very troubled and sad in mind.

Upon the 11th my Lord went from Buckhurst[347] beginning his progress into Sussex, my uncle Neville, my brother Compton, Tom Glemham, Coventry and about thirty horse more, they being all very gallant, brave and merry. Mr Rands brought me a message from Matthew how willing he would be to have my favour, whereto I desired Mr Rands to tell him as I was a Christian I would forgive him and so had some hours' speech with Mr Rands.

About this time I began to think much of religion and do persuade myself that this religion in which my mother brought me up in is the true and undoubted religion so as I am steadfastly purposed never to be a papist.[348]

Upon the 12th or 13th I spent most of the time in playing at glecko and hearing Moll Neville read the *Arcadia*.[349] About this time my Lady Roxburgh that

---

343 Robert Sidney, Lord de L'Isle and later Earl of Leicester, and his wife Barbara Gamage.
344 Lucy Percy. She would marry James Hay, later 1st Earl of Carlisle, on 5 November 1617. She was related to Anne through the Percys.
345 For a description of the King's tour of Westmorland and the festivities at Brougham see NPJ, vol. 3, pp. 391–392.
346 \Upon the 4th ... devices/. See *The Ayres ... played at Brougham Castle* (1618). This marginal insertion is in the Portland MS but does not appear in the nineteenth-century manuscript copies.
347 Sackville's house in Withyham, Sussex.
348 \About this time ... papist/. In 1611 Margaret Russell expressed concern that Anne might be tempted to convert to Roman Catholicism. She asks Sackville to ensure that 'no friend of ally of hers or yours shall resort to her to dissuade her against the religion wherein she was brought up'. Portland MS 23, p. 57. This marginal insertion is in the Portland MS but does not appear in the nineteenth-century manuscript copies.
349 Philip Sidney, *The Countess of Pembroke's Arcadia* (1605). Anne's copy of the *Arcadia*, with annotations in her hand, is Bodleian Library, J-J Sidney 13. Her annotations show

had been so great with the Queen many years, being great with child, went to Scotland in a litter.³⁵⁰

Upon the 19th my Lord wrote me a very kind letter from Lewes to which I wrote an answer. Presently in the afternoon I went to Penshurst on horseback to my Lady L'Isle where I found my Lady Dorothy Sidney, my Lady Manners with whom I had much talk, and my Lady Norris, she and I being very kind.³⁵¹ There was my Lady Wroth who told me a great deal of news from beyond [the] sea, so we came home at night, my cousin Barbara Sidney bringing me a good part of the way.

Upon the 28th Marsh came hither. He told me of a rumour of my brother Sackville's fighting and many other businesses of my Lord of Essex and my Lady Paget.³⁵²

Upon the 29th Dr Carter came hither and told me that my brother Sackville was slain.³⁵³

Upon the 31st my Lord returned to London from his Sussex progress where he had been extraordinary [blank] by all the gentlemen and did go with two or three hundred horse in his company.³⁵⁴

September 1617

Upon the 1st Sir Thomas Wroth and his wife³⁵⁵ came and sat with me most part of the afternoon, they telling me a great deal of news of my Lady Carey the widow.³⁵⁶ Duck³⁵⁷ came from London and told me there was no such thing as my brother Sackville's fighting with Sir John Wentworth.³⁵⁸

 she read this work again in 1651. See Paul Salzman, 'Anne Clifford's Annotated Copy of Sidney's Arcadia' (2009), pp. 554–555. Anne's father also owned a manuscript copy of the *Old Arcadia*, Folger Library, MS H.b.1, fols 2r–216r. This manuscript is in the hand of Richard Robinson, who also provided Anne with a narrative of George Clifford's sea adventures which she included in her *Great Books*.
350 \About this time ... litter/. This marginal insertion is in the Portland MS but does not appear in the nineteenth-century manuscript copies.
351 A large party of the Sidney family had gathered at Penshurst about ten miles from Knole that summer, including Philip Herbert, who would be Anne's second husband.
352 Lady Paget is Lettice Knollys.
353 This rumour regarding a fight between Edward Sackville and John Wentworth was untrue.
354 \Upon the 31st ... party/. Anne would later progress through her Westmorland and Yorkshire estates. This type of display proclaimed one's authority and reminded the inhabitants of their dependence. This marginal insertion is in the Portland MS but does not appear in the nineteenth-century manuscript copies.
355 Margaret Rich, whose grandfather was Richard, Baron Rich.
356 Mary Hyde. Her husband John Carey, 3rd Baron Hunsdon, died in April 1617.
357 A page in the Sackville household.
358 Wentworth, described as a 'person debauched and riotous' (NPJ, vol. 3, p. 106), took part in an illegal interrogation in 1615 of Richard Weston, whose testimony helped convict

Upon the 15th we rid on horseback to my Lady Selby's.³⁵⁹ All this week I being at home and was sad to see how ill things went with me, my Lord being in the midst of his merry progress far out of Sussex where he had hunted in many gentlemen's parks then he went to Woodstock to meet the King, and he stayed up and down at several gentlemen's houses a good while. From thence he went to the Bath where he stayed not above two days but yet returned not to London till about Michaelmas.

Upon the 29th my Lord came home to Knole from his long journey. At this Michaelmas did my Lord receive five thousand pounds of my uncle the Earl of Cumberland which was the first penny that ever I received of my portion.³⁶⁰

October 1617

Upon the 4th came Sir Percival Hart and Sir Ed. [blank] to dine and after dinner my Lord showed them his stables and all his great horses.

Upon the 25th being Saturday came my Lady de L'Isle, my Lady [blank], my cousin Barbara Sidney etc. I walked with them all the wilderness over and had much talk with her of my cousin Clifford and many other matters. They saw the Child and much commended her. I gave them some marmalade of quinces for about this time I made much of it.³⁶¹

Upon the 28th I strung my chains and bracelets with Willoughby.

Upon the 30th fell the Child to be something ill and out of temper like a grudging of an ague which continued with her about a month or six weeks after.

Upon the 31st my brother Sackville spent the day in playing at cards with my cousin Howard.³⁶²

November 1617

Upon the 1st my brother Sackville and I, [and] my cousin Charles Howard went up to London. My Lord stayed behind but went upon Monday after to

---

Robert Carr, Earl of Somerset, of the murder of Thomas Overbury. Edward Sackville was also involved in this illegal interrogation and both Wentworth and Sackville, along with Sir John Lidcot and Sir John Holles were put in prison for a short time for interfering with the judiciary.

359 Ightham Mote, less than five miles from Knole.
360 It would have been customary for Anne's husband to receive this portion (£15,000 according to her father's will) at the time of her marriage in 1609 or shortly after. However, because she contested the will and took legal action to secure the Clifford hereditary lands, her portion was not paid until the legal action was settled by the King's Award. Sackville agreed to this before they married. See Portland MS 23, pp. 57–58.
361 It was common for ladies to make preserves and other high-value food products which were given as gifts and also used in the household.
362 Charles Howard, son of Elizabeth Dacre and Lord Howard of Naworth Castle.

Buckhurst so stayed there and at Lewes till I came hither again. I left Moll Neville and Kate Burton here to keep the Child company.

Upon the 2nd being Sunday I went to church with my sister Sackville to St Bride's, and afterwards my cousin Gorges and I went and dined with my Lady Ruthven, where I met my Lady Shrewsbury.[363] In the afternoon I saw her Lord there. All this time I was at the Court I wore my green damask gown embroidered, without a farthingale.[364] The same day I sent the Queen by my Lady Ruthven the skirts of a white satin gown all pursled[365] and embroidered with colours which cost me five score pounds besides the satin.[366]

Upon the 3rd I went to see my Lady St John. From thence I went to Austin Friars where I wept extremely to remember my dear and blessed mother.[367] I was in the chamber where I was married and went into most of the rooms in the house, but found very little or nothing of the stuff and pictures remaining there. These three days was the last time that ever I was in my mother's chamber in St Austin Friars, which was the same chamber I was married in to Richard Lord Buckhurst who was Earl of Dorset three days after I was married to him.[368] From thence I went to my Lord [blank] and so to Whitehall where my Lady Arundel told me that the next day I should speak to the King for my Lady Arundel was exceeding kind with me all this time.

Upon the 4th I carried my Lady Rich to dine with me to Mrs Watson's where we met my cousin Russell and my cousin Gorges and had an extreme great feast. From thence I went to the Court, where the Queen sent for me into her own bedchamber and here I spoke to the King. He used me very graciously and bid me go to his attorney, who should inform him more of my desires.[369] The 4th day King James kissed me when I was with him, and that was the last time ever

---

363 Mary Cavendish, Countess of Shrewsbury.
364 A hooped petticoat made of a framework of (mainly) whalebone hoops inserted into cloth used to extend a woman's skirts.
365 Pursed, drawn into tight folds or wrinkles, puckered.
366 \which cost ... satin/. This marginal insertion is in the Portland MS but does not appear in the nineteenth-century manuscript copies.
367 This was the London house that Anne shared with her mother for four years after the death of her father.
368 \These three days ... him/
369 This could relate to Anne's intention to claim the hereditary title of Baroness Clifford. In 1628 she would begin a suit to claim this title of honour which was not related to lands and could descend lineally to heirs regardless of gender, see *Great Books*, ed. Malay, pp. 775–776. A number of manuscripts setting out the case for Anne's right to the title of Baroness Clifford survive; the earliest is dated 1606, soon after the death of George Clifford. See for example: Queen's College, Oxford, MS 105; CAS, Kendal, WDHOTH/1/13; Lincoln's Inn, London, MS 104.

I was so near King James as to touch him.[370] All the time of my being in London I used to sup privately and to send for Mr Davis to confer with me about my law business.

Upon the 5th I carried Mr Davis to Gray's Inn to the King's attorney, when I told him His Majesty's pleasure. From thence I went to Mr Walter's to intreat his advice and help in this business and so I came down this night to Knole. The next day my Lord Hay was married to my Lady Lucy Percy.

Upon the 17th in the morning my Lord brought my cousin Clifford (though much against my will) into my bedchamber where we talked of ordinary matters some quarter of an hour and so he went away.

Upon the 19th came John Taylor[371] with whom I had some two hours' talk of ancient matters, of my father and the North.

Upon the 20th I came down to Knole leaving my Lord behind me in London.

Upon the 30th I do not remember whether my Lord went to the church or stayed at home.

December 1617

Upon the 8th I was not very well and Mr Thomas Cornwallis the groom porter[372] came hither.

Upon the 9th I spent time with him talking of Queen Elizabeth and of such old matters at the Court.

Upon the 10th my Lord went away to Buckhurst where all the country gentlemen met my Lord with their greyhounds. All the officers of the house went to Buckhurst where my Lord kept great feasting till the 13th at which time all the gentlemen went away. This time Sir Thomas Parker was there when my brother Sackville and he had much squabbling. From this day to the 20th my Lord lived privately at Buckhurst having no company with him but only Matthew.

Upon the 15th came Sir Henry Neville's Lady.[373] I carried her up into my closet and showed her all my things and gave her a pair of Spanish leather gloves.

Upon the 22nd my Lord and I and all the household removed from hence to London, the Child going two hours before in a litter.

---

370 \The 4th day ... him/
371 John Taylor, a gentleman, was part of George Clifford's retinue in the North. He was also a tenant of the Cliffords in Westmorland.
372 Cornwallis was Groom-Porter from 1597 to 1618. The groom-porter was an officer in the Royal Household whose duties included regulating gaming within the precincts of the royal Court. He supplied cards and dice and decided disputes in Court connected to gaming.
373 Mary Sackville, Richard's aunt.

Upon the 25th being Christmas Day Mr [blank] preached in the chapel and my Lord and I dined below, there being great housekeeping[374] kept all this Christmas at Dorset House.

Upon the 28th I went to church in my rich night gown and petticoat, both my women waiting upon me in their liveries[375] but my Lord stayed at home. There came to dine Mrs Lindsey[376] and a great company of neighbours to eat venison.

Now I had a great desire to have all my father's sea voyages written so I did set Jones etc. to inquire about these matters.[377]

1618

[This year is missing in all extant manuscripts, and is not mentioned in any of Anne's other autobiographical writing or letters. From other sources we know Richard Sackville continued to be favoured at Court, winning £500 at cards in the King's chamber on 7 January. In April he was with the Court in London and participated in a running of the tilt, which Chamberlain describes as an event that was 'meane and poore'. The participants included Philip Herbert, Earl of Montgomery, who would become Anne's second husband in 1630 (LJC, vol. 2, p. 142). Anne's mother-in-law, Anne Spencer, died in September and this would have ended the financial support for her (her jointure) that came from Richard Sackville's estate and also ended the threat of her suit for her thirds as discussed above. Anne's brother-in-law Edward Seymour, Viscount Beauchamp, husband to Anne Sackville, died in October. Anne Clifford had a miscarriage in December of this year. Chamberlain records: 'The countesse of Dorset the last weeke miscaried of a sonne that was borne dead' (LJC, vol. 2, p. 198). In her *Great Books* Anne records that she bore three sons: Thomas Sackville, who was born on 2 February 1620 and died on 26 July 1620, and two other sons to Richard who 'died in their infancy'.[378] The son born in December 1618 was one of these. The dates of the third son's birth and death are unknown.]

---

374 She is referring to the cost of food and entertainment.
375 Liveries were the official uniforms of the household of the Earl of Dorset and advertised Anne's position as a leading noblewoman in the area.
376 The wife of Edward Lindsey, one of Richard Sackville's household officers.
377 This was done, and at least two copies exist. One is held in private hands, the other is CAS, Kendal, WDHOTH/1/7 A988. Earlier copies of George Clifford's voyages include Hertfordshire Archives, Hertford, DE/Lw/F74 (1598) and Lambeth Palace, London, MS 250 (1599). An account of the voyages was also included in the *Great Books*, ed. Malay, pp. 639–655.
378 *Great Books*, ed. Malay, p. 792.

January 1619

The first of this month I began to have the curtain drawn in my chamber and to see light.[379] This day the Child did put on her crimson velvet coat laced with silver lace, which was the first velvet coat she ever had. I sent the Queen a New Year's gift, a cloth of silver cushion embroidered richly with the King of Denmark's arms,[380] and all over with slips of tent stitch. The 2nd the Child grew ill with a cough and a pain in her head so as we feared the smallpox, but it proved nothing for within eight or ten days she recovered.[381]

The 2nd, 3rd, 4th and 5th I sat up and had many ladies come to see me, and much other company and so I passed away the time. My Lord went often to the Court and abroad, and upon Twelfth Eve my Lord lost 400 pound pieces playing with the King.

About this time my Lady Rich was brought to bed of a son, her sixth child. I should have christened it but it died in three or four days.[382]

Upon the 6th the Prince had the masque at night in the Banqueting House.[383] The King was there, but the Queen was so ill she could not remove from Hampton Court. All this Christmas it was generally thought she would have died. About this time my Lady de L'Isle[384] was brought to bed of her first son at Baynard's Castle and within a little while after fell sick of the smallpox.[385]

The 11th my Lord went down to Knole.

The 12th the Banqueting House at Whitehall was burnt to the ground, and the writings in the Signet Office were all burnt.[386] About this time died Tom Robbins my brother Sackville's man, but he left his master no remembrance for they were fallen out.[387]

---

379 The drawing of the curtains suggests she was in the process of recovering from her miscarriage, as does the visit of the ladies later in the week.
380 Frederick II of Denmark, the father of Anne of Denmark, Queen consort of England. Tent stitch work was a pattern in a series of parallel stitches that are arranged diagonally across the intersections of the stitches and is also called petit point.
381 \The 2nd the Child … recovered/
382 \About this time … days/. Anne was asked to stand as godmother to the child.
383 Ben Jonson's masque *Pleasure Reconciled to Virtue*. Chamberlain mentions this event, but says he knew nothing about it (LJC, vol. 2, p. 282).
384 Dorothy Percy. Her husband, Robert Sidney, was elevated to the title of Viscount de L'Isle when his father, Robert Sidney, was made the Earl of Leicester in 1618. Previous to this event, Anne refers to Barbara Gamage as Lady L'Isle in this diary.
385 \About this time … smallpox/. This child did not survive. Anne would spend many years in Baynard's Castle during the Civil Wars of the 1640s.
386 The Signet Office was concerned with the preparation and recording of letters patent, published written orders of the monarch, granting rights, titles etc. to an individual or corporation.
387 \About this time … out/

3 Anne Clifford, by William Larkin (1618)

The 16th came my Lord of Arundel and his Lady. The same day I sent my cousin Hall[388] of Guildford a letter and my picture with it which Larkin drew at Knole this summer.[389] [See Figure 3.]

388 Margaret Hall, Anne's relation.
389 A drawing from this painting by William Larkin now in the National Portrait Gallery, London, NPG 6976.

The 18th my Lady Wotton came to see me and stayed most part of the afternoon with me whom I had much conference of old matters, and of the northern business.

This month died my Lord Cobham,[390] he being lately come out of the Tower, he being the last of the three that was condemned for the first conspiracy against the King at his first coming to England.[391]

The 19th my Lady Verulam came, my Lord Cavendish, his Lady, my Lord Bruce, his sister and much other company, my Lady Herbert, my old Lady Dormer, my young Lady Dormer, with whom I had much talk about religion.[392]

The 20th came my Lord Russell, Sir Edward Gorges, my sisters Beauchamp, Compton and Sackville, and dined with me and in the afternoon came my Lady Bridgewater[393] and much other company, and my Lady of Warwick[394] who told me a great deal of good news.

The 22nd here supped with me my sister Sackville, my sister Beauchamp, Bess Neville,[395] Tom Glemham and my brother Compton and his wife. I brought them to sup there of purpose, hoping to make them friends.

The 23rd I came from London to Knole in a litter, the Child riding all the way in her coach. I went through the City and over the bridge but she crossed the water.[396] We found my Lord at Knole who had stayed there all this time since his coming from London.

I brought down with me my Lady's great trunk of papers to pass away the time which trunk was full of writings of Craven and Westmorland and other affairs with certain letters of her friends and many papers of philosophy.[397]

The 24th being Sunday, here dined Sir William Selby and his Lady and Sir Ralph Boswell.[398]

---

390 Henry Brooke, 11th Baron Cobham.
391 \This month ... England/. The Main Plot of 1603 to put Arbella Stuart on the throne. Also implicated were Sir Walter Raleigh and Henry's brother George Brooke.
392 Alice Barnham, William Cavendish, Christiana Bruce, Thomas Bruce, Janet Bruce, Anne Russell, Elizabeth Browne and Alice Molyneux.
393 Frances Stanley, the daughter of Anne's first cousin Ferdinando Stanley.
394 Frances Wray, who on 24 March 1619 became the Dowager Countess of Warwick, while Frances Hatton, Lady Rich, became the new Countess of Warwick.
395 Elizabeth Neville, Richard Sackville's cousin.
396 Margaret Sackville went across the Thames by one of the many boats that carried passengers across the river. Anne would have gone across London Bridge.
397 Her mother, Margaret Russell. Many of the papers in this trunk would go on to become part of Anne's *Great Books*. All three extant sets are held at CAS, Kendal. A number of letters can also be found there in WD/HOTH/44. For additional copies of her mother's letters see Portland MS 23. The philosophical papers could refer to a manuscript copy of Boetius's *De Consolatione Philosophia*, see above.
398 Ralph Bosville of Brabourne House in Sevenoaks, Anne's near neighbour.

All this week I kept my chamber because I found myself ill and weak.

The 29th in the morning died my sister Beauchamp's daughter Mrs Anne Seymour in the same house her father died five months before. My Lord came into my chamber and told me the news of my sister Beauchamp's child's death.[399] The child was opened, it having a corrupt body, so it was put in lead[400] and the day following Legg brought it to Knole which day was my birthday, I being now 29 years old.

The 31st my cousin Russell's wife[401] was brought to bed of a son, it being her fourth child, at Chiswick, which was christened in the church privately and named Francis.

About this time my sister Compton was reconciled to her husband and went to his house in Finch Lane where they stayed some ten or twelve days and then he brought her into the country to Brambletye.[402]

February 1619

The 1st carried my Lord Beauchamp's child from Knole where it had stood in his chamber to Withyham where it was buried in the vault so that now there was an end of the issue of that marriage which was concluded presently after mine.[403]

About this time my Lord William[404] caused my cousin Clifford to come before the Lords of the Council[405] about northern business, so as the spleen increased more and more betwixt them and bred faction in Westmorland which I held to be a very good matter for me.[406]

The 3rd my Lord went to Buckhurst meaning to lie there private a fortnight or thereabouts.

The 8th my Lady Wotton sent her page to see me, and that day I made pancakes with my women in the great chamber.[407]

My Lady of Suffolk at Northampton House about this time had the smallpox

---

399 \My lord ... death/
400 It was common to open a body and remove the organs before embalming in order to preserve the body for burial. There was also a clear fascination at the time with the state of a body after death as revealed by this 'opening'.
401 Catherine Brydges.
402 \About this time ... Brambletye/. Brambletye House, West Sussex.
403 Edward Seymour and Anne Sackville, Anne's sister-in-law, were married in 1609. Edward died in 1618 and Anne Sackville would later marry Sir Edward Lewis.
404 William Howard of Naworth.
405 The Council of the North, see above.
406 \About this time ... for me/
407 A Shrove Tuesday (the day before Ash Wednesday) tradition.

which spoiled that good face of hers which had brought to others much misery and to herself greatness which ended with much unhappiness.[408]

The 10th Wat Conniston began to read St Augustine's of the *City of God*[409] to me and I received a letter from Mr Davis with another enclosed in it of Ralph Conniston whereby I perceived things went in Westmorland as I would have them.

The 13th Wat Conniston made an end of reading the King's book upon the Lord's Prayer which was dedicated to my Lord of Buckingham.[410]

The 15th Sir Thomas Lake, his Lady and Lady Ros were sent to the Tower. There was nothing heard all this term but this matter between the Countess of Exeter and them, at which hearing the King sat for several days. It was censured on my Lady Exeter's side against them who were fined at great fines both to the King and her. There was spoken extraordinary foul matters of my Lady Ros, and reports went that among others she lay with her own brother so as these foul matters did double the miseries of my Lady Lettice Lake,[411] in her unfortunate match. This business was one of the foulest matters that hath fallen out in our time, so as my Lady Ros was counted a most odious woman.[412] Sara Swarton was fined and censured to be whipped, which answer was not executed by reason she confessed all she knew. In Sir Thomas Lake's place Sir George Calvert was sworn Secretary.[413]

I began and kept this Lent very strictly not eating butter or eggs till the 18th of February. Moll Neville kept it with me, but my Lord persuaded me and Mr

---

408 \My Lady of Suffolk ... unhappiness/. Catherine Knyvet, Countess of Suffolk, used her beauty and position in Court to engage in wide-scale corruption.
409 A volume of Augustine's *City of God* is depicted in Anne's Great Picture.
410 \The 13th Wat ... Buckingham/. James I, *A Meditation upon the Lord's Prayer* (London, 1619). This marginal insertion is in the Portland MS but does not appear in the nineteenth-century manuscript copies.
411 Lettice Rich married Arthur Lake after the death of her first husband in 1616.
412 \This business ... woman/. This marginal insertion is in the Portland MS but does not appear in the nineteenth-century manuscript copies.
413 The marriage of William Cecil, Lord Ros, to Anne Lake was immediately disastrous, with her returning to her mother shortly after the marriage. In May 1617 William Cecil attempted to take his wife home and a brawl ensued. Anne Lake's brother Arthur challenged William to a duel but William fled the country instead. William's grandfather the Earl of Exeter tried to intervene and the Lakes responded by accusing the Earl's young wife Frances Brydges of having an affair with William (which may have been the case, see Anne's comment on 8 April 1617 above). The Lakes went further, accusing Frances of trying to poison Anne Lake. Other accusations flew wildly, including the use of witchcraft, and incest between Anne Lake and her brother Arthur. King James sentenced the Lakes and a number of their servants to imprisonment and other punishments. Sir Thomas Lake lost his post as Secretary of State. William Cecil died abroad in 1619 and was rumoured to have been poisoned.

Smith wrote unto me so as I was content to break it. Besides, I looked very pale and was weak and sickly.[414]

About the 20th the King fell into an extreme fit of the stone at Newmarket so as many doubted of his recovery and the Prince rid down post to him. The 22nd the King came to Royston and there voided a stone and so grew reasonable well.[415]

My Lord should have gone to London the 24th of this month but I entreated him to stay here the 25th because on that day 10 years I was married, which I kept as a day of jubilee[416] to me so my Lord went not up till the 27th at which time he rid on horseback by reason of the great snow, and was so ill and sick after his journey so that whereas he intended to have returned in two or three days he stayed nine or ten days.

The 28th being Sunday, the judges came to Sevenoaks. I did often receive letters from Mr Davis and Marsh by which I perceived my motion to Sir John Suckling on his behalf took good effect[417] and that businesses went well to my liking in Westmorland by reason of differences between my Lord William and my cousin Clifford.

March 1619

Upon the 2nd the Queen died at Hampton Court between two and three in the morning. The King was then at Newmarket. Legg brought me the news of her death about four o'clock in the afternoon, I being in my bedchamber at Knole where I had the first news of my mother's death. Legg told me my Lord was to take some physic of Mr Smith so as he could not come from London these four or five days yet. She died in the same chamber that Queen Jane, Harry the 8th's wife, died in.[418] The Prince was there when the pangs of death came upon her but went into another chamber some half an hour before she died. The old Queen dowager of Denmark was alive when her daughter Queen Anne of England died.[419]

---

414 \I began ... sickly/
415 \About the 20th ... well/
416 A time of reconciliation and celebration.
417 Sir John Suckling (the elder) wished to be appointed a Master of Requests, a Crown office connected to the business of the Court of Requests. He was sworn in as 'master in ordinary' on 9 February 1619. Chamberlain wrote that several men were vying for this position (LJC, vol. 2, pp. 204, 216).
418 Jane Seymour, third wife of Henry VIII and mother of Edward VI. She died shortly after the birth of Edward (1537).
419 \The old Queen ... died/. Sophia of Mecklenburg-Güstrow (d. 1631).

About this time I caused the book of the Cliffords to be newly copied out.[420]

The 4th my Lord Sheffield was married at Westminster in St Margaret's Church to one Anne Irwin,[421] daughter of Sir William Irwin, a Scottish man, which was held a very mean match and undiscreet part of him.

The 5th at night about nine of the clock the Queen's bowels, all saving her heart, were buried privately in the Abbey at Westminster in the place where the King's mother's tomb is. There were none came with it but three or four of her servants and gentlemen ushers which carried it and a herald before it.[422] The Dean of Westminster and about ten others were by.

The 9th the Queen's corpse was brought from Hampton Court to Denmark House by water in the night in a barge with many lords and ladies attending it.[423] Most of the great ladies about the town put themselves in mourning and did watch the Queen's corpse at Denmark House which did lay there with much state.[424]

When my Lord was at London my brother Sackville fell sick of a fever and was dangerously ill. At length it turned to a second ague which continued most of the month so as it was generally reported that he was dead.[425] About the 9th my Lord came down to Knole and continued taking physic and diet.

The 10th Wat Conniston made an end of reading St Austin [Augustine] of the *City of God*.[426]

The 17th my Lord went to Buckhurst to search for armour and provision, which should be laid up by the papists.[427] This day I made an end of my Lady's book in the *Praise of a Solitary Life*.[428]

The 18th I compared the two books of the Cliffords that Mr Knisden[429] sent

---

420 \About this time ... out/. This could be an early version of what would become Anne's *Great Books*, or it could refer to one of the many copies of *The Claim and Title of Lady Anne Clifford* which outlined her claim to the hereditary barony of the Cliffords.
421 Marianna Irwin, daughter to Sir William Irwin who was tutor to Prince Henry. Chamberlain remarks on this wedding: 'The Lord Sheffield in a doating humor hath maried a younge Scottish wentch daughter to one Sir William Urwin, that was a kinde of dauncing schoolmaster to Prince Henry' (LJC, vol. 2, pp. 220–221).
422 It was not unusual to bury internal organs separately from the main corpse. This served two purposes – it allowed a posthumous presence in two places, and allowed a swift burial to the bodily parts more susceptible to decay.
423 \The 9th the Queen's ... it/
424 \Most of the great ... state/
425 \When my Lord ... dead/
426 \About the 10th ... God/
427 In case of an uprising of Roman Catholics after the death of the Queen, who was a Roman Catholic. Sackville was in charge of military affairs for the area. See his letter book on military affairs and readiness (1614–1624), Flintshire Archives, D/HE/732.
428 *The Praise of Private Life* (known as Harington MS), CAS, Kendal, WDHOTH/1/21.
429 St Loe Kniveton. This refers to *The Claim and Title of Lady Anne Clifford*. George

me down. The 20th I made an end of reading the Bible over which was my Lady my mother's. I began to read it the 1st of February so as I read all over the whole Bible in less than two months.

The 24th there was no running at tilt by reason of the Queen's death which I held a good fortune for my Lord because he meant not to run, which I think would have given the King some distaste.[430]

The 24th my Lord of Warwick[431] died in Allington House, leaving a great estate to my Lord Rich and my good friend his Lady,[432] and leaving his wife which was my Lady Lampwell[433] a widow the second time. This day Wat Conniston made an end of reading Mr Sorocold's book of the Supplication of Saints which my Lord gave me.[434]

The 26th being Good Friday, after supper I fell into a great passion of weeping in my chamber, and when my Lord came in I told him I found my mind so troubled as I held not myself fit to receive the communion this Easter which all this Lent I intended to have done.

The 27th in the morning I sent for Mr Rands and told him I found not my self fit to receive the communion. The next day when my Lord heard I had told Mr Rands so much, he sent for him and told him the communion could be put off both for himself and the household except any of them [who] would receive at the church.

The 28th being Easter Day, Mr Rands preached in the chapel but there was no communion in the house but at the church. In the afternoon I began to repent that I had caused the communion to be put off till Whitsuntide, my Lord protesting to me that he would be a very good husband to me, and that I should receive no prejudice by releasing my thirds.

The 29th my Lord went to Buckhurst, and so to Lewes to see the muster which the country prepared in much the better fashion by reason of their affection for him, which was as much as any Lord hath in his own country or can have.[435]

    Williamson mentions a manuscript copy of *The Claim* which he examined around 1922 which is dated 1606. He quotes the inscription in this manuscript which identifies St Loe Kniveton as its producer. See Williamson, *Lady Anne Clifford*, p. 446.
430 \The 24th ... distaste/
431 Robert Rich, 1st Earl of Warwick.
432 Frances Hatton, Countess of Warwick.
433 This is a manuscript error carried in all extant manuscripts so may well have been an error in the source manuscript. The Earl of Warwick's wife Frances Wray was first married to Sir George St Poll, and thus she was the widow St Poll not Lampwell.
434 Thomas Sorocold, *Supplications of Saints* (1612).
435 A calling together of able men of the region for training and military exercises.

April 1619

The first day in the morning I writ in the Chronicles.

The 4th there was a general thanksgiving at Paul's Cross for the King's recovery at which were most of the Privy Council and the Bishop of London[436] preached.

The 5th my Lord Home died in Channel Row, who married Mrs Mary Dudley[437] my old companion, and left her as well as he could possibly.

The 6th my Lord came from Buckhurst to Knole. At his being at Lewes there was great play[438] between my Lord of Hunsdon, my Lord of Effingham,[439] and my Lord who lost there 200 pounds and the town entertained him with fireworks.

The 8th there came a letter to my Lord to advise him to come to Royston to the King, because most of the lords had been with him in the time of his sickness. The 9th my Lord went from Knole to London. The next day he went to Royston to the King with whom he watched that night, my Lord of Warwick[440] and my Lord North[441] watched with him. The King used him very well so that my Lord came not back till the 13th to London. There he stayed till I came up.

The 17th I came to London. Moll Neville, the gentlewomen, and most of the house came with me, so that I left none to wait on the Child but Mary Hutchins.

Sunday the 18th I went to Warwick House to see my young Lady of Warwick[442] where I met my Lord of Warwick, Mr Charles Rich, Mr Nathaniel Rich, Lady Harry Rich.[443] After all the company were gone to the sermon my Lord came in thither.

This day I put on my black mourning attire and went to my sister Beauchamp where I spake with Mrs Bathurst[444] and told her I did both forgive and forget any

---

436 John King, See Morrissey, *Politics and Paul's Cross Sermons* (2011)
437 Alexander Home. His wife was Mary Sutton, daughter of the Edward Sutton, 5th Baron Dudley.
438 Gambling.
439 Henry Carey and Charles Howard, who was Lord Howard of Effingham 1596–1624. In 1624 he became 2nd Earl of Nottingham.
440 This refers now to Robert Rich (d. 1658), the 2nd Earl of Warwick. His father, Robert Rich, 1st Earl of Warwick, died on 24 March 1619, see above.
441 Dudley North,
442 This is now Frances Hatton, wife to Richard Rich, 2nd Earl of Warwick. Frances Wray, who was called Lady Warwick previously in this diary, is now the Dowager Countess of Warwick, because of the death of her husband, Robert Rich, 1st Earl of Warwick, in March 1619.
443 Isabel Cope, wife to Henry Rich, later 1st Earl of Holland. These Rich men are brothers to Robert Rich, 2nd Earl of Warwick.
444 Bathurst had charge of Anne's child, Margaret Sackville, during the period of enforced separation in 1616 described above.

thing she had done against me and that I had spoken to my Lady of Warwick in her behalf.

Monday the 19th I went to Somerset House and sat a good while there by the Queen's corpse and then went into the privy galleries and showed my cousin Mary[445] those fine delicate things there. From thence I went to Bedford House and stayed with my Lady of Bedford a little while and she and I went to Channel Row to see my Lady Home[446] the widow. This day my Lord, my Lord Hunsdon[447] and my sister Sackville christened Hamon's[448] child at St Dunstan's Church.

The 20th I went to Parsons Green to my Lady St John's, where I met the Spanish friar, that is the agent here.[449] This day and the next my Lord had cocking at the cockpit where there met him an infinite company.

The 20th the King was brought in a litter from Royston to Ware and the next day to Theobalds, being carried the most part of the way in a chair by the Guard, for that he was so ill he could not endure the litter.

Thursday the 22nd I went in the morning to see my sister Compton and found my brother Compton there. I was in the room where my Lord's mother-in-law died, the Countess of Dorset,[450] and went up and down the rooms. Afterwards my sister Beauchamp and my sister Sackville came to see me.

Friday the 23rd I went to Blackfriars to see my Lady Cavendish and my Lady Kinloss in that house where my Lady Somerset was brought to bed in her great troubles. Then I went to Denmark House and heard prayers there and this night I watched all night with the Queen's corpse. There watched with me my Lady Elizabeth Gorges and diverse other ladies and gentlewomen, besides there sat up my brother Compton, my cousin Gorges, my cousin Thatcher[451] and Mr Renolds. At the beginning of the night there came thither my Lord of Warwick and his Lady, Sir Harry Rich, Charles Rich, my Lord Carew[452] and Sir Thomas Edmonds, but all these went away before twelve o'clock. I came not away till five o'clock in the morning.

Saturday the 24th my Lord went to Theobalds to see the King, who used him very graciously.

---

445 Mary 'Moll' Neville.
446 Mary Sutton, now Countess Dowager of Home.
447 Henry Carey, 4th Baron Hunsdon.
448 Robert Hammond of Chertsey, Surrey.
449 Diego de Lafuente, 'Padre Maestro', confessor to the Spanish Ambassador Diego Sarmiento de Acuña, Count of Gondomar.
450 Anne Spencer.
451 Possibly Gilbert Thacker of Repton, Derbyshire, or Godfrey Thacker of Repton, high sheriff of Derbyshire (appointed 1619).
452 George Carew, later 1st Earl of Totnes.

This night my cousin Clifford came out of the North where matters went more to my content and less to his than was expected. Either this night or the next morning Sir Arthur Lake's lady[453] was brought to bed of a son.

Sunday the 25th after dinner, I and my Lady of Warwick went to the sermon in the great hall.[454] After sermon my Lord came thither to fetch me so we went to Hyde Park[455] and took the air. After my Lord came home he went to see my brother Sackville who still continueth to look ill, and is very sickly and out of temper in his body.

Monday the 26th my Lord's cocks fought at Whitehall, where my Lord won five or six battles. I went in the afternoon to see my Lady Windsor[456] and my Lady Raleigh in her house which is hard by Austin Friars; then I went to Clerkenwell to that house that Sir Thomas Chaloner built.[457]

Tuesday the 27th I put on my new black mourning night gown and those white things which Nan Home made for me. This day Mr Orfeur[458] brought unto me two of the tenants of Westmorland who craved my assistance in their behalf against my uncle of Cumberland.[459]

The 28th my Lord and I, my cousin Sackville[460] and my Lady Windsor went to see my Lady Somerset[461] where we saw her little child. My Lord went to see the Earl of Northumberland and I and Lady Windsor went to see my Lady Shrewsbury and after supper my Lord and I went by water to Channel Row to see my Lord of Hertford and his Lady[462] where we found my Lady Beauchamp[463] and my Lord of Essex's sister.[464] Then I went to Arundel House

---

453 Lettice Rich. She and the child died shortly after this birth.
454 Probably the Great Hall at Whitehall Palace.
455 Hyde Park was a private hunting preserve of the King and Queens of England at this time. James I allowed limited access to it for recreation.
456 Catherine Somerset.
457 There were several elite homes in Clerkenwell Close and in 1619 Edward Burke, 4th Earl of Clanricarde lived there. Anne spent much of her childhood in another house in Clerkenwell Close.
458 Cuthbert Orfeur was Anne's agent in the North.
459 For a comprehensive account of the dire repercussions of the King's Award on the tenants of Westmorland see John Breay, *Light in the Dales* (1996), pp. 111–131.
460 John Sackville, a relation of Richard Sackville's.
461 Frances Howard, Countess of Somerset. Anne continued on good terms with this woman despite her involvement in the murder of Overbury. Her child is Anne Carr who will marry William Russell, 5th Earl of Bedford.
462 Edward Seymour, 1st Earl of Hertford, and Frances Howard, later Countess of Lennox and Richmond. She was Anne's cousin.
463 Anne Sackville, Anne's sister-in-law.
464 Frances Devereux, married to William Seymour, who was Anne Sackville, Lady Beauchamp's, brother-in-law.

and met with her and talked with her about my Lord's being made Knight of the Garter.⁴⁶⁵

The 30th my Lord Southampton was sworn a Privy Councillor to the King at Theobalds.

May 1619

The 1st after supper Mr Davis came and did read to my Lord and me the bill my uncle of Cumberland and my cousin Clifford put in the Chancery against the tenants of King's Meaburn.⁴⁶⁶

The 2nd when I returned home I found Mr Hammond and his wife⁴⁶⁷ here. I told her that she had made so many scorns and jests of me that for my part she was nothing welcome to me.

The 3rd about two or three o'clock in the morning Sir Arthur Lake's wife died, having been grievously tormented a long time with pains and sores which broke out in blotches so that it was commonly reported that she died of the French disease.⁴⁶⁸

This day one Williams a lawyer was arraigned and condemned at the King's Bench of treason and adjudged to be hanged, drawn and quartered for a certain book he had made and entitled *Balaam's Ass*, for which book one Mr Cotton was committed to the Tower and long time kept prisoner there upon a suspicion to have made it,⁴⁶⁹ but of late he was gotten out upon bail and now well quitted. Williams being condemned was carried to Newgate and the 5th of this month was hanged, drawn and quartered, according to his sentence, at Charing Cross.⁴⁷⁰

This 3rd Monsieur Barnevelt⁴⁷¹ was beheaded at the Hague which is like to

---

465 Here Anne attempts to gain support for Sackville's bid to become a Knight of the Garter, an honour that was never granted to him.
466 King's Meaburn was a manor in Westmorland.
467 Elizabeth Barrett, daughter of Sir Francis Knollys of Reading Abbey.
468 Lettice Rich. Her husband Arthur Lake reportedly suffered from syphilis. Chamberlain comments that 'yt being yet in question among his friends of both sides whether the Lady had them [syphilis 'the pox'] by his guift, or by her owne purchase' or sexual behaviour (LJC, vol. 2, p. 220). Lettice died soon after childbirth.
469 John Cotton, a Roman Catholic, and tenant of the Earl of Southampton, was arrested in 1613.
470 John Williams, a lawyer and a Roman Catholic, was connected to the Knollys family through his wife Anne Weston. *Balaam's Ass*, printed about 1613, prophesied the death of James I. For a contemporary account of the execution see NA, SP 14/109, fol. 17.
471 Johan van Oldenbarnevelt, a statesman and founder of an independent Netherlands. He served as ambassador to England for a time. He was executed in 1619, charged with subverting the religious and political policy of the country.

breed great alteration for the best for this man hath long been a secret friend to the Spaniards and an enemy to the English. About this time Monsieur Tresnel[472] came over to condole for the death of the Queen out of France.[473]

The 5th my Lord of Kent's[474] daughter my Lady Susan Longville and her husband came and dined with me.[475]

The 6th my Lord sat up playing at cards and did not come home till twelve o'clock at night.

The 7th presently after dinner my cousin Clifford came and sat in the gallery half an hour or an hour and so my Lord and he went abroad.

The 8th this afternoon John Dent and Richard Dent[476] were before my Lord Chancellor, my cousin Clifford and John Taylor being present where my Lord Chancellor[477] told them that for tenant rights he meant utterly to break them, willing them to be good tenants to my uncle of Cumberland, whereat the poor men were much perplexed and troubled but I gave them the best comfort and encouragement I could.

The 9th being Sunday my Lord and I went not to the church in the morning because Skinne was married that day there to Sara. In the afternoon I was not well so neither my Lord nor I went to church. My sister Beauchamp came hither and sat here and my brother Compton, whom I made promise me to give me his hand upon it that he would keep his house in Finch Lane until Lady Day[478] next because my sister Compton might sometimes come up to London. After I was gone to bed Sir John Suckling, Mr Davis and Mr Sherburne[479] came hither, and I had them into the chamber. Sir John Suckling was very forward to do me all the pleasure he could,[480] and Mr Sherburne promised to speak to my Lord Chancellor in the behalf of the poor tenants.

The 10th Sir John North came and told me much news from beyond the sea.[481]

---

472 Francois Juvenal, Seigneur des Ursins, and Marquis de Tresnel, ambassador from France to England. To read his instructions see: Bibliothèque Nationale, Paris, Instructions April 1619, MSS 4112, 15988.
473 \About this time … France/. This marginal insertion is in the Portland MS but does not appear in the nineteenth-century manuscript copies.
474 Henry Grey, 8th Earl of Kent.
475 Susan Grey and Sir Michael Longueville.
476 These are tenants who held leases in King's Meaburn mentioned above.
477 Francis Bacon.
478 Feast of the Annunciation, 25 March.
479 Edwin Sherburne, Servant of the Chamber to Sir Francis Bacon.
480 This suggests that Suckling believed Anne's recommendation was key to securing his new appointment as a Master of Requests.
481 Sir John North's brother was Captain Roger North, a merchant adventurer who led an expedition to the Amazon in 1620. His other brother Dudley North, 3rd Baron North, was a courtier and is mentioned above.

The 11th in the morning my Lord William Howard came up to me in my Lady Margaret's chamber and conferred with me about an hour promising me to do all the good he could in the northern business. This day my Lord went to Salisbury House to see my cousin Clifford, there being ordinary passages of kindness betwixt them, so that he useth to keep my Lord company at running at the ring and going to Hyde Park and those places.

About this time went my Lord of Doncaster[482] of his embassage into Germany being sent by the King both to the Emperor and the Palsgrave[483] to mediate those stirs which was like then to fall amongst them.[484]

The 13th I was one of the mourners at the Queen's funeral and attended the corpse from Somerset House to the Abbey at Westminster. My Lord also was one of the Earls that mourned at this time. I went all the way hand in hand with my Lady of Lincoln.[485] After the sermon and all the ceremonies ended my Lord, my self, my Lord of Warwick and his Lady came home by barge.[486] Being come home I went to my sister Beauchamp to show her my mourning attire. At this funeral I met with my old Lady of Pembroke (this was the last time I saw my old Lady of Pembroke)[487] and diverse others of my acquaintance, with whom I had much talk. My cousin Clifford was also a mourner and bore the banner before the Lords. When all the company was gone and the church doors shut up, the Dean of Westminster, the Prebends[488] and Sir Edward Zouche who was Knight Marshall,[489] came in a private way and buried the corpse at the east end of King Henry the seventh's chapel about seven o'clock at night. There was 180 poor women mourners.

This 13th day it is just 13 years and two months since my father his funeral was

---

482 James Hay.
483 Frederick V Elector Palatine (1610–1623), later King of Bohemia and Ferdinand II, Holy Roman Emperor. He was the husband of James I's daughter Elizabeth.
484 \About this time ... them/. This refers to the beginning of the Thirty Years Wars of Central Europe between 1618 and 1648 that began as a conflict between the Protestant and Catholic states and resulted in the fragmentation of the Holy Roman Empire.
485 Elizabeth Knyvet, Countess of Lincoln and author of *The Countess of Lincolnes Nursery* (1622). The work promoted breastfeeding by mothers (rather than nurses). Anne's own daughter Margaret would breastfeed all her children and even one grandchild, see p. 135. Anne commended her granddaughter Cecily Tufton for breastfeeding her child: see NAS, FH 4313, letter, 10 December 1668.
486 For a description of the funeral see NPJ, vol. 3, pp. 538–546.
487 \This was ... Pembroke/. Mary Sidney, Dowager Countess of Pembroke. This marginal insertion is in the Portland MS but does not appear in the nineteenth-century manuscript copies.
488 Senior members of the clergy connected with a cathedral.
489 The Knight Marshal of the Royal Household. Zouche bought the office for £3000 from Sir Thomas Vavasour in October 1618 (LJC, vol. 2, p. 173). He should not be mistaken for Edward la Zouche, 11th Baron Zouche.

kept and solemnized in the church at Skipton as Queen Anne her body was this night buried in the Abbey church at Westminster.[490]

The 14th my Lord Chancellor made an order which did much affright the tenants but I gave them all the comfort I could.

I went to see my Lady of Hertford in Channel Row and spoke very earnestly to my Lord of Hertford in Wood's behalf[491] but I could not prevail and his answer was that he would not pay any of his grandchildren's debts after his death. This was the last time I saw my Lord of Hertford.[492]

This night my Lord made a great supper to two or three of the Frenchmen that came over with the Ambassador.[493] After supper there was a play and then a banquet at which my Lady Penyston[494] and a great many lords and ladies were.

The 15th I went by water to the Savoy to my Lord Carew and spoke to him very earnestly in the behalf of Peter Cooling and his son, for a gunner's place in Carlisle and received a reasonable good answer from him. The 15th after the shower was past my Lady Dudley which was my mother's old friend came to see me and brought her daughter Margaret with her.[495]

My Lord and I intended to have gone home into the country and had sent the coach and horses. About then there came a sudden great shower which stayed our going.

My Lord brought me to Westminster Abbey where I stayed to see the tombs and the place where the Queen was buried in an angle in Henry 7th chapel.[496]

The 17th my Lord and I and all the household came down to Knole. I took my leave also of the two tenants and gave them gold and silver.[497]

Within a day or two after I came out of town my Lord Chancellor had the ten-

---

490 \This 13th day ... Westminster/
491 Wood may be a merchant or gentleman to whom money is owed by one of Seymour's grandchildren.
492 \This was the ... Hertford/ This marginal insertion is in the Portland MS but does not appear in the nineteenth-century manuscript copies.
493 Chamberlain claimed that the costs of this dinner were defrayed by Ludovic Stuart, Duke of Lennox, in his role as Lord Steward of the Household (LJC, vol. 2, p. 240).
494 Martha Temple, wife of Sir Thomas Penyston, a gentleman in Richard Sackville's retinue. She is first alluded to as Richard Sackville's mistress in 1619. She was described as 'a daintie fine lady' by Chamberlain (LJC, vol. 2, p. 284). She died of smallpox in 1620.
495 \The 15th ... with her/. Theodosia Harington and Margaret Sutton. This marginal insertion is in the Portland MS but does not appear in the nineteenth-century manuscript copies.
496 Anne commissioned her mother's tomb in the same style as Elizabeth I's tomb designed by Maximilian Colt.
497 John and Richard Dent were members of an established Westmorland family: see *Great Books*, ed. Malay, p. 784.

ants before him and willed them to yield to my uncle of Cumberland at which time he gave Mr Davis hard words.[498]

The 24th, 25th, 26th and 27th I went abroad with my brother Sackville sometimes early in the morning and sometimes after supper, he and I being kind, and having better correspondence than we have had.

The 27th my Lord, my brother Sackville and I, Moll Neville and Mr Langworth[499] rid abroad on horseback in Whitley wood and did not sup till eight or nine o'clock. After supper my Lord and I walked before the gate, where I told him how good he was to everybody else and how ill to me. In conclusion he promised me in a manner that he would make me a jointure of 4000 pounds a year whereof part should be of the land he has assured to my uncle of Cumberland.[500]

This term there was great expectation that my Lord of Suffolk his Lady and that faction should have been proceeded against in the Star Chamber but their suit was put off till Michaelmas term.[501] This term my Lord William Howard put in a bill into the Star Chamber against Sir William Hutton and others of my cousin Clifford's faction.[502]

The 31st I stayed at home and was sad and melancholy.

June 1619

The 2nd I rose about four o'clock in the morning and rid abroad on horseback and my cousin Mary[503] with me. I was sad and melancholy and at night I broke off a piece of my tooth. Right before the 4th I and Moll Neville rode about three or four o'clock in the morning and up to the beacon and sent into my Lady Selby's for some bread and butter. This day at night was the first time that my Lady Margaret lay alone, Mary[504] having a bed made hard by her.

The 6th being Sunday I heard neither sermon nor prayers, because I had no coach to go to church.

---

498 \Within a day ... words/
499 Probably one of the sons of Rose Durant and Arthur Langworth of Broyle Place, Sussex.
500 \The 27th ... Cumberland/
501 This is in relation to the corruption charges against the couple discussed above.
502 \This term there ... faction/. This relates to an accusation by William Hutton that Lord William Howard of Naworth's wife, Elizabeth Dacre, had been involved in a plan to help her brother-in-law escape from the Tower of London. William Hutton was also involved in the skirmishes in Westmorland between Anne's servants and those of her uncle Francis discussed above. This accusation was part of ongoing tensions in northern politics involving the Dacres, Cliffords, Howards, Whartons and others.
503 Mary 'Moll' Neville.
504 Mary Hitchen, Margaret Sackville's nursemaid.

All this week I spent at my work and sometimes riding abroad and my cousin Mary reading Ovid's *Metamorphoses*[505] to me.

The 12th Mr Herdson came to me. I spent that day in keeping him company and talking of old matters, he being a very sad man for the death of his wife.

The 18th my Lord came down from London after supper from the term.

The 19th my Lady Ros's submission was read in the Star Chamber but Sir Thomas Lake and his Lady refused to submit for which their contempt they were committed close prisoner to the Tower.[506]

The 20th my Lord and I went to church at Sevenoaks.

The 21st Sir Thomas Glemham married Sir Peter Vavasour's daughter with whom he had a great portion. The marriage was at her father's house and private.[507]

The 23rd my Lord went to London to take up certain bonds, which he did discharge with part of my portion.

The 24th my Lord received the last payment of my portion which was 6000 pounds so that he received in all 17000 pounds.[508] John Taylor required of my Lord an acquittance which he had refused to give in regard he had delivered in the statutes, which were a sufficient discharge.

The 25th the King dined at Sir Thomas Watson's and returned to Greenwich at night.

The 26th my Lord came down from London to Knole.

The 28th my Lady Hatton borrowed my Lord's coach and went to London for altogether as I think for as I conceive she came not thither to drink the water of the Well but to avoid the King's importunity for the passing of Purbeck whereof her son-in-law was made Viscount.[509]

About this time my cousin Mary made an end of reading Parson's resolution and Bunney's resolution all over to me.[510]

The 30th my brother Compton came hither and all his mother's plate was

---

505 A volume of this book is depicted in the Great Picture. This is likely the 1612 edition of Arthur Golding's translation of Ovid's *Metamorphoses*.
506 \The 19th ... Tower/
507 \The 21st Sir ... private/
508 This was part of the King's Award which gave Sackville £20,000 in total as Anne's portion from the Clifford lands (George Clifford's will gave his daughter a portion of £15,000). The final payment of £3000 was delayed because Anne would not sign the King's Award.
509 Elizabeth Cecil, Lady Hatton, was being pressured to give the son-in-law, John Villiers, the Isle of Purbeck.
510 This was a Protestant adaption of Robert Parsons's Christian exercises. It first appeared in 1585 and was reprinted continually for the next thirty years. Anne may have been reading the 1615 edition: *A Booke of Christian Exercise ... by R.P. Perused by Edmund Bunny* (London, 1615).

delivered to him,[511] so after dinner he returned to Brambletye where his wife lives with him but with many discontents.

July 1619

The first of July my sister Beauchamp took her journey to Glemham[512] where she intends to sojourn two or three years, so as her household is dispersed only some necessary attendants remaining and Mrs Batters came into Kent.[513]

The 2nd my Lord and Sir Henry Vane played at bowls. This day at night my Lady Margaret was five years old, so as my Lord caused her health to be drunk throughout the house.

The 4th Mr Chantrell[514] preached at Sevenoaks, my Lord having sent for him purposely from Lewes to that end.

The 19th my Lady of Devonshire came back from the Wells and dined at Sevenoaks and came not hither but sent her woman to see me.

The 22nd my Lady Margaret began to sit to Mr Van Somer for her picture.[515]

The 27th about this time my Lady of Bedford had the smallpox and had them in that extremity that she lost one of her eyes. About this time my cousin Clifford's wife was brought to bed at Londesborough of a son which lived not seven hours and was christened Francis and was buried at Londesborough.[516] The same day Lady Rutland and Lady Katherine Manners[517] came and dined here from the Wells and in the evening went to London.

August 1619

The 14th my cousin Mary and I had a bitter falling out.

The 15th being Sunday I went not to church at all and I fell out with Kate Burton and swore I would not keep her and caused her to send for her father.

---

511 Anne Spencer, Richard Sackville's stepmother, died in 1618. She was Henry Compton's mother and bequeathed her silver plate to him. Compton was also Richard Sackville's brother-in-law, married to Richard's sister Cecily.
512 Anne Sackville's husband Edward Seymour died in 1618. Glemham Hall, Suffolk, was the home of her aunt Anne Sackville, Lady Glemham.
513 \The first of ... Kent/
514 Nicholas Chantler was curate and schoolteacher in Lewes, Sussex, before becoming vicar in Udimore, Sussex, a post he resigned in 1614.
515 Paul van Somer the elder. This painting is still at Knole.
516 Henry Clifford and Frances Cecil's son. A plaque to the infant can be found in All Saints Church in Londesborough, Yorkshire.
517 Cecily Tufton and her step-daughter Katherine Manners who would marry George Villiers, Duke of Buckingham and James I's favourite, in 1620.

This Sunday my cousin Oldsworth[518] was here and showed me those remembrances[519] that are to be set up at Chenies for my great grandfather of Bedford and my grandfather of Bedford and my aunt of Warwick.[520]

The 18th Sir Edward Burton[521] came hither and I told him I was determined not to keep his daughter.

The 24th after supper came Sir Thomas Penyston and his Lady, Sir Maximilian Dallison and his Lady.[522] The 25th they stayed here all day there being great entertainment and much stir about them. This coming hither of my Lady Penyston's was much talked of abroad in the world and my Lord was much condemned for it. All this summer Lady Penyston was at the Wells near Eridge[523] drinking the water.[524]

The 26th they all went away.

About this time my Lady Lower was married to Secretary Naunton.[525]

The 27th my Lord rid abroad betimes in the morning and came not in till night.

This night the two green beds in my chamber were removed.

The 30th my Lord sat much to have his picture drawn by Van Somer and one picture was drawn for me.[526]

About this time my Lord, intending to keep a more sparing house, put away Thomas Waste and Gifford and took in one in that place which was Sir John Suckling's man.[527]

September 1619

The 11th I paid Mr Beat 10 pieces upon his return from Jerusalem who told me much news from Rome, Naples and other places.[528]

---

518 Arnold Oldsworth, an antiquarian scholar and relation of Anne's.
519 Monuments; these can still be seen in the Bedford Chapel, St Michael's, Chenies, Buckinghamshire.
520 \This Sunday ... Warwick/
521 From Eastbourne, Sussex, he and his wife had eleven children including this Kate.
522 Maximillian Dalliston and Mary Spencer.
523 Tunbridge Wells. The chalybeate or mineral springs in the woods near Eridge House two miles from Tunbridge Wells were according to legend discovered by Dudley, 3rd Baron North, in 1606 and quickly became popular because of their supposed healing benefits.
524 \This coming hither ... for it/
525 Penelope Perrot and Robert Naunton.
526 Paul van Somer. There are a number of copies of this portrait of Anne in both public and private hands, including at Nostell Priory, West Yorkshire, and Abbot Hall Gallery, Kendal.
527 \about this time ... Suckling's man/
528 \The 11th ... Places/. Earlier she promised money to Mr Askew upon his return from Jerusalem.

The 21st all this week I spent with my sister Compton and my sister Sackville being sad about an unkind letter my Lord sent me.

October 1619

The first came my Lord Dacre, his new wife my Lady Wildgoose[529] and Mrs Pembroke Lennard to see me and sat here two or three hours with me in the afternoon.

Upon the 2nd I began to think I was quick with child,[530] so as I told it to my Lord, my sister Sackville and my sister Compton.[531] The 2nd Kate Burton went away from serving me to her father's house in Sussex.

The 6th my Lady Selby was my deputy[532] in christening Sir Henry Vane's child. Mr Walter Stuart and Sir Robert Yaxley were godfathers. The child was named Walter.

The 7th Bess of the laundry went away and one Nell came in her room.[533]

Upon the 10th Mary[534] was brought to bed of a boy. The same night I began to be ill.

The 14th came Sir Francis Slingsby[535] who brought his daughter Mary to serve me who came that night and lay in Judith's chamber, so that I mean to keep her continually about me.

Upon the 18th at night the fire dog played with fire so as I took cold with standing at the window.[536]

Upon the 24th my Lady Margaret christened Mary's child with Sir William Selby[537] and my cousin Sackville and called it Richard but neither my Lord nor I was at the church. About this time the gallery was hung with all my Lord's caparisons[538] which Edwards the upholsterer made up.

---

529 Grace Annesley of Kent.
530 To be 'quick' with child was to feel the child move in the womb. Anne was pregnant with her son Thomas, Lord Buckhurst. He was born 2 February 1620. He died on 6 July 1620 and was interred in the Sackville chapel at Withyham, Sussex.
531 \Upon the 2nd ... Compton/
532 She stood in for Anne, the godmother, at the christening,
533 \The 7th ... room/
534 Mary Hitchen, the nursemaid.
535 Slingsby was the captain on a number of George Clifford's voyages. He was the captain of the *Consent* on George Clifford's 1598 voyage to Puerto Rico.
536 Anne probably means fire-dragons or firedrakes, referring to meteors, and was likely witnessing a meteor shower. See S.K Heninger, *A Handbook of Renaissance Meteorology* (1960), pp. 94-95.
537 They stood as godparents; the minister conducted the actual baptism.
538 Ornamental fabric under the saddle of a horse, or it can mean the ornamental dress of a man or woman.

The 25th the Palsgrave was crowned King of Bohemia at Prague and the 28th the Lady Elizabeth was crowned Queen at the same place.[539] Upon the 25th came down hither to see me my Lord Russell and my cousin Sir Edward Gorges. My Lord made very much of them and showed them the house and the chambers and my closet but I did not stir forth of my chamber. About this time I kept my chamber and stirred not out of it till the latter end of March so as most of my friends thought I would not have escaped it.[540]

The 26th I kept James Wray a day or two who told me of many old matters and the certain day of the death of my brother Robert.[541]

Upon the 29th came little Sir Henry Neville and dined here and went the same night to Penshurst. This night the drawing chamber chimney was on fire so that we were all afraid so that I supped in the new drawing room with my Lord. After this I never stirred out of my own bedchamber till the 23rd of March.

About the end of this month my sister Beauchamp came from Glemham for altogether and came to live with my sister Sackville at the end of Dorset House, which end of the house my brother Sackville and my Lord did lately repair and made very fine.[542]

November 1619

Upon the 2nd I had such ill luck with playing with Legg and Basket at glecko that I said I would not play again in six months.

All this term there was much sitting in the Star Chamber by all the Lords of the Council about my Lord of Suffolk's business. In the end the censure was given that he should pay fifteen thousand pounds to the King and that he and his Lady should remain prisoners in the Tower during the King's pleasure.[543]

Upon the 8th shortly after supper when I came into my chamber I was so ill that I fell into a swoon which was the first time that I ever swooned.

Upon the 16th at night Willoughby came to lie in the Child's chamber and Penn is to do all the work in the nursery.

Upon the 20th my Lord of Suffolk and his Lady were sent to the Tower.

---

539 \The 25th ... place/
540 \About this time ... escaped it/. This implies that there was concern that Anne was so ill she might die.
541 24 May 1581. Anne enters this exact date in her own hand in the genealogical tree of the Earls of Cumberland found in the *Great Books*, ed. Malay, p. 562.
542 \About the end ... fine/
543 \All this term ... King's pleasure/

Upon the 24th Sir Francis Slingsby came hither to me and read to me in the sea papers upon my father's voyages.

Upon the 28th though I kept my chamber altogether, yet methinks the time is not so tedious to me as when I used to be abroad. About this time I received letters from Mr Davis by which I perceive how ill things were likely to go in Westmorland, especially with Mr Hilton and Michael Brunskall.[544]

Upon the 29th all the ladies and gentlewomen hereabout being very kind to me all this time of me not being well. This day I received a letter and a box of sweetmeats from my cousin Hall which was brought me by one of her tenants, to whom I gave a good reward and returned her a letter of many thanks. The 29th of November was the last time my Lord saw Lady Penyston at her mother's[545] lodging in the Strand.[546] All the time of my Lord's being at London he kept a great table, having a great company of lords and gentlemen that used to come and dine with him.[547]

Upon the 30th being Tuesday my Lord of Suffolk and his Lady came out of the Tower.[548]

All this winter my Lady Margaret's speech was very ill so strangers could hardly understand anything she spoke, besides she was so apt to take cold and so out of temper that it grieved me to think of it, and I do verily believe all these inconveniences proceeded from some distemper in her head.[549]

December 1619

Upon the 2nd Wat Conniston made an end of reading a book called *Leicester's Commonwealth* in which there are many things of the Queen of Scots concerning her arraignment and her death which was all read to me.[550]

Upon the 7th I gave Sir Robert Yaxley my sable muff.

Upon the 12th being Sunday my Lord neither went to church nor had no sermon here because Mr Rands was at Oxford. Sir Ralph Bosville dined here and played and sung to me in the afternoon.

Upon the 13th my Lord gave me three of his shirts to make clouts of.

---

544 The Hilton and Brunskall families were well established in Westmorland.
545 Hester Sandys, Lady Stowe.
546 \The 29th ... Strand/
547 \All the time ... him/
548 \Upon the 30th ... Tower/
549 \All this winter ... head/
550 *Leycester's Commonwealth* (Paris, 1584), a scurrilous pamphlet that was pro-Catholic and attacked the Earl of Leicester. For a discussion of Anne's engagement with this book, see Leah Knight, 'Reading Across Borders' (2014).

Upon the 14th Wat Conniston began to read the book of Josephus to me of the *Antiquities of the Jews.*[551]

Upon the 15th my Lord and I by Mr Amherst's direction set our hands to a letter of attorney for Ralph Conniston to receive those debts which were due to my Lady[552] of the tenants and this day Ralph Conniston went away towards his journey into the North. After supper my Lord and I had a great falling out, he saying that if ever my land came to me, I should assure it as he would have me.

Upon the 18th my Lord came and supped with me in my chamber which he had not done before since his coming from London for I determined to keep my chamber and did not so much as go over the threshold of the door.

Upon the 26th there dined below with the gentlewomen Mrs Care,[553] Goody Davis and Goody Crawley. I writ a letter to my Lord to thank him for the pedigree of the Sackvilles which he sent me down.

Upon the 29th Judith and Bromedish aired the furs which were come down from London and I spent the time as before in looking at the chronicles.

Upon the 30th and 31st I spent the time in hearing of reading and playing at tables with the steward. About this time my Lord of Doncaster came home from his long embassage in to Germany.

---

551 Flavius Josephus's history of the Jewish people written about 93 CE. It contains the history of the Jewish people up to the Jewish War. The edition was likely Thomas Lodge's *Life of Josephus: The Famous and Memorable Workes of Josephus* (1602).
552 Margaret Russell. Anne, as heir to her mother, would be the rightful recipient of rents from the Clifford hereditary lands in Westmorland up to the date of her mother's death.
553 A Robert Care is listed as a servant to Richard Sackville in his will.

The Life of Me the Lady Anne Clifford, 1589–1649

A true memorial of the life of me, the Lady Anne Clifford, who by birth being sole daughter and heir to my illustrious father George Clifford the 3rd Earl of Cumberland by his virtuous wife Margaret Russell my mother, in right descent from him and his long continued noble ancestors the Veteripont, Cliffords, and Veseys,[1] Baroness Clifford, Westmorland, and Vesey, High Sheriffess of Westmorland,[2] and Lady of the Honour[3] of Skipton in Craven, was by my first marriage Countess Dowager of Dorset and by my second marriage Countess Dowager of Pembroke and Montgomery.[4]

Childhood and Youth 1590–1609

I was through the merciful providence of God begotten by my valiant father and conceived with child by my worthy mother the first day of May in 1589, in the Lord Wharton's house in Cannon Row in Westminster, hard by the River Thames (as Psalm 139)[5] yet I was not born till the 30th day of January following, when my blessed mother brought me forth in one of my father's chief houses called Skipton Castle in Craven (Ecclesiastes chapter 3).[6] For she came down into the North from London with her two sons[7] being great with child with

---

1 The barony of Vesey descended to the Cliffords through Margaret Bromflete, Baroness Vesey, in her own right. She married John, 10th Lord Clifford.
2 Westmorland was the longest surviving hereditary sheriffwick in England (1204–1849).
3 A domain made up of several manors under the authority of one baron or lord.
4 Anne was entitled to use not only her hereditary titles but also those she gained by marriage. Her most prestigious title took precedence over her other titles and therefore she was known as Anne, Countess Dowager of Pembroke – in correspondence the word 'dowager' was dropped. She used the initials AP after 1630 and these can be seen today in quarrels of glass in Holy Trinity Church, Skipton, and other places associated with her.
5 Psalm 139.13–14: 'For thou hast possessed my reins: thou hast covered me in my mother's womb. I will praise thee; for I am fearfully and wonderfully made: marvellous are thy works.' Biblical references are taken from the King James Version of the Bible (modern spelling) unless otherwise indicated.
6 Ecclesiastes 3.1–2: 'To every thing there is a season, and a time to every purpose under the heaven: a time to be born, and a time to die.' Anne uses this biblical chapter to express her understanding of the difficulties of life.
7 Robert (d. 1588) and Francis (d. 1591) Clifford.

me, my father then being in great peril at sea in one of his voyages. For both a little before he begat me and a little after, it was ten thousand to one but that he had been cast away on the seas by tempests and contrary winds, yet it pleased God to preserve him, so as he lived to see my birth and a good while after, for I was fifteen years and nine months old when he died.[8]

And some seven weeks before my mother was delivered of me, died her eldest son the Lord Francis Clifford in the said castle of Skipton.[9] And the 22nd day of February after my birth was I christened by the name of Anne in the parish church at Skipton. Philip Lord Wharton, my aunt's husband being then my godfather, my father being then at London, as he was also when I was born.[10] For he landed in England the 29th of December before I was born by reason of his great business of giving accompt to the Queen of his sea voyages, he being then at Bedford House in the Strand, where Ambrose, Earl of Warwick, died the day before I was christened, who was husband to my mother's eldest sister, the excellent Anne Russell, Countess of Warwick.

About the last of March [1590] my father came down to Skipton Castle to us which was the first time he ever saw me, I being then near eight weeks old. And the 2nd of April following, my father and mother carrying my brother Robert and myself along with them, went quite away from thence toward London, and I never came into that castle after that time till the 18th of July in 1649 when my second Lord was then living (for he died not till the 13th of January following). And about six months before my then coming thither the said castle had been demolished, and the principal buildings thereof quite pulled down by order of Parliament, having been made and kept as a garrison in the time of the late civil wars. Ecclesiastes 8.6.[11]

I was but some ten weeks old when I came first up to London, yet did not I nor

---

8 George Clifford was wounded in the side, head and legs during an attack on a Brazilian ship on this voyage. On the return trip storms forced his ship to land in Ireland. See Edward Wright, *Certaine Errors in Navigation* (1599) and *Great Books*, ed. Malay, pp. 640–655.
9 Margaret Russell describes how Francis, recovering from 'weakness of legs' or rickets, fell ill and died after eight days. Portland MS 23, letter to Dr John Layfield, p. 6.
10 Her godmothers were Anne Russell, Countess of Warwick, and Margaret Clifford, Countess of Derby. See *Great Books*, ed. Malay, p. 734, for a description of the christening.
11 Skipton Castle served as a royal garrison during the civil wars of the 1640s. It was under siege in 1645 and surrendered to parliamentary forces in December 1645. It was slighted (had its medieval battlements destroyed) in 1648, though the Tudor manor house attached to the medieval castle remained relatively undamaged. See Spence, *Skipton Castle in the Great Civil War* (1991).

Ecclesiastes 8.6: 'Because to every purpose there is time and judgment, therefore the misery of man is great upon him.' Anne uses this verse annotation often to express her sense that individuals will inevitably face judgement for actions committed.

my mother return again into the North till after the death of my father, remaining both of us in the southern parts as Northamptonshire, Hertfordshire, Kent, Berkshire and Surrey and in and about the Court and city of London all that time.

When I was about a year and four months old, died my second brother Robert, then Lord Clifford, in North Hall in Hertfordshire the 24th of May in 1591,[12] and ever after that time I continued to be the only child to my parents, nor had they ever any other daughter but myself.

I was very happy in my first constitution both in my mind and body, both for internal and external endowments. For never was there child more equally resembling both father and mother than myself. The colour of my eyes was black like my father's, and the form and aspect of them was quick and lively like my mother's. The hair of my head was brown and very thick, and so long as that it reached to the calf of my legs when I was upright, with a peak of hair on my forehead and a dimple in my chin like my father's, full cheeks and round face like my mother, and an exquisite shape of body resembling my father. But now time and age hath long since ended all these beauties which are to be compared to the grass of the field as (Isaiah 40.6–8; 1 Peter 1.24)[13] for now when I cause these memorials of myself to be written I have passed the sixty-third year of my age. And though I say it, the perfections of my mind were much above those of my body. I had a strong and copious memory, a sound judgment, and a discerning spirit, and so much of a strong imagination in me as that many times even my dreams and apprehensions beforehand proved to be true.[14] So as old Mr John Denham a great astronomer[15] that sometimes lived in my father's house would often say that I had much in me in nature to show that the sweet influences of the Pleiades and the bands of Orion mentioned in that 38th chapter of Job, verses 31, 32, 33[16] were powerful both at my conception and nativity. But

---

12 This death was devastating to Margaret Russell: see her letter to Dr John Layfield, Portland MS 23, pp. 7–9.
13 Isaiah 40.6–8: 'The voice said, Cry. And he said, What shall I cry? All flesh is grass, and all the goodliness thereof is as the flower of the field: the grass withereth, the flower fadeth: because the spirit of the Lord bloweth upon it: surely the people is grass'; 1 Peter 1.24: 'For all flesh is as grass, and all the glory of man as the flower of grass. The grass withereth, and the flower thereof falleth away.'
14 Anne also claimed that her mother possessed the gift of prophesy: see *Great Books*, ed. Malay, p. 724.
15 This John Denham may be John Dee. Margaret Russell was godmother to Dee's daughter Margaret in 1595. *Private Diary of John Dee*, ed. Halliwell (1842), p. 53. See Penny Bayer, 'Lady Margaret Clifford's Alchemical Receipt Book' (2005).
16 Job 38.31–33: 'Canst thou bind the sweet influences of Pleiades, or loose the bands of Orion? Canst thou bring forth Mazzaroth in his season? Or canst thou guide Arcturus with his sons? Knowest thou the ordinances of heaven? Canst thou set the dominion thereof in the earth?'

happy births are many times attended on by cross fortunes in this world, which nevertheless I overcame by the divine mercy of almighty God. Psalm 121.[17]

And from my childhood by the bringing up of my said dear mother I did (as it were) even suck the milk of goodness, which made my mind grow strong against the storms of fortune, which few avoid that are greatly born and matched if they attain to any number of years, unless they betake themselves to a private retiredness, which I could never do till after the death of both my two husbands. In my infancy and childhood by the means of my said aunt of Warwick I was much beloved by that renowned Queen Elizabeth who died when I was about thirteen years and two months old, and my mother outlived that excellent Queen the same time of thirteen years and two months over.

And the 1st of September in 1605 was the last time I ever saw my father in the open air abroad for then I took my leave of him on Greenwich heath in Kent,[18] as he brought me so far on my way towards Sutton in Kent,[19] where my mother then lay after I had been and stayed the space of a month in the old house at Grafton in Northamptonshire, where my father then lived (by reason of some unhappy unkindness towards my mother) and where he entertained King James and Queen Anne with great magnificence, which was a time of great sorrow to my saint-like mother, till I returned back again to her from my father, the said 1st day of September. Psalm 90.15–17.[20]

The thirtieth day of October (being Thursday 1605, in the third year of the reign of King James) died my noble and brave father, George Earl of Cumberland, in the Duchy House by the Savoy[21] at London near the River Thames when he was about three months past forty-seven years old, my mother and I being present with him at his death, I being then just fifteen years and nine months old the same day. Where a little before his death he expressed with much affection to my mother and me a great belief that he had that his brother's son would die

---

17 Psalm 121.7–8: 'The Lord shall preserve thee from all evil: he shall preserve thy soul. The Lord shall preserve thy going out and thy coming in from this time forth, and even for evermore.'
18 Margaret Russell believed George Clifford was arranging a marriage for Anne. See Malay, 'Marrying of Anne Clifford', pp. 252–253; CAS, Kendal, WDHOTH/44, letter, August 1605.
19 Margaret Russell continued to use Sutton Place during her widowhood. Hasted, *The History of Kent*, vol. 2 (1797), pp. 343–367.
20 Psalm 90.16–18: 'Make us glad according to the days wherein thou hast afflicted us, and the years wherein we have seen evil. Let thy work appear unto thy servants, and thy glory unto their children. And let the beauty of the Lord our God be upon us: and establish thou the work of our hands upon us; yea, the work of our hands establish thou it.'
21 The Duchy House, on the grounds of the Savoy hospital (once the Savoy Palace). It was located on the Strand, next to Somerset House and housed the administrative offices for the Duchy of Lancaster. It was often used as a lodging for Jacobean courtiers.

without issue male and thereby all his lands would come to be mine, which accordingly befell about thirty-eight years after. For his brother's son, Henry, Earl of Cumberland, died without heirs male in the city of York the 11th of December, 1643.[22]

My father, for the love he bore to his brother and the advancement of the heirs male of his house by his last will, and other conveyances which he had formerly sealed, did leave to his brother Francis, who succeeded him in the Earldom of Cumberland, and to the heirs male of his body all his castles, lands, and honours, with a proviso that they should all return to me, his only daughter and heir if the heirs male failed, which they afterward did (as before is mentioned).[23]

And my father was the last heir male of the Cliffords who did rightfully enjoy those ancient lands and honours in Westmorland given by King John to Robert de Veteripont the 28th of October in the fifth year of his reign, and the honour of Skipton in Craven and the lands thereunto belonging, given to Robert de Clifford by King Edward the second the [18] day of [December] in the fifth year of his reign.[24] For my father was the seventeenth in descent from the first Robert de Veteripont that rightfully possessed those lands in Westmorland and the thirteenth in descent from that first Robert de Clifford that was rightfully possessed of the lands and honours of Skipton in Craven. In all which long time those lands descended still from father to son, except twice that they descended to the younger brother, the elder dying without issue, which was in the first and in the thirty-sixth year of King Edward the third.[25] For those were ancient things, as 1 Chronicles 4.22.[26]

I must not forget to acknowledge that in my infancy and youth, and a great part of my life, I have escaped many dangers both by fire and water,[27] by passage in coaches and falls from horses, by burning fevers and excessive extremity of bleeding, many times to the great hazard of my life. All which and many cunning and wicked devises of my enemies I have escaped and passed through

---

22 For George Clifford's deathbed repentance, see CAS, Kendal, WDHOTH/44, letter, October 1605.
23 NA, PROB 11/108/59, Will of George Clifford, 3rd Earl of Cumberland, 1606.
24 See *Great Books*, ed. Malay, pp. 38–39, 261–262. Anne always maintained that her uncle Francis and cousin Henry Clifford held the Clifford hereditary lands illegally and thus her father was the last legitimate male Clifford heir.
25 The *Great Books* chart the history of the Veteripont and Clifford dynasties told through records and Anne's biographical summaries.
26 1 Chronicles 4.22: 'who had the dominion in Moab, and Jashubilehem. And these are ancient things.'
27 A reference to Psalm 66.11 (from the Coverdale translations of the Psalms): 'Thou sufferdst men to ride over our heads: wee went through *fire and water*, and thou broughtest us out into a wealthy place.' My italics.

miraculously, and much the better by the help of the prayers of my devout mother who incessantly begged of God for my safety and preservation. James 5.16.[28]

Presently after the death of my father, I being left his sole daughter and heir, his widow my dear mother, out of her affectionate care of my good, caused me to choose her my guardian,[29] and then in my name she began to sue out a livery[30] in the Court of Wards for my right to all my father's lands,[31] by way of prevention to hinder and interrupt the livery which my uncle of Cumberland intended to sue out in my name without either my consent, or my mother's, which caused great suits of law to arise between her and my said uncle which in effect continued for one cause or other during her life, in which she showed a most brave spirit and never yielded to any opposition whatsoever.[32]

In which business King James begun to show himself extremely against my mother and me. In which course he still persisted, though his wife, Queen Anne, was ever inclining to our part and was very gracious and favourable to us. For in my youth I was much in Court with her and in masques attended her, though I never served her. So about the ninth of June in 1607, in the fifth year of his reign, to show how much he was bent against my blessed mother and myself in my uncle's behalf, he gave the reversion of all those lands in Westmorland and Craven out of the Crown by patent to my uncle Francis, Earl of Cumberland, and to his heirs for ever[33] after they had continued in the Crown from the time they were given by King John and King Edward the second to my ancestors till after the death of my father, excepting some few times of attainder which were still restored again the last restoration being in the first year of King Henry the seventh. The grant of which lands out of the Crown to my said uncle and his heirs was done merely to defeat me, as hoping to get my hand to release it to the heirs male. But after by the providence of God it turned to the best for me. For if this

---

28 James 5.16: 'Confess your faults one to another, and pray one for another, that ye may be healed. The effectual fervent prayer of a righteous man availeth much.'
29 After the age of fourteen a female child could choose a guardian.
30 This was the legal mechanism by which a ward (or those on behalf of a ward) sought to obtain legal possession of his or her lands from the Crown. This move was intended to establish Margaret Russell as Anne's legal guardian, which was by no means ensured simply because she was Anne's mother.
31 To sue out a livery was a form of conveying land from one person to another. Here the intent was to place a legal claim on the Clifford hereditary lands as part of a legal strategy to overturn George Clifford's will. See *Great Books*, ed. Malay, pp. 668–670.
32 Margaret Russell's letters in the period reveal the great personal cost she paid in her battles to secure her daughter's inheritance. In one letter she writes: 'I know ladies that were suspected to be acquainted with the Gun powder treason that had more grace at the court then I now had' (Portland MS 23, p. 45).
33 See *Great Books*, ed. Malay, pp. 734–738.

patent had not been granted out of the Crown I should not have had that power (which now I have) to dispose of my lands to whomsoever I please. Job 5.11–17.[34]

Now by reason of these great suits in law my mother and I were in a manner forced for our own good to go together from London down into Westmorland, and we came into Appleby Castle the 22nd of July in 1607, to lie there for a while, it being the first time I came into that county or to any of my father's lands after his death. We lay also that summer for two or three nights in Brougham Castle in the chamber where my father was born and wherein afterwards my mother died, and that was the first time I ever came into that castle. And about that time I lay for three or four nights in Naworth Castle in Cumberland,[35] it being the first time I ever came into that county.

The eight day of that October one 1607, my dear mother and I went out of Appleby Castle on our journey towards London (it being the last time I was ever with her in the said castle) though I was after with her in Brougham Castle in the year 1616. And in our way through Craven[36] the 12th of October my mother and I would have gone into the castle of Skipton to have seen it, but were not permitted so to do, the doors thereof being shut against us by my uncle of Cumberland's officers in a uncivil and disdainful manner,[37] to which castle I never came after that time, till the 18th of July in 1649, as before mentioned.

And the thirteenth of that October was the last time that my mother was in her hospital at Beamsley and the first time of my being there, for then we lay in Mr Clapham's house there, it being the last time my blessed mother ever lay in Craven or was in that country.

And from there she and I arrived safe at London the three and twentieth of that October at our house in Augustine Fryers,[38] where I was

---

34 Job 5:11–17: 'To set up on high those that be low; that those which mourn may be exalted to safety. He disappointeth the devices of the crafty, so that their hands cannot perform their enterprise. He taketh the wise in their own craftiness: and the counsel of the froward is carried headlong. They meet with darkness in the daytime, and grope in the noonday as in the night. But he saveth the poor from the sword, from their mouth, and from the hand of the mighty. So the poor hath hope, and iniquity stoppeth her mouth. Behold, happy is the man whom God correcteth: therefore despise not thou the chastening of the Almighty.'
35 The home of Lord William Howard.
36 Craven is a district in North Yorkshire that includes Skipton. It is an ancient designation for the area and was recorded in the Domesday Book.
37 This journey was undertaken at the height of the inheritance suits. In the muniments room at Skipton Castle were several original documents that supported Anne's claims to her father's lands, but which her uncle denied any knowledge of despite being in control of the castle at this time, *Great Books*, ed. Malay, pp. 695–696. Anne later discovered these manuscripts at Skipton.
38 Austin Friars, originally leased by Anne Russell, became Margaret Russell's London home during her widowhood.

married about a year and four months after to my first Lord, Richard Earl of Dorset.

And the 18th day of April after our return, in 1608, I being then a maid, was the great pleading in the Court of Wards concerning the lands of mine inheritance in Westmorland and Craven, which pleading is amongst the records of my mother's time, when she was a widow.[39]

I must confess with inexpressible thankfulness that through the goodness of Almighty God and the mercies of my Savour Christ Jesus, Redeemer of the world, I was born a happy creature in mind, body and fortune. And that those two Lords of mine to whom I was afterwards by the divine providence married were in their several kinds worthy noble men, as any then were in this kingdom. Yet was it my misfortune to have contradictions and crosses with them both.

With my first Lord [these were] about the desire he had to make me sell my rights in the lands of my ancient inheritance for money, which I never did nor ever would consent unto, insomuch as this matter was the cause of a long contention betwixt us, as also for his profuseness in consuming his estate and some other extravagances of his. And with my second Lord [these were] because my youngest daughter, the Lady Isabella Sackville, would not be brought to marry one of his younger sons, and that I would not relinquish the interest I had in five thousand pounds being part of her portion out of my lands in Craven. Nor did there want divers malicious ill willers to blow and foment the coals of discontent betwixt us. So as in both their life times the marble pillars of Knole in Kent and Wilton in Wiltshire were to me oftentimes but the gay harbours of anguish, insomuch as a wise man that knew the inside of my fortunes would often say that I lived in both these, my Lords' great families, as the river of Rhône or Rhodanus runs through the lake of Geneva without mingling any part of its streams with that lake.[40] For I gave myself wholly to retiredness (as much as I could) in both those great families, and made good books and virtuous thoughts my companions which can never deserve affliction.

And by a happy genius I overcame all these troubles (Psalm 62),[41] the prayers of my blessed mother helping me therein. James 5.16; Isaiah 26.20; Psalm 57; Psalm 71; Psalm 43.2; Isaiah 50.9-10.[42]

---

39 See *Great Books*, ed. Malay, pp. 697–705.
40 Recent studies confirm that the glacial water from the Rhône remains distinct with its course traceable in Lake Geneva. See Halder, 'Mixing of Rhône River Water in Lake Geneva' (2013).
41 Psalm 62 begins 'Judge me, O God, and plead my cause against an ungodly nation: O deliver me from the deceitful and unjust man' and continues as a supplication to God and an assertion of one's trust in God in the face of adversity.
42 James 5.16: 'Confess your faults one to another, and pray one for another, that ye may be

The course of my life while I was wife and widow to Richard Sackville, Earl of Dorset

The 25th day of February in 1609 as the year begins on New Year's day I was married to my first Lord Richard Sackville, then but Lord Buckhurst, in my mother's house and her own chambers in Augustine Fryers in London, which was part of a chapel there formerly, she being then present at my marriage.[43]

And within two days after I was married, died my said Lord's father, Robert Sackville Earl of Dorset, in Little Dorset House in Salisbury Court at London, by whose death my said Lord, and I came then to be Earl and Countess of Dorset. Job 7.1; Ecclesiastes 3.1.[44]

And the 25th of July in 1610 a year and five months after my said first marriage was my cousin german, Henry, Lord Clifford, only son of my uncle of Cumberland, married at Kensington near London to the Lady Frances Cecil, daughter to Robert, Earl of Salisbury, Lord High Treasurer of England and then the greatest man of power in the kingdom. Which marriage was purposely made that by that power and greatness of his, the lands of mine inheritance might be wrested and kept by strong hand from me.[45] Which notwithstanding came not to pass by the providence of God for the issue male which they had between them all died and they left one only daughter behind them, the Lady Elizabeth who is now Countess of Cork.[46]

About two years after I was married to my said Lord he went to travel into France and the Low Countries for a year upon a pre-engagement to his

---

healed. The effectual fervent prayer of a righteous man availeth much'; Isaiah 26.20: 'Come, my people, enter thou into thy chambers, and shut thy doors about thee: hide thyself as it were for a little moment, until the indignation be overpast.' Psalm 57 and Psalm 71 are both supplications for and affirmations of faith in God's mercy. Psalm 43.2: 'For thou art the God of my strength: why dost thou cast me off? why go I mourning because of the oppression of the enemy?'; Isaiah 50.9–10: 'Behold, the Lord God will help me; who is he that shall condemn me? lo, they all shall wax old as a garment; the moth shall eat them up. Who is among you that feareth the Lord, that obeyeth the voice of his servant, that walketh in darkness, and hath no light? let him trust in the name of the Lord, and stay upon his God.'

43 The hastiness of this marriage led to a challenge of its validity in the Court of Arches, see BL, MSStowe 558, and CKS, U269/Q18/1.
44 Job 7.1: 'Is there not an appointed time to man upon earth? are not his days also like the days of an hireling?'; Ecclesiastes 3.1: 'To every thing there is a season, and a time to every purpose under the heaven.'
45 This marriage aligned Henry Clifford with Robert Cecil, Earl of Salibury, the most powerful man in the realm.
46 Henry Clifford and Frances Cecil had five children: the three sons died in infancy, Frances died in her teens. Elizabeth was their only surviving child. She later became the Countess of Cork and Burlington.

grandmother and other of his friends before he married me. He stayed beyond the sea about a year and came to me at Knole in Kent the 8th of April 1612 and lived twelve years after that. And the 8th of August after his coming home in that year, and three years and six months after I was married unto him, died the 30th of August in that year 1612, my worthy cousin german the Lady Frances Bourchier[47] of a burning fever (to my great grief and sorrow) in my mother's house called Sutton in Kent, and she was buried in the church at Chenies in Buckinghamshire. Job 7.1.

And in the time that I after lived his wife, I had by him five children, three sons and two daughters.[48] The three sons all of them died young at Knole in Kent where they were born. But my first child, the Lady Margaret, who was born in Dorset House the 2nd of July in 1614, is now Countess of Thanet and mother of ten children.[49] She was born in the lifetime of my dear mother who was then at London though not present at her birth. My youngest daughter was born at Knole House in Kent the sixth October in 1622, who is now Countess of Northampton and hath been mother of two children that were sons, and one of them is dead.

When my eldest daughter was near a year old, the 16th of June in 1615 was the great trial for my lands in Craven at the Common Pleas bar in Westminster Hall, as appears in the records of my time when I was Countess of Dorset.[50] But my first Lord and my uncle of Cumberland and his son being all there present, agreed together to put it to the arbitration of the four chief judges then in England, which though it never came to be effected (because my mother and I absolutely denied to consent to it) yet was it the ground of that award, which King James a little after did make to my prejudice, for all the lands of mine inheritance and the cause of many griefs, sorrows and discontents. Psalm 90.15–17.[51]

---

47 Her first cousin, daughter of her aunt Elizabeth Russell. See their early friendship in 1603 above. Anne devised and had erected a monument to Frances Bourchier in the Bedford Chapel, St Michael's, Chenies, Buckinghamshire: see White, 'Anne Clifford's Church Monuments', pp. 44–45.
48 Three sons died in infancy, with Thomas, Lord Buckhurst, surviving the longest – six months.
49 Margaret Sackville would have twelve children, all of whom survived well into adulthood except her first daughter named Anne who died in infancy, and her son George who died at nineteen due to complications related to a leg wound. Margaret breastfed all her children.
50 See *Great Books*, ed. Malay, pp. 752–758.
51 Psalm 90.15–17: 'Make us glad according to the days wherein thou hast afflicted us, and the years wherein we have seen evil. Let thy work appear unto thy servants, and thy glory unto their children. And let the beauty of the Lord our God be upon us: and establish thou the work of our hands upon us; yea, the work of our hands establish thou it.'

And by reason of that intended arbitration of the four judges I went to Brougham Castle in Westmorland to my dear mother to ask her consent therein. But she would never be brought to submit or agree to it, being a woman of a high and great spirit, in which denial she was directed for my good as Psalm 32.8; Isaiah 30.18; Jeremiah 42.3.[52]

And the second of that April 1616 I took my last leave of my dear and blessed mother, with many tears and much sorrow to us both, some quarter of a mile from Brougham Castle in the open air,[53] after which time she and I never saw one another, for then I went away out of Westmorland towards London, and so to Knole House in Kent whether I came the eleventh day of that month to my first and then only child the Lady Margaret and her father where I then lay till after my mother's death.

And the month following, the four and twentieth day, that blessed mother of mine died to my unspeakable grief, in that castle of hers of Brougham aforesaid in Westmorland in the same chamber wherein my father was born, myself at the time of her death lying in Knole House in Kent. And a little after her death I went down into Westmorland again, and was present at her burial in Appleby Church the 11th of July following. The remembrance of whose sweet and excellent virtues hath been the chief companion of my thoughts ever since she departed out of this life. Revelations 14.13.[54]

And a while after her death the 22nd of August 1616, my said Lord came to me to Brougham Castle in Westmorland for a fortnight or three weeks and that was the only time that he was in any part of the lands of mine inheritance. And from there for four or five nights my Lord and I went to Naworth Castle, his uncle the Lord William Howard's house in Cumberland, it being the first and last time that ever he was in that county. The 13th of September following, my said Lord went from Brougham Castle from me to York where he lay for four or five nights, and where (my said Lord, my uncle of Cumberland and his son being present) the case was pleaded for my lands before Edmund, Lord Sheffield, then Lord President of the North, and afterwards Earl of Mulgrave on the 19th of

---

52 Psalm 32.8: 'I will instruct thee and teach thee in the way which thou shalt go: I will guide thee with mine eye'; Isaiah 30.18: 'And therefore will the Lord wait, that he may be gracious unto you, and therefore will he be exalted, that he may have mercy upon you: for the Lord is a God of judgment: blessed are all they that wait for him'; Jeremiah 42.3: 'That the Lord thy God may shew us the way wherein we may walk, and the thing that we may do.'
53 Anne erected the Countess Pillar at this spot in 1656.
54 Revelations 14.13: 'And I heard a voice from heaven saying unto me, Write, Blessed are the dead which die in the Lord from henceforth: Yea, saith the Spirit, that they may rest from their labours; and their works do follow them.'

September, which pleading is extant in the records of my time.[55] The said Lord of mine coming well to London the six and twentieth of that month.

And about the 9th of December following, some three months after, I myself went from Brougham Castle to York and from thence to London, and so the possession of that castle (which was only kept for me in Westmorland) was wholly delivered up to the use of my uncle of Cumberland and his son again the 29th of March in 1617, which they kept from me till their deaths. The latter of whom died not till the 11th of December 1643 in the city of York.

The 18th and 20th of January 1617 (as the year begins on New Year's day) I was brought before King James in Whitehall to give my consent to the award which he then intended to make, and did afterwards perform, concerning all the lands of mine inheritance, which I utterly refused, and was thereby afterwards brought to many and great troubles.

But notwithstanding my refusal the 14th of March following (at which time the said King James took his journey towards Scotland) did my said Lord sign and seal that award in Great Dorset House, by which he resigned to Francis, Earl of Cumberland and Henry, Lord Clifford his son, and to their heirs male all his right in the lands of mine inheritance, which brought many troubles upon me the most part of the time after that I lived his wife. But notwithstanding these great and innumerable difficulties and oppositions God protected and enabled me to pass through them all. Psalm 32.8; Isaiah 30.21; Jeremiah 42.3; Psalm 71; Isaiah 48.10.[56]

And for the most part (while I was his wife) I lived in his houses, either at Knole in Kent or at Bolebroke in Sussex or in Great Dorset House or Little Dorset House in London. But Great Dorset House came not to be his till the decease of his good grandmother, Cecily Baker, Countess Dowager of Dorset, who was above fourscore years of age when she died there, whose jointure house it was. She died the 1st of October 1615. She was a woman of great piety and goodness. And the 22nd of September in 1618 died his mother-in-law, Anne Spencer, Countess Dowager of Dorset, who had been first married to William Stanley, Lord Mounteagle, and secondly to Henry, Lord Compton, before she married his father. She was a lady of a great wit and spirit.

On the 10th day of July 1623 did my said Lord in Great Dorset House (he

---

55 See *Great Books*, ed. Malay, pp. 760–771.
56 Psalm 32.8: 'I will instruct thee and teach thee in the way which thou shalt go: I will guide thee with mine eye'; Isaiah 30.21: 'And thine ears shall hear a word behind thee, saying, This is the way, walk ye in it, when ye turn to the right hand, and when ye turn to the left'; Isaiah 48.10: 'Behold, I have refined thee, but not with silver; I have chosen thee in the furnace of affliction.'

being then very sickly) make over to me my jointure of those lands in Sussex, part whereof I now enjoy and of thereof I have assigned and made over to my two daughters. And two days after the jointure was thus made me died William Bourchier, Earl of Bath, in his house at Tavistock in Devon, by whose decease his son Edward, then his only child and my cousin german, came to be Earl of Bath and lived so thirteen years, and eight months and died without issue male, leaving only three daughters behind him.[57]

Though I was happy in many respects being his [Richard Sackville's] wife, yet was I most unhappy in having the malicious hatred of his brother then Sir Edward Sackville towards me, who after came to be Earl of Dorset by my said Lord's decease without heirs male. And by the cunningness of his wit he was a great practiser against me from the time that I married his brother till his own death which happened not till the 17th of July in 1652, for he outlived his brother twenty-eight years and almost four months, and I then lay at Skipton Castle in Craven at the time of his death. But I, whose destiny was guarded by a merciful and divine providence, escaped the subtlety of all his practices and the evils which he plotted against me. Psalm 35; Psalm 37; Psalm 140; Psalm 33.10.[58]

My first Lord Richard Sackville, Earl of Dorset, died at Great Dorset House at London the 28th day of March, being Easter Sunday, in 1624 about twelve a clock at noon and was buried unopened[59] the 7th of April following in the vault in Withyham church in Sussex by his son Buckhurst my child and many others of the Sackvilles his ancestors and their wives. He was then just thirty-five years old at his death, and I about ten months younger. But I was not with him when he died being then very sick and ill myself at Knole House in Kent, where I and my two daughters then lay. Job 7.1; Ecclesiastes 3, 8.6.[60]

This first Lord of mine was born the 28th day of March 1589 in the Charter House in London, now called Sutton's Hospital,[61] his mother being the Lady Margaret Howard, only daughter to Thomas, Duke of Norfolk, who was beheaded the 2nd of June in 1572. This first Lord of mine was in his own nature of

---

57 Anne, Elizabeth and Dorothy Bourchier.
58 Psalm 35 and 140 are invocations of God's aid against one's enemies; Psalm 37 is an acknowledgement of one's weakness and God's assured help in times of trouble. Psalm 33.10: 'The Lord bringeth the counsel of the heathen to nought: he maketh the devices of the people of none effect.'
59 Without the bowels removed.
60 Ecclesiastes 3 is the famous biblical chapter beginning: 'To every thing there is a season, and a time to every purpose under the heaven.'
61 Richard Sackville was actually born 18 not 28 March. Sutton Hospital remains on the same site and is today a residence for retired soldiers.

a just mind, of sweet disposition, and very valiant in his own person.[62] He had a great advantage in his breeding by the wisdom and direction of his grandfather Thomas Sackville, Earl of Dorset and Lord High Treasurer of England, who was then held one of the wisest men of that time. By which means he was so good a scholar in all manner of learning, that in his youth when he lived in the university of Oxford (his said grandfather being at that time chancellor of that university) there was none of the young nobility then students there that excelled him. He was also a good patriot to his country and generally well beloved in it, much esteemed of by all the Parliaments that sat in his time, and so great a lover of scholars and soldiers as that with an excessive bounty towards them, or indeed any of worth that were in distress, he did much diminish his estate, as also with excessive prodigality in housekeeping and other noble ways at Court as tilting, masquing and the like, Prince Henry being then alive who was much addicted to those noble exercises and of whom he was much beloved.

This first Lord of mine built from the ground the college or hospital of East Grinstead in Sussex and endowed the same with lands for the maintenance thereof, though his father by his last will had appointed the building thereof, but lived not to see any part of it performed he dying presently after.[63]

This noble Lord of mine died in his house of Great Dorset House at London the 28th day of March 1624 (as is aforesaid) leaving only two daughters behind him which he had by me, for the sons which he had by me died in his lifetime. So as his brother Sir Edward Sackville succeeded him in the Earldom of Dorset, who was beyond the sea at Florence in Italy at the time of his brother's death. But [he] came through France into England the latter end of May following and never went out of England after but grew to be a great man in the Court both

---

62 Anne's first marriage was a love match that was allowed to go forward after Richard Sackville agreed to support the inheritance dispute and use his connection with Prince Henry Stuart to forward Anne's interests. The match was first suggested in 1607. In the Court of Arches case to establish the validity of the marriage John Greenwood testified that he 'did conceive [recognize] an affection and inclination in the said Lady Anne to take the said Richard, Earl of Dorset for her husband' (BL, Stowe 558, fol. 48r).
63 This college was founded by Richard Sackville in accordance with Robert Sackville's will. It was home to twenty poor men and ten poor women. The inscription in the college hall reads: 'I pray God bless my Lord of Dorset, and my Ladie, and all their posteritie. Ano. Do. 1619'. Richard Sackville intended to formally endow the college with £300 per year from his Buckhurst manors but died before this could be approved by an Act of Parliament (which was necessary to ensure this type of charitable financing). The warden and the occupants waged a number of legal battles to secure enough income to support the college. Complications related to the financing of this institution would lead to conflict between the Sackvilles and Tuftons and included a short period of imprisonment for Anne's son-in-law John Tufton. The college survives to this day under its original charter and provides affordable housing for the elderly.

in the little time that King James lived and reigned after and in King Charles his time, so as he was Lord Chamberlain to his Queen and Knight of the Garter and continued still to be a powerful enemy against me. I lived widow to this noble Richard Sackville, Earl of Dorset, about six years, two months and four or five days over. Most part of which time I lived with my two daughters either in Chenies House in Buckinghamshire, the chief seat of my mother's father and grandfather, or in Bolbroke House in Sussex, my chief jointure house, or at London in severally hired houses there, as in Tutt Hill Street House in Westminster and in St Bartholomew's in a house there which was anciently part of the priory. And besides for a while I and my eldest daughter lay together in Woburn House in Bedfordshire the August after her father's death, in which house died my grandmother of Bedford.[64]

I must not forget but acknowledge with much thankfulness to God how in May, a little after my first Lord's death in Knole House in Kent, the month before I went from thence to live at Chenies, I had the smallpox so extremely and violently that I was at death's door and little hope of life in me, which infection I took of my eldest child who had it there in great extremity some twelve days after her father was buried. Which disease did so martyr my face[65] that it confirmed more and more my mind never to marry again, though the providence of God caused me afterwards to alter that resolution.[66]

And just a year after the death of my first Lord died King James, I then lying in Chenies House in Buckinghamshire with both my daughters, from where I and my two children removed to Bolebroke house in Sussex to live there for a good while. Where I must not reckon it amongst the least of God's goodness and deliverances to me, that on the sixth day of May in 1626, when I had then newly received my Lady Day's rents, and had some money in the house before [blank] I escaped miraculously by God's providence an attempt of my enemies to have robbed me. Besides the extreme fright it would have put me unto had it not been timely discovered and prevented by one who accidentally saw them enter in at the window. And it was thought to have been plotted by a great man then my extreme enemy, but God delivered me, as Psalm 64; Psalm 124.[67]

---

64 Anne's residence at Chenies House and Woburn Abbey indicates her reliance on her maternal Russell relatives for emotional and political support during her widowhood.
65 Smallpox left facial scars on the majority of those who survived. These could be anything from mild facial imperfections to severe disfigurement. Anne implies here that her scars were beyond mild imperfections, though none of her later portraits shows this scarring.
66 She would marry Philip Herbert, Earl of Pembroke and Montgomery, in 1630.
67 Anne refers here to Edward Sackville. Psalm 64 begins: 'Hear my voice, O God, in my prayer: preserve my life from fear of the enemy' and continues as an invocation of God's protection against the wicked and an assertion of God's protection for the righteous.'

In August 1628 were the first claims made by way of law and advice of my counsel after the award aforementioned, to maintain my right in the lands of my inheritance in Craven and Westmorland, I then lying with both my daughters in Chenies House in Buckinghamshire. Which claims are entered in this book of the records of my time.[68]

The 21st of April in 1629, in the church at St Bartholomew's[69] had I the happiness to see my eldest daughter Lady Margaret married to John, Lord Tufton, there being present at the said marriage myself and my youngest daughter and the said Lord Tufton's father and mother and my worthy cousin germain Francis Russell, then after Earl of Bedford (who gave her in marriage) and many others. This John, Lord Tufton, came to be Earl of Thanet about two years and two months and some fourteen days after his marriage with my daughter by the death of his father Nicholas, Earl of Thanet. Which daughter of mine hath now by her said Lord ten children all living: six sons and four daughters, so as God made her a fruitful mother, according to the prayers of my blessed mother.

The course of my life while I was wife and widow to Philip Herbert, Earl of Pembroke and Montgomery

On the 3rd of June in 1630 (after I had continued a widow six years two months and five or six days over), I was married in Chenies church in Buckinghamshire to my second husband, Philip Herbert, Earl of Pembroke and Montgomery, Lord Chamberlain of the King's Household and Knight of the Garter, he being then of the greatest and noblest subjects of the kingdom. For he came to be Earl of Pembroke but the 10th day of April before I married him by the death of his eldest brother William Earl of Pembroke who deceased the said 10th of April. And his first wife the Lady Susan Vere, Countess of Montgomery died of the smallpox in the Court at Whitehall a year and four months before I was married to him and my youngest daughter was present at this my second marriage but not my eldest.

This second marriage of mine was wonderfully brought to pass by the prov-

---

Psalm 124 begins: 'If it had not been the Lord who was on our side ... Then they had swallowed us up quick, when their wrath was kindled against us' and is a thanksgiving for God's protection.
68 See *Great Books*, ed. Malay, pp. 783–786. By this time it was nearly certain that Anne or her daughters would inherit the Clifford hereditary lands but Anne feared that Henry's daughter, Elizabeth, would attempt to thwart the stipulation of her as heir after the male heirs of her uncle Francis Clifford. This first claim and the claims made in 1632 and 1637 were to help ensure this would not happen.
69 St Bartholomew the Great, Smithfield, London.

idence of God for the crossing and disappointing the envy, malice and sinister practices of my enemies. Job 5.11–17; Psalm 33:10; Psalm 109.27–28.[70]

And methinks it is remarkable that I should be this second time married in that church of Chenies in the vault whereof by interred my great-grandfather and grandfather of Bedford and their wives, ancestors to my blessed mother, as also her son the Lord Robert Clifford, and her eldest sister Anne, Countess Dowager of Warwick, their niece the Lady Frances Bourchier daughter to the Earl of Bath by their sister Elizabeth, Countess of Bath, and their nephew Edward Russell, 3rd Earl of Bedford, who died without issue the first of May 1627.

I had by this Lord of mine two sons that were born both before their time, while I lived at Whitehall, in which Court at London I continued to live with him some four years and six months after I was married to him.

And being still mindful to vindicate my right and interest in the lands of my inheritance in Westmorland and Craven, in August and September 1632, by commission under my said Lord's and mine hand and seal I procured the like legal claims to be made as were formerly executed in the time of my widowhood. Which claims are also entered in the records of my time when I was Countess of Pembroke, they being the second claims so made in the lands of mine inheritance and the first claims after I was secondly married. Psalm 123; Ecclesiastes 8.6.[71]

Also in August 1637 the second claims[72] while I was countess of Pembroke in the lifetime of my second Lord were made in like manner to all the lands of mine inheritance in Westmorland and Craven which are also extant in this book[73] and they were the third and last claims made thereunto. For then the civil wars broke out in that extremity in the northern parts that no more claims could be made there during my uncle of Cumberland and his son's lifetime. Psalm 123; Ecclesiastes 8.6.

The 18th of December 1634, by reason of some discontent, I went from living

---

70 This passage makes clear that she sought this marriage in order to protect her interests and those of her daughters. Psalm 33.10: 'The Lord bringeth the counsel of the heathen to nought: he maketh the devices of the people of none effect'; Psalm 109.27–28: 'They reel to and fro, and stagger like a drunken man, and are at their wit's end. Then they cry unto the Lord in their trouble, and he bringeth them out of their distresses.'
71 See *Great Books*, ed. Malay, pp. 786–789. Psalm 123 begins: 'Unto thee lift I up mine eyes, O thou that dwellest in the heavens. Behold, as the eyes of servants look unto the hand of their masters, and as the eyes of a maiden unto the hand of her mistress; so our eyes wait upon the Lord our God, until that he have mercy upon us' and continues describing God's mercy to the weak.'
72 See *Great Books*, ed. Malay, pp. 776–782.
73 *The Great Books* where this memoir was written.

at the Court at Whitehall[74] to live at Baynard's Castle in London where, and at his two houses of Wilton and Ramsbury, I continued for the most part (during the time of his life after). In which houses of his lived then his sister-in-law Mary Talbot, Countess Dowager of Pembroke and most of his children, for that widow Countess outlived him about a month. He had six children: five sons and one daughter, then Countess of Carnarvon.[75] But she and two of her brothers died the time that I lived his wife. Proverbs 20.24.[76]

I must not forget God's goodness and mercy to me in sending my eldest daughter the Countess of Thanet her first-born child being a son,[77] whereof she was delivered in Bolebroke House in Sussex the 7th of August 1631 and after that had many more children both sons and daughters to my great comfort so as now she hath ten children alive. Genesis 9.1.[78]

The 5th of June 1635 did my said Lord the Earl of Pembroke in Baynard's Castle make over to me by jointure of those lands of his in the Isle of Sheppey in Kent, which he had formerly made in jointure to his first wife the Lady Susan Vere, Countess of Montgomery. And at the time of his making that jointure he released his right to all my lands in Westmorland and five thousand pounds out of the lands in Craven for a part of my younger daughter's portion, if ever those lands should fall to me in his lifetime as afterwards they did. And this agreement was chiefly made between us by my worthy cousin german Francis, Earl of Bedford.

The 21st of January 1641 died my uncle Francis, Earl of Cumberland, when he was near fourscore and two years old, in Skipton Castle in Craven, I lying then in Ramsbury in Wiltshire. And his only child Henry Lord Clifford, who succeeded him in the Earldom, lived but two years, ten months and some twenty days after him. Job 7.1.

The ninth day of that May, in 1640 died my worthy cousin german Francis

---

74 Anne's letter dated 14 January 1638 reveals that her removal from the Whitehall lodging was more dramatic. In this letter she asks her cousin Francis Russell to procure Philip Herbert's permission for her to come up to London: 'for I dare not venture to come up with out his love lest he should take that occasion to turn me out of this house as he did out of Whitehall and then I shall not know where to put my head', BL, MS Harley 7001, fols 143, 144.
75 This family can be seen in Anthony Van Dyck's painting *Philip Herbert Fourth Earl of Pembroke with His Family* (c. 1636).
76 Proverbs 20.24: 'Man's goings are of the Lord; how can a man then understand his own way?'
77 Nicholas Tufton.
78 Here Anne scores out Proverbs 30:19: 'The way of an eagle in the air; the way of a serpent upon a rock; the way of a ship in the midst of the sea; and the way of a man with a maid' and inserts Genesis 9.1: 'And God blessed Noah and his sons, and said unto them, Be fruitful, and multiply, and replenish the earth.'

Russell, Earl of Bedford, at his house called Bedford House in the Strand, to my extreme grief and sorrow for he was a most worthy man. Ecclesiastes 3, 8.6; Job 7.1.

And when the civil war between the King and Parliament began to grow hotter and hotter in England, my said Lord and I came together from Wilton the 12th of October 1642 with my younger daughter then the Lady Isabella Sackville, and the next day we came to London where my said Lord went to lie at his lodgings in the Cockpit in St James his park over against Whitehall to be near the Parliament. But I and my daughter went to lie at Baynard's Castle, which was then a house full of riches and was the more secured by my lying there, where then I continued to lie in my own chamber without removing six years and nine months which was the longest time that ever I continued to lie in one house in all my life, the civil wars being then very hot in England. So as that I may well say that was then as it were a place of refuge for me to hide myself in till those troubles were over passed. Isaiah 43.2.[79]

About the beginning of the year in 1643 my eldest daughter the Countess Thanet went over into France to her Lord and their eldest son, who were there before, where she stayed some seven or eight months about Paris and Rouen and these places.[80] And in April and May 1644 she returned with her Lord into England to me and four of her younger children, leaving their eldest son the Lord Tufton behind them. Where she was delivered the 30th of August of her seventh child, Mr Thomas Tufton, at her husband's house in Aldersgate Street in London, for she was great with child with him when she came back into England. And she and her Lord and their eldest son were in France when my cousin Henry, Earl of Cumberland, died.

The 11th of December in 1643 in one of the Prebend Houses in York, died my cousin german Henry Clifford, Earl of Cumberland, and which place his wife and widow my Lady Frances Cecil, Countess of Cumberland died the 14th of February following (so as there was little more then two months between their deaths). Which Countess of Cumberland was cousin german to my second Lord's first wife. And this Earl and Countess of Cumberland left but one child behind them, the Lady Elizabeth Clifford now Countess of Cork. So by the death of this cousin german of mine, Henry Clifford, Earl of Cumberland, without heirs male the lands of mine inheritance in Craven and Westmorland

---

79 Isaiah 43.2: 'When thou passest through the waters, I will be with thee; and through the rivers, they shall not overflow thee: when thou walkest through the fire, thou shalt not be burned; neither shall the flame kindle upon thee.'
80 The Tuftons were royalists during the English civil wars of the 1640s and 1650s. Their exile in France was related to their royalist sympathies.

reverted unto me without question or controversy after that his father Francis, Earl of Cumberland, and this Earl Henry his son had unjustly detained from me the ancient lands in Craven from the death of my father, and the lands in Westmorland from the death of my mother till this time. Yet had I little or no profit from that estate for some years after by reason of the civil wars. And by his death was extinct the Earldom of Cumberland in the family of the Cliffords (which had continued from the 18th of June 1525) he being the last heir male of that house.

The 16th day of May in 1645 died Mary Curzon, Countess of Dorset, a virtuous and good woman in Whitehall, she that was my dear and good friend, though her husband, my brother-in-law, was ever my bitter enemy and persecutor. Job 7.1.

About this time, and for some years before, happened a great cause of anger and falling out between my Lord and me because he desired to have one of his younger sons married with my daughter Isabella, which I would no way remedy, my daughter being herself extremely averse from that match, though he believed it was in my power to have brought it to pass (being so persuaded by some of my enemies).

But at length it pleased God that on the 5th of July (being Monday) in 1647, this youngest daughter of mine, the Lady Isabella Sackville, was married to James Compton, Earl of Northampton in the church at Clerkenwell, but I was not then present at the marriage for many reasons. In which church, my mother and I had been parishioners for some seven years together in my childhood.

The 3rd of June in 1649, I took my last leave of my second husband, this Earl of Pembroke, in his lodging at the Cockpit near Whitehall, which was the last time that he and I ever saw one another (it being then Sunday). And the same day I went from there to my daughter Northampton's at Islington, which was the first time I was ever in any of her Lord's houses, nor have I been in any of them since.

And methinks the destiny is remarkable that she should be settled at Islington, so near Clerkenwell where my mother and I lived long in my childhood, and that her Lord's chief house of Ashby should be so near Lillford in Northamptonshire where both my mother and myself in our younger years had our breeding. As also, that my elder daughter of Thanet should be settled at Hothfield in Kent not far from Sutton, where my blessed mother and I lived together a good while whilst I was a maid. So as those countries where my mother lived as a stranger and a pilgrim and in some discontent are now the settled abode and habitations of both her grandchildren, as Knole in Kent was for the most part my habitation during the time I lived to my first Lord. And to my second Lord while I was his wife was Wilton and Ramsbury in Wiltshire the chief places of my abode when I was in the country, not far of Devonshire, where that blessed mother of mine was born (so powerful an influence had her goodness over the destiny of her posterity). Psalm 112, Deuteronomy 11.14.[81]

And the 11th day of July 1649, I having a little afore in that Baynard's Castle taken my leave of my two daughters and their Lords and my grandchildren, did I go out of London onwards on my journey towards Skipton,[82] so as then I went not far from North Hall, where I had formerly lived. And so by easy journeys in that road, I came to Skipton the eighteenth day of that month into my castle there, it being the first time of my coming into it after the pulling down of most of the old castle, which was done some six months before by order of Parliament because it had been a garrison in the late civil war. And I was never till now in any part of that castle since I was nine or ten weeks old.

About the twenty-eight of that month I went unto that old decayed Tower at Barden,[83] it being the first time that I was ever in that Tower. And then I continued to lie in Skipton Castle till the seventh of the month following, which was August. And 7th of that month of August I removed from Skipton Castle to Appleby Castle and lay by the way at Kirby Lonsdale.

So the eight day of that August in 1649 I came into Appleby Castle the most ancient seat of my inheritance and lay in my own chamber there where I used formerly to lie with my dear mother and there I continued to lie till about the 13th of February following, this 8th of August being the first time that I came into the said Appleby Castle ever since I went out of it with my dear mother, the 8th day of October in 1607. So various are the pilgrimages of this human life, as Ecclesiastes 3.1. And from the death of my cousin german Henry, Earl of Cumberland, till this my coming into Appleby Castle was just five years eight months wanting three days. Psalm 21.1.[84]

And the 18th day of this August I went through Whinfell and into Brougham Castle for a while, in which castle and park I had not been since the 9th of

---

81 Psalm 112 begins: 'Praise ye the Lord. Blessed is the man that feareth the Lord, that delighteth greatly in his commandments. His seed shall be mighty upon earth: the generation of the upright shall be blessed' and continues to praise the bounty and protection of God. Deuteronomy 11.14: 'That I will give you the rain of your land in his due season, the first rain and the latter rain, that thou mayest gather in thy corn, and thy wine, and thine oil.'
82 In a letter to Sir John Lowther, 23 November 1647, Anne states she will travel to Skipton Castle as soon as the weather permitted. However, the political unrest of the period delayed her departure until 1649. CAS, Carlisle, DLons/L1/1/28/8.
83 Barden Tower, about five miles from Skipton.
84 Psalm 21.1: 'The king shall joy in thy strength, O Lord; and in thy salvation how greatly shall he rejoice!'

December in 1616 (when I was Countess of Dorset) till this day. And the 15th day of this August I went into my decayed castles of Brough and Pendragon and into Wharton Hall,[85] where I had not been since August or September, 1607 till then. Proverbs 20.24.

---

85   The Whartons of Wharton Hall, Westmorland, were Anne's cousins through the marriage of her aunt Frances Clifford with Philip, 3rd Lord Wharton. It lies between Anne's castle of Pendragon four miles before it and Brough Castle six miles beyond.

The Lady of the North, Yearly Memoirs, 1650–1675

In the year of our Lord God 1650[1]

And the 23rd of January following (as the year begins on New Year's day) died my second Lord Philip Herbert, Earl of Pembroke and Montgomery, in his lodgings at the Cockpit near Whitehall at London, he being then sixty-five years, three months and thirteen days old. And the news of his death was brought down post from London to Appleby Castle the 27th day of that month, being Sunday. For he died upon a Wednesday and his dead body was buried in the great church at Salisbury[2] the 9th of February following by his brother and their father and mother. Job 7.1.[3] And his elder brother's widow, Marie Talbot, eldest daughter and coheir to Gilbert Talbot, Earl of Shrewsbury, died the 25th day of the month following after his death, in Ramsbury house in Wiltshire and was buried a while after by her husband William Herbert, Earl of Pembroke, in the cathedral church of Salisbury.

This second Lord of mine was born a second son the 10th of October in 1584 in his father, Henry Herbert, Earl of Pembroke's house, at Wilton in Wiltshire, which was once a nunnery. His mother was Mary Sidney, only daughter to Sir Henry Sidney and only sister to the renowned Sir Philip Sidney. He [Philip Herbert] was no scholar at all to speak of, for he was not past three of four months at the university of Oxford, being taken away from thence by his friends presently after his father's death in Queen Elizabeth's time at the latter end of her reign to follow the Court (as judging him fittest for that kind of life)[4] when he was not passing fifteen or sixteen years old. Yet he was of a very quick apprehension, a sharp understanding, very crafty[5] withal and of a discerning spirit,

---

1 In these memoirs Anne dates her years beginning on 1 January. Officially England still used the Julian calendar in which the new year began on 25 March. This would not change until 1752, but in practice, as Anne shows here, many had begun to use 1 January to date the beginning of the new year in the seventeenth century.
2 Salisbury Cathedral.
3 Job 7.1: 'Is there not an appointed time to man upon earth? are not his days also like the days of an hireling?' Most biblical references are entered into this autobiography in Anne's hand in at least one set of the *Great Books*. For details of this see *Great Books*, ed. Malay, pp. 814–905.
4 The life of a courtier.
5 This term could carry a positive connotation suggesting cleverness and ingenuity as well as the negative connotation of trickery.

4 Anne Clifford, Countess of Pembroke, by John Bracken (1670), from *The Great Picture Triptych* (1646), attributed to Jan van Belcamp

but extremely choleric[6] by nature which was increased the more by the office of Lord Chamberlain to the King, which he held many years. He was never out of England but some two months when he went into France with the other Lords in the year 1625 to attend Queen Mary[7] at her first coming over into England to

6 The choleric temperament, drawn from the theory of the four humours, is characterized as aggressive with a quick and passionate temper. Anne was on the receiving end of his choleric nature on several occasions.
7 Henrietta Maria of France. She came to England to marry Charles I in 1625.

be married to King Charles her husband. He was one of the greatest noblemen of his time in England in all respects and was generally throughout the realm very well beloved.[8] He spent most of his time at Court and was made Earl of Montgomery by King James the 4th of May in 1605 and Knight of the Garter a little after, the year after he was married to his first wife.[9] But she died before he came to be Earl of Pembroke, for his elder brother Earl William died but the 10th of April in 1630, a little before I was married to him.

This second husband of mine died the 23rd of January in 1650, as the year begins on New Year's day and was buried the 9th of February following in the great church at Salisbury, I lying then in my castle of Appleby in Westmorland. Job 7.1.[10]

A little after my second Lord's death, on the 13th of February following, I removed from Appleby Castle in Westmorland, to my castle of Skipton in Craven, lying one night by the way at Kirkby Lonsdale, and so the 14th I came thither, and continued to lie in my said castle for a whole year together. And this was the first time I came to Skipton where I was born when I was the second time a widow, I being then Countess Dowager of Pembroke and Montgomery, as well as Countess Dowager of Dorset. And I did not return from thence, till the 18th of February some twelve month after. And this was the first time that I lay for twelve months together in any one of my own houses and there I found by experience in a retired life that saying to be true Ecclesiastes 7.13; Psalm 104.13, 24: Psalm 16.5,6.[11]

And this time of my staying there I employed myself in building and reparations at Skipton and Barden Tower and in causing the bounders[12] to be ridden and my courts kept in my several manors in Craven[13] and in those kind of

---

8 Anne is quite generous here. Philip Herbert was a controversial figure, often involved in quarrels, and was dismissed from his position as Lord Chamberlain. Despite this his temperament he remained politically powerful throughout his life.
9 Susan De Vere.
10 Anne and Philip Herbert lived apart for a number of years before his death, though he was always her staunch ally in matters related to her claims to the Clifford hereditary lands.
11 Ecclesiastes 7.13: 'Consider the work of God: for who can make that straight, which he hath made crooked?'; Psalm 104.13, 24: 'He watereth the hills from his chambers: the earth is satisfied with the fruit of thy works; O Lord, how manifold are thy works! in wisdom hast thou made them all: the earth is full of thy riches'; Psalm 16. 5, 6: 'The Lord is the portion of mine inheritance and of my cup: thou maintainest my lot. The lines are fallen unto me in pleasant places; yea, I have a goodly heritage.'
12 The boundaries.
13 Manor courts were local courts organized by manor and were chiefly concerned with the preservation of the rights of the lord and maintaining peaceful relations between tenants. At this time it was important for Anne to re-establish her authority in local matters and to affirm her rights as lord of each manor.

5 Skipton Castle, by Thomas D. Whitaker (1878) from *The History and Antiquities of the Deanery of Craven in the County of York*

country affairs about my estate, which I found in extreme disorder by reason it had been so long kept from me as from the death of my father till this time, and by occasion of the late civil wars in England. And in this time the suits and differences in law began to grow hot betwixt my tenants in Westmorland and some of my tenants in Craven, and me. Which suits with my Westmorland tenants are still depending and God knows how long they may last, but the differences with my tenants in Craven were for the most part by compromise and agreement reconciled and taken up.[14] And while I now abode there was my eldest daughter the Countess of Thanet delivered of her son George Tufton at Hothfield House in Kent the 30th of June. I accounting it a great blessing to have a grandchild of mine to bear my noble father's name, Genesis 26.22.[15] And she hath had two daughters since.[16]

And about the beginning of this September did my cousin Elizabeth Clifford, Countess of Cork, with her two sons and four daughters[17] come to lie at her house at Bolton in Craven near to me at Skipton for a month, she that was daughter and heir to my cousin german Henry late Earl of Cumberland. During which time there passed many visits and civilities betwixt her and me, I dining sometime at Bolton with her and she sometime at Skipton with me, notwithstanding that by reason she was heir to her father Henry, Earl of Cumberland, and I to my father

14 For a discussion of the suits against her tenants see Spence, *Anne Clifford*, pp. 114–159.
15 Genesis 26.22: 'For now the Lord hath made room for us, and we shall be fruitful in the land.'
16 \And she hath had two daughters since/ WD. Mary and Anne Tufton.
17 Charles, Richard, Mary Anne, Frances, Henrietta and Elizabeth Boyle.

George, Earl of Cumberland, there were divers differences then a foot betwixt us,[18] but we passed them by as Proverbs 19.11.[19] And the tenth of that month was the first time I saw her or any of her children in the northern parts, for then I dined at Bolton with them. And the 26th of that month was the last time I saw that Countess of Cork, my cousin, at my castle of Skipton. For then she took her leave of me there and went a little while after to Londesborough[20] and so up to London where she and her children remained until about the beginning of September 1652 and went with her Lord and six children out of England into Ireland to his great estate there. But in this year 1650, her husband the Earl of Cork continued to lie at Bolton for some two or three months and often saw me and my first grandchild at Skipton. For the 18th day of December did my said first grandchild Nicholas Lord Tufton come thither to me and stayed there till the 20th day of the month following, that he returned up to London and from thence went beyond sea to travel into Italy to Rome, and to other places abroad. And this was the first time that I saw him or any of my grandchildren at Skipton or in any part of the lands of mine inheritance. Psalm 45.16.[21]

And about August this summer did Francis Thorpe, one of the Barons of the Exchequer, and Mr Justice Warburton,[22] the two judges of the assizes for the Northern Circuit come to keep the assizes[23] at Appleby where they now lay in the castle some three or four nights. Ecclesiastes 3.

In the year of Our Lord God 1651

The next year 1651 and one about the 18th and 19th of February, as the year begins on New Year's day, I returned back to Appleby Castle in Westmorland (lying one night by the way at Kirkby Lonsdale) in which castle of mine I continued to

---

18 Anne brought suit in 1650 against Elizabeth in an attempt to lay claim to land in Skipton which had belonged to her father. See Spence, *Anne Clifford*, pp. 121–126.
19 Proverbs 19.11: 'The discretion of a man deferreth his anger; and it is his glory to pass over a transgression.'
20 The Londesborough estate came to the Clifford family through the marriage of Margaret Bromflete with John, 9th Lord Clifford, in the fifteenth century. Henry, 12th Lord Clifford, left Londesborough to Francis Clifford, Anne's uncle, and the property descended from him to his granddaughter Elizabeth Clifford, Countess of Cork.
21 Psalm 45.16: 'Instead of thy fathers shall be thy children, whom thou mayest make princes in all the earth.'
22 Peter Warburton.
23 Periodic courts. Assize courts held in England and Wales made judgements on both civil and criminal causes. They heard the most serious cases coming out of the quarter sessions (held by local county courts four times per year). They were presided over by judges appointed by the Crown in order to ensure ideally that cases were heard by consistent judicial expertise throughout the country.

6 Appleby Castle, from Samuel and Nathanial Buck, *A Collection of Engravings of Castles, and Abbeys in England* (1726–1739)

lie for a whole year, without removing any whither and spent much in repairing of my castle of Appleby and Brougham, to make them as habitable as I could though Brougham was very ruinous and much out of repair. And in this year the 21st of April, I helped to lay the foundation stone of the middle wall in the great tower of Appleby Castle in Westmorland, called Caesar's Tower to the end it may be repaired again and made habitable if it pleases God, Isaiah 58.12; Ezekiel 36.33, 36,[24] after it had stood without a roof or covering or one chamber habitable in it ever since about 1569, a little before the death of my grandfather of Cumberland, when the roof of it was pulled down in the great rebellion time in the North in 1569.[25] Which tower work [was] wholly finished and covered with lead the latter end of July 1653.[26]

And the 23rd day of the said April two days after, I was present at the laying of

24 Isaiah 58.12: 'And they that shall be of thee shall build the old waste places: thou shalt raise up the foundations of many generations; and thou shalt be called, The repairer of the breach, The restorer of paths to dwell in.' Ezekiel 36.33,36: 'Thus saith the Lord God; In the day that I shall have cleansed you from all your iniquities I will also cause you to dwell in the cities, and the wastes shall be builded; Then the heathen that are left round about you shall know that I the Lord build the ruined places, and plant that that was desolate: I the Lord have spoken it, and I will do it.'
25 The Rising of the North of 1569 (also called Revolt of the Northern Earls or Northern Rebellion) occurred when Catholic nobles in the North attempted to remove Queen Elizabeth and place Mary, Queen of Scots, on the throne. Henry Clifford, 2nd Earl of Cumberland (whose daughter Margaret was next in the line of succession according to Henry VIII's will through her mother Eleanor Brandon), and Henry's father-in-law William Dacre refused to join the rebellion.
26 \Which tower work ... end of July 1653/ WD.

the first foundation stone of my hospital or almshouse here in Appleby town,[27] for which I purchased lands in the manor of Brougham the 4th day of February following, and the lands called Saint Nicholas near Appleby the 29th day of December, in 1652. Which almshouse was quite finished and the mother and twelve sisters placed therein in January and March 1653. [28]

And about this April and May in 1651, were the bounders ridden for me in my lands here in Westmorland, which (as I was informed) had not been done since my mother had those lands in jointure till this time. Proverbs 22.28.[29]

And this summer Major General Thomas Harrison came hither with his forces for then the war was hot in Scotland, so as then many places of Westmorland and especially my castle of Appleby was full of soldiers who lay here a great part of that summer.[30] But I thank God I received no harm or damage by them nor by the King [Charles II] and his army who that August came into England and within six or seven miles of Appleby Castle though they came not to it.[31] And that Christmas I kept here in Appleby Castle (as I had done the Christmas before at Skipton), but by reason of the wars and troubles in the North this summer no assizes were this year kept either at Appleby or any where else in these northern parts.[32]

And in this settled abode of mine in these three ancient houses of mine inheritance: Appleby Castle and Brougham Castle in Westmorland, and Skipton Castle or house in Craven,[33] I do more and more fall in love with the

27 St Anne's Hospital, Appleby, continues to provide housing for retired single women who can demonstrate need, at a nominal rate.
28 \which almshouse was ... and March 1653/ WD.
29 Proverbs 22.28: 'Remove not the ancient landmark, which thy fathers have set.'
30 In response to Charles II's march into England with a Scottish army. Cromwell sent Harrison to the North to report on Charles's progress and to impede their march, which was why he was stationed at Appleby that summer. In September he joined Major-General John Lambert and took part in the Battle of Worcester.
31 The tension of this situation is not fully expressed here, as the possibility of a damaging military engagement involving Appleby, where she was lodging at the time, was a real possibility. She was also essentially under house arrest during this period. In her eulogy Bishop Edward Rainbow describes how Harrison 'quartered himself under the roof of this Noble Lady and had made suspicious inquiries ... of her sending assistance privately [to the royalists] but being not able to make proof he would needs know her opinion and dispute out of her Loyalty; at which time when she slept, and lived but at his mercy, giving her Alarms night and day when he listed', *A Sermon Preached at the Funeral of the Right Honorable Anne, Countess of Pembroke*, p. 49.
32 \But by reason ... northern parts/ H1, H2; this insertion comes at the end of 1651 in WD. Charles II's campaign in 1651 resulted in a number of military actions in the North that summer.
33 Anne often refers to Skipton Castle as a house. This was strategic on her part because of the ongoing threat that the castle would be slighted again after she had rebuilt it. In 1659 she wrote to Captain Adam Baynes, 'I assure you Sir the addition I have made in this castle is

contentments and innocent pleasures of a country life, which humour of mine I do wish with all my heart (if it be the will of Almighty God) may be conferred on my posterity that are to succeed me in these places, for a wise body ought to make their own homes the place of self-fruition and the comfortablest part of their life. But this must be left to a succeeding Providence for none can know what shall come after them. Ecclesiastes 3.22.[34] But to invite them to it, that saying in the 16th Psalm verses 5, 6, 7 and 8 may be fitly applied: 'The lot is fallen unto me in a pleasant place, I have a fair heritage.'[35] And I may truly say that verse:

> From many noble progenitors I hold
> Transmitted lands, castles, and honours which they swayed of old.[36]

All which benefits have been bestowed upon me for the heavenly goodness of my dear mother, whose fervent prayers were offered up with great zeal to Almighty God for me and mine, and had such return of blessings followed them, as that though I met with some bitter and wicked enemies, and many great oppositions in this world, yet were my deliverances so great as could not befall to any who were not visibly sustained by a divine favour from above. Psalm 41.[37]

And in this country life of mine I find also that saying of the Psalmist true: 'The Earth is full of the Goodness of the Lord.' Psalm 33.5; Psalm 104.24; Psalm 119.64.[38]

The 29th of December in this year did I sign and seal a patent to Mr Thomas Gabetis to be my deputy sheriff for the county of Westmorland for the execu-

---

only a slight superstructure upon some parts of the old wall not above two foot thickness and no way considerable at all for strength' (BL, Add. MS 21425, fol. 127).

34 Ecclesiastes 3.22: 'Wherefore I perceive that there is nothing better, than that a man should rejoice in his own works; for that is his portion: for who shall bring him to see what shall be after him?'

35 The wording of this quotation is derived from the Geneva Bible of 1561, Psalm 16: 'The Lord (is) the porcion of mine inheritance and of my cup thou shalt mainteine my lot / The lines are fallen unto me in pleasant places yea, I have a faire heritage' (Geneva, 1561, sig. PPiiiv). Anne was also quite familiar with Coverdale's translations of the psalms, a copy of which she includes in her Great Picture. During her weekly devotions (Wednesday and Sunday) the minister would have read from this psalter which after 1662 was included in the Book of Common Prayer.

36 It is unclear where this passage comes from. It may be Anne's own composition.

37 Psalm 41 begins: 'Blessed is he that considereth the poor: the Lord will deliver him in time of trouble' and continues to praise God's protection of the persecuted.

38 Psalm 33.5: 'He loveth righteousness and judgment: the earth is full of the goodness of the Lord'; Psalm 104.24: 'O Lord, how manifold are thy works! in wisdom hast thou made them all: the earth is full of thy riches'; Psalm 119.64: 'The earth, O Lord, is full of thy mercy: teach me thy statutes.'

7 Brougham Castle, from Samuel and Nathanial Buck, *A Collection of Engravings of Castles, and Abbeys in England* (1726–1739)

tion of which office he had the Council of State's order[39] for his approbation bearing date the 21st of November before.

In the year of our Lord God 1652

The 24th of February in 1652 as the year begins on New Year's day did I remove from this Appleby, lying one night by the way at Kirkby Lonsdale, and the next day being the 25th I came to Skipton Castle after I had lain in the said castle in Westmorland a year and four days over. And when I now returned to Skipton I continued to lie in my own chamber there till the 29th of November following, when I returned to Appleby again. So as I stayed this time at Skipton nine months and odd days.

The 19th of this May did my grandchild Mr John Tufton, second son to my eldest daughter and her Lord the Earl of Thanet, come down hither to me, which was the first time I saw him at Skipton. And here in Craven and in Westmorland he continued to lie till the 28th day of March in 1653, on which day he went from Appleby Castle into the South to see his father and mother and so to Eton College[40] there to study for some time and to live as a scholar.

---

39 The Council of State was appointed by Parliament in 1649 to act as the country's executive in place of the King and Privy Council. In 1651, Anne's stepson, Philip Herbert, 5th Earl of Pembroke, was the president of the Council. The order mentioned here validated Gabetis in his role to act as Anne's deputy in matters relating to the office of sheriff which she held by hereditary right.
40 Eton College came to prominence as an educational establishment for the elite in the seventeenth century, and remains so today.

The 17th of this July being Saturday died Edward Sackville, Earl Sackville, Earl of Dorset, in Great Dorset House in London and he was buried within a while after in the vault in Withyham church in Sussex by his wife and his eldest brother, my first Lord and many of their ancestors. Of whose death Mr Christopher Marsh brought me word to Skipton the four and twentieth day of that month when he then came to lie there in my family[41] till the 30th day of September following. Which Edward Sackville of Dorset was the most bitter and earnest enemy to me that ever I had, but Almighty God delivered me most miraculously from all his crafty devices as Deuteronomy 23.5[42] for without the merciful power of that God it had been impossible for me to have escaped them as Psalm 18.42; 43, 47, 48; Psalm 116.8; Psalm 124; Isaiah 13.2; Job 28.3; Psalm 92.2.[43] And now on this 24th day of July did Mr George Sedgewick[44] come hither from London to me to serve me as my secretary and one of my chief officers. [45]

On the 2nd day of August this year was born the Lady Mary Tufton, my grandchild, in her father the Earl of Thanet's house of Hothfield in Kent (she being the eleventh child to her mother) so as I accompted myself happy to have a grandchild of mine of that blessed name. Luke 1.48.[46]

And in the month of August in this year did Judge Puleston and Serjeant Parker come to Appleby Castle to keep the assizes there in their Northern Circuit where they now lay some four or five nights together at my

41 Anne refers to the personal servants of her household with this phrase.
42 Deuteronomy 23.5: 'Nevertheless the Lord thy God would not hearken unto Balaam; but the Lord thy God turned the curse into a blessing unto thee, because the Lord thy God loved thee.'
43 Psalm 18.42, 43, 47, 48: 'The sorrows of death compassed me, and the floods of ungodly men made me afraid; Thou hast delivered me from the strivings of the people; and thou hast made me the head of the heathen: a people whom I have not known shall serve me; It is God that avengeth me, and subdueth the people under me; He delivereth me from mine enemies: yea, thou liftest me up above those that rise up against me: thou hast delivered me from the violent man'; Psalm 116.8: 'For thou hast delivered my soul from death, mine eyes from tears, and my feet from falling'; Isaiah 13.2: 'Lift ye up a banner upon the high mountain, exalt the voice unto them, shake the hand, that they may go into the gates of the nobles'; Job 28.3: 'He setteth an end to darkness, and searcheth out all perfection: the stones of darkness, and the shadow of death'; Psalm 92.2: 'To shew forth thy loving kindness in the morning, and thy faithfulness every night.' The theme of Psalm 124 is clear in verses 2 and 3: 'If it had not been the Lord who was on our side, when men rose up against us, then they had swallowed us up quick, when their wrath was kindled against us.'
44 George Sedgewick often served as Anne's amanuensis, and his hand is found in her letters and throughout the *Great Books*. He also wrote an account of his life and his relationship with Anne: CAS Carlisle, DLons/L12/2/16, Life of George Sedgewick. An abridgement of this autobiography can be found in Joseph Nicholson and Richard Burn, *History and Antiquities of the Counties of Westmorland and Cumberland* (1777), vol. 1, pp. 294–303.
45 \And now one … my chief officers/ WD.
46 Luke 1.48: 'For he hath regarded the low estate of his handmaiden: for, behold, from henceforth all generations shall call me blessed.'

charge, myself and my family then lying in my castle of Skipton in Craven. Ecclesiastes 3.

And it was about the 8th day of September did my cousin, the Countess of Cork, with her six children go from Bristol over sea into Ireland to Lismore and Cork and those places in Munster to her husband Richard, Earl of Cork, who went thither a few months before her. But in the year 1656 she came with her two sons and daughter Elizabeth into England again for a while and left her two sons at Queen's College in the University of Oxford to study there for a time, herself and her daughter Elizabeth going over sea into Ireland again in October in the same year to her husband the Earl of Cork. [47]

The 6th of November was my cause in Chancery between me and my tenants in Westmorland dismissed out of that court and I was left to my remedy at Common Law, to which business God send some good conclusion for it hath been both chargeable and troublesome unto me.

And the 29th of this month of November I with my grandchild Mr John Tufton[48] and my family came from Skipton lying one night by the way at Kirkby Lonsdale and so the next day we came into Appleby Castle, where this grandchild and I kept our Christmas this year, and this was the first time that any of my grandchildren were with me in Westmorland. Psalm 123.[49]

The numerousness of my posterity, and all other benefits whatsoever, I believe were bestowed upon me for the heavenly goodness of my dear mother whose fervent prayers were offered up with great zeal to Almighty God for me and mine and had such a return of blessings followed them, as that though I met with some wicked and bitter enemies and many great oppositions in this world, yet were my deliverances so great as could not befall to any that were not visibly sustained by a divine favour from above, Psalm 41.[50] And in this country life of mine I find that saying of the Psalmist true: 'The Earth is full of the goodness of the Lord.' Psalm 33.5; Psalm 104.24; Psalm 119.64.[51]

---

47 \But in the … the Earle of Cork/ WD.
48 John Tufton was being groomed to be heir of the Clifford hereditary lands in Westmorland. At Anne's death the lands descended instead to his older brother Nicholas and next to him at his brother's death.
49 This is a short psalm of thanksgiving.
50 Psalm 41 begins: 'Blessed is he that considereth the poor: the Lord will deliver him in time of trouble' and continues on this theme.
51 Psalm 33.5: 'He loveth righteousness and judgment: the earth is full of the goodness of the Lord'; Psalm 104.24: 'O Lord, how manifold are thy works! in wisdom hast thou made them all: the earth is full of thy riches'; Psalm 119.64: 'The earth, O Lord, is full of thy mercy: teach me thy statutes.'

In the year of Our Lord God 1653

In the beginning of this year 1653, as the year begins on New Year's day, did I cause several courts to be kept in my name in divers of my manors within this county of Westmorland. But the tenants being obstinate and refractory, though they appeared, would not answer as they were called. And also many leases of enactment did I cause to be sealed in this county in order to a trial with my tenants at common law. God send them good success. Isaiah 30.21.[52]

And the 30th day of this January (being my birthday) did I pass my climacterically year of sixty-three[53] the year amongst physicians accompted so remarkable. Psalm 123.

The 28th of this March, my grandchild[54] went from Appleby Castle to York from thence to London and so to Hothfield in Kent, to see his father and mother, brothers and sisters and within a while after to Eton College there to study, where he now remained from the 25th of April for the most part, till the 5th of July in the year following that he went to Skipton, and from thence to Oxford, the 2nd of August to be a student there.

And in the beginning of this year was my almshouse here at Appleby quite finished, which had been almost two years abuilding. So as I now put in to it twelve poor women, eleven of them being widows and the twelfth a maimed maid, and a mother, a deceased minister's widow.[55] Some of whom I put into the said house in December and the rest in January and the beginning of March following. Luke 7.5; Psalm 116.12–14.[56]

The 27th of this May was my youngest daughter the Countess of Northampton[57] delivered of her second child, which was also a son[58] in her Lord's house called Canonbury [Tower] by Islington near London who was christened there the next day after by the name of William, I lying then in my castle here at Appleby in Westmorland. The birth of which child I account as an extraordi-

---

52 Isaiah 30.21: 'And thine ears shall hear a word behind thee, saying, This is the way, walk ye in it, when ye turn to the right hand, and when ye turn to the left.'
53 The climacteric years of a person's life according to ancient Greek philosophy and astronomy were believed to be periods when an individual was at greater risk. The sixty-third year was often called the grand climacteric.
54 John Tufton.
55 The 'mother' was head of the almshouse.
56 Luke 7.5: 'For he loveth our nation, and he hath built us a synagogue'; Psalm 116.12–14: 'What shall I render unto the Lord for all his benefits toward me? I will take the cup of salvation, and call upon the name of the Lord. I will pay my vows unto the Lord now in the presence of all his people.'
57 Isabella Sackville.
58 William, Lord Compton (d. 1661).

nary great blessing and seal of God's mercies to me and mine. Jeremiah 29.6 the latter part of it; 30.19; Genesis 1.28; 26.22; Psalm 116.12–14.[59] But he died to my great grief and sorrow the 18th day of September 1661 in his father the Earl of Northampton's house in Northamptonshire called Castle Ashby.[60]

The 15th of June following did her husband James Compton, Earl of Northampton, come from his journey from London, over Stainmore to my castle of Appleby to me. Where he now lay in the Baron's Chamber for the most part till the 29th of the same month (excepting two nights that he went to Carlyle and Naworth Castle and those parts). And the 15th of this month was the first time that I saw him or any son-in-law of mine here in Westmorland or in any parts of mine inheritance. And the 29th day of this month, when he went from hence he went into my house or castle of Skipton and into my decayed house of Barden, into my lordship of Silsden[61] and the most remarkable places of my inheritance in Craven. And the 2nd day of the month following he went away from thence toward his house at Islington by London[62] and came thither to his wife about ten days after. Ecclesiastes 3; 8.6.[63]

The 25th day of this June died at her house in Rainham in Kent, Frances Cecil Countess Dowager of Thanet, daughter to Thomas, Earl of Exeter, who was mother to my son-in-law, the Earl of Thanet. And she was buried a little after at Rainham church in Kent by her husband Nicholas, Earl of Thanet, and her grandchild and mine the Lady Anne Tufton. Job 7.1; Ecclesiastes 3; 8.6.

The 18th of July was my grandchild the Lady Margaret Tufton married in her father's house in Aldersgate Street in London to Mr George Coventry, eldest son to Thomas, Lord Coventry, whose father Thomas, Lord Coventry, was Lord Keeper of the Great Seal of England. And she went from thence about ten days after her marriage with her husband and his father down into the country to

---

59 Jeremiah 29.6: 'give your daughters to husbands, that they may bear sons and daughters; that ye may be increased there, and not diminished'; 30.19: 'And out of them shall proceed thanksgiving and the voice of them that make merry: and I will multiply them, and they shall not be few; I will also glorify them, and they shall not be small'; Genesis 1.28 and 26.22: 'And God blessed them, and God said unto them, Be fruitful, and multiply, and replenish the earth, and subdue it: and have dominion over the fish of the sea, and over the fowl of the air, and over every living thing that moveth upon the earth; And he removed from thence, and digged another well; and for that they strove not: and he called the name of it Rehoboth; and he said, For now the Lord hath made room for us, and we shall be fruitful in the land.'
60 \But he died ... Northamptonshire called Castle Ashby/ WD.
61 Silsden sits between Keighley and Skipton.
62 Canonbury Tower, manor house, built between 1509 and 1532, that was to granted Thomas Cromwell and later came to the Earls of Northampton.
63 Ecclesiastes 8.6: 'Because to every purpose there is time and judgment, therefore the misery of man is great upon him.'

their house at Croome in Worcestershire to live there with them. Which marriage I accounted as a great blessing of God Almighty to me and mine. Psalm 116.12–14; Psalm 68.18.[64]

About the latter end also of this July was the great tower here at Appleby called Caesar's Tower covered with lead, which had lain open and uncovered as a ruinous place ever since the year of our Lord 1569 (being the year before my grandfather of Cumberland died)[65] till this time. The middle wall of which tower and repairing of it I began in April the year 1651 and finished now. Isaiah 58.12; Ezekiel 36.33, 36. And in this year about the beginning of March was my new stables begun to be built without the castle and adjoining to the barn, built there about two years since by my directions where there never was any building before. Proverbs 20.24.

The 17th day of August did Judge Puleston and Judge Parker come hither and lay in Appleby Castle for five nights and kept the assizes here in the moot hall.[66] So as on the 20th day the cause between me and my Westmorland tenants came before Judge Parker, but was dismissed by reason of a general exception taken against most of the jurors. And the 22nd day these judges went away from hence towards Lancaster. And this was the first time that I lay in Appleby Castle when there was an assize held here, Ecclesiastes 8.6.

And about the time of the keeping of these assizes did my cousin, Philip, Lord Wharton, with his now second wife[67] and his eldest daughter by his first wife[68] and his brother Sir Thomas Wharton and his wife[69] and their mother the Lady Philadelphia Wharton[70] the widow come to lie for a few nights in Wharton Hall in Westmorland. So as I went to them to Wharton and they came hither to me to Appleby. And this was the first time that I saw any of them here in Westmorland. Ecclesiastes 3.

The 1st day of September following did my son-in-law, the Earl of Thanet and my daughter his wife and their eldest son Nicholas Lord Tufton come from London over Stainmore hither to Appleby Castle to me where they continued to lie eleven nights together, my daughter and her Lord in the chamber under the Drawing Room and my Lord Tufton in the Baron's Chamber, this being

---

64 Psalm 68.18: 'Thou hast ascended on high, thou hast led captivity captive: thou hast received gifts for men; yea, for the rebellious also, that the Lord God might dwell among them.'
65 Henry Clifford, 2nd Earl of Cumberland.
66 A building for local meetings and assemblies. This moot hall in Appleby survives today.
67 Jane Goodwin.
68 Elizabeth Wharton, daughter of Elizabeth Wandesford.
69 Mary Carey.
70 Philadelphia Carey.

the first time that this first child of mine or her Lord or any of my own children came to me into Westmorland or into any part of the lands of mine inheritance, excepting her second son John Tufton who had been with me in Westmorland before last year. Psalm 116.12–14; Psalm 45.16.

And the 7th day of this month I went with them into Brougham Castle and into Whinfell, it being the first time they were ever in those places. So as now I had the happiness to see this first child of mine and her first child her eldest son in the chamber where my father was born and my blessed mother died. Psalm 16.5–7.[71]

And the 12th day of this September my daughter of Thanet and her Lord and their eldest son went away from me out of Appleby Castle in Westmorland into Worcestershire, passing thorough Lancashire and those parts so through the city of Worcester unto their daughter[72] at the Lord Coventry's house at Croome in that county. So as they came thither the 17th day of this month and lay there nine nights as they were in their journey towards London and their house of Hothfield in Kent,[73] this being the first time that any child of mine came into Worcestershire, or so near the River Severn. Ecclesiastes 8.6; Psalm 116.12–14.

The 9th day of November following (being Wednesday) came my cause between me and my Westmorland tenants to be heard at the Common Pleas bar[74] in Westminster before three of the judges of that court, Puleston, Atkins,[75] and Warburton, in the case of Skayfe of Stainmore,[76] which was given against me by the jury against evidence, direction of court and the judgement of all that hear the same debated. Psalm 7.9.[77]

The 9th day of December I removed from Appleby Castle into Brougham Castle in Westmorland where I continued to lie in the chamber where my

---

71 Psalm 16.5–7: 'The Lord is the portion of mine inheritance and of my cup: thou maintainest my lot. The lines are fallen unto me in pleasant places; yea, I have a goodly heritage. I will bless the Lord, who hath given me counsel: my reins also instruct me in the night seasons.'
72 Margaret Tufton.
73 Anne took details of these return journeys from letters she received.
74 This common law court in the English legal system emerged in the early thirteenth century. It became one of the central English courts for nearly six hundred years. Its jurisdiction was over real property and thus it was the appropriate place for Anne and her tenants to bring their differences. The court sat in Westminster Hall as stipulated by the Magna Carta, in a space marked off by a wooden bar, thus the term Anne uses here.
75 John Puleston, Edward Atkins and Peter Warburton. Note that Warburton and Puleston had enjoyed Anne's hospitality at Appleby Castle earlier.
76 Margaret Russell had engaged in an earlier suit against Skayfe in 1611: NA, STAC 8/89/11, Countess of Cumberland v Skayfe, 1611.
77 Psalm 7.9: 'Oh let the wickedness of the wicked come to an end; but establish the just: for the righteous God trieth the hearts and reins.'

father was born and my blessed mother died, till the 11th of April following that I removed from thence to Skipton. And I had not lain in this Brougham Castle in thirty-seven years till now, for the 9th of December in 1616 (when I was then married to Richard Earl of Dorset) I went out of it up towards London to him and never lay in it after till this night. In which long time I past through many strange and hard fortunes in the sea of this world for as I may well apply that saying to myself: Psalm 107 and Psalm 109.27.[78] And the repairing of this Brougham Castle, which had lain as it were ruinous and desolated ever since King James his lying in it in 1617 till I made it lately habitable causing me now to apply to myself that saying in Isaiah 58.12; Ezekiel 36.28, 33, 36,[79] as also in my repairs of the great tower called Caesar's Tower at Appleby.

And in this year also was built and finished at my own charge a new water corn mill (which was begun to be erected there the year before) within my manor of Silsden in Craven in High Holden, not far from the place where the windmill formerly stood, that was built there by my ancestors. Psalm 121.[80]

In the year of Our Lord God 1654

The 18th of March in 1654 (as the year begins on New Year's day) died in one of the new built houses in Queen's Street [London] Mary Beaumont, Countess Dowager of Northampton, mother to my son-in-law James Compton, Earl of Northampton. And she was buried a while after in Compton church in Warwickshire, Job 7.1; Ecclesiastes 3; 8.6.

And the 11th of April I removed from Brougham Castle in Westmorland and lay one night by the way at Kirkby Lonsdale and came the next day (being the

78 Psalm 107 begins: 'O give thanks unto the Lord, for he is good: for his mercy endureth for ever. Let the redeemed of the Lord say so, whom he hath redeemed from the hand of the enemy' and carries on the theme of God's mercy and protection for the oppressed.
79 King James's visit at that time (see p. 66) was in celebration of the King's Award and was particularly bitter for Anne. Here she affirms what she always believed was the error of that decision, and accused her uncle and cousin of ravaging the land after they had attained it (a view supported by John Breay, *Light of the Dales*, pp. 122–131). She emphasizes her role as the restorer with her favourite quotation: Isaiah 58.12: 'And they that shall be of thee shall build the old waste places: thou shalt raise up the foundations of many generations; and thou shalt be called, The repairer of the breach, The restorer of paths to dwell in.' Ezekiel 36.28, 33, 36: 'And ye shall dwell in the land that I gave to your fathers; and ye shall be my people, and I will be your God. Thus saith the Lord God; In the day that I shall have cleansed you from all your iniquities I will also cause you to dwell in the cities, and the wastes shall be builded. Then the heathen that are left round about you shall know that I the Lord build the ruined places, and plant that that was desolate: I the Lord have spoken it, and I will do it.'
80 Psalm 121 begins: 'I will lift up mine eyes unto the hills, from whence cometh my help. My help cometh from the Lord, which made heaven and earth' and emphasizes God's care and protection.

12th) to Skipton to lie here again in it after I had lain in Westmorland without removing out of that county for a year and four months. And so I now continued to lie here in the Round room, where I used to lie, till the 2nd day of August following that I came back again into Westmorland. Proverbs 20.24; Ecclesiastes 3.

The 26th day of May did my daughter of Northampton and her Lord and their little son the Lord William Compton, come hither to me to Skipton where they now continued to lie for a while in this house or castle of mine, my daughter and her Lord in the Round Chamber above mine and the little Lord in the chamber next to the Old Castle. So this 26th day was the first time that ever I saw my daughter of Northampton or her Lord or their child here at Skipton, and the first time that I ever saw this younger daughter of mine or any child of hers in any of the lands of mine inheritance, which gave me occasion to apply myself to that saying of Israel unto Joseph, Genesis, for I never saw any child of hers till now, Genesis 48.11; [81] Proverbs 20.24. And he wanted but a day of a year old when I first saw this grandchild of mine. And his father's second brother, Sir Charles Compton, came hither now with them. Isaiah 21.16.[82]

And the 5th day of June following I went with my daughter of Northampton and her Lord into my mother's almshouse at Beamsley[83] and into my Lady of Cork's house at Bolton (though she herself was then in Ireland) and into my decayed tower of Barden, it being the first time that ever I was in any of those places with any child of my own. Psalm 116.12–14.

And the 8th day of this month was my grandchild the little Lord Compton carried away from hence by his nurse that gave him suck (who was born in Scotland) to Otley where he lay this one night and where the next day his father and his mother overtook him. Proverbs 20.24.

For the 9th day of this month my youngest daughter and her Lord and his brother Sir Charles Compton went away from me from Skipton Castle, to Otley and so took the child away with them to York, for there they lay one night in their journey homeward and they came well (I thank God) the 17th day to their house of Castle Ashby in Northamptonshire, Ecclesiastes 8.6.[84]

---

81 William, Lord Compton. Genesis 48.11: 'And Israel said unto Joseph, I had not thought to see thy face: and, lo, God hath shewed me also thy seed.'
82 This quotation from Isaiah 21.16 was inserted into the text by Anne after 1661 and refers to the death of this child, William, in 1661: 'For thus hath the Lord said unto me, Within a year, according to the years of an hireling, and all the glory of Kedar shall fail.'
83 Beamsley almshouse or hospital. See *Great Books*, ed. Malay, pp. 658–660, for the charter founding Beamsley.
84 Ecclesiastes 8.6: 'Because to every purpose there is time and judgment, therefore the misery of man is great upon him.' Anne uses this biblical quotation often to express grief at some event.

The 22nd of this month was my daughter of Thanet delivered of Lady Anne Tufton, her sixth daughter and twelfth child and second of that name,[85] at Hothfield House in Kent. And the 5th of July following did her son, my grandchild John Tufton, come from Eton College, from studying there to Skipton, to me for a little while, from whence he went immediately up to Oxford and was settled there in Queen's College, the 2nd of August following. Isaiah 58.12; Ezekiel 36.33, 36.[86]

The 2nd day of this August I and my family removed from my house and castle of Skipton in Craven unto Kirkby Lonsdale where I lay in the inn there all night. And the next day (being the 3rd) I came into Appleby Castle in Westmorland after I had lain there in Skipton Castle from the 12th day of April last till now. And I returned to lie in Appleby Castle till the 25th of this month that I removed into Brougham Castle. Ecclesiastes 8.6; Psalm 121.

And while I now lay in Appleby Castle did the two judges, Hugh Windham and Richard Newdigate,[87] come hither in their circuit where they now lay five nights together, Judge Newdigate in the Baron's Chamber and Judge Windham in the great tower called Caesar's Tower, this being the first time that any of the judges or any person of note or quality lay there since I lately repaired it to my exceeding great cost and charge. Ecclesiastes 8.6.

And the 12th day, while these judges now lay here was my cause between me and my Westmorland tenants heard in the moot hall in Appleby before Judge Newdigate, where it was conceived I had a reasonable good success having obtained a special verdict against them, though my tenants still persisted in their wilful refractoriness and obstinacy against me. Job 5.12–15.

The 25th day of this month being Friday I removed from Appleby Castle with my family into my castle of Brougham in Westmorland where I now continued to lie till the 8th day of January following when I removed from thence back again into Appleby Castle, I having time now in this private life of mine at Brougham to contemplate the great mercies of God in delivering me from so many evils as I had passed over and crowning me with his blessings, in this my

---

85 Margaret Sackville bore a daughter, Anne, in 1634, who died in infancy. It was not unusual to use the name of a child who had died previously for subsequent children.

86 These oft-quoted biblical references are used as a shorthand in this text to emphasize Anne's role in 'raising the foundations' for many generations. Anne planned for John Tufton to be her heir after her daughter, Margaret, and states this in her will, NA, PROB 11/350/488, Will of Anne Clifford, 1676. Nicholas Tufton, his elder brother, challenged this after Anne's death and inherited the Clifford hereditary lands after the death of his mother Margaret in 1676, just months after Anne's death. John Tufton inherited the lands in 1679 after Nicholas's death, but died the following year.

87 Newdigate moved in a circle that included Mary Curzon, Anne's sister-in-law, so he would have been known to her socially.

old age, to live happily and peaceably in these ancient places of my inheritance. Isaiah 26.8, 9.[88]

And whilst I now lay here in Brougham Castle in my own chamber where my father was born and my mother died, I had the joyful news how that on the 2nd day of this September (being Saturday) my grandchild the Lady Margaret Coventry, wife to Mr George Coventry, was delivered of her first child, which was a son, in her father-in-law the Lord Coventry's house of Croome in Worcestershire, which child was christened there the 17th day following (being Sunday) by the name of John.[89] This being the first child that made me a great-grandmother, which I accompt as a great blessing of God. Psalm 116.11–15. And my daughter of Thanet was there at the birth and christening of this first grandchild of hers, so as he sucked the milk of her breast many times, she having there with her now youngest child the Lady Anne Tufton being about nine weeks old. But my grandchild the Lady Margaret Coventry, after my daughter of Thanet's departure from Croome, gave this child of hers suck herself as her mother had done to most of her children.[90] Jeremiah 29.6 the latter part of it; 30.19.

In the year of Our Lord God 1655

The 8th day of January in 1655 (as the year begins on New Year's day) I removed from Brougham Castle with my family to my castle of Appleby in Westmorland again and lay in it till the 18th of September following, and then I removed to Skipton. Ecclesiastes 3; 8.6. In which time on the 10th day of August did two judges of the assize, the Lord Chief Baron Steele[91] and Sergeant John Parker, come hither to Appleby to meet in their circuit and lay here in Appleby Castle six nights together and kept the assizes in the town, I lying then with my family in Appleby Castle, Ecclesiastes 3; Proverbs 20.24.

The 18th day of September following I removed again with my family out of Appleby Castle in Westmorland towards Skipton Castle in Craven (lying all night by the way at Kirkby Lonsdale) and came safe thither the 19th, I having

---

88 Isaiah 26.8, 9: 'Yea, in the way of thy judgments, O Lord, have we waited for thee; the desire of our soul is to thy name, and to the remembrance of thee. With my soul have I desired thee in the night; yea, with my spirit within me will I seek thee early: for when thy judgments are in the earth, the inhabitants of the world will learn righteousness.'
89 John Coventry, 4th Baron Coventry.
90 Elizabeth Clinton, Countess of Lincoln, published *The Countesse of Lincolnes Nurserie* in 1622 advocating the breastfeeding of children by their own mothers. This was an ongoing discussion in the period. Isabella Sackville did not follow her sister's example and instead used a wet nurse, see above. Clinton was a friend of Anne's, see p. 85.
91 William Steele.

not been in the castle of Skipton since the 2nd day of August till now. So I lay then in my said castle of Skipton till the 1st day of August next following, which was about six months and ten days over, at which time I removed the said 1st of August 1656 out of my said castle of Skipton towards Brougham Castle in Westmorland to lie there in it for a while (lying all night by the way in the inn at Kirkby Lonsdale). So as I continued to lie in my said castle of Brougham till the 2nd of October following, at which time I with my family removed to Appleby Castle in Westmorland. Ecclesiastes 3; Psalm 123.

About the tenth of this March in this year 1655 as the year begins on New Year's day, while I lay in Appleby Castle, did I cause a great part of Appleby church to be taken down (it being very ruinous and in danger of falling of itself) and so I caused a vault to be made in the north-east corner of the church for myself to be buried in, if it please God.[92] And the repairing of the said church cost me about some six or seven hundred pounds (being finished the year following). Ecclesiastes 3; Psalm 116.12–14.

And about the 20th of this March was my first grandchild, the Lord Nicholas Tufton, sent as a prisoner into the Tower of London by command of the Lord Protector and his Council upon suspicion that he had a hand in the late plot.[93] So as this grandchild of mine continued to lie in it as a prisoner nine months and four days. For the 24th of December following he was enlarged out of his imprisonment in the said Tower of London and went home to his father and mother again, this being the first time of his imprisonment in that Tower, notwithstanding he was committed again to the same Tower as a prisoner, the 11th or 12th of September in the year following. Psalm 105.19.[94]

The 16th day of this April was my grandchild the Lady Frances Tufton sent from her father and mother from their house in Aldersgate Street in London over sea unto Utrecht in Holland to be cured of the rickets, which she had in great extremity, where she remained in that city of Utrecht till about the 8th or 9th of May in 1657. At which time she came over in a Dutch man of war to Gravesend[95] when she and her brother John Tufton, with George Sedgewick[96] his governor and others in their company, came back to their father's house in Aldersgate Street at London to their father and mother, Ecclesiastes 8.6.

---

92 Anne's monument can be seen in St Lawrence's church, Appleby.
93 Penruddock's uprising of 1655.
94 Psalm 105.19: 'Until the time that his word came: the word of the Lord tried him.'
95 \At which time … war to Gravesend/ H1. A man of war was a large warship or frigate armed with cannon and propelled with sails.
96 See Sedgewick's manuscript diary for a description of his travels with John Tufton, CAS, Carlisle, DLons/L12/2/16.

And the 14th of this July when I now lay in this Appleby Castle was my daughter of Northampton delivered of her third child, the Lady Anne Compton, who was her first daughter, in her Lord's house at Canonbury near Islington by London. Jeremiah 29.6 the latter part of it; 30.19 the latter part of it. Which Lady Anne Compton died in her father's house in Lincoln's Inn Fields at London the 15th day of December in 1660. I then also lying in Appleby Castle in Westmorland. [97]

And this summer by my appointment was the wall of the little park at Appleby made new and higher round about save only towards the waterside. Psalm 90.17.[98] This summer also though I lay in Appleby Castle in Westmorland yet by my appointment and at my own charge was the steeple of Skipton church on the east and north part of it, which had been pulled down in the time of the late civil war, built up again, repaired, and leaded all over and some part of the church itself to be also repaired with a tomb to be erected and set up in it in memory of my noble father.[99] Ecclesiastes 3; Psalm 116.12–15.

And about the 1st of this October in 1655, when I lay now in my house here at Skipton, did I begin to make the rubbish to be carried out of the old castle at Skipton, which had lain in it since it was thrown down and demolished in December 1648 and the January following. And in the year 1659 the said old castle was very well finished and new built up, though I came not then to lie in it by reason of the smell and unwholesomeness of the new walls. Ezekiel 36.36[100] the latter part of it; Isaiah 58.12.

In the year of Our Lord God 1656

In this year 1656 (as the year begins on New Year's day) about the 13th of January did my grandchild John Tufton, after he had continued, about a month at my house or castle of Skipton in Craven go away from thence from me back to Queen's College at Oxford to lie in that University as a student till the 6th of May following, at which time he went quite away from living as a student there towards London, to his father and mother and most of their children, whether he came well to them the next day into their house at Aldersgate Street there.

---

97 \Which Lady Anne … December in 1660/ WD; \I then also … Castle in Westmorland/ H1.
98 Psalm 90.17: 'And let the beauty of the Lord our God be upon us: and establish thou the work of our hands upon us; yea, the work of our hands establish thou it.'
99 This monument along with a number of earlier Clifford monuments can still be seen in Holy Trinity church, Skipton. For documents relating to the installation of the tomb see YAS, DD121/109.
100 Ezekiel 36.36: 'Then the heathen that are left round about you shall know that I the Lord build the ruined places, and plant that that was desolate: I the Lord have spoken it, and I will do it.'

And from thence about the 14th of June following he went out of England into the Low Countries with George Sedgewick whom I had appointed to be his governor. So as they stayed now in Holland and these provinces till the beginning of May following in 1657 (having spent most of their time in the city of Utrecht) and came safe into England, and arrived at London the 9th of May in 1657 from whence he came hither to me to Skipton Castle the 12th of June following and with him George Sedgewick his governor and Alexander Whitchard, my grandchild's man, to live there with me as they had done formerly. And my grandchild the Lady Frances Tufton came then also over with her brother John Tufton from Utrecht in the Low Countries into England to her father and mother after she had remained there at Utrecht all the while her brother John stayed there and a good while before for the cure of the rickets, which she had in extremity. Ecclesiastes 3.

The 1st day of April I with my family removed out of my house or castle of Skipton in Craven into the inn at Kirkby Lonsdale in Westmorland from whence the next day I continued my journey to my castle of Brougham in the said county where by the way I went into Mr Dalston's house in Melkinthorpe[101] and stayed there a while, which was the first and last time that ever I was in that house. And so that evening from thence I came well into my said castle of Brougham, where I lay in the chamber which my noble father was born in and in which my blessed mother died, for some six months: April, May, June, July, August and September, which was the first time that I lay those few months altogether in that castle, though I have formerly lain in it in September and the rest of the months. And the 2nd of October following I removed with my family out of that Brougham Castle into my castle of Appleby in Westmorland. Ecclesiastes 8.6; Psalm 121.

And the 16th day of May was the cause between me and my Westmorland tenants heard at the Common Pleas bar in Westminster Hall, before four of the chief judges there, to wit my cousin Oliver St John Lord Chief Justice of the Common Pleas, Judge Atkins, Judge Hugh Windham and Judge Matthew Hale[102] where a jury appeared being sworn and my cause was openly pleaded by Sergeant Maynard, Sergeant Newdigate and Sergeant Bernard,[103] who were the counsel for me and Sergeant Earl and Sergeant Evers[104] who were of counsel for my said

---

101 Sir John Dalston was related to Anne through his wife Lucy Fallowfield.
102 This panel of judges was made up of Anne's cousin St John and Matthew Hale, Anne's lawyer and a long-term adviser and friend.
103 Bernard's son married Elizabeth, the daughter of Elizabeth Cromwell and Oliver St John, in 1655 and was thus connected to the Anne through the St Johns.
104 Sir Erasmus Earle and Sir Samson Eure (Evers). Both these men were eminent lawyers,

tenants. At which time they put me upon all manner of proofs being plaintiff in the cause though they were made forth by my witnesses very fully to the satisfaction of the court, so that the juries gave in a verdict for me against my said tenants. And the next day being the 17th of that month, another jury appeared for the second trial but the same went by default of the tenants, who only appeared but would not plead at all. So that the jury did not go from the bar but immediately gave in another verdict on my behalf, and the court thereupon awarded me costs which the said causes to the value of two hundred and fifty pounds, and two verdicts exemplified under the seal of the court. Psalm 116.12–13.

The 2nd day of this July died betimes in the morning in Baynard's Castle, to my great grief, my chief officer for my estate in Sussex and dear friend, Mr Christopher Marsh, who was buried the same night in the church there called St Bennett by Paul's Wharf, my daughter Thanet and her eldest son the Lord Nicholas Tufton being at his burial, he being near fifty years old at his death. Job 7.1.

And the day after being the 3rd of this month did my daughter of Thanet with her four youngest children, namely Cecily, George, Mary and Anne, begin their journey in the coach out of London town towards the North, who came safe and well to me with her children (for which, I thank God) to Brougham Castle in Westmorland the 11th of that month.

And Richard Clapham came along with them, who first of all told me the sad news of the said Mr Marsh's death and this was the first time I saw three of my said grandchildren, to wit George, Mary and Anne Tufton, as also the first time I saw my grandchild the Lady Cicely, in the North, though I have seen her before at London. Job 7.1; Ecclesiastes 3. So they continued with me in my said castle for seventeen nights together during which time my daughter Thanet with my grand child the Lady Cecily and her brother George went for a while in their coached into Edenhall in Cumberland and into Lowther Hall[105] in Westmorland. And whilst they were with me did Charles Stanley, Earl of Derby, come to Brougham Castle to visit me and lay there some three or four nights, being the first time that he was ever in the castle where his great grandmother,[106] my father's sister by the half blood[107] was born.

And the 28th of this July did my daughter of Thanet with four of her

    with Earle holding several offices under Oliver Cromwell. Eure was also distantly related to Anne so, while it appears that Anne may have had the advantage of her opponents because of her connections with the judges, the tenants also had lawyers with important connections with the judges and others with power.
105 Now referred to as Lowther Castle.
106 Margaret Clifford, Countess of Derby.
107 They shared the same father, thus were siblings by the 'half blood'.

children, Cecily, George, Mary and Anne, go out of my castle of Brougham in Westmorland from me (where I took my leave of them in the open air in the court there), and so through Whinfell Park into my castle of Appleby in the said county, where they lay in it one night, and so they went the next day after from thence out of Westmorland over Stainmore onwards on their journey towards London, whither they came safe and well the 5th day of the month following unto their house in Aldersgate Street where they continued to lie for some eight nights together. And when they were past on the 13th of the same month they went from thence unto the inn at Rochester in Kent, where they lay that night and the next day they went into Hothfield House in the said county to my Lord of Thanet and three of his sons my grandchildren, Richard, Thomas and Sackville. For which safe coming home of theirs from me out of these northern parts I praise God with my heart. Jeremiah 29.6 latter part of it. And I had not seen my daughter of Thanet since the 12th of September in 1653 when she went then from Appleby Castle from me till this 11th day of July that she came to me to Brougham Castle. Jeremiah 30.19 the latter part of it.

And the 29th of August in 1656 when I lay at Brougham Castle did the two judges for the Northern Circuit, John Parker esquire sergeant at law and then of the Barons of the Exchequer, who lived near Rochester in Kent, and Erasmus Earle[108] esquire sergeant at law who lives in Norfolk, came into Appleby Castle in Westmorland to keep the assize in the said town for the said county where in the castle they continued to lie for five nights together at my charges, Parker in the Baron's Chamber and Earle in Caesar's Tower. And the 3rd day of the month following they went away from thence to Kendal and so forward on their circuit. And during the time they kept the assizes at Appleby did my cousin Philip Lord Wharton lie for some three or four nights together in the chamber of the said castle where I used to lie myself, he having some business at the assizes. And the same 3rd day did my said cousin the Lord Wharton come to Brougham Castle to me for a while, it being the first time that ever he was with me in the said castle wherein his uncle George Wharton[109] was born, though I had seen him before in Appleby Castle in 1653. Ecclesiastes 3.

And the 11th day of this September, by the command of my Lord Protector[110] and his council was my first grandchild the Lord Tufton[111] the second time put

---

108   Earle had just recently argued against Anne in her suit with her tenants, see above.
109   George Wharton was the son of Frances Clifford, Anne's aunt, and Philip, 3rd Lord Wharton. He was killed in a duel with Sir James Stewart, Master of Blantyre, who was also killed in the duel.
110   Oliver Cromwell.
111   Nicholas Tufton.

up as a prisoner in the Tower of London where he lay under restraint till the 25th day of June in 1658 that he was released of his said imprisonment. Psalm 105.19.

The 28th of July was my grandchild the Lady Margaret Coventry delivered of her second child Mistress Anne Coventry, who died the next day.[112]

And the 2nd day of October did I and my family remove out of Brougham Castle in Westmorland to my castle of Appleby in the same county where I then continued to lie for about six months, till the 14th day of April following, when I then removed from thence in two days into my castle of Skipton in Craven. Ecclesiastes 8.6.

And about Midsummer this year, did my cousin Elizabeth Clifford of Cork come from her husband Earl of Cork out of Ireland with their two sons and their daughter Elizabeth for a while into England, whether neither she nor any of her children had been since about September in 1652 till now. And now about the beginning of this October she and her daughter Elizabeth went again out of England over sea into Ireland to her husband the Earl of Cork. But the Countess now left behind her in England her two sons, Charles Lord Dungarvan and his brother Richard Boyle, at the University of Oxford to lie there as a student in the Queen's College for a time. Ecclesiastes 3.

And on November the 12th day was the cause between me and my Westmorland tenants heard in Westminster Hall before the four judges of the Common Pleas: Lord St John Lord Chief Justice, Judge Atkins, Judge Windham and Judge Hale. In which cause James Walker was defendant against me on the tenants' behalf. The jurors all appearing being sworn and empanelled and the cause called, the defendant appeared not, nor any for him so as he was nonsuited[113] one hundred pounds costs recovered against him and the land adjudged to be mine and not the tenants', which since I leased out to another for one and twenty years. Proverbs 20.24.

And the 16th day of this December whilst I lay in Appleby Castle was my daughter of Northampton delivered of her second daughter and fourth child, the Lady Isabella Compton, in her Lord's house at Castle Ashby in Northamptonshire. Which Lady Isabella died the 3rd day of March in 1657 in the late Countess Dowager of Rivers'[114] house in Queen Street, London, where her father and mother then lay, she being a year and about three months old, and was buried in the vault of Compton church in Warwickshire, I then lying in Appleby Castle. Job 7.1.

---

112 \The 28 of July ... the next day/ WD.
113 A nonsuit was the ending of a suit by the judge because there was not sufficient evidence to make a case. To 'nonsuit' a person is to end the suit.
114 Mary Ogle.

In the year of Our Lord God 1657

The 3rd day of February in this year 1657 did Mr Thomas Gabetis, my deputy sheriff for the county of Westmorland, and Mr John Turner, Mr Thomas Johnson, John Darby and Thomas Carlton head bailiff for the West Ward enter into James Walker's house in Nether Brough commonly called Kirk Brough in the said county where they fairly and gently dispossessed the said James Walker's wife and her family of the said house and all lands thereto belonging.[115] The said sheriff by virtue of a writ issued out of the Common Pleas at Westminster delivering ever the same to the said John Darby my servant who was the lessee upon the ejectment for my use. And within a while after I did lease out the said James Walker's house and tenement to John Salkeld of Brough for one and twenty years, at a rack rent,[116] the same being held before at a finable rent as other the lands and tenements in the county of Westmorland are held of me, and by that means I altered the tenure of this land, which was the principal thing I aimed at in my suits in law with my Westmorland tenants as being a great benefit and advantage to me and my posterity and to all the landlords and tenants in that county, Isaiah 30.21; Jeremiah 42.3; Psalm 32.8.[117]

About the 30th of this January in her house called Chiswick near London died that Catherine Brydges, Countess Dowager of Bedford, who was wife to my cousin german Francis, Earl of Bedford, and was married to him two days after I was married to my first Lord. And her dead body was buried in the church at Chenies in Buckinghamshire, I then lying in Appleby Castle in Westmorland, Job 7.1.

And the 14th day of April did I remove with my family out of my castle of Appleby in Westmorland, towards Skipton in Craven whither I came safe and well the next day being the 15th day, having lain by the way all night at Kirkby Lonsdale in the inn there as I usually do in my journey between Westmorland

---

115   Anne would later employ an Isaac Walker from 1665 until her death. She housed Amy Walker in her almshouse at Appleby and bought goods from both a James and a William Walker. This James, Anne's tenant, appears to be a substantial and influential man in the area and likely had a number of other holdings. He is possibly James Walker of Sharrow Bay, near Penrith.

116   Anne uses this term to indicate the usual market rent of a property taking into consideration improvements and maintenance. A finable rent was a fixed low rent which included the right of inheritance of the leasehold land, with a fine paid to the new lord following the death of the previous lord. These finable rents could be historically low, though, as would be the case after Anne's death, when a number of lords died in quick succession, the fines could add up to a substantial amount in a short time.

117   Psalm 32.8: 'I will instruct thee and teach thee in the way which thou shalt go: I will guide thee with mine eye.'

and Craven. And I continued to lie in my said castle of Skipton till the 7th day of October. Following that I removed from thence towards Appleby Castle in Westmorland again, Ecclesiastes 3.6.

About the 25th or 26th of April aforesaid did Gabriel Vincent, now steward of my house and gentleman of my horse (by my directions), set the masons and carpenters on work in the further repairing of Skipton Castle, which he performed so as that the Michaelmas following (or but a few days after) there were fifteen rooms finished, seven whereof were upper rooms (in one of which I was born and my uncle of Cumberland died) and the rest lower rooms, also a little closet built on the north wall, the coining house new repaired and slated and the conduit court cleansed of all the rubbish that was thrown in at the demolishing of the castle. Which rooms were all covered over with slate about Michaelmas, also with gutters of lead about the rooms that are covered with slate, for I was not permitted to cover all with lead.[118]

And the April, about the 23rd day was another trial between me and my Westmorland tenants at the Common Pleas bar in Westminster Hall before my cousin Lord St John Lord Chief Justice, Judge Atkins, Judge Windham and Judge Hale where the verdict passed for me, and was so recorded in court, this being the fourth trial I have had and the fourth verdict I have had against my said tenants at the said Common Pleas bar in Westminster, Psalm 116.12, 13.

And this summer while I lay in my house or castle of Skipton in Craven about this time was the tomb quite finished which I caused to be erected and set up for myself in the north-east corner of Appleby church, here in Westmorland over the vault there which by my directions had been made in 1655, when I then repaired the said church, in which vault I intend to lie buried myself, Psalm 123.4.[119]

And about the 9th day of May following did my grandchild Mr John Tufton and his governor George Sedgewick and his man Alexander Whitchard come over sea in a Dutch man of war out of the Low Countries with my grandchild, the Lady Frances Tufton his sister and her woman, with others in their company and arrived the said 9th day safe at London, Psalm 121. From whence my said grandchild Mr John Tufton, George Sedgewick and my grandchild's

---

118 There was great concern that Anne's restoration of Skipton Castle would make it defensible again and so restrictions were placed on the kinds of material and the manner in which she rebuilt the destroyed portions of the castle.

119 Anne changed her mind and erected a tomb for herself in St Lawrence's church, Appleby, near her mother, not in Skipton near her father. Psalm 123.4: 'Our soul is exceedingly filled with the scorning of those that are at ease, and with the contempt of the proud.'

man Alexander Whitchard came to me to Skipton the 14th of June following. [120]

And the 19th day of June did my daughter of Northampton and the Earl her husband with their eldest son William, Lord Compton, and his uncle Mr Henry Compton,[121] the said Earl's youngest brother, come to me, and my grandchild John Tufton, from their house at Castle Ashby in Northamptonshire to my house or castle of Skipton in Craven, where they now lay for eleven nights, this being the first time that young Mr Henry Compton was ever there. But my Lord of Northampton, my daughter his wife and their son the Lord William Compton had been once there with me about three years before. And this 19th day was the first time that my said daughter, her Lord or any of their children ever saw any of her sister, my daughter of Thanet's, children in any part of my inheritance in the North, Proverbs 20.24.

And the 4th day of the next month my daughter of Northampton and her Lord and their eldest son the Lord Compton and Mr Henry Compton, my Lord of Northampton's brother, came safe to their house at Castle Ashby in Northamptonshire to my two grandchildren, Lady Anne and Lady Isabella Compton, their two daughters, to lie there again with them in the said castle, Proverbs 20.24; Ecclesiastes 8.6.

And in August this year did Baron Parker[122] and Unton Croke sergeant at law, the two judges of assize for the Northern Circuit come to Appleby Castle to keep the assizes there, where they lay some five nights, I lying then with my family at Skipton Castle in Craven, Ecclesiastes 3.

The 14th day of September was my grandchild the Lady Margaret Coventry delivered of a daughter in her father, the Earl of Thanet's, house at Hothfield in Kent, which was christened the day after by the name of Margaret (it being her second daughter, the third child, for her second son and eldest daughter are dead). And this was the first time she was delivered of any of her children in the said house wherein herself was born and wherein her father and mother and their younger children and her own eldest son John Coventry now lay (I lying now in my house or castle of Skipton in Craven) Jeremiah 29.6, the latter part of it; 30.19.

The 1st of October did Mr John Turner with his wife Elizabeth Turner, who was a Nicholls and had served me from her childhood till now, since the latter end of May 1629, and their daughter Elizabeth go quite away from my house or castle of Skipton and from further serving me, onwards on their journey

---

120 \From whence my ... of June following/ H1.
121 He would become Bishop of London in 1675.
122 John Parker.

towards London.[123] Whither they came safe and well the 15th day following to Baynard's Castle (having lain some three or four nights by the way in their house in Oxfordshire). But notwithstanding her husband is to continue my office for the receiving of my jointure rents in the Isle of Sheppey in Kent as long as he shall please, Ecclesiastes 8.6.

The 7th day of the said October did I and my family, with my grandchild John Tufton, remove out of my house or castle of Skipton in Craven towards Appleby Castle in Westmorland, whither I came safe and well the day following, being the eight day (having lain one night as I usually do at Kirkby Lonsdale by the way, in the inn there). And so I now lay in this Appleby Castle till the 23rd day of April following that I removed from thence with my family to my castle of Brougham in Westmorland. But while I now lay in Appleby I had news of the sad loss and death of the Lady Isabella Compton, second daughter to my daughter of Northampton and her Lord. Which Lady Isabella died the 3rd day of March in the late Countess Dowager of Rivers's house in Queen Street, London, where her father and mother now lay, she being a year and about three months old at her death, and was buried in the vault of Compton church in Warwickshire, Proverbs 20.24; Job 7.1.

In the year of Our Lord God 1658

And the 23rd day of April, after I had lain in Appleby Castle from the 8th day of October last till this time did I remove with my grandchild, Mr John Tufton, and my family into my castle of Brougham in Westmorland. Where I now lay till the 30th day of October following that I removed from thence with my family to Appleby Castle again. Isaiah 26.8–9.

And the 17th day of February, while I lay at Appleby Castle before my now coming to Brougham did I send my grandchild Mr John Tufton with his two men to Croome house in Worcestershire to see his sister Coventry her husband and children, and her father-in-law the Lord Coventry, where he lay for a few nights with them and returned to me back again to Appleby Castle the 29th day of March following. So he went thither by Lancaster, Preston, Manchester, Chester, Flint Castle, Denbigh, and other parts of North Wales and South Wales, and came back again by Warwick, Coventry, Lichfield and

---

123 Elizabeth Nicholls would return for future visits and Anne would later rebuild Julian Bower in Whinfell forest to house her and her second husband John Gilmore, whom she made under-keeper of Whinfell forest. There are numerous entries related to Elizabeth in Anne's account books and it is clear Elizabeth was dear to Anne, who treated her as an adopted daughter.

those parts. This being the first time he was ever in those places in Wales. Ecclesiastes.

The 16th day of June this summer did my said grandchild Mr John Tufton go for one night to Corby Castle in Cumberland to my cousin, Sir Francis Howard's house, where he lay that one night and returned back again the next day to me to Brougham Castle. Ecclesiastes 8.6.

The 25th day of this June was my first grandchild Nicholas, Lord Tufton, released of his restraint and imprisonment in the Tower of London, where he had lain the second time as a prisoner ever since the 11th of September in 1656. Psalm 105.19.

And the same 25th day of June after I had taken leave of him the night before, did my grandchild Mr John Tufton go away from me, from Brougham Castle towards London, to his father and mother. Whither he came well to them to their house in Aldersgate Street the 1st day of the month following and lay there till the 10th day of August that he went over sea into the Low Countries with his sister the Lady Frances Tufton, where they remained about some two months and returned again together into England the 7th of October following. Proverbs 20.24.

And this summer did I cause great repairs to be made upon the old walls of Skipton Castle in Craven, as also at Barden Tower, my steward Gabriel Vincent lying in both these places a great part of the summer to take order about the said repairs. So as most of the stonework of this ancient decayed castle tower of mine was finished (I thank God) to my good liking and content the beginning of the next summer in 1659. Ezekiel 36.33, 36; Isaiah 25.12.

And the beginning of this spring, did I cause Bongate church near Appleby to be pulled down and new built up again at my own charge. And it was wholly finished about the later end of April in 1659, for which God be praised. Psalm 116.11–14.

This summer also I caused the chapel at Brougham to be pulled down and new built up again larger and stronger then it was before at my own charge. And it was wholly finished about the latter end of April in 1659, for which God be praised. Psalm 116.11, 12, 13, 14.

This summer on the 19th, 20th and 21st of August was the assizes kept at Appleby by John Parker, one of the Barons of the Exchequer and Richard Newdigate, one of the judges of the Upper Bench, where they now lay three nights in Appleby Castle, Judge Parker in the Baron's Chamber and Judge Newdigate in the great tower. And by the way thither as they came from Carlyle they both of them came to see me at Brougham Castle and dined there with me. Ecclesiastes 3.

And at these assizes my cousin Philip, Lord Wharton and his brother Sir

Thomas Wharton lay both in Appleby Castle, where my Lord Wharton had some trials. And after both he and his brother came two or three times to Brougham Castle (where I now lay) to see me, this being the first time I saw my said cousin the Lord Wharton after the death of his second wife.[124] And he and his brother went, both of them, out of Westmorland a while after. Ecclesiastes 8.6.

An the 28th of this August did my daughter the Countess of Thanet come hither to me to Brougham Castle from London with three of her younger sons: Richard, Thomas and Sackville, this being the first time I ever saw these three sons of hers here in Westmorland or in any other part of the lands of mine inheritance, and the third time of her coming into this county to me. And I saw her not since the 28th of July in 1656 till this 28th of this month that she now came hither to me, where she and her three sons now lay nine nights together. So as I have now seen nine of my said daughter's children here in Westmorland, which I account as a great blessing and singular goodness of God towards me. And they went away from me the 6th day of September following through Whinfell to Appleby Castle, where they lay that night, and the next day went over Stainmore, towards London. Whither they got well to their house in Aldersgate Street the 14th day of the same month and the 17th day they went down to their house at Rainham in Kent and there lay all night, from whence they got well to Hothfield the next day, to my Lord of Thanet, my son-in-law and to his eldest son my Lord Tufton and four other of his youngest children, who are all of them his wife, my eldest daughter's children also, for which God be praised. Genesis 1.28; 26.22 the latter part of it; Isaiah 49.21–22;[125] Jeremiah 29.6 the latter part of it; 30.19; Psalm 116.12–14.

This summer by some few mischievous people secretly in the night, was there broke off and taken down from that tree near the pale of Whinfell Park (which for that cause was called the Hart's Horn Tree) one of those old hart's horns, which (as is mentioned in the summary of my ancestor Robert Lord Clifford's life) were set up in the year 1333 at a general hunting when Edward Balliol then King of Scots, came into England by permission of King Edward the third and lay for a while in the said Robert Lord Clifford's castles in Westmorland.[126]

---

124 Jane Goodwin.
125 Isaiah 49.21–22: 'The children which thou shalt have, after thou hast lost the other, shall say again in thine ears, The place is too strait for me: give place to me that I may dwell. Then shalt thou say in thine heart, Who hath begotten me these, seeing I have lost my children, and am desolate, a captive, and removing to and fro? and who hath brought up these? Behold, I was left alone; these, where had they been?'
126 See *Great Books*, ed. Malay, p. 350.

Where the said King hunted a great stag which was killed near the said oak tree. In memory whereof the horns were nailed up in it, growing as it were naturally in the tree and have remained there ever since, till that in the year 1648 one of those horns was broken down by some of the army and the other was broken down (as aforesaid) this year. So as now there is no part thereof remaining. The tree itself being now so decayed and the bark of it so peeled of that it cannot last long. Whereby we may see that time brings to forgetfulness any memorable things in this world be they never so carefully preserved, for this tree with the hart's horn in it was a thing of much note in these parts. Ecclesiastes 3.

And whilst I now lay in Brougham Castle did my grandchild Mr John Tufton and the Lady Frances Tufton his sister come away from the city of Utrecht in the Low Countries and took shipping at the Brill in Holland the 7th day of October and landed the 8th day at Deal in Kent, and so came safe with their company on the ninth day following to their father's house at Hothfield. Ecclesiastes 8.6.

And the 30th day of this October did I and my family remove from my castle of Brougham to Appleby Castle again after I had lain in this Brougham Castle from the 23rd day of April until now. And I continued to lie in this Appleby Castle till the 5th day of May in 1659, at which time I removed from thence with my family to my castle of Skipton in Craven. Psalm 121.

And in the beginning of this summer was finished by my direction the new wall about the little park adjoining to Brougham Castle, the old low wall being before pulled down. And this new wall joins on the one side to the garden wall, and on the other side to the castle. Ecclesiastes 3.

In the year of Our Lord God 1659

And while I now lay in Appleby Castle in Westmorland upon Thursday the 14th day of April was my younger daughter Isabella, Countess of Northampton, brought to bed of her third son and her fifth child in a hired house where she and her Lord and their family new lay, in Lincoln's Inn Fields at London, who was christened the day after by the name of James, this being the first time that she had two sons alive together at one time. Genesis 1.28; 26.22 the latter part of it; Isaiah 49.20–21; Jeremiah 29.6; 30.19; Psalm 116.12–14. But this grandchild of mine died in Canonbury by Islington the 1st day of August in 1662 being a good while after the death of his mother.[127]

And the 5th day of this May being Thursday did I remove with my family from Appleby Castle towards Skipton in Craven, whither I came well the next day

---

127 \But this grandchild ... death of his mother/ WD.

having laid one night by the way in the inn at Kirkby Lonsdale. And I had not lain in this Skipton Castle, nor been at it, since the 7th day of October in 1657, when I removed thence with my family to Appleby Castle in Westmorland being about a year and six months. And now did I continue to lie in this Skipton Castle in the Round Chamber (where I have lain, at such times as I have lived there ever since I first came to lie there in 1649) until the 9th of December following at which time I removed from thence to Barden Tower to lie there in it for a time, this being the first time since I was born that I came to lie in this Barden Tower. Ecclesiastes 8.6; Ezekiel 36.33, 36; Isaiah 58.12.

And the 23rd day of this May my grandchild Mr John Tufton, and his sister the Lady Frances Tufton with Mistress Sibilla Baker, her gentlewoman that had been abroad with her in the Low Countries, and Henry Hatfield that now serves my grandchild Mr John Tufton in Alexander Whitchard's place, lately deceased, did come hither to me unto my house or castle of Skipton in Craven from there journey from York and from London. And this was the first time that I saw this grandchild of mine, the Lady Frances Tufton, either in Craven or in any of the lands of mine inheritance. And I had not seen her brother John since Midsummer last that he went from me from Brougham Castle toward London till now. Isaiah 49.20–21; Jeremiah 29.6; 30.19.

So these two grandchildren of mine lay here in Skipton Castle until the 4th of July, that they went from hence to the Wells at Knaresborough,[128] where they lay for seventeen days to take the waters. And the one and twentieth of the same month they returned back to me to Skipton again and stayed there till the 10th of September following when they went away from hence with their two servants in my coach and six horses, to York lying there all day on Sunday. And the next day, being the 12th of the same month, they went away in a hired coach towards London, whither they came well to their mother to her house in Aldersgate Street the 17th day of this month. And three days after Lady Frances went down to her sister Lady Margaret Coventry to Croome in Worcestershire whither she came well the 24th day of the said September. Proverbs 20.24.

And the beginning of this summer, a little before my coming out of Westmorland, did I cause the church of Ninekirks[129] to be pulled down and new built up again in the same place, larger and bigger then it was before, which was finished the latter end of this summer (though myself and my family were then at my castle of Skipton in Craven). And this church of Ninekirks would, in all

---

128 Mother Shipton's well, or the Dripping or Dropping Well. John Leland in his travels in the 1530 and 1540s described it as 'a well of a wonderful nature' (*Leland's Itinerary*, p. 86).
129 The bowels of Margaret Russell were buried in Ninekirks church.

likelihood have fallen down, it was so ruinous, if it had not been now repaired by me. Psalm 116.12–14.

And this April, after I had first been there myself to direct the building of it, did I cause my old decayed castle of Brough to be repaired, and also the old tower, called the Roman Tower in the said castle and a courthouse for keeping of my courts in, with some dozen or fourteen rooms to be built in it upon the old foundation.

The 21st of August this summer by reason of the trouble now afoot in these northern parts[130] though it were Sunday, yet did two judges of assize for the Northern Circuit, Francis Thorpe and John Parker, come that night from Carlisle to my castle of Appleby in Westmorland, where they continued to lie till Friday morning following. From whence they then went to Kendal that night and the next day to Lancaster to keep the assizes there also. And notwithstanding these judges now lay here, yet was there then a garrison of soldiers in the castle. Ecclesiastes 8.6.

And the 27th of this August being Saturday was my grandchild the Lady Margaret Coventry delivered of a son which was her fifth child and is now her second son, in her father-in-law the Lord Coventry's house at Croome in Worcestershire, I then lying at Skipton Castle in Craven as also did her brother John Tufton and her sister Lady Frances Tufton, this being the first time that my said grandchild Lady Margaret Coventry had the blessing and happiness to have two sons alive together at one time. Genesis 1.28; 26.22 the latter part of it; Isaiah 49.20–21; Jeremiah 29.6; 30.19; Psalm 116.12–14. Which son Thomas died at Croome where he was born the 17th of June 1660.[131]

And about the 4th day of this August was my son in law the Earl of Northampton committed close prisoner to upon some suspicion that he was engaged in the late insurrection in England.[132] My daughter his wife being also there in his lodgings, where he continued prisoner till the 2nd day of November following that he was released of his said imprisonment in the Tower and went to live with my daughter, his wife, in that house in Lincoln's Inn Fields in London where they lived before. Ecclesiastes 3; Deuteronomy 23.5.

And this summer my eldest grandchild, Nicholas, Lord Tufton, went from his father and mother and having lain for some time at the Wells at Epsom in

---

130 Richard Cromwell resigned, ending the Protectorate, in May 1659. A number of plots intended to restore Charles II to the throne developed in the summer. As a result the Council of State mobilized the militia, reinforcing strategic garrisons throughout the country, including, as Anne notes below, Appleby Castle.
131 \Which son Thomas … of June 1660/ WD.
132 Booth's Uprising in July and early August 1659.

Surrey he went over secretly into France. Ecclesiastes 8.6. From whence in the winter following he came over again to his father and his mother and his brothers and his sisters.

And this summer though I found the castle of Skipton for the most part well finished and better then I expected it could have been, yet I could not lie in it partly by reason of the smell and unwholesomeness of the new walls, and partly by the reason of the garrison of foot soldiers, which was put in there, about the 4th of August under the command of Ensign Robert Fener for securing thereof by reason of the trouble now in England. Ecclesiastes 3; 8.6; Proverbs 20.29; Ezekiel 36.33, 36; Isaiah 58.12.

And about the said fourth of August was there also a garrison of foot soldiers put into Appleby Castle in Westmorland into the great tower there called Caesar's Tower, which I lately repaired. But after they had lain a while there they went away and quitted it and after they were gone, others came in their room but stayed not long, as likewise into Brougham Castle for a while. Both which castles these soldiers not long after quitted and went away. Deuteronomy 23.5.[133]

And the 9th of this December, after I had lain in this house or castle of mine of Skipton ever since the 6th of May last did I remove from thence with my family to Barden Tower to lie in it for a time, which was the first time that I did ever lie in this Barden Tower, having lately repaired it, to my great costs and charges when it was then a most ruinated decayed place. For my mother had never lain in it since she was with child with me, nor my father in a good while before, neither did my uncle of Cumberland or my cousin his son ever lie in it after they came to this estate in Craven. And I lay now in this Barden Tower till the 8th day of October, following that I removed thence with my family towards Appleby Castle in Westmorland.

So this year I had the blessing to have two male children born into the world of the generation of my body: the one James Compton, now youngest son to my daughter of Northampton and the other Thomas Coventry, now youngest son to my grandchild, the Lady Margaret Coventry. Psalm 116.12–14; Ecclesiastes 3. But this Thomas Coventry died at Croome in Worcestershire (where he

---

133 Anne does not mention here a greater threat emerging from the political uncertainties of the period. There had been some concern about her rebuilding work at Skipton Castle. In the autumn of 1659 the castle was again under threat of being 'slighted' or having its walls and ramparts brought down again. Two letters by Anne to Captain Adam Baynes ask for his help in convincing the parliamentarian authorities in London that her rebuilding efforts were only intended to make the house habitable and, as Anne puts it, 'I am confident this Castle if mine will never bee found to be any such place of strength if it were viewed by persons of judgement' (BL, Add. MS 21425, fol. 127, see also fol. 148).

was born) the 17th day of June in 1660 and this James Lord Compton died at Canonbury near Islington the 1st of August 1662 after the death of his mother, so as they both died in their infancy.¹³⁴

January 1660 as the year begins on New Year's day

And the 25th day of April this year a new Parliament began to sit at Westminster wherein were chosen, most part by my means, knights of the shire for Westmorland: my two cousins Sir Thomas Wharton and Sir John Lowther of Lowther knight and baronet and for burgesses of the borough of Appleby: my cousin Sir Henry Cholmley and Christopher Clapham esquire.¹³⁵ Which Parliament proved to be a happy Parliament by calling in our rightful Prince King Charles the second into England, wherein also General George Monck the general of the army in Scotland was a great and a happy instrument. His Majesty, with his two brothers the Dukes of York and Gloucester,¹³⁶ coming out of the Low Countries by sea into England about the 25th day of May and landed at Dover in Kent and so went by land to Canterbury and Rochester and the 29th day following (being his Majesty's birthday) he made his triumphant entry through the city of London to Whitehall to lie there again. But this great joy was clouded with sorrow for the death of his younger brother Henry, Duke of Gloucester, who died the 14th day of September following of the smallpox at Whitehall in the Prince's lodging there and was buried a while after, in King Henry the seventh's chapel at the abbey church in Westminster amongst many of his ancestors. And his eldest sister, Mary, Princess of Orange,¹³⁷ died at Whitehall the 24th day of December following and was buried by him in the said Henry the 7th's chapel, she that was widow to William, last Prince of Orange.

And in April and May this year did the masons begin to build up again and repair my castle of Brough in Westmorland, a good part whereof had been repaired the last summer and the remainder thereof now this summer being taken in hand after it had lain ruinous ever since the year 1521 that it was burnt down in Henry, Lord Clifford's time, about two years and a little more before his death, he dying in this 15th of Henry the 8th. And this Brough Castle and the

---

134 \But this Thomas ... in their infancy/ WD.
135 The 1660 Convention Parliament enacted a number of important legal statutes, including the Tenures Abolition Act 1660 which most closely affected Anne. Through these four men, Anne was able to exert some influence on the work of this parliament, as she would continue to do with later ones. Clapham was related to Anne, and his family had long been associated with the Cliffords.
136 James Stuart (later James II of England) and Henry Stuart.
137 Mary Stuart.

8 Brough Castle, from Samuel and Nathanial Buck, *A Collection of Engravings of Castles, and Abbeys in England* (1726–1739)

Roman Tower in it was so well repaired by me that on the 16th of September in the next year I lay there for three nights together which none of my ancestors had done in 140 years before till now.

And in June this year by my directions was also my old decayed castle of Pendragon in Mallerstang in the said county of Westmorland begun to be repaired, which had lain waste (as appears by many records in Skipton Castle before the late civil wars) ever since the 15th of Edward the 3rd when the Scots did then burn down the timber of it and demolished it, with their often inroads and incursions into England, there being in his time sharp and bitter wars between the two nations. And it was so well repaired by me that on the 14th of October in the following I lay there for three nights together which none of my ancestors had done since Idonea de Veteripont lay in it, who died eighth [year of] Edward 3rd without issue.[138]

The 17th day of June being Trinity Sunday, died little Thomas Coventry, second son to my grandchild the Lady Margaret Coventry, in his grandfather the Lord Thomas Coventry's house at Croome in Worcestershire, where this child to whom I was great-grandmother was born into the world but the 27th of

---

138 Idonea and her sister Isabella (Sheriffess of Westmorland in her own right and wife of Roger de Clifford III) were important influences on Anne. Idonea's heir was her great-nephew Robert, 3rd Lord Clifford, and thus at Idonea's death the Veteripont inheritance of Westmorland, including Brough, Brougham, Appleby and Pendragon, passed into the Clifford line. Anne had dreamed of rebuilding Pendragon Castle since childhood. Her mother mentions in a letter to her in 1615 that 'you were wont to say you would if even you came to it repair Pendragon Castle to make a Library of it for Mr Christopher Worlidge [or Woolridge]' (Portland MS 23, letter, 1615, p. 66).

August before, and his dead body was buried in the church there, whose death I esteemed as a loss and cross to us all. And then did his little sister Margaret and their father lie in the said Croome House in Worcestershire. But his mother and his eldest brother lay then in Thanet House in Aldersgate Street, London, with her father and mother.

The 10th day of March in this year a little before the King came into England died my virtuous and good cousin german Margaret Wharton then the widow Lady Wotton in her house at Canterbury, formerly a part of the Priory there,[139] she that was born in Skipton Castle in Craven in July 1581. And she was buried a while after near to her husband Edward, Lord Wotton, in the church of Boughton in Kent[140] and when she died did I lie in Barden Tower in Craven.

The 27th day of July in this year 1660 did my youngest daughter Isabella, Countess of Northampton, with her two eldest children William, Lord Compton, and Lady Anne Compton, come hither to me into Barden Tower in Yorkshire, from their journey from Edington in Wiltshire and Compton in Warwickshire, where they now lay in this Barden Tower with me ten nights together in the four rooms on the west side of the Great Chamber. This being the first time that I ever saw Lady Anne Compton or of any of my said daughter of Northampton's daughters. And while they were here, did my daughter of Northampton with these two children of hers, go the 31st day of this month into Skipton Castle for a while to see it, this being the first time she ever saw it since I last repaired the decayed part of it, and the first time her daughter Lady Anne was ever in this Skipton Castle. Neither had my said daughter or her eldest son the Lord Compton been in it since the 30th day of June 1657 till now. And on the 6th day of August following my said daughter of Northampton and her two eldest children and servants went away hence towards her Lord's house of Compton in Warwickshire,[141] whither they came safe and well about five or six days after with their whole company, my Lord of Northampton himself meeting them there from London. And this 6th day of August was the last time I saw these two grandchildren of mine, William, Lord Compton, and Lady Anne Compton his sister, for she died the 14th of December following, and he died on the 14th of September 1661 just nine months after his sister's death to my unspeakable grief and sorrow and it was likewise the last time I saw their mother my youngest daughter.[142]

The 5th day of September, being Wednesday, did the King's two judges of assize

139 St Augustine's Abbey, Canterbury, Kent.
140 Boughton Malherbe, Kent.
141 Compton Wynyates, Warwickshire.
142 \and it was ... my youngest daughter/ WD.

for the Northern Circuit, Sir Thomas Twisden[143] and Sir Robert Bernard, come into my castle of Appleby in Westmorland where they now lay five nights together, Judge Twisden in the Baron's Chamber and Judge Bernard in the chief chamber in Caesar's Tower. And when they were past the 10th of the same month they went away from thence forward on their circuit. And this was the first time that this Sir Thomas Twisden was ever in Appleby Castle or any part of mine inheritance, whose great-grandfather was that Sir Thomas Heneage that was Vice Chamberlain to Queen Elizabeth and in great favour with her the most part of her reign. And my father and mother loved that Vice Chamberlain extremely and he them.

Towards the latter end of this summer [I caused] my mill about a mile from Barden Tower in Yorkshire called Hough Mill to be pulled down and new built up again with stone and wood at my own charge, for before it was so ruinous as it was like to fall down having not been repaired in many years before till now.

The 2nd day of this October in 1660 did Richard Earl of Cork and his two sons, my cousins Charles, Lord Dungarvan, and Mr Richard Boyle come hither to me into this Barden Tower and dined with me, but went back again the same day into their house at Bolton, some two miles hence, where they now lay for a little time and I had seen none of them, since about last summer [which] was ten years, when they were at Skipton Castle with me sometimes, and I with them at Bolton, till this day that they came hither to me again.

And the 8th of October in this year did I and my family remove out of my tower of Barden in Craven towards Appleby Castle in Westmorland and lay three nights by the way, the first night at Pateley Bridge, the second night at Street House not far from Bedall, and the third night at Bowes, and so over Stainmore to Appleby Castle and came safe and well thither the 11th day following, after I had lain in that tower of Barden ever since the 9th day of December 1659 till now.

And by the way in this my journey from Barden to Appleby Castle I went hard by Snape House of the Earl of Exeter's.[144] And I had not been at Bowes nor on Stainmore nor in those ways since the 9th day of December in 1616 when I then went up from Brougham Castle in Westmorland to London to my first Lord, Richard Earl of Dorset and the Lady Margaret Sackville my then only child, till the 11th day of this October that I came to lie in this Appleby Castle again, where I had not lain since about the 5th day of May in 1659 till now. And I had not lain three nights together out of some of my houses in Craven

---

143 His grandmother, Elizabeth Heneage, is mentioned as one of the party of women including Anne who stayed at North Hall in 1603, see p. 17.
144 Snape Castle, Yorkshire. This Earl of Exeter was John Cecil, 4th Earl of Exeter.

or in Westmorland since the year 1649 when I then came from London into the North till this time that I lay out three nights as I was in my journey from Barden Tower to Appleby Castle. For heretofore I used but to lie out one night in my removes between Craven and Westmorland, since my said coming down and that was at Kirkby Lonsdale.

And when I now came to lie in Appleby Castle in Westmorland I continued to lie in it till the 29th of October 1661 excepting six nights, three whereof I lay in Brough Castle and the other three in Pendragon Castle in that county. And that 29th day of October in 1661 I removed with my family from Appleby Castle into my castle of Brougham in the same county.

And the 15th day of this December (being Saturday) while I then lay in this Appleby Castle in Westmorland, died my grandchild the Lady Anne Compton, eldest daughter to my daughter of Northampton and her Lord, in her father's house in Lincoln's Inn Fields at London when she was five years and about five months old, to my great grief and sorrow for she was a child that promised much goodness. And the 6th day of August before, she went away from me from Barden Tower in Craven with her eldest brother the Lord Compton and their mother towards London, it being the last time I ever saw this grandchild of mine, the Lady Anne Compton. And she was buried in the vault of Compton church in Warwickshire[145] by her father's ancestors. [146]

About the 2nd of November this year did Queen Marie, Queen Dowager of England, daughter to King Henry the 4th of France, widow to our late King, and mother to our now King Charles the 2nd, come over seas out of France into England with her youngest daughter, the Princess Henrietta. And she now lay in her own lodgings there about some two months, for on the second of January following she went away from thence with her said youngest daughter to Portsmouth and so over seas into France again. And this Queen had not been in England since July in 1644 till now. And a little after their coming again into France was the said Princess Henrietta married to her cousin german the Duke of Orleans and Anjou, he that is second and only brother to the now King of France.[147]

And this 2nd of November was the first time the said Queen Dowager came into England after her son King Charles was restored to his crown and though she went soon after into France as above said yet she came again into England the 28th of July 1662 and stayed till 1665. [148]

145 A chapel is adjacent to the house at Compton Wynyates.
146 \and she was ... her father's ancestors/ WD.
147 \And a little ... King of France/ WD.
148 \And this 2nd ... stayed till 1665/ H1.

About the 7th day of December did three of my daughter of Thanet's younger sons, that is to say John, Richard and Thomas Tufton, go from their father and mother, and their eldest brother, and their two youngest brothers, and their four younger sisters out of Thanet House in Aldersgate Street and out of London town and so after a short stay at their father's house at Hothfield in Kent they went to Dover, and from thence, in the packet boat, to Calais in France and from thence they went to Paris, so to Orleans and from thence to Blois, where they intend to live for a time. This being the first time that my daughter of Thanet's said two sons Richard and Thomas were ever beyond the seas, but their brother John had been twice before this beyond the seas into the Low Countries, though never before in France. And they all three came over well into England again to their father and mother and some of their brothers and sisters at Hothfield in Kent[149] about the beginning of March in 1663 as the year begins on New Year's day.

In the year of Our Lord God 1661

The 14th day of March in this year, my daughter of Northampton was delivered of her third daughter and sixth child, the Lady Alethea Compton, in her Lord's house in Lincoln's Inn Fields at London, which child was christened about two days after, I then lying in Appleby Castle in Westmorland. And the 14th day of October following died her mother my daughter of Northampton in the said house in Lincoln's Inn Fields after she had but awhile before come from Castle Ashby in Northamptonshire from her last seeing her eldest son William, Lord Compton, whom she left there behind her and from Woburn, the Earl of Bedford's house in Bedfordshire, up thither to London to take physic.

And about the 21st day of May was the decayed mill at Brough pulled down, and is to be new built again by my directions, which was done so well and in so good a manner that I was in it myself, and liked it very well, on the 16th day of September when I went to lie in Brough Castle. [150]

The 23rd of April in this year (I then lying in Appleby Castle in Westmorland) was our King Charles the 2nd crowned King of England in the Abbey church at Westminster with great solemnity, for which God be praised. [151]

---

149 \to their father ... Hothfield in Kent/ H1.
150 \which was done ... in Brough Castle/ WD.
151 \The 23 of ... God be praised/ WD. Thomas Machell describes a lavish celebration in Appleby on the day of the coronation, which Anne presided over: 'the aged countess seeming young again to grace the solemnity', Nicholson and Burn, *History and Antiquities of the Counties of Westmorland and Cumberland*, vol. 1, p. 316.

And the 17th of May this year did Elizabeth, the widow Queen of Bohemia,[152] come over seas, out of the Low Countries into England to the city of London to see her two nephews, Charles the 2nd and our King of England and James, Duke of York, after she had been out of England forty-eight years and a month over. And she now continued to be at London for the most part in the Lord Craven's house in Drury Lane till the 13th of February following that she died in the new-built house called Leicester House in the Fields[153] not far from Charing Cross, to which house she removed about a month before her death. And none of her children were with her when she died but her son Prince Rupert who was then in England and present at her death.[154] Job 7.1.

And the 9th day of August, this year did my daughter of Thanet come hither to me over Stainmore into this Appleby Castle in Westmorland from her journey from London, with her three youngest daughters: Lady Cecily, Lady Marie and Lady Anne Tufton, to my great joy and comfort. Where she and her daughter Lady Cecily now lay together in the Baron's Chamber and her two younger daughters in the next chamber to it, for eleven nights together. In which time, they went with me the 11th day of this month into Appleby church and the 18th of it into Bongate church.

And on the 20th day they went away from me from this Appleby Castle, after I had taken my leave of them in my own chamber, onwards on their journey towards London over Stainmore. And by the way they went for a while into my castle of Brough in Westmorland to see the new buildings there, which was the first time that ever any of my posterity came into that castle since it was lately repaired by me.

And I had not seen this eldest daughter of mine since the 6th of September in 1658, when she went away with three of her younger sons from my castle of Brougham in Westmorland towards London, till now. And I had not seen these three youngest daughters of hers since the 28th of July in 1656 till this time. And this is the fourth time my daughter of Thanet hath come into Westmorland to me. And the 6th day of July was my grandchild the Lady Margaret Coventry delivered of her third son and fifth child, Mr William Coventry, who died the 14th of July 1662. [155]

And the 24th day of August this year (being Saturday) did Sir Christopher Turnor, one of the Barons of his Majesty's Court of Exchequer and Sir Robert Bernard knight and sergeant at law, his Majesty's justices for the Northern

---

152 Princess Elizabeth Stuart.
153 Now the site of Leicester Square, near St Martin's-in-the-Fields.
154 \and she now continued to be at London … England and present at her death/ WD.
155 \And the 6th day … dyed the 14 of July 1662/ WD.

Circuit, come from Carlisle hither to Appleby Castle, where they now lay five nights together, Judge Turnor in the Baron's Chamber, and Judge Bernard in the best room in Caesar's Tower. And on Thursday following (the 29th day) about nine o'clock, they went away from hence towards Lancaster to keep the assizes there also, lying at Kendal that night by the way. And I lay now here in this Appleby Castle while these judges stayed here, which I had not done since August in 1653 till now.

The 10th day of September this year, I sent down to my almshouse here at Appleby the King's letters patents under the Great Seal of England for making the said almshouse a corporation, being a perpetuity granted to me for the foundation thereof dated at Westminster the 2nd day of the last month in the 13th year of his Majesty's reign, which was now laid up in the chest or trunk in the mother's chamber there under lock and key, to be kept amongst the rest of the writings and evidences concerning the foundation of the said almshouse and the lands of St Nicholas near Appleby and the manor of Brougham which I purchased for the maintenance thereof.[156]

On Saturday the 18th day of September about two o'clock in the afternoon died my most dear grandchild William, Lord Compton, in his father's house at Castle Ashby in Northamptonshire, when he was eight years, three months and about eighteen days old, he being a child of great hopes and perfection both of body and mind. And his brother and his sister and their father then there with him. But his mother was then at London under the physicians' hands, and lay in her Lord's house there in Lincoln's Inn Fields, I then lying in the Roman Tower at Brough Castle in Westmorland and stirred not out of it all that day. And this sad news was brought me by a letter from his father the 27th day of the said September to Appleby Castle where I then lay.

And the 16th day of this month did I remove out of Appleby into Brough Castle in Westmorland where I now lay for three nights together, the first night in that half round tower called Clifford's Tower, and the other two nights in the second room of the great tower called Roman Tower, both which towers and castle there were repaired by me lately to my exceeding great costs and charges, after they had lain desolate ever since the timber thereof was casually burnt in the year 1521 some two years and a little more before the death of that Henry, Lord Clifford, my ancestor who was father to Henry, Lord Clifford, 1st Earl of Cumberland. So as none of my ancestors have lain in it since it was so consumed by fire till I now lay in it myself. And I had not been in it since about the 14th or 15th of April in 1659 when it was then a-repairing till this time that I now lay in it.

---

156 St Anne's continues in operation today in general accordance with this letter patent.

And the 18th day of this month about four o'clock in the afternoon whilst I lay in the great tower at Brough Castle in Westmorland called the Roman Tower, died my dear grandchild William, Lord Compton, in his father's house at Castle Ashby in Northamptonshire and his dead body was opened and afterwards buried in the vault in Compton church in Warwickshire, where his sisters Anne and Isabella, and many of their father's ancestors the Comptons and their wives, lie also interred.

And the 14th of October this year about eight o'clock in the morning died his mother, my youngest daughter Isabella, Countess of Northampton, in her Lord's house in Lincoln's Inn Fields at London, when she was thirty-nine years old and some thirteen days over, her two children that are now only left alive James, Lord Compton, and Lady Alethea Compton and their father the Earl of Northampton lying then in that house and then did I lie in my own chamber in Appleby Castle in Westmorland from whence I removed the same day some two or three hours after into Pendragon Castle in Westmorland to lie there for three nights. But I did not hear the sad news of her death till after I came from thence into Appleby Castle again.

Also the same 14th day of this October, about nine o'clock in the morning, after she was dead (though I knew it not) did I remove out of Appleby Castle in Westmorland, into Pendragon Castle in the same county, where I now lay in the second storey that looks east and south for three nights together, and when they were past, I came from thence into this Appleby Castle again to lie in it as before, this being the first time I lay in the said Pendragon Castle since it was lately repaired and made habitable by me, to my great costs and charges, after it had lain desolate ever since about the 15th year of Edward the 3rd in 1341 which is 320 years ago. For then (as by old records and chronicles it appears) the Scots made an inroad into the West of England, totally destroying it, and pulling down all the timber, and a great part of the stone building of it. But before that, it was the chief and beloved habitation of Idonea the younger daughter and coheir of Robert de Veteripont, my ancestor. She dying without issue, as appears by inquisitions taken after her death in the 8th year of Edward the 3rd,[157] and then all her inheritance in Westmorland came to her older sister Isabella's grandchild Robert Lord Clifford, and his posterity, to whom I am heir by a lineal descent.

And after I came from Pendragon Castle in Westmorland, I lay now in Appleby Castle some twelve nights before I removed from thence to Brougham Castle in the said county, whither I and my family came safe the 29th day of this

---

157 See *Great Books*, ed. Malay, pp. 130–141.

9 Pendragon Castle, from Samuel and Nathanial Buck, *A Collection of Engravings of Castles, and Abbeys in England* (1726–1739)

October, to lie there in it for a time in the same chamber wherein my noble father was born and my blessed mother died. After I had lain in Appleby Castle ever since the 11th of this October was a twelvemonth (excepting only six nights, three whereof I lay in Brough Castle and the other three in Pendragon Castle in Westmorland, as is before mentioned).

And the 27th day of this October whilst I lay in Appleby Castle in Westmorland died Thomas, Lord Coventry, in his house in Lincoln's Inn Fields at London of the gangrene that was in several of his toes, he whose eldest son now George, Lord Coventry, did marry about eight years, three months and some days over, my grandchild the Lady Margaret Tufton, then and now eldest daughter to my daughter of Thanet and her Lord.

And the 29th day of this October (as is above written) did I and my family remove out of Appleby Castle in Westmorland into my castle of Brougham in the same county to lie there for a time in the same chamber wherein my noble father was born and my blessed mother died. After I had lain in Appleby Castle aforesaid ever since the 11th of this October was a twelvemonth excepting only six nights, three whereof I lay in Brough Castle, and the other three in Pendragon Castle in Westmorland.

And I now continued to lie in the said chamber in Brougham Castle in Westmorland for nine months and two days over, till the first day of August. Following that I removed from thence into my said castle of Appleby again to lie in it for a little time. And during that time of my lying at Brougham Castle I received the sacrament there once at Christmas in the chapel at Brougham Castle, once at Ninekirks on Easter Sunday and once at Brougham Chapel the

27th of July which chapel I have lately built and this was the first time since the death of my mother that I ever received the blessed sacrament in this Brougham Chapel. And I seldom else went out of my chamber or upon the leads of the castle as I used to do, but only into the Painted Chamber to hear prayers.

In the year of our Lord God 1662

On the 13th day of February died Elizabeth Queen Dowager of Bohemia[158] she that was aunt to our King Charles the second and James, Duke of York. And she died in Leicester House in the fields near Charing Cross at London and was buried in Henry the seventh's chapel in the abbey church at Westminster, near to her father and mother and her nephew Henry, Duke of Gloucester and the Princess Elizabeth his sister, after she had now lived in England since about the 17th day of May last. And she died the even of that day was forty-nine years that she was married to Frederick Prince Elector Palatine her husband. I now lying in Brougham Castle in Westmorland when she died.

And the 22nd day of March in this year I had a swounding[159] fit whereby I was in great danger of death, but it pleased God to restore me to life and health again in a very short space. And the 30th day of this March being Easter I received the blessed sacrament in the church called Ninekirks, this being the first time I came into it after I had repaired and new built the said church.

The 12th day of April in this year my son-in-law James, Earl of Northampton, came hither to me from his journey from Castle Ashby in Northamptonshire and the southern parts by Skipton (where he had not been since the latter end of June in 1657 when he was there with his wife and his eldest son William, Lord Compton) and he went into the castle to see the rooms there in it. And in his journey from Skipton he lay at Ingleton by the way. And the same 12th day came hither to me into this Brougham Castle in Westmorland with his cousin Mr John Mordaunt, son to Mr James Mordaunt, a younger brother to the last Earl of Peterborough, and they stayed here with me at Brougham Castle seven nights together, his Lordship lying in the Baron's Chamber, and his cousin Mordaunt in Graystock Chamber. And when those seven were past they went away from hence to Carlisle and so to Edinburgh in Scotland and other places where they lay a good while but returned back by Carlisle hither the 11th day of May following, though it were Sunday. And then they lay here again in the same chambers in this Brougham Castle for eight nights together. And this was the

---

158 Elizabeth Stuart.
159 Swoon or fainting fit.

first time that my Lord of Northampton did ever lie in this Brougham Castle. And he went the 13th day of April being Sunday in the afternoon, into the chapel at Brougham to hear the sermon there, that being the first time he was ever in that chapel. And the 18th of May following he went into the church at Ninekirks in the forenoon to the sermon there, that being also the first time he was ever in that church of Ninekirks. And the 19th day of May they went away from me from Brougham Castle to Kirkby Lonsdale where they lay the 19th day at night, and the next night they lay in Barden Tower in Craven, this being the first time that either my Lord of Northampton or his cousin Mordaunt ever lay in that Barden Tower. From whence the 21st day they went onwards on their journey southwards. And he came well to his house at Castle Ashby in Northamptonshire a while after, and the 30th day of the month he came well to his house in Lincoln's Inn Fields at London, to his two children James, Lord Compton, and the Lady Alethea Compton his sister.[160]

Our young Queen Catherine the Infanta of Portugal, daughter to the late King and sister to this King of Portugal, after she had taken her leave of the Queen Dowager her mother, this King of Portugal her brother, and her younger sisters aboard one of our King's great ships riding near Lisbon, took her voyage and landed safely about the 14th of May at Portsmouth in Hampshire, after she had lain upon the seas in her journey from Lisbon ever since about the 23rd of April till now. And our King Charles the second came to her to Portsmouth about the 20th day of this month and married her there in a public manner, the next day being the 21st. And so from thence he and she went the 28th day to Winchester, and so by Farnham Castle to Hampton Court whither they came to lie the 29th of this May. And thither my daughter of Thanet and Lady Frances her daughter went to see this new Queen the 4th of June following, I then lying in Brougham Castle in Westmorland.

This summer did I cause a new brewhouse and bakehouse to be built up in the court within the walls of Brougham Castle in Westmorland whereof one side was built on the old wall towards the north, and the other side on the old wall towards the west. And now also did I cause the old brewhouse and bakehouse to be taken down and the ground to be levelled, which old brewhouse and bakehouse stood near to the Tower of League, so as this removing of it made the

---

160 Compton's son James was now heir to Anne's property in Yorkshire, including Skipton Castle. After his death his sister Alethea became heir to the Yorkshire property. Her death in 1678 reunited the Clifford hereditary lands in the hands of Anne's grandson Nicholas Tufton. Compton's visit was not just social. It was part of his parental duty to safeguard his children's inheritance. Because of the King's Award, Anne was free to leave her property where she desired as the award removed the royal entail.

court larger and handsomer than it was before. And this summer did I cause a kitchen, a stable, a bakehouse and a brewhouse to be built in the court of my castle of Brough in Westmorland within the walls that were lately built there by me, the kitchen, bakehouse, and brewhouse being on the north side and the stable on the south side thereof.

Also this summer did I cause a wall of lime and stone to be built round about that piece of ground which I had taken in about Pendragon Castle in Westmorland being ten quarters in height and about ninety roods in compass with two gates to let in horses or coaches. And within the said wall I caused to be built a stable and coach house, a brewhouse, bakehouse and washhouse, and a little chamber over the gate that is arched.

And on the 1st day of August this year being Lammas day[161] about noon I removed with my family from Brougham Castle in Westmorland to my castle of Appleby in the said county after I had lain in Brougham Castle ever since the 29th of October last till this time, being nine months and two days over. And in this remove of mine I went through Whinfell Park where I had not been during the time of my last lying at Brougham Castle till now. So I now lay in this Appleby Castle till the 15th day of September following that I removed from thence with my family to Brough Castle in the said county and so to Pendragon Castle and so to Barden Tower in Yorkshire whither I came the 26th of the same September to lie there in it.

And this same 1st day of August while I lay in Brougham Castle some [blank] or five hours before my remove from thence to Appleby Castle about seven o'clock in the morning died my dear grandchild James, Lord Compton, in his father's house at Canonbury by Islington near London, he being then the only surviving son of his mother, being about three years and three months old and sixteen days over at his death, and he was buried the 8th of this month at night in the church at Compton in Warwickshire, his dead body being first opened and his lungs found much annoyed with glandells[162] and sticking to his ribs. His sister Lady Alethea Compton being then also at Canonbury at his death, she being the now only surviving child of her mother but his father my Lord of Northampton was then either in Northamptonshire or Warwickshire.

And the 14th day of the month before died that William Coventry who was the third son to my grandchild the Lady Margaret Coventry in her husband the Lord Coventry's house at Croome in Worcestershire being about a year old and was buried the night after in the church there at Croome, I then lying in

---

161 1 August, the feast of St Peter in Chains. It was connected to the end of the hay harvest.
162 Small tumours, from the French *glande*.

Brougham Castle in Westmorland. And the news of his death came first of all to me to Appleby Castle in Westmorland the 5th of this month by a letter from my daughter of Thanet the same day that I heard of my Lord, James Compton's death.

And the 16th day of this August did Sir Christopher Turnor knight, one of the Barons of his Majesty's Exchequer and judge of the assize for this Northern Circuit, come hither to Appleby Castle from Carlisle and he lay here six nights together in the Baron's Chamber, and on Friday following, being the 22nd day about ten o'clock, he went away from hence from me and us here out of this Appleby Castle to Kendal and so to Lancaster to keep the assizes there also. And I now lay here myself in this Appleby Castle while the judge stayed here. And this Baron Turnor was now the only judge of assize for this Northern Circuit though heretofore two judges used to always to come the circuit hither.

The 28th of July in this year a little before I removed from Brougham Castle did our Queen Marie the Frenchwoman,[163] mother to our now King Charles, land at Greenwich in Kent newly come from her journey from Calais in France in a great ship over the seas and so up the river of Thames thither, where she lay for a little while and afterwards continued her journey from thence up the said river of Thames in her ship to London, to her two sons the King and the Duke of York and their wives, I then lying in Brougham Castle in Westmorland. And this Queen had not been in England since about the latter end of January 1661 when she took ship at Portsmouth with her youngest daughter the Princess Henrietta, and so went out of England over seas into France, till this time. And she stayed in England from the said 28th day of July till the [blank] day of [blank] in 1665 that she went over again then into France.[164]

And on the 15th day of September following did I remove with my family out of Appleby Castle in Westmorland into my castle of Brough in the same country where I now lay three nights together, one night in the highest room in Clifford's Tower, and two other nights in the great tower called the Roman Tower, as I did the last time I lay there before. And from thence out of that Brough Castle I removed the 18th day of the same month (going through Kirkby Stephen and Wharton Park near Wharton Hall) into Pendragon Castle in Westmorland where I lay for six nights in the chamber within the Great Chamber, the windows whereof look towards the west and the south, though the three nights that I lay there before I lay in the chamber that is now the Great Chamber there.

And from this Pendragon Castle I removed the 24th day of this month

---

163 Henrietta Marie, Queen consort of Charles I.
164 \And she stayed … then into France/ WD.

and went through Ravenstondale into Mr John Otway the lawyer's house at Ingmer[165] by Sedbergh in Yorkshire where I lay in it that one night. And I was not out of Westmorland since the 11th of October in 1660 till now. And the 25th day from Mr Otway's house I went near Kirkby Lonsdale, within sight of it, and so by Cowan Bridge, Ingleton and Clapham and those ways I had formerly gone, into the inn at Settle where I lay that night and never lay there before. And the next day being the 26th day I came over the moor by Mowlam Water Tarn, where I had not been in nine or ten years before and so into my house called Barden Tower and lay in the same room where I used to lie, and continued to lie in it till the 6th day of May following in 1663 when I then removed from thence with my family into Skipton Castle where I then begun to lie in the chamber wherein I was born into the world, in that part of the castle which was lately repaired by me. And I had not been in this Skipton Castle since the 9th of December 1659 that I removed from thence into Barden Tower, it being a strange and miraculous Providence of God that I should at this great age of seventy-three years come to lie again in the same chamber where I had not lain since I was a child of eight weeks old till now. Proverbs 20.24; Ecclesiastes 8.6; Psalm 116.12–15.

And some five or six weeks before my coming out of Westmorland did my cousin Elizabeth Clifford, Countess of Cork, and her husband Richard Boyle, Earl of Cork, with their five youngest children, two sons and three daughters, go from their house in Whitefriars at London wherein Elizabeth, Countess of Kent,[166] formerly died, onwards on their journey towards Bristol and those parts and so into Wales where at Milford Haven in Pembrokeshire they all went into a ship on the seas wherein they passed over to Ireland either to Cork, Youghall or Lismore where they have houses and arrived safe there within a while after, after they had resided in England for the most part of two years and six months, excepting a little while that my Lord of Cork and his two sons went over into Ireland either the last summer or the summer before, but they came quickly into England again. And now that they all went into Ireland did this Earl of Cork's eldest son's wife, she that was the Lady Jane Seymour and youngest daughter to the widow Duchess of Somerset and her deceased husband the Duke,[167] go over also into Ireland with her husband this Charles Boyle, Lord Dungarvan, by whom she hath had one child already (a daughter) which she left behind her at London with her mother, it being not a year old.[168]

165 Ingmire Hall, build by Otway in 1640.
166 Elizabeth Talbot.
167 Frances Devereux and William Seymour.
168 Elizabeth Boyle, later Countess of Barrymore (1662–1703).

And it was the first time that ever this Lady Dungarvan came into Ireland or went beyond the seas. And her sister Marie is now beyond the seas in Turkey at Constantinople.[169] But they came into England again in the year 1663 and so to their house in Whitefriars where, and in other places in England, they continued till their second daughter Elizabeth came to be married the 11th of April in that year to my eldest grandson Nicholas, Lord Tufton, who by the death of his father the 7th of May following came to be Earl of Thanet. And a little after that marriage in July following they all came down into the North to their house at Londesborough in Yorkshire, from whence, after a while, my Lord of Cork and his Lady with most of their children came to Bolton Abbey in Craven to lie there for a time and in that time they went also into my castle of Skipton and tower of Barden for a while to see them. And about that time did their said second daughter, and her Lord, my grandchild the Earl of Thanet, come hither into this Appleby Castle in Westmorland for a few nights.

In the year of Our Lord God 1663

The 2nd day of April in this year did my grandchild Mr John Tufton come from his journey from London hither unto this Barden Tower to me where I now kissed him with much joy a little before supper, and he now told me how he set forwards on his journey from London hitherwards, from his mother and two of his sisters, Lady Frances and Lady Cecily, the 26th day of March last. For he and they came up thither from Hothfield in Kent from my Lord of Thanet the 16th of the same month, whither his mother and two sisters returned back again the 27th day. And when he now came hither to me, he begun to lie in the best room in this Barden Tower at the end of the Great Chamber where my daughter of Northampton lay when she was last here, and his man John Gently (who is newly come to him) in the room within it. And I had not seen any grandchild of mine since the death of my daughter of Northampton and three of her children till now that I saw this John Tufton, and this was the first time that any of my daughter of Thanet's children ever lay in this Barden Tower. And this grandchild of mine was the more welcome to me in regard he had escaped death very narrowly by a dangerous sickness he had in France the last year, which causes me to have in a thankful remembrance God's great mercies to me and mine. Psalm 23.4–5; Psalm 116.12–13.[170]

169 Mary Seymour, Countess of Winchilsea.
170 Psalm 23.5–6: 'Thou preparest a table before me in the presence of mine enemies: thou anointest my head with oil; my cup runneth over. Surely goodness and mercy shall follow me all the days of my life: and I will dwell in the house of the Lord for ever.' Psalm

And the 6th day of May in this year being Wednesday did I with my grandchild Mr John Tufton and my whole family remove from Barden Tower in Craven (after I had now lain in it ever since the 26th of September last till now) and came the nearest way through the Haw Park to Skipton Castle into the new repaired old buildings there, to lie now for a time in the chamber there wherein myself was born. For though that and the chief parts of the castle were pulled down by command of Cromwell about the end of December 1648 yet did I cause it to be rebuilt in the years 1657, 1658 and 1659. And I was not in this Skipton Castle since the 9th of December 1659 when I went out of it in haste to lie first of all in Barden Tower, till this time that I now came to lie in it again. And though I was near the said castle of Skipton and about the walls of it with my blessed mother about the 12th of October in 1607 when we were then in our journey out of Westmorland towards London, yet did I not come to lie in this old part of the castle wherein I was born since I was carried out of it when I was about eight weeks old with my father and mother and my brother Robert, Lord Clifford, from thence towards London, till this 6th day of May. And it is to be accounted a great and wonderful providence of God that now in the 73rd year of my age, I should come to lie again in that chamber wherein I was born into the world.

And the 25th of January in this year as the same begins on New Year's day died that Mr John Turner, the receiver of my jointure rents in the Isle of Sheppey in Kent, who was husband to Mistress Elizabeth Turner that was a Nicholls, and had served me so many years. And he died in his house at Ramsbury in Wiltshire.

And the 22nd day of May in this year did my grandchild Mr John Tufton go away from hence from me and us here out of this Skipton Castle over Cotter and those ways to Pendragon Castle in Westmorland, this being the first time that either he or any grandchild of mine ever lay in that castle of mine which was lately repaired by me. And from thence he went into Appleby Castle and lay there two nights and the next day he went to Brough Castle where he lay one night, this being the first time that he or any grandchild of mine lay in that Brough Castle, for I repaired it but lately. And from thence the day after he went through Whinfell Park into Brougham Castle where he lay one night. And while he was now in Westmorland he went also into Lowther Hall, Acorn Bank[171] and other places and was at the horse race on Lanwathby moor[172] and came home

---

116.12–13: 'What shall I render unto the Lord for all his benefits toward me? I will take the cup of salvation, and call upon the name of the Lord.'

171 Acorn Bank House, once a medieval Templar hospital much rebuilt by the Dalston family.

172 Five miles north-east of Penrith on the River Eden. Horse racing took place on the moors

well again to me (I thank God) the 29th day of the same month following. And he had not been in Westmorland since the 25th day of June in 1658 that he went thence from Brougham Castle, towards London till now.

The 24th day of July in this year did Mistress Elizabeth Turner,[173] the widow that had served me so many years, come from her journey from London and from York hither to Skipton Castle in the chamber where I was born into the world, so she lay here eighteen nights, the first seven or eight nights in the best chamber in the great half-round tower, and the rest in the chamber called Mistress Widdrington's chamber below.[174] And I had not seen her since the 8th of May in 1660 that she and her husband Mr John Turner and their daughter went away then from me from Barden Tower in Craven towards London till now. And I never saw her husband since then, for he died in his house at Ramsbury in Wiltshire the 25th day of January last.

And there came now hither with her Mr William Edge, the receiver of my Sussex jointure rents, and he lay here in the withdrawing chamber next the gallery the time of his staying here, saving six nights that he went to Manchester in Lancashire amongst his friends and kindred. And the 11th day of August following he and Mistress Turner went from hence from me and my daughter of Thanet, and us here onwards on their journey towards London.

And the 3rd day of August this summer, being Monday, did my daughter the Countess of Thanet with four of her younger sons: Richard, Thomas, Sackville and George Tufton, and her daughter Lady Frances Tufton come hither from their journey from York and from London hither into Skipton Castle in Craven to me about eight o'clock at night into the chamber where I then lay and where I was born into the world. And I then kissed them all with much joy and comfort, it being the first time that I saw my daughter of Thanet or these four younger sons of hers in Skipton Castle or in Craven for it was the first time that my daughter of Thanet or these her four youngest sons ever came to into Craven. Neither did I see her daughter Lady Frances Tufton since she went from me from Skipton Castle the 10th day of September 1659 till now. Nor had I seen my three grandsons Richard, Thomas and Sackville Tufton since they went away with their mother, my daughter of Thanet, from Brougham Castle

---

from at least 1585 though likely much earlier and was patronized by the aristocracy and the gentry by this time.
173   Elizabeth Nicholls.
174   This chamber could have been allocated for the use of a female from the family of Mary Widdrington who married Anne's cousin Sir Francis Howard. The Widdringtons were a long-established family in the area and had a number of connections to the Cliffords in addition to this marriage.

in Westmorland from me the 6th day of September 1658 till now. Nor had I seen my said youngest grandchild George Tufton since the 28th day of July 1656 when he then went away from me from the said Brougham Castle with his mother and his three youngest sisters towards London. And I had not seen my daughter of Thanet herself since she went from me from Appleby Castle in Westmorland towards London with her three youngest daughters, Lady Cecily, Lady Marie and Lady Anne Tufton, on the 20th day of August in 1661 till now.

So as this journey of hers now this August from London to Skipton Castle to me was the fifth journey that she had taken into the North to see me, for she had been four several times with me before in Westmorland. And my daughter of Thanet and these four younger sons of hers and her daughter Lady Frances continued to lie with me in the said Skipton Castle, herself and her daughter Frances lying in the two best rooms in the chief round tower in the old building in Skipton Castle lately repaired by me, and her two youngest sons, Sackville and George, lying in the upper great round room at the end of the gallery, and their brother Thomas in the round room below it, where I formerly used to lie myself, and their brother Richard lying with his brother John Tufton in the great room over the gatehouse all the time (save one night that he lay in the drawing room next the gallery). For their brother John Tufton met his mother and four brothers and sister at York and came hither to Skipton Castle with them and continued to lie in it as formerly all the while they stayed here.

And the 10th day of this August my daughter of Thanet and these five younger sons of hers and her daughter Lady Frances went from Skipton Castle into Barden Tower to see it, which was the first time that she or her four younger sons ever came into this Barden Tower, but they came all back again the same night to me to Skipton Castle. And so after they had lain here twelve nights on the 15th day of the said August about ten o'clock (after I had first kissed her and then her children in the chamber wherein I was born) they went away from me out of this Skipton Castle onwards on their journey towards London. And my grandchild, her son John Tufton, went also with his mother and his brothers and sister the first day's journey to Wetherby but returned back again to me to Skipton Castle the 17th day of that August at night. And the 22nd of the said August my daughter of Thanet and these four younger sons of hers, with her daughter Lady Frances Tufton, came all well to Thanet House in Aldersgate Street at London where they now lay for two nights together because the next day was Sunday. And on the 24th day they went away from thence down into the county towards Hothfield House in Kent whither they came well the next day, being the 25th day, to my Lord of Thanet and his three youngest daughters.

The 29th day of this August did Sir Thomas Twisden and Sir Christopher

Turnor, the King's two judges of assize appointed this year for the Northern Circuit, come from their journey from Carlisle into my castle of Appleby in Westmorland where they lay for four nights together, Judge Twisden in the Baron's Chamber and Judge Turnor in one of the best chambers in Caesar's Tower in which time they kept the assizes at the moot hall in Appleby town. And the 2nd of September following being Wednesday they went away from thence to Kendal in the same county where they lay that night and the next day to Lancaster where they finished their circuit.

And the 7th day of this September in this year did my grandchild Mr John Tufton ride away from this Skipton Castle from me and us here with his man John Gently towards London and so into Kent to his father and mother and many of their children. And I did not see him again till after his father's death which was on the 7th of May 1664, for he came not to me till the 8th of July next following that he came from his journey from thence and from London hither to Appleby Castle in Westmorland to me. And the 30th of this September (a little before my removal from this Skipton Castle) did my cousin Philip, Lord Wharton, and three of his daughters by his second wife, Anne my goddaughter and Margaret and Mary Wharton[175], came from his house called Helaigh Manor[176] in Yorkshire to Skipton as aforesaid to me, where they lay two nights together and then went home again to Helaigh Manor aforesaid.

And the 6th day of this October 1663, after I had lain in Skipton Castle in the chamber there wherein I was born just five months from my coming from Barden Tower, did I remove from thence onwards on my journey towards Westmorland, so as I went to Mr Cuthbert Wade's house at Kilnsey,[177] and lay there that night and the next day from thence, through Kettlewelldale, up Buckden Rakes, and over the Stake into Wensleydale to my cousin Mr Thomas Metcalfe's[178] house at Nappa where I lay also that night and the next day, being the 8th day from thence I went over Cotter in my coach (where I think never coach went before) and over Hellgill Bridge into Westmorland, and so by the chapel of Mallerstang (which I lately repaired), I came into this Pendragon Castle to lie in it again.

And this was the first time I was ever in Kettlewelldale, or went over Buckden Rakes, or the Stake, or Cotter or any of those dangerous places wherein yet God

---

175   Philip, 4th Baron Wharton, his wife Jane Goodwin and their daughters.
176   Healaugh Park Priory, Yorkshire.
177   Kilnsey Old Hall, Yorkshire.
178   His grandmother was Anne's great-aunt, Elizabeth Clifford, who married Sir Christopher Metcalfe of Nappa.

was pleased to preserve me in that journey.[179] And I was not in Westmorland since the 25th day of October in 1662 till now. So now I kept Christmas here in this Pendragon Castle this year, and this was the first time that I ever kept Christmas in it or any of my ancestors before me for three hundred years before or more. And I now lay in it till the 27th day of January that I removed from thence with my family into Appleby Castle in Westmorland.

And while I lay in Pendragon Castle was my son-in-law John Tufton, Earl of Thanet, committed prisoner to the Fleet at London the 21st of December about the business of Sackville College in Sussex.[180] In which imprisonment he continued to lie till the 21nd of January next after that he was released from thence and came home again to his house in Aldersgate Street to my daughter his wife and some of their children.

In the year of Our Lord God 1664

The 27th day of January in this year about ten o'clock in the forenoon did I go out of Pendragon Castle in Westmorland in my coach drawn with six horses and most of my family with me on horseback into Appleby Castle, after I had lain in the said Pendragon Castle ever since the 8th of October last that I came to it with my family from my journey from Skipton Castle in Craven, until now. And now I began to lie in the same chamber in this Appleby Castle where I used formerly to lie, and where I had not been since the 18th of October in 1662 till now. And in which I now continued to lie till the 16th of September following that I removed from thence into Brough Castle in the same county, where I lay for eight nights together till the 24th of that September, and then returned back from thence to this Appleby Castle again.

And before I came away from Pendragon Castle did I, upon the 12th day of this January, purchase of Reynald Cocke of Cawtley near Sedbergh in Yorkshire, lands to the value of eleven pounds per annum for which I paid two hundred and twenty pounds. Which lands I gave for the maintenance of a person qualified to read prayers and homilies of the church of England, and to teach the children of the Dale to write and read English in Mallerstang Chapel for ever. And I did put in to officiate in the said chapel of Mallerstang, Rowland Wright

---

179 This is still a challenging journey over very rugged countryside, but with magnificent views.
180 The financial provision for Sackville college, set up by Richard Sackville's will according to his father Robert's bequest, later came under dispute between the heirs of Edward Sackville 4th Earl of Dorset, and Anne Clifford, John Tufton, and James Compton. This imprisonment was part of the ongoing dispute.

who had been at the said chapel some three or four years before to teach scholars there.

And the 17th day of this March, being Thursday in the evening, did Sir Thomas Twisden, one of the judges of the Court of Common Pleas, at Westminster and Sir Christopher Turnor one of the Barons of the Exchequer, come hither from Kendal and so from Lancaster the day before, into this Appleby Castle where they lay for five nights together, Judge Twisden in the Baron's Chamber and Judge Turner in the best room in Caesar's Tower, sitting here by special commission from the King upon the trials of divers of the traitors in this county that were engaged in the late plot and rising against his Majesty,[181] so as three of them were hanged, drawn and quartered here at Appleby. For otherwise except upon such an occasion, the assizes are but kept once a year for this county. And the 22nd day these judges went away from hence on their journey towards York to keep the assizes there also. And I lay in my own chamber in this Appleby Castle all the time that the judges now lay here.

The 11th day of April being Easter Monday was my first grandchild Nicholas, Lord Tufton, married in a chamber in Clifford's Inn in London town to the Lady Elizabeth Boyle my cousin and goddaughter, second daughter to Richard, Earl of Cork, by his wife my cousin Elizabeth Clifford, Countess of Cork.[182] And my said first grandchild and the said Lady Elizabeth Boyle were married together by one Mr Byfield who is chaplain to her said father, I then lying in my own chamber in Appleby Castle in Westmorland.[183] And this new married couple begun first of all to lie together in that house in Whitefriars at London,

---

181 The Kaber Rigg plot. This plot was part of northern republican resistance to the government of Charles II. The Kaber Plot leaders, including Robert Atkinson, Anne's tenant, intended to force Charles to fulfil the promises outlined in the Treaty of Breda. When few men joined the rebellion the plot dissipated, and a number of their leaders, including Atkinson, were arrested. Atkinson was executed for his part in this plot, see below. See NA, ASSI 45/6/3, Northern Circuit: Criminal Depositions and Case Papers, 1663.

182 Nicholas Tufton had long resisted this marriage to his cousin, Elizabeth Boyle, granddaughter to Henry Clifford, 5th Lord Clifford, which reunited the Clifford lines of Anne's father George and her uncle Francis Clifford. Instead he pursued Annabel Benn, Countess of Kent, who was widowed in 1651. He agreed to the marriage with Elizabeth only after Annabel made clear she would never marry him. See CAS, Kendal, WDHOTH/44, letter, 17 May 1664.

183 The bride's mother, Elizabeth Clifford, Countess of Cork, describes the wedding in her diary: 'April the 11th 1664 being Easter Munday my Daughter Bettye [Elizabeth] was marryed to the Ld: Tufton in my Chamber at Clifforde's Inne, by Mr Byfield our owne Chaplain there being present my Ld: [Richard Boyle], my self, my son Richard, Sir Henry Jones & honest Graham our Sollicitor, God of his mercy blesse them with long life & many happye dayes, Amen.' Chatsworth House, Derbyshire, Cork MSS, misc. 5, Diary of Elizabeth Clifford, fol. 8r.

which was once part of the priory there where her father and mother and most of their family now lie.

And the 7th day of May being Saturday about three o'clock in the morning died my son-in-law John Tufton, Earl of Thanet, in his house called Thanet House in Aldersgate Street at London, in those lodgings that look towards the street which he had built about twenty years since with freestone very magnificently, and my first child, his wife the Lady Margaret, Countess of Thanet, and their five youngest sons and four youngest daughters, lay in that house of his when he died. And he was fifty-five years old the 15th day of December last before his death.

And the 11th day of this month was the dead body of my son-in-law John Tufton, Earl of Thanet carried out of his house in Aldersgate Street where he died the 7th of that month and so over London Bridge down into the country into the church at Rainham in Kent and was buried unopened in the vault there by his father and mother and his second child my grandchild the Lady Anne Tufton, his brother and his five younger sons and his daughters Lady Frances and Lady Cecily Tufton being there present at his burial, but his eldest son was not, I lying in my own chamber in Appleby Castle in Westmorland both when he died and when he was buried.

And the 8th day of July following did his second son, my grandchild John Tufton, come from his journey from Thanet House in Aldersgate Street in London town, from his mother and some of his brothers and sisters, hither to Appleby Castle in Westmorland to me, to my great joy and comfort, I having not seen him since the death of his father, my son-in-law John Earl of Thanet, not in eight months before till now for the 7th day of September last in 1663 [when] this grandchild of mine went from Skipton from me onwards on his journey towards London. And now, in this journey of his from thence hither he lay two nights by the way the 5th and 6th of this month, in the highest chamber of the great round tower at Skipton Castle, over that round chamber at the end of the long gallery there where I formerly used to lie. And the 7th day at night he lay in the inn at Kirkby Lonsdale from whence the next day (as aforesaid) he came hither to Appleby Castle where he now continued to lie till the 20th day of this month. Following that he went with his mother and his three youngest sisters from hence to Brougham Castle and lay there with them four nights, till the 24th of the same month that he came back again hither with them to this Appleby Castle. From whence, after he had lain two nights more in it, on the 26th day he went away from me and from his mother and sisters up towards London, about four days before they went and he came well to Thanet House in Aldersgate Street there the 2nd day of the month following.

29th of this July did my grandchild Nicholas Tufton, Earl of Thanet, and his wife my cousin and goddaughter the young Countess of Thanet come hither to me and to his brother John Tufton, into my chamber in this Appleby Castle in Westmorland about seven o'clock in the evening, where I kissed them both with much joy and comfort, it being the first time I saw any grandchild of mine that was an Earl. Neither had I seen him since I saw him in the court of this Appleby Castle when he went away from hence with his father and mother towards Croome in Worcestershire, and from thence up to London in 1653 till this day. And it was the first time this new married wife of his ever came into Westmorland, neither had I seen her since I saw her and her father and mother (the Earl and Countess of Cork) and her brothers and sisters in Craven in 1650, when they were then with me at Skipton Castle and I with them at Bolton Abbey, till this time. And this Earl my grandchild and his wife came now hither to me from Londesborough, York, and Topcliffe and came today over Stainmore hither, lying the night before in the poor inn at Bowes and by the way hither from Bowes they went into Brough Castle for a while to see it. And now my said grandchild the Earl of Thanet and the Countess his wife continued to lie in this Appleby Castle for eleven nights together in the Baron's Chamber. And whilst they now lay here they went into Brougham Castle for a good while and into Edenhall, Lowther Hall and Acornbank. And he and his brother John Tufton went into Pendragon Castle to see it, but his wife did not go with them, she being a little indisposed that day. And upon the 9th of August following after I had then kissed them in my chamber in Appleby Castle, did this Earl of Thanet and the Countess his wife with their company go away again from hence out of Westmorland over Stainmore into the inn at Cataract Bridge towards York and Londesborough.[184] But my grandchild John Tufton returned back again to me to Appleby Castle after he had brought his brother and sister onwards upon their journey as far as Brough. And some two days after, my said grandchild the Earl of Thanet and his wife met my Lord of Cork and his wife about York, and went with them to their house at Londesborough for they were lately come from Bolton Abbey and out of Craven thither again.

The 16th day of August in this year, about six or seven o'clock in the evening, did my daughter Margaret, Countess Dowager of Thanet, with her three youngest daughters: Lady Cicely, Lady Marie and Lady Anne Tufton, and their company,

---

184 This visit is also described by Elizabeth Clifford, see Diary of Elizabeth Clifford, fol. 9r–v. The marriage of Nicholas Tufton and Elizabeth Boyle and the subsequent visits between the two families were intended to heal the rift in the family caused by the inheritance battles at the beginning of the century.

come from their journey from London over Stainmore, and those ways, hither to me into this Appleby Castle in Westmorland, where I now kissed them with much joy and comfort, it being the first time I saw this daughter of mine, or any of her daughters since she was a widow by the death of her Lord the late Earl of Thanet (who died the 7th day of May last) or in some time before, for I had not seen her since the 15th of August last in 1663 that she went away from me from Skipton Castle in Craven with her four youngest sons: Richard, Thomas, Sackville and George Tufton, her daughter Lady Frances Tufton up towards London, until now. Nor had I seen these three youngest daughters of hers since the 20th day of August in 1661 that they went from me from this Appleby Castle in Westmorland up towards London, with my said daughter their mother (who had been then here to see me with them) till now.

And now they continued to lie in the Baron's Chamber here for four nights together. And the 20th day, by reason of the two judges coming hither to keep the assizes they went from hence with my grandchild John Tufton, into Brougham Castle in this county, where they lay for four nights more, during the time of the assizes, my daughter of Thanet and her youngest daughter Lady Anne lying in the chamber there wherein I formerly used to lie, wherein my noble father was born and my blessed mother died (which was the first time that she or any of her children ever lay in that chamber) and Lady Cecily and Lady Mary lying in the middle chamber of the greatest tower there. And my daughter of Thanet had not been in Brougham Castle since the 6th of September 1658 that she went from thence from me with her sons Richard, Thomas and Sackville Tufton up towards London, till now this 20th of August. Nor had her said three youngest daughters been in that castle since the 28th of July 1656 that they went from thence with their mother, my said daughter, up towards London until now. And this was the first time that any of them lay in that castle when I lay not there myself. But on the 24th of this August, when those four nights were past, they and their company came from thence back again into this Appleby Castle, where they lay for six nights more, all save my said grandchild John Tufton who lay but two nights in this castle, for the 26th day he began his journey from hence up towards London (as aforesaid). And upon this 30th day of the same August, my daughter of Thanet and her said three youngest daughters and their company, after I had first kissed them as taking my leave of them, went away from me out of this Appleby Castle, about eight or nine a clock in the morning, onwards on their journey towards London again, whither they came safe and well the 8th day of the month following to Thanet House in Aldersgate Street in London town to lie there in it for a time.

And the 20th day of this August being Saturday in the evening did the two judges of the assize for this Northern Circuit, Sir Thomas Twisden and Sir Christopher Turnor, come hither from Carlisle and Newcastle and those places, to keep the assizes here at Appleby for this county of Westmorland as usually. And they lay here in this Appleby Castle for four nights together, Judge Twisden in the Baron's Chamber and Judge Turnor in the best room in Caesar's Tower. In which time they kept the assizes in the moot hall in Appleby town where Robert Atkinson, one of my tenants in Mallerstang and that had been my great enemy, was condemned to be hanged, drawn and quartered as a traitor to the King for having a hand in the late plot and conspiracy[185] so as he was executed accordingly the 1st day of the month following.

And the 24th of this August being Wednesday they went away from hence to Kendal in this county where they lay that night and the next day to Lancaster to keep the assizes there also and to finish their circuit, I lying in my own chamber in this Appleby Castle all the time of these assizes.

The 16th day of September in this year, after I had lain in my chamber in Appleby Castle in Westmorland ever since the 27th of January last that I came to it from Pendragon Castle, did I remove with some of my family out of my said castle of Appleby into my castle of Brough in the same county where I lay for eight nights together, the first four nights in the uppermost chamber in that they call the Clifford's Tower there, and the other four in the middle chamber of the great Roman Tower there. And when they were past, on the 24th of the same month, I returned back into my castle of Appleby again, into my chamber in it, where I now continued to lie for thirty-one nights. And when they were past on Tuesday the 25th of the month following I removed from Appleby Castle into Brougham Castle in the same county. And I had not been in Brough Castle aforesaid since the 18th day of September in 1662 till this 16th day.

The 8th day of July in this year after they had taken their leaves of their mother, and most of their younger brothers and sisters a day or two before at Thanet House in Aldersgate Street in London town, did my two grandchildren Mr Sackville Tufton and Mr George Tufton embark themselves at Dover in Kent, and so sailed over the seas into France whither they came safe and well to Paris within a while after, this being the first time these two grandchildren of mine were ever beyond the seas or out of England. And Sir Thomas Billingsley

---

185 Robert Atkinson had served as the Parliamentarian governor of Appleby Castle. He was one of the leaders of the tenant disputes with Anne. His involvement with the Kaber Rigg plot was his downfall. See CAS, D/MUS 5/5/6/3, Execution of Captain Robert Atkinson, 1664.

who had served their grandfather of Dorset,[186] went along with them as their governor. And after a short stay at Paris they went from thence to Sedan.

The 25th day of October in this year being Tuesday, after I had lain in Appleby Castle in Westmorland ever since the 27th of January last past that I came to it from Pendragon Castle (excepting only eight nights that I lay in Brough Castle, from the 16th of the last month till the 24th of the same), did I this 25th day of October (as aforesaid) remove with my family out of my said castle of Appleby into my castle of Brougham in the same county where I had not lain since the 1st of August in 1662 till now. And where I now continued to lie in the chamber wherein my noble father was born and my blessed mother died, till the 1st day of August in the year following that I removed from thence into Appleby Castle with my family to lie there for a time. So as I now continued to lie in this Brougham Castle for nine months together and seven days over.

In the year of our Lord God 1665

The 23rd day of February in this year between eleven and twelve o'clock in the forenoon was my grandchild the Lady Frances Tufton, now second daughter to my daughter of Thanet and her deceased Lord, married in the chapel in Thanet House in Aldersgate Street at London by Mr Hinde,[187] my daughter of Thanet's chaplain, to Mr Henry Drax.[188] Which grandchild of mine had been once or twice in the Low Countries for the cure of the rickets, but thanks be to God she came now to be well married. And after she and her said husband had lain in Thanet House in Aldersgate Street some eight or nine nights they went away from thence into her husband's house in Lincoln's Inn Fields to live there in it fore a while, and afterwards they went into his house at Hackney some three or four miles from London to live there in it, I lying at the time of her marriage in Brougham Castle in Westmorland in the chamber there wherein my father was born and my blessed mother died. And she died in labour of her first child (to my great grief) the 22nd of November following at Buckwell in Kent, the child dying in her a little before. And she and it were buried together in Rainham church in Kent the 15th of December after that.[189]

186 He is listed in the Knole catalogue, seated at the parlour table.
187 Likely Samuel Hinde, incumbent of St Mary's church, Dover, and later chaplain to Charles II.
188 This was a love match. Margaret Sackville wrote to Anne Clifford, 'I hope in God it will be happy for her, she liked well of it herself'. CAS, Kendal, WDHOTH/44, letter, 23 February 1665.
189 \And she died … December after that/ WD. Frances's sister-in-law Elizabeth Boyle wrote to Cecily Tufton, Lady Hatton (Frances's sister), describing Frances's labour and death:

About the 29th day of June in this year being St Peter's day did our Queen Marie the French woman, Queen Dowager and mother to our King Charles the 2nd, go out of Somerset House and out of London town, cross over the River Thames to Lambeth and so by easy days' journeys to Dover in Kent, her two sons, our King Charles and James, Duke of York; Prince Rupert, the Duke of Monmouth, and many others of the nobility bringing her onwards on her journey as far as Dover aforesaid where they then all took their leaves of her as she was on shipboard in the seas. From whence she crossed the seas in one of the King's ships and landed safely at Calais, and from thence went to Paris in France in the beginning of July following. And this Queen Marie had stayed in England ever since the 28th of July in 1662 that she then came out of France into England, this being the eleventh or twelfth time that she hath passed and crossed the seas to and fro between England and beyond the seas, so as from her first coming into England to this going over of hers now into France was just forty years the 12th of this month of June. And some few days before her going from London this Queen Dowager took her leave of Queen Catherine, her son our King's wife at Hampton Court.

And this year 1665 and the beginning of the year following was there a great plague in the city and suburbs of London, whereof there died for several weeks together above 8000 a week, the like whereof was never known in London before.[190]

> 'She had pains a Saturday and Sunday, but Mrs Baker [the midwife] believed it was not her labour; and so made nothing of it. When I came a Monday morning I found her in great pain, which continued till night when her water broke, and the midwife said the Child came wrong. I had prevailed with Mr Drax to send to Canterbury for a Doctor Peters who is very famous for his skill, and he was in the house ready, if there were reason, but we were desirous if possible to save the life of the child by not using forcible means till it needs must, but her pains continuing all Monday night without any profit to her labour and the midwife finding by some tokens the child was dead, she desired Doctor Peters would make use of his skill, for it was past hers. My poor sister [Frances] seemed content that he should, only desired him to put her to as little pain as her could and seemed very little discouraged but prayed as she had done all along'. Elizabeth Boyle continues to describe in harrowing detail Frances's suffering as the doctor attempted to extract the child. She recalls that finally 'the Doctor having told me that all hopes of her life was gone, I desired the minister to advertise her of her end ... she told him she was very willing to die and hoped God would receive her'. Elizabeth Boyle notes that Henry Drax never left his wife's side throughout this whole period, but 'held one of her knees in her greatest torment'. She ends this sad tale by observing that 'the day after she died she was opened and the child lay a very right at the birth [but] ... her backbone was so bowed, as he [Dr Peters] said it was impossible to make passage so much as for a limb of the child' (NAS, FH 4412, letter, November 1665). Frances Tufton, as Anne's records above, suffered from rickets that resulted in a curvature of her spine making Frances unable to deliver the child. The complications related to childbirth in rickets sufferers were known in the period, see Wendy D. Churchill, *Female Patients in Early Modern Britain* (2012), p. 42.

190 The London death toll was somewhere between 80,000 and 100,000 in 1665. See A. Lloyd Moote and Dorothy C. Moote, *The Great Plague* (2004), p. 11.

The 1st day of August this year after I had lain nine months and seven days over in Brougham Castle in Westmorland in the chamber where my noble father was born and my blessed mother died, did I remove with my family out of the said Brougham Castle into my castle of Appleby in Westmorland. And I came by the way thither through some part of Whinfell park where I had not been since this day three years till now. And I now continued to lie in this Appleby Castle, till the 10th day of November following that I removed from hence with my family into Brough Castle in the same county.

And this first of August also did my daughter of Thanet and her three youngest daughters, Cicely, Marie and Anne, with her family remove from out of their hired house at Epsom in Surry where they drunk the waters into Bolebroke House in Sussex, her house of inheritance by her father where they now continued to lie.

And this was the first time my daughter of Thanet came to lie in the Bolebroke House after she was first a widow or in a good many years before, and the first time her three youngest daughters were ever in it. And her eldest son the Earl of Thanet and his lady and her other three sons that are now in England and her daughter Lady Frances Drax and her husband came thither to see her for a time in the said Bolebroke House, where she [Margaret Sackville] had been delivered of her said first son now Earl of Thanet, whose wife came then also thither with him to see her. [191]

The 19th day of this August did Sir Richard Rainsford, one of the Barons of his Majesty's Exchequer and now judge of the assize for this Northern Circuit, come hither from Carlisle to keep the assizes here at Appleby, where he now continued to lie in the Baron's Chamber for five nights together, till the 24th of this month that he went from hence to Kendal and the next day to Lancaster to keep the assizes there also, and to finish his circuit. And my cousins Sir Philip Musgrave and his son Christopher and my cousin Sir John Lowther of Lowther lay here also most part of the assizes.

And while the assizes were kept here did my cousin Charles Howard, Earl of Carlisle, and young Mr Fenwick that married his eldest daughter come hither to me into this Appleby Castle the 21st of this month, and lay here that night in the Great Tower as they were in their journey to York, to attend the Duke of York there, which was the first time I saw my said cousin the Earl of Carlisle since he was ambassador for our King in Muscovia, Sweden and Denmark, or in some five or six years till now.

The 10th day of November in this year being Friday after I had lain in Appleby

---

191 \whose wife came ... to see her/ H1.

Castle in Westmorland ever since the 1st of August last being three months and some nine days over, in the chamber in it where I formerly used to lie, and wherein I have lain long since with my blessed mother when I was a maid, did I remove from thence with my family out of the said Appleby Castle into my castle of Brough in the same county where I had not been since the 24th day of September in the last year 1664 till this day. And where I now begun to lie in the highest round chamber in Clifford's Tower till the 19th of April following that I removed from thence with my family into Pendragon Castle in the same county. And during the time I lay in this Brough Castle did I keep my Christmas in it which was the first Christmas that I ever kept in the said castle nor had any of my ancestors done it since the year 1521, it being then burnt down, when Henry, Lord Clifford my father's great-grandfather, then lay in the said castle about two years and somewhat more before the said Henry, Lord Clifford's death.

The 22nd day of November in this year about one o'clock in the afternoon (to my unspeakable grief) died my dear grandchild the Lady Frances Drax who was my daughter of Thanet's third daughter but sixth child, and was born in her father's house called Thanet House in Aldersgate Street in London town the 23rd of March in 1642 as the year begins on New Year's day, I then lying in a hired house in the city of Bath in Somersetshire. And she was married in the same Thanet House the 23rd of February last to Mr Henry Drax. And she died (as aforesaid) this 22nd of November in a hired house of her husband's at Buckwell in Kent near Hothfield, being then in labour of her first child which was a son, of whom she could not be delivered for the child was dead within her a few hours before her own death. And whilst she was in labour did my daughter of Thanet her mother begin her journey from Bolebroke in Sussex toward Buckwell aforesaid to her, but hearing of her death before she came thither, she returned immediately back to Bolebroke again, where she lay when her said daughter was buried which was on the 15th of December being the month next following. And her child was buried there together with her in the vault of Rainham church in Kent by her father and grandfather, there being present at their burial several of her brothers and sisters as namely the Earl of Thanet and his Lady, Mr John Tufton, Mr Richard Tufton, Mr Thomas Tufton and Lady Cecily Tufton, and also many of their neighbours and relations. And both when she died and was buried did I lie in my own chamber in Clifford's Tower in Brough Castle in Westmorland where I heard first of all the sad news of her death the 6th day of the said December.

In the year of our Lord God 1666

The 2nd day of January in this year about six or seven o'clock in the evening did there a great fire happen in the highest chamber but one of the Great Roman Tower here in this Brough Castle in Westmorland, which burnt a bed and the curtains and valance and all the furniture belonging to it, and a tapestry hanging that hung behind the bed. But before it got any further hold it was, by God's merciful Providence, discovered and quenched so as the tower itself received no harm. And I then lay in my own chamber in Clifford Tower in the said castle.

The 19th day of April in this year did I remove with my family out of Brough Castle in Westmorland and so went through Wharton Park near to Wharton Hall, into my castle of Pendragon in the same county, after I had lain in the said Brough Castle in the uppermost room of Clifford's Tower since the 10th day of November last till now, being five months and some nine days over. And at the time of my now lying in Brough Castle died my dear grandchild the Lady Frances Drax the 22nd of November in a hired house of her husband's at Buckwell in Kent near Hothfield (as is above mentioned). And the said 19th day in the morning before I came away from the said Brough Castle did I go for a while into the great Roman Tower there, into the best room in it, where I used sometime to lie, and into the lower room where Gabriel Vincent died the 12th of February before to my great grief and sorrow.[192] And I had not been in that great Roman Tower since the 24th of September 1664 (when I had then lain in it for four nights, and removed thence to Appleby Castle) till now that I came into it again for a while. And I had not been in this Pendragon Castle since the 27th of January 1664 as the year begins on New Year's day, till this 19th of April that I now came into it again, and where I continued to lie in my own chamber there that looks to the south and west till the six day of August following that I removed from thence with my family towards Skipton Castle in Craven.

And a little before my coming away from Brough Castle in the latter end of March or beginning of April did my two grandchildren, Mr Sackville Tufton and his brother Mr George Tufton with their governor Sir Thomas Billingsley, go from Sedan in France into upper Germany to the Prince Elector Palatine's

---

192 He was her steward and the director of her building works in the north. He was buried in St Michael's church, Brough, and the inscription on his tomb reads: 'Gabriel Vincent, Steward to the Right Hon: Anne Clifford, Countess Dowager of Pembroke, Dorset and Montgomery, Chief Director of all her buildings in the North, who died in the Roman Tower of Brough Castle like a good Christian 12 Feb. 1665, looking for the Second Coming of Our Saviour'.

Court at Heidelberg.[193] And the reason of this their so sudden departure out of France into Germany was because of the wars that are now between England and France. And in that time that they remained at Heidelberg was my said grandchild George Tufton sorely shot and wounded in the wars there.[194]

And the 6th day of this August, after I had lain in Pendragon Castle ever since the 19th of April before, did I remove out of the said Pendragon Castle and went into the chapel of Mallerstang by the way for a while, it being the first time I was ever in that chapel, and so over Cotter and those dangerous ways into one Mr John Coleby's house near Bambridge[195] in Wensleydale where I lay that night with my women servants and some three of my men servants (my other servants lying at Askrigg and Bambridge). And this was the first time I ever lay in the said house. And the next day being the 7th of August I went over the Stake and down Buckden Rakes and so into Mr Wade's house at Kilnsey where I then lay in it that one night (having lain in it one night before in my former remove from Skipton Castle to Pendragon Castle in Westmorland). And from thence the next day being the 8th of this month, I came safe and well into my said castle of Skipton in Craven and so into my own chamber in it wherein I was born into the world, where now I continued to lie for five months and two days that is to say from this 8th of August till the 10th of January following that I then removed with my family to Barden Tower in Craven to lie in it for a time. And I had not been in these ways over Cotter and the Stake since the 6th, 7th and 8th days of October in 1663 till now, neither was I in Skipton Castle since the said 6th of October in 1663 till now.

The 27th day of this August being Monday did my daughter Margaret now Countess Dowager of Thanet, with her three youngest daughters: Lady Cecily, Lady Mary and Lady Anne Tufton, come hither to me from their journey from London and today from the inn at Wetherby into this Skipton Castle a little before supper where I kissed them all with much joy and contentment in the chamber here wherein I was born into the world, I having not seen any of them since the 30th day of August in 1664 when they went away from me from Appleby Castle in Westmorland back towards London until now. And now they continued to lie here in this castle for twelve nights together, my daughter and her daughter Lady Cecily in the middle round room at the end of the long gallery here (where formerly I used to lie myself) and Lady Marie and Lady

---

193 Charles Louis was the Elector Palatine (from 1648 to 1680) when Anne's two grandsons went into Germany. He was the son of the Princess Elizabeth Stuart, whom Anne knew in her youth.
194 This wound would ultimately kill the young George, see below.
195 Coleby Hall, Askrigg, Yorkshire (also called Bowbridge Hall).

Anne in the room above it, which was the first time my daughter of Thanet or these three daughters of hers ever lay in that round tower, though her daughter Lady Frances Tufton (since deceased) had lain in it when she was here.

And this is the seventh time that my said daughter hath come into the North to see me, where she hath been five times with me in Westmorland, and this is the second time she hath been with me here at Skipton. But it is the first time these three youngest daughters of hers were ever here, though they had been with me before in Westmorland both at Brougham Castle and Appleby Castle. And the 31st of this month during their stay here these three young ladies my grandchildren with their three women – Mistress Jane Paulett, Mistress Bridget Billingsley and Katherine Preston – went in my daughter, their mother's coach, with six horses out of this Skipton Castle into my tower of Barden where they dined, and from thence into Mr Sheffield Clapham's house at Beamsley where they stayed a while and from thence into my blessed mother's almshouse there at Beamsley and returned back again into this Skipton Castle a little before supper time, this being the first time that any of my said three grandchildren were ever in Barden Tower or in Beamsley Hall or in the almshouse at Beamsley, which was founded by my blessed mother. So when these twelve nights were past my daughter of Thanet and her said three daughters and their company went away from hence from me after I had first kissed them, as taking my leave of them and so from this Skipton Castle the 8th day of September following about nine o'clock in the morning onwards on their journey towards London again.

And the 1st day of June in this year, whilst I lay in Pendragon Castle with my family, did Mr William Russell, second son to my cousin the now Earl of Bedford and his wife,[196] come from his journey from their house called Woburn in Bedfordshire thither to Pendragon Castle to me where he lay that one night and the next day he continued his journey into Scotland, calling by the way at Naworth Castle in Cumberland to see my cousin the Earl of Carlisle and his Lady that is his cousin.[197] And this was the first time that ever my said cousin Russell was in Westmorland or in any part of my inheritance or so far northward. And about the latter end of that month or the next after he came well home again to his father and mother to their said house at Woburn in Bedfordshire.

And whilst my daughter of Thanet and her said three youngest daughters were with me here at Skipton Castle did the two judges of assize for this Northern Circuit, Sir Christopher Turnor and Sir Richard Rainsford, two of the Barons of

---

196 William Russell, Lord Russell, and Rachel Wriothesley. William Russell was executed in 1683 after being implicated in the Rye House Plot to assassinate Charles II.
197 Charles Howard, 1st Earl of Carlisle, and Mary Howard, daughter of Mary Butler and Edward Howard, 1st Baron Howard of Escrick.

his Majesty's Exchequer, come into Appleby Castle in Westmorland the 1st day of this September in the evening (being Saturday) where they now lay for four nights together, Judge Turner in the Baron's Chamber and Judge Rainsford in the best room in Caesar's Tower. And after those four nights were past and that they had ended the assizes there at Appleby, those two judges of [the assizes] went away from thence on Wednesday following, being the 5th of that month about two o'clock, towards Kendal where they lay that night, and the next day to Lancaster to keep the assizes there also and to end their circuit.

The 2nd day of this September being Sunday about two o'clock in the morning, whilst my daughter of Thanet and her three youngest daughters lay here in Skipton Castle with me, and whilst the said judges of assize for this Northern Circuit lay in my castle of Appleby in Westmorland to keep the assizes in the town there, did there a great fire break out in several places and houses within the walls of the city of London,[198] which continued raging there for about four days together before it could be quenched. And in that time this terrible fire consumed and burnt down not only Baynard's Castle, but also Great Dorset House and Little Dorset House, which Little Dorset House was once my jointure house, and in all which three places I had spent much of my time when I was wife to my first and second husbands. And eighty parish churches with most of all their parishes were consumed, whereof the great Cathedral church of St Paul was one, which had been one of the stateliest and ancientest fabrics when it was standing in all Christendom. But in all this great desolation Thanet House in Aldersgate Street, my daughter of Thanet's jointure house, was then preserved.

In the year of our Lord God 1667

The 10th day of January in this year (after I had lain in Skipton Castle in that chamber within the old walls of it wherein I was born into the world, ever since the 8th of August last) did I remove from thence with my family, and so went through the Haw Park and by Shibden and Halton and those ways, I in my horselitter, and some of my chief women in my coach, into my house or tower of Barden in Craven where I had not been since the 6th day of May in 1663 till now and where I now continued to lie (in the same chamber I formerly used to lie in) till the 29th day of July following that I removed from hence with my family towards Pendragon and Appleby Castles in Westmorland.

And so this late Christmas did I lie all the time of it in my own chamber

---

198   The Great Fire of London raged from 2 to 5 September. Many of the places that Anne knew in her youth and her married life were destroyed.

within the old walls of Skipton Castle where I was born into the world which was the first Christmas I ever kept in that chamber since I was born, though I had lain for several Christmases since I was last a widow (by the death of my Lord the Earl of Pembroke) in the other part of that castle which was built by my great-grandfather of Cumberland,[199] in the middle chamber in the great round tower at the east of that long gallery there.

And about the beginning of this June in this year 1667 did my cousin Elizabeth Clifford, Countess of Burlington and Cork, and the Earl her husband and their eldest and now only son[200] and their youngest daughter save one, the Lady Anne Boyle, come from that house called Berkshire House at Saint James at London down to their house at Londesborough in Yorkshire to lie there in it for a time.

And about the 19th day of the same month of June did the said Richard, Earl of Burlington and Cork, go from his said house at Londesborough, from his wife and daughter Anne and two of his son's children,[201] either to Chester or to Liverpool in Lancashire, from whence he crossed the seas in a ship to Dublin in Ireland and after some stay there he went to some of his own houses in Ireland.

And about the [blank] day of this June did my grandchild Nicholas, Earl of Thanet, and his wife come from their house at Hothfield in Kent to Gravesend in the same county and from thence by water in a barge up to London where they lay two or three nights in a lodging there and then he went down again to his said house at Hothfield. But his wife came down from London to Londesborough house in Yorkshire to her mother and sister Anne, and two of her eldest brother's children for a time.

And the 29th day of this June at night, the said young Countess of Thanet came from Londesborough house in Yorkshire and from York, to me, to Barden Tower in Craven in that county, where she stayed with me for four nights together, she and her two women lying in the two low rooms at the west end of the Great Chamber there, which are over the kitchen, and when those four nights were passed she and her company went away from thence, from me and my family, back to Londesborough again. And from thence about Michaelmas following she went with her mother the Countess of Cork and Burlington up to her father where, after a short stay at Berkshire House with her mother, the said young Countess of Thanet went down to Hothfield House in Kent to her Lord.

199 She is speaking of the Tudor wing of Skipton Castle built by Henry, 1st Earl of Cumberland, for the royal bride Eleanor Brandon (niece to Henry VIII) who married his son, Henry, 2nd Earl of Cumberland.
200 The Boyles' second son, Richard, died at the Battle of Lowestoft in 1665.
201 The sons of Charles Boyle: Charles Boyle, later 4th Viscount Dungarvan, and Henry Boyle, later 1st Baron Carleton.

And the 29th of July in this year, after I had lain in my house or tower of Barden in Craven, ever since the 10th day of January last (being six months and some nineteen days over) did I remove from thence with my family towards my castle of Pendragon in Westmorland. So as that day I went into one John Symondson's house at Starbotton[202] in Craven, when I lay that one night (which was the first time I ever lay there). And from thence, the next day being the 30th day, I went up Buckden Raikes and over the Stake and so out of Craven, into Mr John Coleby's house in Wensleydale, where I lay that one night (which was the second time I had lain there). And from thence the next day (being the 31st day) I went up Cotter Hill and over Hellgill Bridge, and by Mallerstang chapel, and those ways, into my said castle of Pendragon, where I had not been since the 6th of August last in 1666 until now, and where I now continued to lie (in the chamber within the Great Chamber there, the windows whereof are towards the south and west) but for eight nights together.

And when they were past upon the 8th day of August in this year I removed from my said castle of Pendragon with my family, into my castle of Appleby in the same county, where I had not been since the 10th day of November in the year 1665 till now, and where I now continued to lie in the same chamber I used to lie in till the 18th day of October following that I removed from thence to Brougham Castle in the same county to lie in it with my family for a time. And in all these late journeys of mine from Skipton to Barden, and from thence to Pendragon and so to Appleby, I rid all the way in my horselitter.

And the 24th day of August, being Saturday in the evening, did the two judges of assize for this Northern Circuit namely Sir Christopher Turnor and Sir Richard Rainsford, two of the Barons of his Majesty's Exchequer, come from the city of Carlisle in Cumberland from holding the assizes there hither into this Appleby Castle in Westmorland, where I and my family now lie and where they now lay for four nights together, Judge Turnor in the best room in Caesar's Tower and Judge Rainsford in the Baron's Chamber. And after those four nights were past (the assizes here at Appleby being ended) they went away from hence from me on Wednesday the 28th of this month about eleven o'clock towards Kendal where they lay that night. And the next day they went to Lancaster to keep the assizes there also and to end their circuit. And these two judges have come this circuit several times before. And my cousins Sir Philip Musgrave of Edenhall in Cumberland and Sir John Lowther of Lowther in this county lay here also, most part of these assizes as usual.

---

202 Starbotton Old Hall was the property of the Symondson family, but was heavily damaged in the great storm of 1686 which damaged much of the village of Starbotton.

And presently after these assizes ended was the peace proclaimed in Appleby, as elsewhere throughout the kingdom, which had been concluded of but last month at Breda between our King Charles the second (by his Ambassadors Denzill Lord Hollis and Mr Henry Coventry)[203] on the one part, and the States of the United Provinces and the two kings of France and Denmark, on the other part, to the general good of Christendom, and to the joy and satisfaction of our King and all his good subjects after there had been hot wars between them by sea for almost three years last past.

And the 18th of October in this year, after I had lain in Appleby Castle in Westmorland (in the chamber wherein I used to lie) ever since the eight day of August last, being two months and some ten days over, did I remove from thence in my horselitter with my family (going along the usual high road and not through Whinfell Park) into Brougham Castle in the same county, in which castle of Brougham I had not been since the 1st day of August in 1665 till now and where I now continued to lie, as I use to do, in the same chamber wherein my noble father was born and my blessed mother died, till the 26th day of June next following that I removed from thence back again into Appleby Castle aforesaid, to lie there in it for a time.

In the year of our Lord God 1668

The 12th day of February in this year, I then lying in Brougham Castle in Westmorland, I first of all came to know that my grandchild the Lady Cecilia Tufton, my daughter of Thanet's fourth daughter and seventh child, was married to Mr Christopher Hatton, eldest son to Christopher, Lord Hatton of Kirkby in Northamptonshire,[204] privately the 12th day of February in the last year 1667 as the same begins on New Year's day, I then lying in Barden Tower in Craven. And that they were married together by Doctor Evans, one of the Duchess of York's chaplains, in Sir Charles Littleton's house in the Mews, he that is cupbearer to the King, none but he and his Lady[205] being present at the marriage.

And on the 2nd day of March this year when I then also lay in Brougham Castle in Westmorland, my grandchild Mr Thomas Tufton was chosen burgess for the town of Appleby to serve in the House of Commons in Parliament then assembled and sitting in Parliament at Westminster in the place of Mr John

---

203 Henry Coventry, Secretary of State, was the uncle of George Coventry, Lord Coventry, the husband of Anne's granddaughter Margaret Tufton.
204 Sir Christopher Hatton was a collector of books and antiquities. He contributed material to Anne's *Great Books of Record*, see *Great Books*, p. 103.
205 Anne Temple, maid of honour to Catherine of Braganza, Queen consort of England.

Lowther, eldest son to my cousin Sir John Lowther of Lowther. Which Mr John Lowther died but a while before at London so as this Thomas Tufton my grandchild began first of all to sit in the said House of Commons at Westminster as a member thereof the 10th day of March instant, which Parliament had begun to sit again the 14th day of February before, he being the first grandchild of mine that ever sat in that House of Commons in the Parliament at Westminster.[206]

The 11th day of May in this year did my old servant Mistress Elizabeth Gilmore, whose first husband was Mr John Turner, come from her son-in-law Mr Killawaye's house at Week in Wiltshire to an inn at Reading in Berkshire and from thence the next day to London, where she stayed till the 5th day of the month following. In which time her second husband Mr John Gilmore, with their maid and a man called John Walter and one Thomas Kingston came up thither to her, and from thence the same 5th day of June they came down together in a hired coach towards York, whither they got well the 9th day. And then and there my servants George Goodgion[207] and John Hall, by my appointment, met them with some of my horses to bring them from thence hither to Brougham Castle. And accordingly they set forth from York the 11th day and came that night to Greta Bridge, and the next day over Stainmore by Brough Castle into my castle of Appleby where they lay all night, Mistress Gilmore and her husband lying in the Baron's Chamber there. And from thence the 13th of June they came by Julian Bower (where they alighted to see all the rooms and places about it)[208] and so through Whinfell Park hither into this Brougham

---

206 Underlying this statement was a fraught period in which Henry Bennet, 1st Earl of Arlington and Secretary of State to Charles II, sought to place his man, Joseph Williamson, as MP for Appleby. Anne refused to consider this as she intended her grandson Thomas Tufton to serve as MP. She was not intimidated by the flurry of correspondence that was sent to her and her daughter Margaret in order to persuade them to step aside and allow Williamson the place. In the end Anne had her way for, as Dr Thomas Smith, brother to the mayor of Appleby, explained to Williamson, while the 'whole county wishes to have you chosen ... they of Appleby, having so absolute a dependence upon her (as indeed they have) it would be vain to strive against that stream'. For a discussion of this episode with copies of the original letters see Malay, 'Beyond the Palace: The Transmission of Political Power in the Clifford Circle' (2017), pp. 153–169.
207 George Goodgion was one of Anne's chief servants. He performed a wide number of duties for her. He is listed as a slaughterer (or butcher) and chief director of her kitchen at Brougham. But he also procured all sorts of goods for her, from petticoats and foodstuffs to a coach from London. He accompanied George Sedgewick on rent days, he met important visitors, he helped serve at communion (or Eucharist) services, and he was the one who cut Anne's hair. He was one of the witnesses to her will and was also a beneficiary of that will. He is one of the most often mentioned individuals in her accounts from 1665 until her death.
208 Anne's accounts for this period reveal that Anne made extensive repairs to a house at Julian Bower, in Whinfell forest, which was to become the Gilmores' home. She records giving John Gilmore £20 for his moving and travel expenses in June 1668 when he and

Castle to me, where I kissed Mistress Gilmore, I having not seen her since the 11th day of August 1663 when she had been for a while at Skipton Castle with me, till now this 13th of June.

The 26th day of June in this year, after I had lain in Brougham Castle in Westmorland in the chamber wherein my noble father was born and my blessed mother died ever since the 18th of October last, being eight months and some eight days over, did I remove from thence in my horselitter (my women riding in my coach drawn with six horses and my menservants on horseback) through Whinfell park and by the Hart's Horn Tree, and by the house called Julian Bower in my said park to see it (though I did not alight to go into it) and so from thence through Temple Sowerby, Kirkbythure and Crackenthorp, and over Appleby Bridge into my castle of Appleby in the same county, where I now began to lie in the same chamber wherein I formerly used to lie and now lay in it till the [19th of October 1669].

The 21st of July in this year did my daughter the Countess Dowager of Thanet, with her two youngest daughters Lady Mary and Lady Anne Tufton, go out of Thanet House in Aldersgate Street (leaving there behind them Mr Sackville Tufton, her youngest son save one, and her daughter Lady Cecily Hatton and her husband) and so out of London town down into the country towards Croome House in Worcestershire. And, having lain two nights by the way, the first at Wickham in Buckinghamshire, and the second at Enstone in [Oxfordshire] they came safe and well thither to Croome the 23rd of that month, to her daughter the Lady Margaret Coventry and her Lord, and their two children, where they stayed with them for seven nights together, till the 30th of the same month, and then returned from thence back towards the said Thanet House at London again. Whither they came well the 1st of August following having lain two nights by the way the first at Stow-on-the-Wold in Gloucestershire (from thence going by Oxford to see the most remarkable things there) and the next night at Tetsworth in [Oxfordshire]. And her daughter the Lady Margaret Coventry with her daughter Margaret came up thither with them, that journey from Croome, leaving behind them my Lord Coventry and his eldest and now only son.

> Elizabeth came 'down from Ramsbury to live at Julian Bower'. Gilmore entered Anne's service at this time and remained at Julian Bower until Anne's death, though Elizabeth returned south to her daughter in April 1671, CAS, Kendal, WD HOTH/17. Anne may have had the new house built on the foundations of the original Julian Bower as she notes in the *Great Books* in 1653 that 'the lower foundacion of which howse standeth still and is yet to be seene, though all the walles bee downe long since'. Julian Bower was originally built about 1318 by Roger, 2nd Lord Clifford, for his mistress, whom Anne describes as 'a meane [or low-status] womman who was called Julian of the Bower', *Great Books*, ed. Malay, p. 319.

And on Friday the 31st of this July did my eldest grandchild, Nicholas Tufton, Earl of Thanet, come hither into this Appleby Castle in Westmorland late in the evening, so as I saw him not till the next day in the morning that he came up to me into my chamber where I then kissed him with much joy and comfort, I having not seen him since the 9th of August in 1664 (when he had been here with me with his wife, my cousin and goddaughter, and that they then took their leaves of me in this same chamber of mine and went towards her father the Earl of Burlington and Cork's house at Londesborough in Yorkshire, and so to their own house at Hothfield in Kent) until now. And now this Earl my grandchild came from his journey from the said Hothfield House, and by the way from the Lord Viscount Dunbar's house in Holderness,[209] and from Scarborough Wells and Bolton in Yorkshire, and today[210] from the inn at Kirkby Lonsdale in Westmorland hither into this Appleby Castle as aforesaid, where he now continued to lie in the Baron's Chamber for seven nights together. And when they were past on the Friday following being the 7th of August, betimes in the morning before I saw him, he (having taken his leave of me the night before in my chamber) went away again from hence with his company by the same ways that he came, onwards on his journey back towards his said house at Hothfield to his wife.

And the 8th of this August being Saturday in the evening, did the two judges of the assize for this Northern Circuit, namely Sir Christopher Turnor and Sir Richard Rainsford, two of the Barons of his Majesty's Exchequer, come from the city of Carlisle in Cumberland from holding the assizes there hither into this Appleby Castle in Westmorland, where I and my family now lie, and where they now lay for four nights together, Judge Turnor in the best room in Caesar's Tower, and Judge Rainsford in the Baron's Chamber. And when they were past, the assizes here at Appleby being ended, they went away from hence from me on Wednesday the 12th of this month to Kendal where they lay that night, and the next day they went to Lancaster to keep the assizes there also and to finish their circuit. And my cousin Sir Philip Musgrave of Edenhall in Cumberland, and my cousin Sir John Lowther of Lowther in Westmorland, lay here also in this castle, most part of the time of these assizes as usual.[211]

209 John Constable, 2nd Viscount Dunbar, Benningholme Grange, Holderness.
210 Occasionally the appearance of the present tense reveals that the source of much of the material in these yearly summaries was taken from Anne's daybooks, now lost except for the Daybook of 1676 below.
211 Lowther records that in 1668 Anne gave him 'a grant or warant for my lodging for my self and servants in the Green Chamber and that adjoyneinge, for my life, as a testimony of her love and affection. In return wereof I do usually send her a buck at the assizes as being better than hers that lie abroad and not so quiet', *Lowther Family Estate Books*, p. 185.

And on Monday the 21st of September in the afternoon did my grandchild Mr Thomas Tufton, the fourth son and seventh child to my daughter the Countess Dowager of Thanet, and now one of the burgesses[212] in Parliament for this corporation of Appleby, come hither into this Appleby Castle in Westmorland, and so up into my chamber to me where I kissed him with much joy and comfort, I having not seen him since the 15th of August in 1663 when he with his mother and some of his brothers and his sister Lady Frances went from Skipton Castle from me up towards London, until now. And now this grandchild of mine came from his journey out of Kent, and so by London, York and Ripon, and today from the inn at Bowes in Richmondshire hither into this Appleby Castle (as aforesaid) where he now lay in the Baron's Chamber for ten nights together. During which time he went to visit several of the gentry, my neighbours and friends in this country.[213] As on the 23rd of September [he went] to Acorn Bank to Mr John Dalston his fellow burgess, and to my house at Julian Bower in Whinfell Park, and the 24th day to Edenhall in Cumberland to my cousin Sir John Lowther, and so to my castle of Brougham to see it, and the 26th day to Howgill Castle to the widow Lady Sandford[214] and Sir Richard Sandford her eldest son and the rest of her children, and the 28th day being Monday to my castle of Pendragon and Brough to see them. At none of which houses and places above mentioned he had ever been before, except at Brougham Castle where he had been once with me for a time in August and September 1658 with his mother and some other of her children. And when these ten nights were over on Thursday the 1st of this October in the morning before I saw him, he (having taken his leave of me the night before) went away again from hence by Brough and over Stainmore into the inn at Bowes aforesaid where he lay one night, and so continued his journey up towards London.

And the 9th day of October in this year being Friday about four a clock in the morning, in Thanet House in Aldersgate Street, London, where her husband Mr Christopher Hatton and her mother my daughter of Thanet and most of her younger children then lay, was my grandchild the Lady Cecilia Hatton delivered of her first child which was a daughter, and was christened the 18th of that month being Sunday by the name of Anne, myself by deputy[215] and my said daughter

212 Member of Parliament.
213 Thomas Tufton, later 6th Earl of Thanet and Baron Clifford, inherited the Clifford hereditary lands in 1684 and held them until his death in 1729, longer than any other of Anne's grandchildren. He modelled himself in many ways on Anne and his entries in the *Great Books* (pp. 907–935) show his admiration for her. He was known as the 'Good Earl'.
214 Bridget Dalston.
215 Anne proposed herself as godmother to this child, and was pleased to have the child named after her. See BL, Add. MS 29551, letter, 26 August 1668, fol. 453.

the Countess Dowager of Thanet, being the two godmothers, and Christopher Lord Hatton of Kirby grandfather to the said child being the godfather.

And I lay all this Christmas, in this year, in my own chamber in Appleby Castle in Westmorland where I use to lie.

In the year of Our Lord God 1669

The 22nd of March in this year, the Prince of Tuscany, who is eldest son to Cosmo de Medici the great Duke of France in Italy,[216] and some years since married the then Duke of Orleans's daughter by his second wife, by whom he hath already had some children, came from his voyage from Corunna and from his visits of several princes in Christendom at their several Courts hither into England, landing then at Plymouth in Devonshire. From whence the 27th of the same month he went to Exeter and so by continued days' journeys, to Salisbury in Wiltshire, where whilst he lay he was magnificently entertained the 2nd of the month following by the now Earl of Pembroke, at his house at Wilton[217] in that county. And the 5th of the same he arrived safe at London, and came to the Court at Whitehall to the King and Queen and the Duke of York, where he lay for some time in the house called the Pall Mall near St James's and then went to see the two universities of Oxford and Cambridge, and other remarkable places in this kingdom and on Friday the 4th of June following, having before taken his leave of our said King and the rest, he came to Harwich where he embarked for Holland.

And the 29th day of May in this year did my daughter the Countess Dowager of Thanet and her son Sackville Tufton and her two youngest daughters Lady Mary and Lady Anne Tufton go from Thanet House in Aldersgate Street in London town, from her daughter Lady Cecily Hatton, and her husband and their little daughter Anne, down into the country to Bolebroke House in Sussex where they continued to lie till the 8th of the month following, and then returned back again to her said house in Aldersgate Street to lie in it as before.

And on Friday the 4th of June this year did our Queen Catherine wife to our now King Charles the second, in her lodging in the Court at Whitehall near Westminster and London, miscarry of a child which she had gone about nine weeks withal, to her great grief this being the second or third child that she hath miscarried of.

---

216 Cosimo III de Medici, who was the son of Ferdinando III de Medici, not Cosimo.
217 Philip Herbert, 5th Earl of Pembroke and 2nd Earl of Montgomery. He was Anne's stepson from her second marriage. She spent much time at Wilton during this marriage.

The 5th of this June did my cousin and godson Mr Edward Russell, third son to the now Earl of Bedford, come from his journey from his said father's house at Woburn in Bedfordshire, from him and his Lady[218] and some of their other children and their family hither into this Appleby Castle in Westmorland late in the evening so as I saw him not till the next morning that he came up into my chamber to me, where I then kissed him, it being the first time I ever saw him in any part of the lands of my inheritance, or that ever he was so far northwards, though his elder brother, William, the second son, had been with me before at Pendragon Castle in this county in June 1666. And this Mr Edward Russell now lay here in the Baron's Chamber for ten nights together, in which time he went to see my castles of Brougham, Brough and Pendragon and other the chief places of this county. And on Tuesday the 15th of this month in the morning, after he had taken his leave of me, he went away from hence by Brough and over Stainmore and those ways (though in his journey hither he came by Lancaster and Kendal) and so went now onwards on his journey home towards the said Woburn House in Bedfordshire, whither the said Mr Edward Russell came safe to his father and mother and some other of their children about them.

And the 7th of this June whilst my said cousin and godson Mr Edward Russell was here, did my grandchildren Mr John and Mr Richard Tufton, second and third sons to my daughter the Countess Dowager of Thanet, come hither into this Appleby Castle in Westmorland to me, where I then in my own chamber and kissed them both with much contentment, I having not seen my said grandchild John since the 16th of August 1664 when he went away from hence from me and from his mother and three youngest sisters (who were then also here with me) onwards on his journey towards London, until now, nor had I seen his brother Richard since the 15th of August 1663 (which was almost nine months before his father died) when he went away from Skipton Castle in Craven from me with his mother and some of his brothers and his sister Lady Frances up towards London, until now. And now these two grandchildren of mine came from their journey from Great Chart, near their eldest brother the Earl of Thanet's house at Hothfield in Kent, and from London, after some six weeks' stay there and today from Bowes, and over Stainmore, and by Brough and those ways, hither into this Appleby Castle (as aforesaid) where they now lay together in the Green Chamber, which is under the withdrawing room, for seven nights together. In which time they went with my said cousin Russell to my castles of Brougham, Brough and Pendragon, to show him them and some other remarkable houses and places of this county. And when those seven

---

218 Anne Carr.

nights were past, on Monday the 14th of this month in the morning, after they had taken their leaves of me and my said cousin Russell (who stayed with me a day longer), they went away from hence by the same ways they came onwards on their journey towards London. And this was the first time that ever my grandchild Mr Richard Tufton was in Pendragon Castle aforesaid, whither he went with his brother and Mr Edward Russell the 11th of this June.

And the 11th of this June, whilst my said two grandchildren and my cousin and godson Mr Edward Russell were here, there came hither to me to Appleby Castle from his own house at Edlington in Yorkshire over Stainmore and those ways, my cousin Sir Thomas Wharton who is second and only brother to the now Lord Wharton. And so this Sir Thomas now lay with us for two or three nights in Caesar's Tower here, which was the first time he ever lay in that tower and about the 16th of this June he went away again.

And the 20th or 21st day of May in this year did my grandchild George Tufton, youngest son to my daughter Margaret, Countess Dowager of Thanet, take his leave of her and some of his brothers and sisters at Thanet House in Aldersgate Street in London town and go from thence to Dover in Kent and after some few days' stay there for a fair wind, he took shipping for France. In which ship he went well and safe to Rochelle in France where he arrived and landed safely about the [blank] and from thence he went to Bordeaux and so to the baths called Muds in France. And about the beginning of September following he came from the hot baths in France upon the frontiers of Spain, took ship at Rochelle, and landed the 19th day at Dover in Kent, and so came safe to his brother Mr John Tufton's house in Kent and from thence to his eldest brother the Earl of Thanet's house at Hothfield in that county and so to Bolebroke House in Sussex to his mother and his two youngest sisters to stay there with them for some while. But my said grandchild received little or no benefit by the said baths.[219]

The 3rd of August in this year being Tuesday about six o'clock in the evening did my daughter Margaret, Countess Dowager of Thanet, with Mr Sackville Tufton her youngest son save one and her two youngest daughters Lady Mary and Lady Anne Tufton and their company, come from their journey from my said daughter's house called Thanet House in Aldersgate Street at London and this day came over Stainmore, and those ways hither into this Appleby Castle in Westmorland and so up into my chamber to me, where I now kissed them

---

219 George Tufton, suffering the effects of the leg wound he received in 1666, visited the cluster of baths in the south of France including Bagneres en Bigorre, Cauterets, Bareges and Eaux-Chaudes. These were also frequented by the aristocracy of France.

with much joy and comfort, I having not seen this daughter of mine nor her said two youngest daughters since the 8th of September in 1666 when they with Lady Cecily, another of her daughters, went away from me from Skipton Castle in Craven (where I then lay) back towards London until now. Nor had I seen her son Sackville Tufton since the 15th of August 1663 when he with my said daughter his mother and three of his brothers, namely Richard, Thomas and George and his sister Lady Frances (since deceased), went away from me from Skipton Castle aforesaid (where I then also lay) back towards London again, until now.

And now they continued to lie here (my daughter with her youngest daughter Lady Anne in the Baron's Chamber, and Lady Mary with her woman in the Sheriff's Chamber near to it and Sackville Tufton in the best room in Caesar's Tower here) for ten nights together. In which time, on Monday the 9th of this August, they went in my coach to my castle of Pendragon in this county to see it, which was the first time my daughter or any of these her three children were ever in it, though most of her other children had been in it before. And on Friday the 13th of this month about nine o'clock in the morning, after I had kissed them as taking my leave of them, they with their company went away hence from me to Brough, my said grandchild Mr Sackville Tufton going a little before to see my castle there, and the Roman Tower (for he had never been in them before) and afterwards, meeting his mother and sisters and their company again, they rid together over Stainmore, and so onwards on their journey towards London, whither they came safe and well to Thanet House in Aldersgate Street there the 21st of that month and lay there in it for a time.

And the 21st of this August being Saturday in the evening did the two judges of the assize for this Northern Circuit, namely Sir Christopher Turnor, one of the Barons of his Majesty's Exchequer (who hath come hither often on the same occasion), and Thomas Waller esquire, sergeant at law, come from the city of Carlisle from holding the assizes there and so out of Cumberland over the river near Brougham Castle hither into this Appleby Castle in Westmorland, where I and my family now lie and where they now lay for four nights together, Judge Turnor in the Baron's Chamber and Sergeant Waller in the best room in Caesar's Tower. And when they were past (the assizes here at Appleby being ended) they went away from hence from me on Wednesday the 25th of this month to Kendal, where they lay that night and the next day they went to Lancaster to keep the assizes there also and to finish their circuit. And my cousin Sir John Lowther of Lowther in this county lay here also in this castle, most part of the time of these assizes as usual.

And a little before this, on the 14th of May last, did there come into this Appleby Castle in Westmorland to me from their journey out of Derbyshire, Sir Francis Rodes and his sister Mistress Jane Rodes, whose mother was the widow

Lady Rodes my cousin german, she having been youngest daughter to my uncle of Cumberland and this was the first time I ever saw any of his generation in Westmorland.[220] And with them there came hither to me Mr Roger Molineux who had been a colonel, and now also lives in Derbyshire. So these three lay here for three nights and on the 17th of this month they went away from hence from me back again towards their own homes in Derbyshire.

And the 26th of August, in this year being Thursday about noon, did my grandchild the Lady Margaret Coventry and her two children now only living, namely Mr John and Mistress Margaret Coventry and their company, come from their journey from her Lord's house called Croome in Worcestershire, from whence they set forth on Thursday the 19th instant, and came by Nottingham, Doncaster and over Stainmore and this day from Brough in Westmorland, hither into this Appleby Castle in the same county, and so up into my chamber to me where I now kissed them, with much joy and contentment, this being the first time that ever any of them were in Westmorland or in any part of the lands of my inheritance, as also the first time that ever I saw any to whom I am great-grandmother. And I had not seen my grandchild the Lady Margaret Coventry since she was married nor in a good while before. For I had not seen her since about the beginning of July 1649 when she was with me at Baynard's Castle in London a little before I came quite away from thence, hither into the North to Skipton and Westmorland until now, Genesis 48.11.[221] And now they continued to lie here (my said grandchild the Lady Margaret Coventry in the Baron's Chamber and her daughter Mistress Margaret Coventry with her mother's gentlewoman in the Sheriff's Chamber near to it and Mr John Coventry in the Green Chamber which is under the withdrawing room) for eight nights together. In which time, on Monday the 30th of this August, they went in their coach from hence to Julian Bower in Whinfell Park to see it and from thence by the Three Brothers Tree in that park,[222] into Lowther Hall to my cousin Sir John Lowther and his Lady, where they dined. And from thence after dinner they went into my castle of Brougham in this county to see it, but came back again the same night hither into this Appleby Castle from whence on Friday the 3rd of the month following, about nine o'clock in the morning after I had kissed them, as taking my leave of

---

220 Oddly for Anne, she has this wrong. The widow Rodes is Anne Clifton, daughter of Anne's first cousin or cousin german Frances Clifford and thus Rodes is the granddaughter of Anne's uncle Francis Clifford, not his daughter.
221 Genesis 48.11: 'And Israel said unto Joseph, I had not thought to see thy face: and, lo, God hath shewed me also thy seed.'
222 The Three Brothers Tree was the remaining tree where once three massive oaks stood in Whinfell forest called the Three Brethren.

them, they with their company went from me by Brough and over Stainmore and those ways to the inn at Greta Bridge and the next day to the city of York to see it, where they lay two nights (the latter being Sunday). And on Monday the 6th of the same September they continued their journey from hence homewards towards her Lord's house at Croome in Worcestershire, whither they came safe and well, I thank God, to her Lord and husband, the 9th of the same, lying one night by the way (amongst other places) in the city of Coventry in Warwickshire. Jeremiah 29.6; 30.19; Psalm 116.12–14.[223]

The 10th day of September in this year, being now Friday, died Henrietta Maria, Queen Mother of England, in her house called Colombes in France some four miles from Paris,[224] which house she had lately caused to be built herself, who if she had lived till the 16th of November next, would have been sixty years old. She came first into England and was married in July 1625 to our King Charles the 1st, who was afterwards unfortunately beheaded the 30th of January in the year 1649 as the same begins on New Year's day. During which time she had many children by him and amongst the rest our now King Charles the 2nd. She was a woman of excellent perfections both of mind and body and was youngest child to Henry of Bourbon, the 4th King of France who was treacherously killed when she was but about five months old. And on Wednesday the 10th of November following in this year (according to the accompt of the Church of England) was performed the solemn funeral service for the said Queen Mother of England, in the abbey church of St Dennis near Paris in France, where her dead body was then buried after the form and magnificence as had been formerly used at the funeral of the Queen Mother of France. Job 7.1; Ecclesiastes 3; 8.6.

And the 7th of this September in this year, being now Tuesday about five or six o'clock in the evening, did my son-in-law James Compton, Earl of Northampton, with his company, come from his journey from his own house at Castle Ashby in that county from my grandchild the Lady Alethea Compton his daughter and from his second wife and his children by her,[225] hither into this

---

223 Jeremiah 29.6: 'Take ye wives, and beget sons and daughters; and take wives for your sons, and give your daughters to husbands, that they may bear sons and daughters; that ye may be increased there, and not diminished'; 30.19: 'And out of them shall proceed thanksgiving and the voice of them that make merry: and I will multiply them, and they shall not be few; I will also glorify them, and they shall not be small'; Psalm 116.12–14: 'What shall I render unto the Lord for all his benefits toward me? I will take the cup of salvation, and call upon the name of the Lord. I will pay my vows unto the Lord now in the presence of all his people.'
224 The Château de Colombes.
225 Mary Noel. Their daughter Mary Compton would married Charles Sackville, 6th Earl of Dorset. Their third son Spencer was Prime Minister of Great Britain from 1742 to 1743 and in 1730 he was created Earl of Wilmington.

Appleby Castle in Westmorland. For he set forth from Castle Ashby aforesaid on Tuesday the 31st of the last month and lay two nights by the way (the 4th and 5th of this month, the latter being Sunday) in my castle of Skipton in Craven in the highest chamber of the great round tower there in which castle he had not been since the 11th of April 1662 (as he was then in his journey to Brougham Castle in Westmorland to me) until now. And the 6th of this month from thence he came to Kirkby Lonsdale and the 7th day (as aforesaid) hither into this Appleby Castle in Westmorland to me, where I now kissed him in my own chamber, I having not seen him since the 19th of May in the said year 1662 when he was then but newly a widower, by the death of my dear daughter his first wife and when he then went from me from Brougham Castle aforesaid, through Craven, by Barden Tower and those ways up towards London and the southern parts, until now. And now he lay here for three nights in the Baron's Chamber, till the 10th of this September, that he went from hence onwards on his journey towards Liddesdale in Scotland to see his aunt the Countess [Clanricarde] of Liddesdale,[226] where he also lay three nights and two nights by the way at Carlisle in his going and coming. And on the 15th instant returned back hither to Appleby Castle aforesaid to me where he lay in the Baron's Chamber for five nights more. And when they were past, on Monday the 20th of this month, in the morning before I saw him (for he took his leave of me in my chamber the night before), he went away again from hence with his company by Brough and over Stainmore and those ways, onwards on his journey towards his said house at Castle Ashby in Northamptonshire.

And the 9th of this September in the forenoon, whilst my Lord of Northampton was here (so as it was now their fortune to meet together here), did my second Lord, the Earl of Pembroke's, youngest son but one called Mr James Herbert with one Mr Thomas Saunders come from their houses in Oxfordshire to me into this Appleby Castle in Westmorland where I now kissed them both, it being the first time that ever I saw any of my second husband's children in Westmorland or any part of my inheritance. And they now lay in Caesar's Tower here for five nights together and on Tuesday the 14th instant betimes, in the morning before I saw them, they (having taken their leaves of me the night before) went away from hence over Stainmore to the city of York and so onwards on their journey towards Oxfordshire again.

About the latter end of August in this year did my daughter the Countess

---

226 Anne Compton, Marchioness of Clanricarde, was James Compton's great-aunt, daughter to his grandfather William Compton, 1st Earl of Northampton. She was living in Liddesdale, in Scotland, at the time, just across the Cumberland border so not too distant from Westmorland.

Dowager of Thanet's two youngest daughters, Lady Mary and Lady Anne Tufton, go from her out of her house called Thanet House in Aldersgate Street (by reason the smallpox was then so rife in that part of London) down into the country to Bolebroke House in Sussex, whither their said mother my daughter went down to them the 6th or 7th of the month following, to lie there in it with them for a time, till the 16th of November following (as hereafter written) that she and they returned back to the said Thanet House again to her daughter Lady Cecily Hatton and her husband, and their little daughter Anne to lie there in it with them as before.

And the 1st day of October this year did there come hither to me to Appleby Castle from their house not far from Naworth Castle in Cumberland, Edward Lord Morpeth (eldest son to my cousin Charles Howard, Earl of Carlisle) and his Lady[227] who was one of the younger daughters to Sir William Uvedale by his second wife Victoria Cary, and widow to one of the Berkeleys that was killed at sea in the late wars. So she and her husband lay that one night in the Baron's Chamber and they next day in the morning before I saw them, they and their company went away onwards on their journey towards London.

And the 19th of this October about eleven o'clock in the forenoon did I and my family remove out of Appleby Castle to Brough Castle in Westmorland and coming out of my own chamber there I passed through the Great Chamber, and went into the chapel and through the hall, took my litter at the hall door in the court, and so passing through the town of Appleby, over the bridge and Sandford more, went through Warcop town into the said Brough Castle. And I had continued to lie in the said castle of Appleby in my chamber there from the 26th of June 1668 till the time of my now removal, being a year and four months wanting some seven or eight days. And I had not lain in Brough Castle since the 19th of April 1665, being three years and six months complete. And I now began to lie again in the round tower called Clifford's Tower in the upper room next the leads in that Brough Castle where I did always use to lie since the repair of that castle, excepting some few nights that I lay in the Roman Tower. In which chamber of mine in Clifford's Tower I now continued to lie for twenty-eight weeks together, till the 3rd of May in the year following, that I removed from this Brough Castle into my castle of Pendragon in the same county to lie in it for a time.

And the 16th of November this year did my daughter Margaret, Countess Dowager of Thanet, with her two youngest daughters Lady Marie and Lady

---

227 Elizabeth Uvedale, who was married first to Sir William Berkeley.

Anne Tufton, after they had lain in Bolebroke House in Sussex ever since about the latter end of August and beginning of September before, remove from thence up to London again to my said daughter's house called Thanet House in Aldersgate Street there, to her daughter Lady Cecily Hatton and her husband and their little daughter Anne and to her youngest son George Tufton, who then also lay there, though he had been down at Bolebroke aforesaid with his said mother and sisters but a little before when he was then but newly come from his journey from the hot baths in France near the borders of Spain, which he went to make use of for his lameness, though it seems they did him little good.

In the year of Our Lord God 1670

The 3rd day of May, being Tuesday in this year, after I had lain in Brough Castle in Westmorland in the highest chamber in Clifford's Tower there ever since the 19th of October last, being six months and some fourteen days over, and after I had been a while in the forenoon in the Roman Tower there to see it, did I remove from thence to my horselitter (my women riding in my coach drawn with six horses and men servants on horseback) through Brough, Sowerby and Kirkby Stephen and within sight of Wharton Hall (though not through Wharton Park). I came safe and well into my castle of Pendragon in the same county and so up into my own chamber in it wherein I formerly used to lie and where I now continued to lie till the three day of August following that I removed from thence into my castle of Appleby in the same county to lie in it for a time.

The 29th day of April in this year was Cardinal Paulus Emelius Alteiri elected and proclaimed Pope at Rome by the name of Clement the tenth, after there had been a vacancy ever since the 9th of December last, which was the longest vacancy that hath been in the papacy, since the reigns of Henry the 4th, Henry 5th and Henry the 6th.[228]

The 16th of May in this year being Monday did the Princess Henrietta Maria, wife to the Duke of Orleans, who was youngest daughter to our late King and Queen and youngest sister to our now King Charles the 2nd, come from her journey out of France from the said Duke her husband, and so from Dunkirk over sea into England and landed this day at Dover in Kent. Whither our said King, her brother, with the Duke of York and Prince Rupert, went to meet her.

---

228 Clement X was born Emilio Bonaventura Altieri. The College of Cardinals took a little over four months to choose a new pope after the death of Clement IX.

And afterwards on the 18th instant the Queen and Duchess of York went also towards Dover to visit her. And after this Princess Henrietta had made a short stay there she returned back into France, and being arrived at St Cloud which is within four or five miles of Paris, she was taken with a sudden and violent distemper (thought to be a kind of bilious colic) whereof she died there on Monday the 20th of the month following about four o'clock in the morning. Which sad news was brought into England to Whitehall the 22nd of the same month by an express from Mr Montague our King's Ambassador at Paris,[229] to the great grief of his Majesty and the rest of her relations.

And the 20th of this May being Friday, before nine o'clock in the morning, was my grandchild the Lady Cecily Hatton delivered of her second child, which was also a daughter, in Thanet House in Aldersgate Street in London town where she and her husband then lay. Which child was christened the next day by the name of Margaret, her two grandmothers (namely my daughter Margaret, Countess Dowager of Thanet and my Lord Hatton's Lady)[230] being her godmothers and my Lord Fanshawe[231] her godfather.

The 10th day of June in this year being Friday did my dear grandchild Lady Alethea Compton, youngest and only surviving child to the now James, Earl of Northampton, by my deceased daughter his first wife, come from her journey from her said father's house at Castle Ashby in Northamptonshire, from him and his now wife and their children and family, hither into this Pendragon Castle in Westmorland to me where I now kissed her in my own chamber with much joy and comfort, it being the first time I ever saw her, though she be now nine years and three months old wanting but some four days. And this grandchild of mine set forth from Castle Ashby aforesaid, on Thursday the 2nd of this month in her coach (attended by four gentlewomen, a gentleman, and other servants and also by Colonel Carr that lives at Skipton in Craven) and so came by Stamford, Newark, Doncaster, Wetherby, Knaresborough, and by my almshouse at Beamsley (which she went into to see it) into my castle of Skipton in Craven,[232] where she lay for two nights together in the highest room of the great round tower at the end of the long gallery there (where her father and mother have lain formerly). And in that time, the 8th instant, went for a while into my house or tower of Barden to see it and the next day being the 9th day

---

229 Ralph Montagu, later Duke of Montagu.
230 Elizabeth Montagu.
231 Thomas Fanshawe.
232 Margaret was to inherit this castle from Anne, and after her death in August 1676 it descended first to Alethea Compton and at her death in 1678 to Margaret's son Nicholas Tufton, 3rd Earl of Thanet.

she came from Skipton to Kirkby Lonsdale, where she lay one night and from thence the 10th day (as abovesaid) came safe, God be thanked, hither into this Pendragon Castle to me, where she now lay in that chamber over the Great Chamber which hath windows to the east and south, for thirty-three nights together. During which time, the 1st of July, she went with her gentlewomen and my two gentlewomen to Hartley Castle to my cousin Mr Richard Musgrave and his wife and daughter for a while, and to Kirkby Stephen and Wharton Hall to see those places but came back again to me about six o'clock the same evening. And another time she went to see Mallerstang Chapel which I not long since had caused to be new builded.

And the 13th of July this grandchild of mine, after I had kissed her and she taken her leave of me and after she with her company had lain here over since the 10th of the last month, went from hence to my castle of Brough to see it and the Roman Tower there and so from thence over Stainmore onwards on her journey towards Castle Ashby in Northamptonshire, whither she came safe and well (I thank God) the 23rd of that month to her father. Jeremiah 29.6; 30.19; Psalm 116.12–14.

And the same 10th of this June a little after she was come hither did my dear grandchild Mr Thomas Tufton, fourth son and seventh child to my daughter Margaret, Countess Dowager of Thanet, and now one of the burgesses in Parliament for the corporation of Appleby, come from his journey from London and the southern parts and to day from the inn at Greta Bridge and so over Stainmore hither also into this Pendragon Castle in Westmorland and so up into my chamber to me, where I kissed him with much joy and contentment I having not seen him since the 30th of September 1668 that he went the day following from Appleby Castle (where I and my family then lay) up towards London, until now. And now he lay in this Pendragon Castle in the chamber over the great chamber which adjoins to my grandchild Lady Alethea's chamber for ten nights together, in which time, the 13th of this month, he went to see several remarkable places about this castle as namely Wildboar Fell, Hugh Seat Morville,[233] and Hellgill Bridge. And the 16th of this month he went to Edenhall in Cumberland to my cousin Sir Philip Musgrave, calling by the way at Acorn Bank in this county to see Mr John Dalston. And the 18th of this month he went

---

233 Wildboar Fell is the fourth highest fell in the Yorkshire Dales. Hugh Seat is the high point above Black Fell Moss, near Wildboar Fell. Anne had a cairn pillar erected at Hugh Seat in 1664 and the engraving 'AP1664' can still be seen. The seat is named after Hugh de Morville, one of the assassins of Thomas Becket. Anne's ancestor Robert de Veteripont was granted some of Hugh de Morville's holdings in this area of Westmorland and was made guardian of Hugh Morville's daughter Ada: see the *Great Books*, ed. Malay, p. 84.

to Kendal in this county to see it and into the ruinous castle and the church there and to Mr George Sedgwick's house at Collinfield,[234] where he dined with him and came back also the same night into this Pendragon Castle again. From whence on Monday the 20th instant betimes in the morning before I saw him, he went away onwards on his journey towards Scotland (by the city of Carlisle and those ways) and saw most of the remarkable cities and places in that kingdom as namely Dumfries, Douglas, Hamilton, and the Duke's palace there (where he was nobly treated by Duke Hamilton)[235] and from thence went to the city of Glasgow, where he gave a visit to the Archbishop[236] at the castle, and saw the university there, and thence went to the town and castle of Dumbarton, thence to the town of Stirling thence to the city of Edinburgh, thence to a place called Bask Island (which is so remarkable for Soland Geese). And so from thence out of Scotland he returned back by the town of Berwick upon Tweed, Newcastle and Barnard Castle, hither into Pendragon Castle to me the 7th of the month following, where he lay for about eleven nights more. In which time, the 15th of the same July, he went with some of my chief folks through Whinfell Park and by my castle of Brougham into Dacre Castle in Cumberland, then to Dunmallerd Hill[237] and so down to Ullswater to see those places, but they came back to Brougham Castle aforesaid where they lay that one night (my grandchild lying in the Baron's Chamber). And the next day from thence by Julian Bower and the same ways they went, he and they came back into this Pendragon Castle again. And on the 18th of this July betimes in the morning after I had kissed him and he taken his leave of me in my chamber, he rid away from hence from me and so over Stainmore onwards on his journey towards London. Jeremiah 29.6; 30.19; Psalm 116.12–14.

The 3rd day of August in this year being Wednesday, after I had lain in Pendragon Castle in Westmorland (in the same chamber wherein I formerly used to lie) ever since the 3rd of May last being a just quarter of a year, did I remove from thence in my horselitter, and my family towards my castle of Appleby in the same county, so as we now went within sight of Wharton Hall, Brough Castle and Hartley Castle and through Wateby and Soulby and over Soulby Mask to my said castle of Appleby safe and well I thank God. Where I

234   Anne bought this property for George Sedgewick in recognition of his service to her and her family. Her initials can still be seen above the original oak door.
235   William Douglas-Hamilton. He became Duke of Hamilton for his life upon his marriage to Anne Hamilton, 3rd Duchess Hamilton in her own right. He also took the Hamilton name, as did his children.
236   Robert Leighton's stepmother was Isabel Musgrave and thus related to Anne.
237   Or Dunmallet, near Pooley Bridge. The remains of an Iron Age fort were discovered here.

alighted, and came through the hall, the chapel, the Great Chamber, and the withdrawing room (in every of which I stayed a while to see them) and so up into my own chamber in it wherein I formerly used to lie, and where I had not been since the 19th of October last that I removed from thence to Brough Castle and from thence the 3rd of May last to Pendragon Castle aforesaid, until this 3rd of August that I came hither again. And I now continued to lie in this Appleby Castle till the 14th of October following that I removed from thence with my family into my castle of Brougham in the same county to lie in it for a time.

The 13th day of August being Saturday in the afternoon did the two judges of assize for this Northern Circuit, namely Sir Christopher Turnor and Sir Timothy Littleton, two of the Barons of his Majesty's Exchequer, come from the city of Carlisle in Cumberland, from holding the assizes there and so out of that county, over the river, near my castle of Brougham, hither into my castle of Appleby in Westmorland, where I and my family now lie and where these judges now held the assizes for this county also in the town hall here in Appleby, which was the first time that ever the said Sir Timothy Littleton came hither on this occasion, though the other hath come this circuit for several years last past. And they now lay here in this castle for four nights together, Judge Turnor in the Baron's Chamber and Judge Littleton in the best room in Caesar's Tower. And when they were past (the assizes here being ended) they went away hence from me on Wednesday the 17th of this month to Kendal where they lay that night. And the next day they went to Lancaster, where also they stayed some days to keep the assizes for that county and so finished their circuit.

The 8th day of September being Thursday did Mr William Edge, who had been formerly my domestic servant and is now receiver general of my southern rents, come with his second and new married wife who was a widow and whom I never saw before, from their journey from London (where they live) through Staffordshire and Lancashire, and today from Kendal hither into this Appleby Castle in Westmorland to me, where they now lay for seven nights together in the Baron's Chamber. And when they were past on Thursday the 15th of this month, after they had taken their leaves of me in the morning, they went away from hence onwards on their journey towards London again. And I had not seen William Edge these good many years before, till now.

And this September whilst I lay in Appleby Castle a little before my removal thence to Brougham Castle did my daughter Margaret, Countess Dowager of Thanet, go from Thanet House in Aldersgate Street in London town down into the country to Kirkby in Northamptonshire (which is not far from Lilford) to her daughter Lady Cecily Hatton and her two little children, Anne and Margaret, whither she came to them the 22nd of that month. But her son-in-law the now Lord Hatton was then beyond the seas in the Isle of Guernsey, which island the King lately made him governor of.[238] And after my daughter had lain at Kirkby aforesaid for four or five nights she came back again to her said house called Thanet House at London.

And the 14th day of October being Friday about nine or ten o'clock in the forenoon, after I had lain in Appleby Castle ever since the 3rd of August last that I came from Pendragon Castle thither, did I remove with my family from thence, coming through the withdrawing chamber, and Great Chamber into the chapel for a while, and so through the hall, took my litter at the hall door in the court, in which I rid through the town of Appleby, over the bridge, and so through Crackenthorp, Kirkbythure, Temple Sowerby, Woodside and by the Hart's Horn Tree (which I looked upon a while). I came safe and well, I thank God, into my castle of Brougham in the same county about three o'clock in the afternoon having been accompanied hither by several of the gentry of this county and of my neighbours and tenants both through the Great Chamber, and Painted Chamber, and the little passage room into my own chamber where I formerly used to lie, and where my noble father was born and my blessed mother died. And I had not been in this Brougham Castle since the 26th of June 1668 when I removed thence to Appleby Castle aforesaid until now. And I now continued to lie in my said chamber in Brougham Castle till the 17th of August following that I removed with my family to the said Appleby Castle again, so as the time of my stay at Brougham was ten months and three days. In which time, the 12th of December in this year (as is hereafter written), died my dear grandchild Mr George Tufton, youngest son to my daughter Margaret, Countess Dowager of Thanet.[239]

And before I removed (as abovesaid) from Appleby Castle to Brougham Castle, on the eighth of September in this year, being Thursday, was my grandchild the Lady Mary Tufton, youngest daughter and child but one to my daughter Margaret, Countess Dowager of Thanet, married to Mr William Walter, eldest son to Sir William Walter of Sarsden, not far from Woodstock in Oxfordshire, whose father was that Sir John Walter that was Lord Chief Baron of the Exchequer in the time of our late King Charles the 1st. And this young couple were married together in St Botolph's church in Aldersgate Street at

---

238   Christopher Hatton succeeded his father 4 July 1670, becoming the 2nd Baron Hatton. This appointment as Governor of Guernsey was to have disastrous personal consequences for his family as Anne relates below.

239   His death was caused by complications related to his leg wound received in the fighting in Germany in 1666, see above.

London, by Doctor Wells,[240] minister of that parish, there being present at the marriage Christopher Lord Hatton her brother-in-law (who gave her in marriage) and her mother my daughter of Thanet, and the Lady Diana Curson,[241] Mr Cecil Tufton and his wife and son and daughter,[242] and Mr Offlet Groom Porter and others. And the said new married couple lay for five nights together in my daughter of Thanet's house in Aldersgate Street aforesaid. And when they were past, the 13th of this month, they went down towards their father's house at Sarsden in Oxfordshire to live there with him.

The 24th of October in this year being Monday the two Houses of Parliament, the Lords and Commons (according to their adjournment), reassembled at Westminster, where our now King Charles was then present in the House of Lords habited in his royal robes, and crown upon his head. And having taken his place with the usual ceremonies in the Chair of Estate, his Majesty made a gracious speech, in short, to both the Houses leaving the Lord Keeper to open the particulars more at large.

And the 27th of this October did his Highness William of Nassau, Prince of Orange,[243] eldest and only child to our now King of England's eldest sister deceased,[244] take ship at the Briel in Holland in which he came over sea into England, and landed at Margate the 29th of the same month in the morning from whence immediately he rid post to Canterbury, and thence passed by coach to Rochester where he lay that one night. And the next day being the 30th day he came to Gravesend, and so from thence in a barge along the river of Thames to Whitehall to his uncle our said King of England and Her Majesty and to the Duke and Duchess of York, who all of them received him with great demonstration of affection and joy, this being the first time that ever this young prince came into England. And he now begun to lie in those lodgings by the Cockpit at Whitehall wherein my late Lord the Earl of Pembroke did use to lie, and wherein that Lord of mine died. And in a short time after this young Prince went to Windsor Castle, where he lay one night and then to both universities of Oxford and Cambridge and to Audley End House to see them, and other remarkable houses and places in this kingdom. And on Monday the 13th of February following, he with the Earl of Ossory[245] (whom the King appointed to

---

240 Dr John Wells.
241 Diana Tufton.
242 Cecil Tufton, his wife Mary Lloyd, his son Charles Tufton and an unknown daughter. Cecil and Diana were brother and sister to John Tufton, Margaret Sackville's husband.
243 Later William III of England as co-monarch with his wife Mary II.
244 Mary, Princess Royal, daughter of Henrietta Maria and King Charles I of England.
245 Thomas Butler.

attend him in the voyage) went from Whitehall and so from London down by Rochester in Kent to Sheerness, where he took shipping that evening in one of His Majesty's yachts, and so went safe and well over seas into his own country, to the Hague in Holland, to live there again, and in other places in the Low Countries as before.

And the 12th day of December being Monday about twelve o'clock at noon, to the unspeakable grief of me, and his mother my daughter the Countess Dowager of Thanet, died my dear grandchild Mr George Tufton, her youngest son, in Thanet House in Aldersgate Street in London town, when he was twenty years old and almost six months over. For he was born into the world in Hothfield House in Kent the 30th day of June in 1650 and he died of a wound which he got about four years since by a shot in the wars in Germany, so as his dead body was opened and inward parts taken out and viewed by a physician and surgeon and found to be so much decayed by reason of the said wound that they wondered he should live so long after having received it. And afterwards his dead body, with the bowels enclosed again in it, was buried in the church at Rainham in Kent, by his father and two of his sisters, namely the first Lady Anne Tufton[246] and the Lady Frances Drax. And both when he died and was buried did I lie in my chamber in Brougham Castle in Westmorland wherein my noble father was born and my blessed mother died.

In the year of Our Lord God 1671

The 31st day of March in this year, being Friday, in the King's house at St James's near Whitehall and the river of Thames and not far from London town, died that Anne Hyde that was Duchess of York in one of the chambers wherein had formerly died Queen Mary and Prince Henry, James, Duke of York, her husband being present at her death and her three children that are living (whereof two are daughters and one a son)[247] being then also in the house. And on the fifth of the month following betwixt nine and ten of the clock at night, her dead body, after it had been opened, was accompanied from the Painted Chamber in the palace at Westminster by his Highness Prince Rupert who appeared a chief mourner and most of the English nobility and was buried in a large vault on the south side of Henry the 7th's chapel in Westminster Abbey.

And the 17th day of August being Thursday in the forenoon, after I had lain

---

246 This Anne Tufton died as an infant; a second daughter was subsequently named Anne. This Anne married Sir Samuel Grimston.
247 Mary Stuart, later Mary II of England; Anne Stuart, later Anne of England; Edgar Stuart, Duke of Cambridge, who would die in this year.

in my castle of Brougham in Westmorland, in the chamber wherein my noble father was born and my blessed mother died ever since the 14th of October last, did I go for a little while out of it into the room adjoining being the middle room in the great Pagan Tower, and into that part of it where my old servant Jane Bricknell died, and so came into my own chamber again. Where after a short stay, I went from thence about eleven o'clock of the same day through the little passage room, and the Painted Chamber, and Great Chamber, and the hall, down into the garden for a while, and from thence back into the court of that castle, where I took my horselitter in which I rid by the pillar that I erected in memory of my last parting there with my blessed mother,[248] and so, through part of Whinfell Park to Julian Bower and from thence out of that park I went over Eden Bridge, and through the towns of Temple Sowerby, Kirkbythure and Crackenthorp, and down the Slape Stones, and over Appleby Bridge, and near the church, and through Appleby town. I came safe and well, I thank God, into my castle of Appleby in the same county about four o'clock in the afternoon (my women attending me in my coach drawn with six horses, and my menservants on horseback, and a great many of the chief gentry of this county, and of my neighbours, and tenants accompanying me in this my removal). So after I was now alighted in this Appleby Castle I went through the hall up into the chapel for a while, and into the Great Chamber, and so up the green stairs, and through the withdrawing chamber, into my own chamber where I formerly used to lie, and where I had not been since the said 14th of October last until now. And I now continued to lie in this chamber of mine for three months together, till the 17th of November following, that I removed from hence with my family to my castle of Pendragon in the same county to lie in it for a time.

And the 25th of this August whilst I lay in Appleby Castle in Westmorland did my daughter Margaret, Countess Dowager of Thanet, and her youngest daughter the Lady Anne Tufton, after they had lain [blank] nights in Bolebroke House in Sussex, remove with her family from thence up into her house in Aldersgate Street in London town to lie in it as before.

And the 2nd day of September in this year being Saturday did Sir Timothy Littleton, who is one of the Barons of His Majesty's Exchequer and now one of the judges of assize for this Northern Circuit, come from the city of Carlisle in Cumberland (from his fellow judge Sir William Wilde, who was detained there longer by occasion of much business) and so over the rivers of Emont and Lowther near my castle of Brougham in Westmorland where he was met by my undersheriff Mr Thomas Gabetis and several of my servants with my coach and

---

248 The Countess Pillar.

10 The Countess Pillar, Brougham, Westmorland (now Cumbria)

six horses, in which he came about five o'clock in the afternoon hither into this Appleby Castle in the same county.

And on the Monday following being the 4th of the same month did the said Sir William Wilde, who is one of the justices of His Majesty's Court of Common Pleas and now the other judge of assize for this Northern Circuit, come from the said city of Carlisle, being met by the way at Emont Bridge by my said sheriff and others with my coach, in like manner as the former judge was and so came in it hither into Appleby Castle to him, and me, and us here. So these two judges now lay here till the 6th day of this month, Judge Littleton four nights in the best room in Caesar's Tower, and Judge Wilde two nights in the Baron's Chamber, during which time they held the assizes in the moot hall in Appleby town and dispatched business for the people of this county as usual. And on the said 6th instant being Wednesday (having taken their leaves of me in my chamber), they went away from hence part of the way in my coach attended by some of my servants towards Kendal, intending to lie there one night and the next day to go to Lancaster to hold the assizes for that county also, and so to finish their circuit. And this was the first time that ever Sir William Wilde came hither on this occasion, though the other judge had been here the year before.

And whilst the assizes were held here at Appleby as aforesaid, on Monday the 4th of this September, did my cousin Philip Lord Wharton and his two eldest sons, Thomas and Goodwin, and a grandchild of my Lord Wenman's[249] come hither into Appleby Castle to me, but went that night to Wharton Hall in this county. Also my cousin Sir Philip Musgrave of Edenhall came hither to me the same day with them, and lay in one of the best upper chambers in Caesar's Tower one night, and the next day went away again. And the said Lord Wharton's three daughters that are unmarried whom he had by his second wife were also here with me for a while these assizes. For during the time of these assizes did I lie in my own chamber in Appleby Castle in Westmorland.

And the 3rd day of this September being Sunday about seven o'clock in the morning was my grandchild the Lady Mary Walter, fifth daughter and ninth child to my daughter the Countess Dowager of Thanet, brought to bed of her first child, which was a son, in Thanet House in Aldersgate Street in London town where her husband Mr William Walter and her said mother and youngest sister Lady Anne Tufton then lay. And the 7th of that month in the same house was this child christened by the name of William after his father, my said daughter standing as deputy godmother in my stead, and the child's father standing as deputy godfather in his father's stead, and Mr David Walter was the other godfather. And the 21st of the same month (to my great grief and sorrow) this little William Walter my godson died, being but three weeks old wanting two days, and his dead body was opened and towards the latter end of the same month was carried to Church Hill near Sarsden in Oxfordshire, and buried in the church there where his father's relations lie buried. And so, both when this

---

249 Sir Richard Wenman, who was likely an associate of Anne's father.

child was born, christened and died, and was buried did I lie all the time in my own chamber in Appleby Castle in Westmorland.

And the 17th of November in this year being Friday about ten o'clock in the forenoon, after I had lain in my chamber in Appleby Castle in Westmorland ever since the 17th of August last being just three months, did I remove with my family from thence, coming through the withdrawing chamber and Great Chamber into the chapel for a while, and so through the hall I took my litter at the hall door in the court, in which I rid by the High Cross in Appleby, and through Scattergate and over Soulby Mask, and through Soulby and Wateby, and over Ashfell into the forest of Mallerstang and so came safe and well, I thank God, into my castle of Pendragon there in the same county about four o'clock in the afternoon having been accompanied in the way by several of the gentry of this country and of my neighbours and tenants both of Appleby, Kirkby Stephen and Mallerstang etc. And my two gentlewomen and women servants rid in my coach drawn with six horses and my menservants on horseback, but we had a great storm of rain and wind towards the latter end of the journey. And after the company had taken their leaves of me here at Pendragon Castle, I came up the stairs, and through the Great Chamber into my own chamber on the west side of it, where I formerly used to lie, and where I had not been since the 3rd day of August 1670 (being a year, three months and some fourteen days) until now, and where I now continued to lie for five months and two days, till the 19th of April following (being in the year 1672) that I removed from hence again into my castle of Brough in the same county to lie in it for a time.

In the year of Our Lord God 1672

For on this 19th of April 1672 (as aforesaid) being Friday, about ten o'clock in the forenoon after I had lain in my chamber in Pendragon Castle in Westmorland ever since the 17th of November last, did I remove out of it, and came through the Great Chamber, down the stairs into the court, where at the hall door, I went into my horselitter, in which I rid through the gatehouse there, and through the river of Eden, and over a part of Askfell, and through Wharton Park, and in sight of that Hall, and through Kirkby Stephen, and Brough Sowerby to my castle of Brough in the same county, my gentlewomen and maidservants attending to me in my coach drawn with six horses, and my menservants on horseback and a great many of my tenants and neighbours of Mallerstang, Kirkby Stephen, Brough and Appleby and other places in this county coming along with me. And so we came to my said castle of Brough about one o'clock in the afternoon where in the court of it I alighted out of my litter, and came up stairs into the hall, where all the strangers that accompanied me took their leaves of me, and went away to their several homes and from thence I came up stairs into the Great Chamber and through it and the chamber adjoining, I came into my own chamber in Clifford's Tower where I formerly used to lie, and where nor in this castle, I had not been since the 3rd of May in 1670 until now. And now I continued to lie in it till the 15th of August following (being just four months but for four days) and then I removed from hence again (as shall be here under written) into my castle of Appleby in the same county to lie in it for a time.

And the 30th day of July in this year being Tuesday whilst I lay in Brough Castle as aforesaid did my daughter Margaret, Countess Dowager of Thanet, and her youngest child the Lady Anne Tufton and second son Mr John Tufton with their servants, come from their journey from Thanet House in Aldersgate Street at London, and the last night from the inn at Greta Bridge in Yorkshire, and over Stainmore into Brough Castle in Westmorland, and so into my chamber in Clifford's Tower there to me, where I kissed them with great satisfaction and joy, I having not seen my said dear daughter, nor grandchild Lady Anne, since the 13th of August 1669, when they with other two of my grandchildren, namely Mr Sackville Tufton and Lady Mary Tufton, went away from me from Appleby (as where I then lay) back towards London, until now. Nor had I seen my said grandchild Mr John Tufton since the 14th of June in the said year 1669 that he and his brother Mr Richard had been with me in Appleby Castle aforesaid for about a week and then went back again towards London, until now. And they now lay in Brough Castle, my daughter, and her daughter with their women lying in the room at the north-west corner of the Great Chamber and her said son Mr John with their menservants lying in the great Roman Tower there for seven nights together. And when they were past, on Tuesday the 6th of the month following, in the morning, I having kissed them in my said chamber, as taking my leave of them, they went away from thence over Stainmore again, and so onwards on their journey towards London, whither they came safe and well (I thank God) the 14th day of the same month to Thanet House in Aldersgate Street there.

The 15th day of August in this year did I remove with my family out of the said Brough Castle into my castle of Appleby in the same county, coming along in my horselitter attended by my women servants in my coach, and my menservants on horseback, with a great many of my neighbours and tenants of both places through Warcop, Bongate and over Appleby Bridge, through the town, up into the court of the said Appleby Castle, where I alighted and went through the hall up into the chapel for a while, and then through the Great Chamber and withdrawing chamber. I came into my own chamber where I formerly used to lie, and where I had not been since the 17th of November last, till now, and where I now continued to lie till the 28th of January following (being five months and about a fortnight over) that I removed from thence into my castle of Brougham in the same county to lie in it for a time.

The 28th of this August did Mr Richard Sackville, third son to the now Earl and Countess of Dorset, come from his journey out of Scotland from his sister Homes[250] (who lives there) and from the city of Carlisle (where he lay the night before) hither into Appleby Castle in Westmorland, though I saw him not till the next day that he came up into my chamber to me, where I kissed him, it being the first time I ever saw him, or that he or any of his parent's children were in any part of the lands of my inheritance, so [he] now lay in the Baron's chamber here for three nights together and on Saturday the 31st of the same month he went away from hence again, to Kendal, and so onwards on his journey towards London.

The same 31st of August in the evening did Sir William Wilde, one of the justices of the Court of Common Pleas, and Sir Timothy Littleton, one of the Barons of His Majesty's Exchequer, who are now the two judges of assize for this Northern Circuit (as they also were the last year) came from their journey from Carlisle, hither into Appleby Castle in Westmorland where they now lay, the first in the Baron's Chamber, and the other in the best room in Caesar's Tower for four nights together. In which time they held the assizes for this county in the town hall here and on Wednesday the 4th of the same month they (having taken their leaves of me in my chamber) went away towards Kendal intending for Lancaster tomorrow to keep the assizes there also, which is the last place they have to go to in this circuit.

Also my cousin Sir Philip Musgrave of Edenhall and my cousin Sir John Lowther of Lowther lay in this Appleby Castle most part of the time of these assizes as usual.

And the 11th of October in this year being Friday did my daughter Margaret, Countess Dowager of Thanet, with her youngest daughter and child the Lady Anne Tufton remove out of Thanet House in Aldersgate Street at London and so in their coach over London Bridge into her house at Bolebroke in Sussex to lie there in it for a time, which was the first time they came to that house after they and my said daughter's second son Mr John Tufton, had been with me at Brough Castle in Westmorland but the August before. For they went from thence from me but the 6th of that month towards London. And my said daugh-

---

250 Anne Sackville, Countess of Home.

ter continued to lie in Bolebroke House aforesaid till the 26th day of December following that she removed from thence back again to Thanet House aforesaid. But by the way she lay one night in the inn at Croydon in Surrey, which was the first time she ever lay in that inn wherein her father's dead body did lie one night many years before, as he was carried from Dorset House in London to his burial in Withyham church in Sussex.

And the 29th of December in this year being Sunday about midnight did there fall a violent storm of thunder and lightning upon the island of Guernsey, which taking hold of the magazine powder blew up and destroyed Cornet Castle, which was the garrison of that island. By the ruins whereof were killed (to my great grief and sorrow) my dear grandchild the Lady Cecily Hatton, wife to Christopher, Lord Hatton, the governor there.[251] And with her the old Lady Dowager Hatton his mother, [252] and many of his officers, soldiers and attendants. But by God's merciful providence my said dear grandchild's children that she left behind her, which are three daughters as also their said father and some relations of theirs that were there, were preserved alive. But the dead bodies of my said grandchild and her Lord's mother were brought over into England to Portsmouth etc. and interred in the abbey of Westminster the 11th of the month following.

In the year of our Lord God 1673

The 28th day of January in this year being Tuesday, about one o'clock after noon, I removed out of Appleby Castle in Westmorland with my family after I had lain in it ever since the 15th of August before, into my castle of Brougham in the same county, where I had not been since the 17th of August 1671 till now. And now as I came from Appleby Castle I went through the withdrawing chamber and Great Chamber into the chapel for a while, where being taken with a swooning fit, I was carried into the Green Chamber and after I was by God's blessing recovered of it, I came from thence again down the stairs through the hall into the court, from whence, being a-taken by another fit of swooning, I was carried up for a while into the Baron's Chamber, but having also by God's

---

251 Thomas Dicey describes the death of Cecily Tufton in the 1672 explosion in Cornet Castle, Guernsey: 'Her Ladyship being greatly terrified at the Thunder and Lightning, insisted (before the Magazine blew up) upon being removed from the Chamber she was in, to the Nursery, where having caused her Women to come also to be with her in order to have joined in Prayer, in a few minutes after, that noble Lady and her Women fell a Sacrifice, by one Corner of the Nursery Room falling in upon them; and were the next Morning both found Dead'. *Historical Account of Guernsey* (1651), p. 125.

252 Elizabeth Montagu.

blessing got well past it, I went down again into the court where I took my horselitter, in which I rid through Appleby town, and over the bridge there, and through Crackenthorp, Kirkbythure, Temple Sowerby and Woodside into the court of Brougham Castle aforesaid whither I came safe and well, I thank God, about four o'clock that afternoon. And there I alighted and went upstairs into the hall, where all the company of my neighbours and tenants and others that came along with me took their leaves of me and went away. And I came upstairs through the Great Chamber and Painted Chamber, and that passage room, into my own chamber in the said Brougham Castle wherein my noble father was born and my blessed mother died, and where I now continued to lie till the 30th of July following that I removed from thence with my family to Appleby Castle in the same county to lie in it for a time.

The 23rd of February in this year being Sunday about seven o'clock in the morning was my grandchild the Lady Mary Walter[253] brought to bed and safely (I thank God) delivered of her second child, which is her first daughter, in her mother my daughter of Thanet's house in Aldersgate Street at London. Which child was christened the 26th of that month by the name of Mary, the Countess of Kent[254] (whose mother[255] was my god-daughter) being the one godmother and my said daughter of Thanet the other and Sir William Walter the godfather.

The 17th day of April in this year was my dear grandchild the Lady Anne Tufton, youngest child to my daughter Margaret, Countess Dowager of Thanet, married in St Botolph's church, Aldersgate Street at London, to Mr Samuel Grimston, a widower, whose first wife was daughter to Sir Heneage Finch the King's Attorney General by whom he had one only daughter now living, and himself is only son to Sir Harbottle Grimston, Master of the Rolls,[256] who with his Lady[257] and many others of his relations were present at the marriage as also my said grandchild's relations, her sister the Lady Margaret Coventry and her children, and three of her brothers, Mr John, Mr Richard and Mr Thomas Tufton and others, I then lying in Brougham Castle in Westmorland as I also did at the time of their removal, which was the 8th of the month following. For then this new married couple went from her mother my said daughter's house in Aldersgate Street aforesaid, to his father's house at the Rolls[258] to live there

253 Mary Tufton.
254 Mary Grey, Baroness Lucas in her own right and great-aunt to the child.
255 Anne Neville, daughter of Sir Christopher Neville and Mary D'Arcy,
256 The Master (or Keeper) of the Rolls was a judicial post and had administrative responsible for the records of the Court of Chancery. He oversaw Chancery clerks and at times acted as Keeper of the Great Seal.
257 Anne Bacon.
258 Rolls House, Chancery Lane, London.

with him and his Lady. Ecclesiastes 3; 8.6; Proverbs 20.24; Psalm 26.11–13;[259] Psalm 121.

The 13th day of June in this year were my great-grandchildren, my Lord Hatton's three little daughters that he had by my deceased grandchild the Lady Cecily Hatton, carried from Cornet Castle in the Isle of Guernsey from their said father the now governor of that island to the seaside, where they took ship in the Hatton yacht and landed in England at Portsmouth the 15th of that month, from whence they continued their journey towards London and came well thither the 18th of that month to Thanet House in Aldersgate Street to their grandmother, my daughter of Thanet, to live there with her. And that was the first time she ever saw those three grandchildren of hers since their mother's death by the unhappy accident herein above related. Psalm 90.15–17.[260]

The 17th day of July in this year did my daughter the Countess Dowager of Thanet, with her daughter the Lady Mary Walter and her husband Mr William Walter, go from Thanet House in Aldersgate Street at London (leaving behind her there her said three grandchildren my Lord Hatton's daughters) down to Sir Harbottle Grimston, the Master of the Rolls, [to] his house called Gorhambury near St Albans in Hertfordshire,[261] to her youngest daughter the Lady Anne Grimston wife to the Master of the Rolls's only son, where they lay for thirteen nights together. And the 30th of the same month they returned back from thence to Thanet House again.

And the same 30th of July being Wednesday in the forenoon, after I had lain in Brougham Castle in Westmorland in the chamber wherein my noble father was born and my blessed mother died for about half a year, ever since the 28th of January last, did I go for a while out of it into the middle room in the great Pagan Tower, where my old servant Jane Bricknell died and then came into my own chamber again. Where after a short stay I went from thence through the

---

259 Psalm 26 does not have a verse 13. All three manuscript editions of the *Great Book* include this reference, though none is in Anne's hand as was usual for biblical quotations. Psalm 26.11–12 reads: 'But as for me, I will walk in mine integrity: redeem me, and be merciful unto me. My foot standeth in an even place: in the congregations will I bless the Lord.' It may be that Anne meant Psalm 25.11–13: 'For thy name's sake, O Lord, pardon mine iniquity; for it is great. What man is he that feareth the Lord? him shall he teach in the way that he shall choose. His soul shall dwell at ease; and his seed shall inherit the earth.' This seems more likely given its reference to 'his seed' as this entry concerns marriage.
260 Psalm 90.15–17: 'Make us glad according to the days wherein thou hast afflicted us, and the years wherein we have seen evil. Let thy work appear unto thy servants, and thy glory unto their children. And let the beauty of the Lord our God be upon us: and establish thou the work of our hands upon us; yea, the work of our hands establish thou it.'
261 Grimston bought Gorhambury, once the estate of the Bacon family including Sir Nicholas and his son Sir Francis Bacon. His second wife was the great-granddaughter of Sir Francis Bacon.

little passage room and the Painted Chamber and Great Chamber and the hall down into the court of that castle, where I went into my horselitter in which I rid (being attended by my women in my coach drawn with six horses, and my menservants on horseback) along by the Pillar (that I erected in memory of my last parting there with my blessed mother) and through Whinfell Park and by the Hart's Horn Tree and the Three Brothers Tree and Julian Bower and through the entry, and so out of that park (crossing the two rivers of Lyvennett and Eden). I went through Kirkbythure, Crackenthorp, Battleburgh and over Appleby Bridge and through the town into Appleby Castle, whither I came well (I thank God) about three in the afternoon having been accompanied most part of the way by many of the chief gentry of this country and others and by my neighbours and tenants hereabouts. And so after I was now alighted in the court of this Appleby Castle, I came through the hall, and upstairs into the chapel and Great Chamber and from thence up the green stairs and through the withdrawing room into my own chamber, where I formerly used to lie and where I had not been since the said 28th of January last, till now and where I now continued to lie till the 20th day of March following that I removed from hence with my family to my castle of Pendragon in the same county to lie in it for a time.

The 9th day of August in the evening did Sir William Wilde baronet, one of the justices of the King's Bench, and Sir William Ellis knight, one of the justices of his Majesty's Court of Common Pleas, and now the two appointed judges for this Northern Circuit, come from their journey from Carlisle in Cumberland from holding the assizes there for that county, hither into this Appleby Castle in Westmorland, where they now lay the first in the Baron's Chamber and the other in the best room in Caesar's Tower, for four nights together, and in that time kept the assizes in the moot hall in Appleby town. Which being ended they went away from hence from me on Wednesday the 13th of the same. And my cousin Sir John Lowther of Lowther lay here most part of the time of these assizes as usual, but not my cousin Sir Philip Musgrave though he was here on Monday the 11th instant most part of the day and went home in the evening.

The 21st day of November in this year did the Duchess of Modena[262] with her daughter and many persons of quality come from their journey out of Italy (their own country) and landed at Dover in Kent, where His Royal Highness, the Duke of York, met them and married the said Duchess's daughter for

---

262 Laura Martinozzi and her daughter Mary of Modena, who married James Duke of York, later James II, in September 1673.

his second wife. And they all came together to London and Whitehall and St James's the 26th of that month. And the 30th day of the month following did the said Duchess of Modena, mother to the now Duchess of York, go from her and her husband the Duke, from St James's and Whitehall, and so out of England, onwards on her journey back into Italy to her own home there.

In the year of Our Lord God 1674

The 20th day of January in this year beginning Tuesday, between one and two o'clock in the afternoon, was my grandchild the Lady Mary Walter brought to bed of her third child, which was her 2nd son in Thanet House in Aldersgate Street at London, which child was christened the next day by the name of John, Sir William Walter the grandfather and Mr William the father being the two godfathers and myself (by deputy) the godmother. But my said dear grandchild the day after her delivery as aforesaid was taken with the disease of the smallpox, whereof she died there (to my great grief and sorrow) the 31st of the same month, at the age of twenty-one years and about six months over. And her dead body was carried the 5th of the month following to Church Hill near Sarsden in Oxfordshire and buried the 7th of the same in the vault of the church there, where her eldest son and her husband's relations lie buried. And during that time of her delivery, death and burial, as aforesaid, did I lie in my own chamber in Appleby Castle in Westmorland.

And the 23rd of this January died in Arundel House of a fit of the stone Elizabeth Stuart, Countess Dowager of Arundel, and was buried in Arundel church or chapel in Sussex by her husband Henry Howard, Earl of Arundel, by whom she had eight sons and two daughters. And part of her jointure was the castle and barony of Greystoke in Cumberland.

And the 20th day of March being about ten o'clock in the forenoon after I had lain in my chamber in Appleby Castle in Westmorland ever since the 30th of July last did I remove with my family out of it and came down through the withdrawing chamber, Great Chamber, and hall into the court, where I went into my horselitter in which I rid (being attended by my women in my coach, and my menservants on horseback, with several of my neighbours and tenants) through Scattergate, and over Soulby Mask, and through Soulby, and Wateby, to my castle of Pendragon in the same county, whither I came safe and well, I thank God, about three o'clock in the afternoon. And there, after those of the gentry and other my neighbours and tenants that accompanied me had taken their leaves of me, I came upstairs through the Great

Chamber into my own chamber on the west side of it, where I had not been since the 19th of April in 1672 till now, and where I now continued to lie till the 24th of September following, being about half a year, and then I removed from thence to my castle of Brough in the same county, to lie in it for a time.

And the 29th of May did my grandchild Mr Thomas Tufton, fourth son and seventh child to my daughter of Thanet, and one of the burgesses in Parliament for the corporation of Appleby, come from his journey from London hither into this Pendragon Castle to me where I kissed him with great satisfaction, I having not seen him since the 18th of July 1670 that he had been at this same castle with me till now. And now he lay here seven nights together in which time he went to Appleby to see the mayor and aldermen and to Acorn Bank to see my cousin Dalston his fellow burgess. And the 5th of the month following after I had kissed him and he taken his leave of me, he rid away from hence from me onwards on his journey towards London again and the southern parts.

And the 27th of July about eight o'clock in the evening was my grandchild the Lady Anne Grimston, youngest child to my daughter of Thanet and second wife to her husband Mr Samuel Grimston, brought to bed in her own chamber at the Rolls in Chancery Lane at London of her first child, which was a son who was christened there the 4th of the month following by the name of Edward.

The 31st day of August being Monday did Sir Richard Rainsford, one of the justices of the King's Bench, and Sir Timothy Littleton, one of the Barons of His Majesty's Exchequer, they being appointed the two judges this year for this Northern Circuit, come from the city of Carlisle in Cumberland from holding the assizes there and so by Brougham Castle and those ways into my castle of Appleby in Westmorland, whither I had sent some of my servants before to entertain them (myself with the rest remaining still at Pendragon Castle). And there at Appleby the said judges held the assizes for this county, and lay two nights in my castle there, Judge Rainsford in the Baron's Chamber and Judge Littleton in the best room in Caesar's Tower. And when they were past the 2nd day of the month following they with their attendants went away from thence to Kendal where they lay one night and the next day they went to Lancaster to hold the assizes there also for that county and so to finish their circuit. And my cousin Sir John Lowther of Lowther in Westmorland and my cousin Sir Philip Musgrave of Edenhall in Cumberland lay most part of the time of these assizes in my castle of Appleby as usual at such times.

And the 21st of May in this year did my honourable cousin (to whom I was godmother by deputy) Mr Robert Stanley, second brother to this Earl of

Derby,²⁶³ born at Knowsley in Lancashire, come hither to Pendragon to see me and lay here one night and the next day went away again homewards to the Countess Dowager of Derby his mother.²⁶⁴

And the 26ᵗʰ of August did my cousin Philip Lord Wharton's two eldest sons, Thomas that was lately married and Goodwin who is yet unmarried, come from their father to his house at Wharton Hall in this county where they lay for about a week. In which time, the 29ᵗʰ and 31ˢᵗ of the same month, they came severally hither to Pendragon Castle to me for a while.

The 24ᵗʰ of September being Thursday about eleven o'clock in the forenoon, after I had lain in my chamber in Pendragon Castle in Westmorland ever since the 20ᵗʰ of March last, did I remove from thence being attended by my gentlewomen and maidservants in my coach and my menservants on horseback and some of the gentlemen as also of my neighbours and tenants of Mallerstang, Appleby, Brough and other places. And so I rid in my horselitter [a]cross the river of Eden and through Wharton Park, Kirkby Stephen, Brough Sowerby and part of Brough town into my castle of Brough, whither I came safe and well I thank God about three o'clock in the afternoon and so up into my own chamber in Clifford's Tower where, nor in this castle I had not been since the 15ᵗʰ of August 1672 until now, and where I now continued to lie till the 11ᵗʰ day of May following that I removed to Appleby Castle to lie there for a time. ²⁶⁵

And the 19ᵗʰ day of October about two o'clock in the morning, in her father the Lord Hatton's house at Kirkby in Northamptonshire died my great-grandchild Mistress Elizabeth Hatton, third and youngest daughter and child to my late dear grandchild the Lady Cecily Hatton deceased. And the 27ᵗʰ of November about ten o'clock at night in the same house at Kirkby in Northamptonshire died her sister Mistress Margaret Hatton, second daughter and child to my said dear grandchild the Lady Cecily Hatton deceased.

And the 23ʳᵈ of December about twelve o'clock at noon died at the Rolls in London my great-grandchild and godson Mr Edward Grimston, first and only child to my dear grandchild the Lady Anne Grimston, and was buried the 28ᵗʰ of the same month in the vault of St Michael's church at St Albans in Hertfordshire, where some of his father's ancestors were buried before him, and where also was buried my ancestor Thomas Lord Clifford who was killed there in the first battle between the two houses of York and Lancaster, in Henry the 6ᵗʰ's time.²⁶⁶

263 William Stanley, 9ᵗʰ Earl of Derby.
264 Dorothea Helena Kirkhoven.
265 \till the 11ᵗʰ ... there for a time/ H1.
266 Thomas, 8ᵗʰ Lord Clifford, died in the Battle of St Albans, 22 May 1455. His uncle,

And when (to my great grief and sorrow) these three great-grandchildren of mine died, as aforesaid did I lie all the time in my chamber in Clifford's Tower at Brough Castle.

In the year of our Lord God 1675

The 24th day of March in this year [1675] died in his house at Sarsden in Oxfordshire Sir William Walter who was grandfather to two of my great grandchildren, for my grandchild the Lady Mary Tufton had been married to his son Mr William Walter above four years ago, and died (his wife) of the smallpox about two years ago, leaving two children behind her who are still living, namely Mistress Mary Walter who was two years old the 23rd of February last and Mr John Walter who was one year old the 20th of January last. And now at the time of his death, his said son their father, was in Italy.

The 11th day of May 1675 about ten o'clock in the forenoon, after I had lain in my chamber in Clifford's Tower in Brough Castle in Westmorland ever since the 24th of September last, did I remove from thence with my family going by Warcop, Bongate and over Appleby Bridge, into my castle of Appleby in this same county, whither I came safe and well I thank God about two o'clock in the afternoon having been accompanied by several of the gentry, and of my neighbours and tenants who took their leaves of me there. And then I went through the hall, and up through the Great Chamber, and withdrawing chamber, into my own chamber there, where I had not been since the 20th of March 1674 till now and where I now continued to lie till the 5th of October following that I removed from thence to Brougham Castle in the same county to lie in it for a time.

The 18th day of June in this year was conferred upon my noble son-in-law James Compton, Earl of Northampton, by our now King Charles the 2nd, the command and trust of Constable of the Tower of London.

The 3rd day of August did my dear daughter Margaret, Countess Dowager of Thanet, and her grandchild Mistress Anne Hatton (the only surviving child of Lady Cecily her deceased mother) come from their journey from Thanet House in Aldersgate Street at London hither into this Appleby Castle in Westmorland to me, where in my own chamber I kissed them with much joy, I having never seen this grandchild of mine before, nor had I seen my daughter since the 6th day of August in 1672 when she was with me at Brough Castle till now. So they now lay here in the Baron's Chamber eight nights together, and when

---

Henry Percy, 2nd Earl of Northumberland, was also killed in this battle. See *Great Books*, pp. 481–482.

they were past the 11th instant they began their journey towards London again, whither (I thank God) they came safe and well on Friday the 20th of the same month.

And the 23rd of this August being Monday did Sir Richard Rainsford and Sir Timothy Littleton, the two judges of assize for this Northern Circuit, come from holding the assizes at Carlisle in Cumberland, hither to me to Appleby Castle in Westmorland where they now lay, the first in the Baron's Chamber, the other in the best room in Caesar's Tower, for two nights together. In which time they held the assizes for this county in the moot hall in Appleby town. And on Wednesday the 25th instant they went to Kendal and the next day to Lancaster where they likewise held the assizes for that county and so ended their circuit.

The 1st day of September about noon did Henry Howard, Earl of Norwich and Lord Marshal of England, and his eldest son the Lord Henry Howard[267] and Charles Howard, Earl of Carlisle (my cousins), come into this Appleby Castle in Westmorland to me for a while. So I kissed them it being the first time I saw this Lord Marshal since he was a child or that I ever saw this son of his. And after they had dined here with several of the gentry of this county and of Cumberland they went away from hence onwards on their journey towards London.

The 15th day of this September did my dear grandchild the Lady Alethea Compton, youngest and only surviving child to my deceased daughter Isabella, Countess of Northampton, come from her journey from her father's house at Castle Ashby in Northamptonshire hither into this Appleby Castle in Westmorland to me, where I kissed her with much joy, I having not seen her since the 13th of July 1670 that she was at Pendragon Castle with me, till now. And she continued to lie here in the Baron's Chamber eight nights together. And when they were past on the 23rd instant, she began her journey from hence towards Castle Ashby again, whither she came safe and well, I thank God (with her company), the 29th of the same month.

The 23rd of this September about ten o'clock at night, was my grandchild the Lady Anne Grimston, twelfth and youngest child to my daughter Margaret, Countess Dowager of Thanet, delivered of her second child, which was a daughter, in her husband's house at Gorhambury in Hertfordshire. Which child was christened there the 6th of the month following by the name of Mary. The Master of the Rolls (the child's grandfather) and my said daughter of Thanet and the Lady Diana Curson being witnesses to it.

267 Henry Howard, 7th Earl of Norfolk.

And about that time was my grandchild Mr Thomas Tufton, fourth son and seventh child of my said daughter of Thanet, sworn Groom of the Bedchamber to the Duke of York.[268]

The 5th day of October being Tuesday about ten or eleven o'clock in the forenoon, after I had lain in my chamber in Appleby Castle ever since the 11th of May last, did I remove with my family from thence by ways of Crackenthorp, Kirkbythure, Temple Sowerby and Woodside etc. into my castle of Brougham in the same county where I had not been since the 30th day of July 1673 till now and where I now continued to lie, as usual, in the chamber wherein my noble father was born and my blessed mother died till the [22 March 1676].[269]

The last day of November about seven o'clock in the evening died my worthy cousin Sir John Lowther Baronet in his house at Lowther Hall in this county of Westmorland when he was about seventy-three years old, and was buried the 4th of the month following in the church there at Lowther where many of his ancestors lie interred. And by his death his grandchild and heir John Lowther my godson came to be Baronet who that day, as chief mourner attended the corpse to the church, where Doctor Smallwood, parson of Greystoke, preached the funeral sermon, there being present at the whole solemnity a great many of the gentry of this and the neighbouring counties, as also most of my chief servants

This noble and pious Lady, after a happy and retired life in these northern parts ever since the year 1649 where she repaired all those ancient castles and houses of her inheritance after they had lain ruinous many years, built and repaired several churches, chapels, bridges, and other structures of public benefit, built and endowed almshouses in both counties, making acts of charity and goodness the delight of her life, and with such great care and resolution preserved and defended her undoubted right to this northern estate, and so settled the same (which by her father was left in great confusion and disorder) that it is now lineally descended to the Right Honourable Thomas, Earl of Thanet, her now surviving heir and grandson), died in her castle of Brougham in Westmorland

---

268 This passage, 'And about that time … Duke of York', is heavily scored out, completely obscuring the text, in WD and H2. This was likely done by Thomas Tufton after the accession of William and Mary to the throne in 1689.

269 This statement was not completed because Anne died at Brougham Castle on 22 March 1676. Her body was taken to Appleby where she was interred in her tomb in St Lawrence's church there, near her mother where her monument and body remain today. Anne never strayed far from Brougham Castle during this last period of her life, and it seems clear that she hoped to die in the chamber where her father was born and her mother died, as she did.

the [22ⁿᵈ] day of [March] 1675 [1676] in the eighty and seventh year of her age and was buried in the vault in Appleby church (where her mother also lies) to whose virtuous and excellent memory, her succeeding posterity owe many great obligations.[270]

---

270 This paragraph was composed by Thomas Tufton, 6ᵗʰ Earl of Thanet, and inserted at his request.

Countess of Pembroke's Daybook, 1676

January 1676

The 1st day, and this forenoon there came hither from her house at Setterah Park, Mrs Winch[1] that is mother to Mr Thomas Sandford of Askham,[2] so I had her into my chamber and kissed her, and she dined without with my folks in the Painted Room, and after dinner I had her again into my chamber and talked with her a good while, and I gave her four pairs of buckskin gloves that came from Kendal. And with her I had also Mrs [Anne] Gabetis into my chamber and spoke to her a good while, and a little after they went from me.

And this morning about ten of the clock did some of my chief folks, Mr Thomas Gabetis my sheriff, Mr George Sedgwick,[3] Mr Edward Hasell, Mr Henry Machell[4] and the men to the first three, ride on horseback out of this Brougham Castle to my cousin Mr John Dalston at Millrigg, and dined there with him and his wife and children, but came back hither again about five of the clock at night. I went not out of the house nor out of my chamber today. Psalm 121.[5]

And this evening, about seven o'clock after I was in bed, did Allan Strickland[6] commit some disorders in my house of which I was acquainted next morning by Mr Thomas Gabetis my sheriff, but he showing a great regret

---

1 Mary Aglionby was related to Anne through the Musgraves.
2 This Thomas Sandford died 19 February 1676.
3 Anne was patron of George Sedgewick from the 1630s until his death, see above.
4 The Machell family was long connected with the Cliffords, with a Thomas Machell part of the famous hunting party during the visit of Edward Balliol to Robert, 1st Lord Clifford, at Brougham Castle in 1333. In her accounts for 1675 Henry Machell is described as the steward of Anne's house and gentleman of her horse. His nephew is Thomas Machell, the antiquarian, See Thomas Machell's manuscript history of the region, CAS Carlisle, D/CHA/11/4/1.
5 Reference to this psalm ends many daily entries (and was likely meant in places where there is a blank). It is an eight-line assertion of the belief in God's care and begins, 'I will lift up mine eyes unto the hills, from whence cometh my help' and ends 'The Lord shall preserve thy going out and thy coming in from this time forth, and even for evermore'. Reference to this verse is her way of commending herself to God's care at the end of each day.
6 Allan Strickland, Anne's steward, was likely connected to Thomas Strickland, the receiver of Anne's rents in Westmorland. Allan first appears in Anne's accounts in 1669. She was clearly fond of him or she would not have forgiven him his transgression.

and compunction for those misdemeanours, I was moved upon his ingenious acknowledgement and confession to pardon him.

The 2nd day being Sunday, yet I went not out of the house nor out of my chamber today. But my two gentlewomen Mrs [Frances] Pate[7] and Mrs Susan [Machell][8] and Mr Thomas Gabetis my sheriff and his wife, and three of my laundry maids[9] and most of my chief servants went to Ninekirks,[10] where Mr Grasty the parson preached a sermon to them and the congregation.[11]

And today there dined without with my folks in the Painted Room,[12] and with the sheriff and his wife, Mr Grasty the parson, my two farmers here, William Spedding and his wife, and Jeffrey Blamire and his son.[13] So after dinner I had them into my room and kissed the women and took the men by the hand. And a little after Mr Grasty the parson said Common Prayers[14] and read a chapter and sang a psalm as usual to me and them and my family, and when prayers were done they went away. I went not out of the house nor out of my chamber today.

3rd day, and this forenoon a little before dinner did I see John Webster[15] paid

---

7   Frances Pate was Anne's chief gentlewoman, likely the widow of Edmund Pate of Burton upon Trent. She was the mother of Marmaduke Pate, who first went to school at Kendal and later to Oxford where he took his B.A. in 1673. Anne supplemented Marmaduke's income during his education and may have paid his school fees. She is consistently generous to Frances Pate in her accounts and leaves Frances £50 in her will. Her salary was £10 per year from at least 1668 until 1676. Anne's chief gentlemen Hasell, Machell and Strickland were paid twice this yearly sum, i.e. £20.
8   Niece to Anne's gentleman servant, Henry Machell mentioned above. Susan Machell's yearly wage was £10.
9   Anne's laundry maids were Margaret Dargue, Jane Sledall, Dorothy Demain and Anne Chippendale. These were all from lower gentry or farming tenant families and so should be classed more as a lady's maids than maids of all work. They received generous wages at £4 per year, the equivalent wage to Anne's under-butler or chief groom. Anne also regularly gave gifts to them and their families.
10 Anne rebuilt the church of St Ninian's, called Ninekirks, after it lay in a ruinous state in 1659, see above. Her mother's bowels were buried there and her body buried in St Lawrence's church, Appleby, in a tomb designed by Anne.
11 Samuel Grasty was appointed Vicar of Brougham (which includes Ninekirks church) in 1664. He appears in the accounts of July 1665 administering the sacrament to Anne and her family at Brougham Castle.
12 The Painted Chamber was on the second floor of Brougham Castle and connected with Anne's chamber through a small passage. In the 1660s she used the Painted Chamber for Wednesday and Sunday prayers. Lower-status individuals ate their meals in the Great Hall below.
13 These are Anne's tenants and farmers. They appear to be closely connected with each other. They appear often in Anne's accounts from 1669 to 1675.
14 The Book of Common Prayer (London, 1662), which emerged from the political settlement after the Restoration. Prior to the Restoration she used the 1559 Book of Common Prayer.
15 John Webster appears often in this daybook and in Anne's accounts. He was a versatile man and performs a wide number of services for Anne. It may be that there was more than

for drawing over a copy of [blank] of St Nicholas belonging to my almshouse at Appleby and he dined without with my folks. And there also dined here with my folks and with Mr Thomas Gabetis my sheriff and his wife, Mr Lancelot Machell of Crackenthorp, so after dinner I had him into my chamber and took him by the hand and talked with him, and I gave him a pair of buckskin gloves and afterwards he went away. I went not out of the house nor out of my chamber today.

4th day, and this morning I saw Thomas Wright the Quaker[16] (who lay here the last night), paid in my chamber for twelve bushels of malt for beer for my house, and I took him by the hand and talked with him and a little after he went away. And afterward I had Mr Bracken of Kirkby Stephen the painter[17] into my chamber, and took him by the hand and talked with him, and saw him paid for drawing over two copies of the picture of my cousin german Francis, Earl of Bedford,[18] and he dined without with my folks and with Mr Thomas Gabetis my sheriff and his wife, and after dinner he went away.

And this forenoon about ten o'clock did my steward Mr Henry Machell ride on horseback out of this Brougham Castle toward Edenhall in Cumberland to my cousin Sir Philip Musgrave, but he came back again hither at night. And by the [London] Gazette this day received by the post from London I came to know that the Danes had taken Wismar from the Swedes,[19] and the King by his proclamation doth forbid all coffee houses or the selling of coffee publicly.[20] I went not out of the house nor out of my chamber all this day. Psalm 121.

The 5th day, and by a letter I received this morning from my daughter Thanet[21] dated the 30th of December I came to know that she is much troubled with pain in the head, but all that her posterity are well, and that Lord Hatton was mar-

one John Webster though this seems unlikely. He procures grain and other farm produce for her, is called her tenant and her woodward for Whinfell and Flakebridge. He makes locks and frames, he also draws maps of her manors.

16 Thomas Wright was nephew to Robert Atkinson who was executed for his part in the Kaber Rigg plot, see above. Wright alerted authorities to the plot.

17 Bracken copies a number of portraits for Anne including four copies of a series of four pictures of herself that she calls 'The four ages of her life' in 1674. She also has copies made of her father's portrait, her two husbands' portraits and several others. Bracken also painted forty-two coats of arms for her to be hung in Brougham Castle. See Accounts 1669–1675; M.E. Burkett, *John Bracken* (1976).

18 Francis Russell.

19 *London Gazette*, November 1675. Wismar is a port and city in northern Germany on the Baltic Sea, in the state of Mecklenburg-Vorpommern. It was given to Sweden under the Peace of Westphalia in 1648.

20 Charles II objected to coffee houses because of fears that they made people idle and were places where sedition was fomented: see *Proclamation for the Suppression of Coffee-Houses* (1675).

21 Margaret Sackville.

ried to his second wife Mrs Yelverton the 21st day of that last month,[22] being St Thomas Day, his first wife being my grandchild who was blown up with gunpowder in the Isle of Guernsey. And this afternoon did my housekeeper Richard Lowes come into my chamber to prayers, whom I had not seen in two months by reason of his great sickness, so I took him by the hand and talked with him. I went not out of the house nor out of my chamber today. Psalm 23.

The 6th day, being Twelfth Day, I remembered how this day was fifty-four (1620) years at night, at a masque performed in the King's Banqueting House at Whitehall and in the Privy Galleries there, did I see King James the Scotchman, and it was the last time I ever saw him or he me. Proverbs 20.24; Ecclesiastes 3; 8.6.

And this morning, before I saw him, did Mr Thomas Gabetis my sheriff ride away on horseback from his wife and me and us here, out of this Brougham Castle towards Appleby where the County Court is kept in the moot hall therein. And this morning after I was out of my bed I had seven or eight great loose stools downwards, which I thought did me much good, but withal weakened my body so much that it cast me into a swooning fit. But God be praised I recovered soon after. Psalm 23. And this morning I set my hand to three good letters of Hasell's writing for me:[23] one to my daughter Thanet, one to my Lord Northampton[24] and one to Mr William Edge, all in answer of letters I received from them by the last post.

And this 6th day there dined here with my folks and sheriff's wife, Mr Samuel Grasty our parson, and Mr James Buchanan the parson of Appleby and his second son,[25] and also John Webster. So after dinner I had them into my chamber and took them by the hand. And afterwards Mr Grasty said prayers and read a chapter (which he usually did upon a Wednesday) to me and them and my family, and when prayers were done they all went away. I went not out of the house all this day. Psalm [blank].

The 7th day. And this morning and today there dined here without in the Painted Room with my folks and Mr Thomas Gabetis my sheriff and his wife, Justice William Musgrave of Penrith. And I had him into my chamber and took him by the hand and talked with him awhile and I gave him a pair of gloves and then he went away.

22 Frances Yelverton, Christopher Hatton's first wife, was Cecily Tufton, who was killed in the 1672 explosion at Cornet Castle, see above.
23 Hasell has become her main secretary at this point. This daybook was dictated to him and is written in his hand.
24 James Compton, Earl of Northampton, whose first wife was Anne's daughter Isabella. They remained in close contact throughout Anne's life. Compton's daughter Alethea was heir to the Yorkshire estates, including Skipton Castle, after Margaret Tufton.
25 Charles Buchanan.

And there also dined here Mr Robert Willison of Penrith the Postmaster,[26] and after dinner I had him into my chamber and took him by the hand and saw him paid for a rundlet of sack[27] and another of white wine, and after he went away. And a little after did Mr Hugh Wharton come hither and brought me a letter from my Lord Wharton's eldest son, wherein he desires, if there be a new Parliament, to serve as knight for this year.[28] And I caused Mr Hasell to write an answer wherein I gave my consent and promise of my assistance to it, and gave him three shillings and then he went away.

And this 7th day in the afternoon, a little after dinner did Mr Thomas Gabetis my sheriff and his wife and servants, after I had taken my leave of them in my chamber, and after they had lain here with me during Christmas, for fourteen nights together, they rid away on horseback from me and us here towards their own homes at Crosby Ravensworth.

The 8th day, I remembered how this day was fifty-nine years[29] my first Lord and I and our first child the Lady Margaret went out of Great Dorset House in London town to Knole House in Kent to lie there for a time, which was the first time I came thither after my coming but the month before from my journey from Brougham Castle and so out of Westmorland and from the city of York, up to the said Great Dorset House to him and her, who then lay there. Psalm 55.17;[30] 121. Proverbs 20.24; Ecclesiastes 3; 8.6.

And this forenoon I had six or seven loose stools downwards which I thought did me good though it brought me into a swooning fit. And this day in the afternoon did George Goodgion pay me the kitchen stuff money and Mr Hasell received it off him in the Painted Room. I went not out of the house nor out of my chamber today. Psalm [blank]

The 9th day, being Sunday, yet I went not out of my chamber all this day. Ergo, consequently, Ecclesiastes [3], but my two gentlewomen and three of my laundry maids and most of my menservants went to the church of Ninekirks where Mr Grasty our parson preached a good sermon to them and the congregation. And today there dined without in the Painted Room with my folks Mr Grasty the parson, and my two farmers here, namely William Spedding and his wife,

26 He is a wine merchant and is listed as a gentleman.
27 A rundlet was approximately 68 to 84 litres. Sack was a fortified Spanish wine.
28 He is asking for her to support his bid to be a Member of Parliament for the area.
29 The events of 1616 and 1617 appear much on Anne's mind in these last months of her life and provide additional information on those years covered by her diary of the time above. Unfortunately, as no other daybook survives we do not know if it was her practice to remember the events of 1616 and 1617 each year.
30 Psalm 55.17: 'Evening, and morning, and at noon, will I pray, and cry aloud: and he shall hear my voice.'

and Jeffrey Blamire and his son, and John Webster. And after dinner I had them into my chamber and kissed her, and took them by the hand and talked with them. And afterward Mr Grasty our parson said Common Prayers and read a chapter and sang a Psalm, as usual upon Sundays, to me and them and my family, and when prayers was done they went away. And this 9th day, first of all did I fix a day to receive the blessed Sacrament with my family, which I intend, God willing, shall be upon the 25th day of this month.[31] I went not out of the house nor out of my chamber today. Psalm 23.

The 10th day, and this morning about nine o'clock, after I had taken my leave of him [George Sedgwick] in my chamber, and after he and his man had lain here in the highest chamber in Pagan's Tower (as usually for twenty-one nights together during which time I kept my Christmas here) did Mr George Sedgwick and his man Thomas Whalley ride on horseback out of this Brougham Castle from me and us here towards his own house near Kendal. And today there dined here with my folks in the Painted Room Mr Thomas Sanford's wife from Askham and her 2nd son,[32] so after dinner I had them into my chamber and kissed her and took him by the hand, and I gave her a pair of buckskin gloves and him 5^s and then they went away. And there also dined without Doctor Smallwood's wife of Greystoke and her eldest son and daughter,[33] and after dinner I had them into my chamber and kissed them and took him by the hand and talked a good while with them, and I gave her two pairs of buckskin gloves, and each of them one pair, and then they went away. And about five of the clock this evening did George Goodgion bring me twenty-eight books of devotion he bought for me at Penrith, and I then saw them paid for and gave them all away but six to my domestic servants. I went not out of the house nor out of my chamber today. Psalm 121.

The 11th day, and this morning I saw William Spedding, one of my farmers and others paid for loading of a cartload of wood out of Whinfell Park to this Brougham Castle, and likewise for riving[34] of wood for firing for my house here. And he dined here in the Painted Room, and after he went away, John Webster being by, he also dined here. I went not out of the house nor out of my chamber all day. Psalm [blank]

The 12th day, I remembered how this day was fifty-nine years [1617] my first and then only child the Lady Margaret, after she had been in the garden of

---

31 Anne and her household, or, as she calls them, her 'family', received communion four times per year.
32 Elizabeth Orfeur and her son John Sandford (b. 1653).
33 Dorothy Pursglove, Charles Smallwood and Catherine Smallwood.
34 splitting.

Knole House in Kent, did in the night fall desperately sick of her long ague of which she was in great danger of death, she then lying in a chamber in the tower there, which was underneath my chamber. Proverbs 20.24; Ecclesiastes 3; 8.6.

And today there dined here in the Painted Room with my folks Mrs Jane Carlton, the widow, sister to Sir William Carlton deceased, so after dinner I had her into my chamber and kissed her and talked with her a while. And I gave her 5ˢ and a little after (before prayers) she went away. And Mr Grasty our parson also dined here, and after dinner he came into my chamber and said Common Prayers as usual upon Wednesdays to me and my family, and after prayers was ended he read the Exhortation[35] for receiving the Sacrament which I intend, God willing, to receive the 25th of this month with my family. And then he went away. I went not out of the house nor out of my chamber today. Psalm 23.

The 13th day, and this morning I set my hand to three good letters of Hasell's writing for me, one to my daughter Thanet, one to my Lord Northampton and one to Mr William Edge, all in answer to letters I received from them by the last post. I went not out of this house nor out of my chamber today.

The 14th day, and this 14th day of this month I remembered how that day was fifty-nine [1617] years my first and only child the Lady Margaret, now Countess Dowager of Thanet, was removed out of the chamber in the tower at Knole House in Kent which was underneath mine into another chamber in the same house which looks towards the east, she then continuing to have her ague in great extremity. Ecclesiastes 3; 8.6; Proverbs 20.24.

And this morning after the week book was paid, did Mr Henry Machell my steward ride away on horseback out of this Brougham Castle towards Crakenthorp to see his brother and sister, and he lay there one night, and the next day towards evening he came back again hither to me. And today there dined here with my folks in the Painted Room Mr John Gilmore my Keeper of Whinfell, and his man William Labourne dined in the Hall, so after dinner I had them into my chamber and took them by the hand and talked with them, and then they went away.

And there also dined without John Webster, whom after dinner I had into my chamber and so paid him for drawing over the copy of the map of Harwood belonging to my almshouse at Beamsley, and then he went away. And there also dined here Mrs Elizabeth Atkinson, daughter of Mr Fairer of Warcop,[36]

---

35 This is the instruction or 'Exhortation' in the 1662 Book of Common Prayer that announces when holy communion will next be celebrated and gives those intending to receive it ways to prepare themselves spiritually. See Brian Cummings, ed., *The Book of Common Prayer* (2011), pp. 395–396.
36 Elizabeth Fairer, daughter of William Fairer (d. 1637) of Warcop Tower.

so after dinner she came into my chamber and I kissed her and gave her 2ˢ and then she went away. I went not out of the house nor out of my chamber today.

The 15th day, and this morning I had Thomas Wright the Quaker of Mallerstang (who lay here last night in the Bannister Room) into my chamber and took him by the hand and discoursed with him a while, and saw him paid for twelve bushels of barley malt, and afterwards he went away.

[She was told by letter] of my Lord Northampton's brother being made Dean of the Chapel, Bishop of London and Privy Counsellor. And about four months since was Dr Henry Compton, Bishop of Oxford, youngest brother to my son-in-law, the Earl of Northampton, made Dean of the King's Chapel, and about a month since he was translated to the Bishopric of London, and now lately sworn one of his Majesty's Privy Councillors. I went not out of the house nor out of my chamber today. Psalm [blank].

The 16th day being Sunday, which though it was yet I went not to church nor out of my chamber today. Psalm 23. But my two gentlewomen rode horseback thither, and my chief menservants went a foot and three of my laundry maids, to Ninekirks where Mr Grasty preached to them and the congregation.

And today there dined without with my folks in the Painted Room as usual, Mr Grasty our parson and my two farmers here, namely William Spedding and his wife, and Jeffrey Blamire and his son, and John Webster, so after dinner I had them all into my chamber and kissed the woman and took them by the hands. And a little after, Mr Grasty said Common Prayers and read a chapter and sung a Psalm, as usual upon Sundays, to me and them and my family, and after prayers was ended he read the Exhortation for the worthy receiving of the Holy Sacrament to me and them, which I intend God willing, to receive the 25th day of this month, and then they all went away. I went not out of the house nor out of my chamber today, though it was Sunday.

The 17th day being Monday, I remembered how this day was fifty-nine years [1617] I went out of Knole House in Kent from my first and then only child the Lady Margaret up to Great Dorset House at London to her father, my first Lord, the occasion of that journey of mine being an award that King James would have made concerning the lands of my ancient inheritance, so I lay there with him four nights together, and then returned back to Knole again to my said daughter. Ecclesiastes 3; 8.6; Proverbs 20.24.

And today there dined without in the Painted Room with my folks my cousin Mr Thomas Birkbeck of Hornby and his wife and their little daughter,[37] and his

---

37 Margaret Catterick, the younger, and Mary Birkbeck.

father-in-law Mr Catterick and his wife, and his mother.[38] And there also dined here Mr Robert Carlton, only son to the widow Lady Carlton.[39] So after dinner I had them all into my chamber, and kissed the women and took the men by the hand and I gave to my cousin Mr Birkbeck and his wife each of them 10^s and his mother 10^s and his father-in-law Mr Catterick and his wife each 10^s and 6^d to the child, and I gave Mr Carlton a pair of buckskin gloves, and then they all went away. I went not out of the house nor out of my chamber today. Psalm 121.

The 18th day I remembered how this day was fifty-nine years [1617] I went with my first Lord, Richard Earl of Dorset, before King James, into his inner drawing chamber at Whitehall where the King earnestly desired me to subscribe to an award which he intended to make betwixt me and my said Lord on the one part, and my uncle of Cumberland and his son Henry Lord Clifford on the other part, concerning the lands of my ancient inheritance in Craven and Westmorland. But (by God's Grace) I began to deny it, it being the first time I was ever before that King. Ecclesiastes 3; 8.6; Proverbs 20.24. And that same day in Knole House in Kent, where she then lay, had my first and then only child the Lady Margaret a fit of her long ague whereby she was in great danger of death. Psalm 23.4, 5.

And this 18th day, a little before dinner, did John Webster come hither, so I had into my chamber and took him by the hand and saw him paid for a drawing over the copy of a map of the lands of Temple Sowerby, and he dined without in the Painted Room with my folks. And there also dined here Mr Webster's two sons from Dufton, who brought me news that the parson of Dufton was sadly deceased at London, so I took them by the hand and talked awhile and then they went away.[40] I went not out of the house nor out of my chamber today.

The 19th day I remembered how this day was fifty-nine years [1617] and then Sunday in the afternoon in the withdrawing chamber of Queen Anne the Dane in the Court at Whitehall, did that Queen admonish me to persist in my denial of trusting my cause concerning my lands of Inheritance to her husband King James's award, which admonition of hers and other of my friends did much confirm me in my purpose, so as the next day I gave that King an absolute denial accordingly, which by God's Providence tended much to the good of me and mine.

And today there dined here with my folks in the Painted Room Mr Grasty our parson, so after dinner I had him into my chamber and took him by the hand and talked with him. And a little after he said Common Prayers, as usual

---

38 Margaret Catterick, the elder (maiden name unknown).
39 Barbara Delaval.
40 John Webster, Vicar of Dufton.

upon Wednesdays, to me and my family and when prayers was done he also read the Exhortation for worthy receiving the blessed sacrament of bread and wine, and when that was ended he went away.

And this afternoon, a little after dinner, did Mr James Bird[41] the attorney come hither to me for a little while, as he was in his journey to London, intending shortly to go up tomorrow. So I took him by the hand and discoursed with him awhile, and gave him 10^s as I used to do, and then he went away from me with reference to the prosecution of his intended journey. I went not out of this house nor out of my chamber today. Psalm [blank]

The 20th day, I remembered how this day was fifty-nine years [1617] I went with my first Lord to the Court at Whitehall, where in the inner withdrawing chamber King James desired and urged me to submit to the award which he would make concerning my Lands of Inheritance, but I absolutely denied to do so, wherein I was guided by a great Providence of God for the good of me and mine. And that day also had my first and then only child a dangerous fit of her long ague in Knole House in Kent, where she then lay. Psalm 23.4, 5; Ecclesiastes 3; 8.6; Proverbs 20.24.

And this morning I set my hand to three good letters of Hasell's writing for me, one to my daughter Thanet, one to my Lord Northampton and one to Mr William Edge, all in answer of letters I received from them by the last post. And today there dined without with my folks Mr Thomas Gabetis the sheriff, so after dinner I had him into my chamber and took him by the hand and talked with him awhile, and a little after he went away. And today there also dined with my folks in the Painted Room Mr Richard Pinder the Quaker, who lives now near Newcastle, so after dinner I had him into my chamber and took him by the hand and talked with him. And today I had a very ill fit of the wind yet slept well in the night. Psalm [blank]. I went not out of the house nor out of my chamber today. Psalm [blank]

The 21st day, I remembered how this day was fifty-nine years [1617] I went out of Great Dorset House in London town from my first Lord down to my first child the Lady Margaret to lie there in Knole House in Kent for a good while. I thanked God I found her alive though extremely weak and ill with her long

---

41 James Bird was a gentleman who served as attorney and steward for Anne in these last years and later served as lawyer and steward to her grandson, Thomas Tufton, Earl of Thanet. He also bought Anne's portion of Brougham Hall (not Castle) and the manor attached to it after Anne's death, uniting the manor under one owner. He also made some modifications of the hall. He served a number of families in the area including the Dacres, Lowthers and Otways. He was an antiquarian and amassed a large archive of material concerning Westmorland history.

ague, of which she had been in great danger those four nights I was from her. Psalm 23.4, 5; Ecclesiastes 3; 8.6.

And this morning, Thomas Wright the Quaker, I saw him paid for twelve bushels of malt for my house, he having lain here the last night, and then he went away. And this forenoon did John Webster come hither to me into my chamber, so I took him by the hand and talked with him and gave him a quarter of scarlet[42] and he dined without with my folks and afterwards he went away. I went not out of this house nor out of my chamber today. Psalm 121.

The 22nd day, and today there dined here without with my folks in the Painted Room Mr Robert Willison of Penrith, the postmaster, so after dinner I had him into my chamber and took him by the hand and talked with him, and saw him paid for a rundlet of sack, another of white wine and a gallon of claret against my receiving the Holy Sacrament,[43] and then he went away. I went not out of the house nor out of my chamber today. Psalm 121.

The 23rd day being Sunday I remembered how this day was fifty-two years [1624] in the chapel in Great Dorset House in London Town was I godmother to him that was christened by the name of Edward Sackville,[44] who was younger son to my first Lord's younger brother,[45] from whence I went down the next day from thence to Knole House in Kent to my two daughters and their father, to lie there.

And this 23rd day I remembered how this day was twenty-six years [1650] died my second Lord Philip Herbert, Earl of Pembroke and Montgomery, in his lodgings near the Cockpit at Whitehall, I then lying in my own chamber in Appleby Castle in Westmorland, whither John Turner (whose wife then served me) brought me the news of it the 27th day following. And my said husband's dead body being unopened was wrapt in cere cloth and lead and so carried down and buried in the cathedral church at Salisbury in Wiltshire by his brother and father and mother. Job. 7.2;[46] Proverbs 20.4; Ecclesiastes 3; 8.6.

And though it was Sunday yet I went not to church, nor out of my chamber all this day, nor neither of my gentlewomen, but most of my chief menservants and three of my laundry maids went to Ninekirks where our parson, Mr Grasty, preached there a good sermon to them and the congregation. And today there

---

42 A rich cloth, often of a bright red colour though it could be of other colours.
43 To be used in the communion cup.
44 He was wounded at the Battle of Newbury on 20 September 1643 and taken prisoner by Parliamentary forces. He died in 1646 during his imprisonment and some report that he was murdered by his captors.
45 Edward Sackville, 4th Earl of Dorset.
46 Job 7.2: 'As a servant earnestly desireth the shadow, and as an hireling looketh for the reward of his work.'

dined here in the Painted Room with my folks Mr Grasty the parson, and William Spedding and his wife, and Jeffrey Blamire and his son, and John Webster. So after dinner I had them into my chamber and kissed the woman and took the men by the hand. And after Mr Grasty said Common Prayer and read a chapter and sung a psalm as usual upon Sundays to me and them and my family, and also read the Exhortation for receiving the Holy Sacrament, and a little after they all went away. I went not out of the house nor out of my chamber today, though it be Sunday. Psalm 121.

The 24th day, and this day there was none that dined here or visited me, so as I spent the time hearing some chapters read to me and in preparing my self to receive the Holy Sacrament of Bread and Wine, which I intend, God willing, to receive tomorrow with my family. I went not out of the house nor out of my chamber all this day. Psalm 121.

The 25th day I remembered how this day was fifty-two years [1624] in the withdrawing chamber at Knole House in Kent, as we sat at dinner, had my first Lord and I a great falling out, when but the day before I came from London from being godmother to his brother's youngest son. Deuteronomy 23.5;[47] Proverbs 20.25; Ecclesiastes 3; 8.6

And this 25th day in the morning did Mr Samuel Grasty our parson preach a good sermon and administered the blessed sacrament to me and my family in my chamber at the Brougham Castle which I nor they had not received since the 3rd of November lastly that then we received of him here it until now. And this morning about eight o'clock did Mr Samuel Grasty our parson preach a good sermon in my chamber to me and my family, and a little after he administered the Sacrament of bread and wine to me and them: to my two gentlewomen Mrs Frances Pate, Mrs Susan Machell, Dorothy Demain, Margaret Dargue, Anne Chippindale and Jane Sleddall, my four laundry maids, Isabell Jordan my washwoman, Mr Edward Hasell, Mr Henry Machell, George Goodgion, Edmund Sort, Allan Strickland, William Dargue, John Hall, Abraham Fittin, Isaac Walker, Richard Reynoldson, William Buckle, Richard Lowes my housekeeper, Cuthbert Rawling, Jacob Murgatroyd, Arthur Swindin, George Lough, clerk, which I nor they received since 3rd November last. And Parson Grasty dined here with my folks in the Painted Room and then he went away. And there also dined in the Painted Room with my folks Mr Charles Crow the parson of Warcop, so after dinner I had him into my chamber and took him

---

47 Deuteronomy 23.5: 'Nevertheless the Lord thy God would not hearken unto Balaam; but the Lord thy God turned the curse into a blessing unto thee, because the Lord thy God loved thee.'

by the hand and talked with him, and I gave him 2ˢ 6ᵈ and then he went away. I went not out of this house nor out of my chamber today. Psalm 121.

The 26ᵗʰ day, and this morning by letters I received from my daughter Thanet and by the packet of this week from London, I came to know that she herself, my said daughter, was well, and most of her generation and posterity in their several places and homes. And though today I had a very ill fit of the wind, yet I slept well in the night notwithstanding, I thank God. I went not out of the house nor out of my chamber all this day. Psalm [blank]

The 27ᵗʰ day, I remembered how this day was twenty-six years [1650] did John Turner (who is since deceased, and his wife⁴⁸ who then served me secondly married to John Gilmore) come from his journey from London to Appleby Castle in Westmorland, and in my own chamber there did first of all tell me of the death of my second husband, Philip Earl of Pembroke and Montgomery, and how he died the 23ʳᵈ of that month in his lodgings by the Cockpit at Whitehall. Job 7.1; Ecclesiastes 3; 8.6.

And this morning I set my hand to three good letters of Hasell's writing for me, one to my daughter Thanet, one to my Lord Northampton and one to Mr William Edge, all in answer of letters I received from them by the last post. And today there dined here with my folks besides John Webster, Mr Robert Hilton of Murton.⁴⁹ So after dinner I had them into my chamber and took them by the hand and talked with them, and I gave Mr Hilton a pair of buckskin gloves, and I saw John Webster paid for drawing over the copies of two maps of Southfield, and then they went away. I went not out of this house nor out of my chamber today. Psalm [blank].

The 28ᵗʰ day, and this day did Mr Thomas Gabetis my sheriff and auditor after he had dined with my folks he read over to me Mr Edge and Mr Lane's accounts for Michaelmas 1675 which then I allowed and set my hand and they were witnessed by Mr Edward Hasell, Mr Henry Machell, George Goodgion, Edmund Foster, and John Preston. And when I had paid him [Gabetis] as usual for that service he went from here to his house at Crosby

And today I had a very ill fit of the wind, but yet never the less I slept well in the night, I thank God. Psalm 23. I went not out of the house, nor out of my chamber all this day. Psalm 121.

The 29ᵗʰ day, and yesternight late did John Bradford come from Skipton and over Cotter and Stake afoot hither to this Brougham Castle, but I did not see

---

48 Elizabeth Nicholls.
49 A gentry family of Hilton Bacon, near Appleby, Westmorland. They were long-time tenants of the Cliffords in Westmorland. Members of the family acted as Anne's agents from time to time.

him till this morning. And he brought the news of Mrs Sutton's death, mother of my almshouse at Beamsley.

And this morning about six o'clock, before I was out of my bed, did I pare the tops of my nails of my fingers and thumbs and burnt them in the fire after I was up.

And today there dined without with my folks in the Painted Room Mr John Gilmore, my Keeper of Whinfell Park, and Mrs Saul.[50] So after dinner I had them into my chamber and kissed her and took him and his man, William Labourne, who dined below in the Hall, by the hand and talked with them a good while, and I gave Mrs Saul, whose grandmother I knew well when I lived at Court, 5^s and then they went away, I went not out of the house nor out of my chamber today. Psalm [blank].

The 30th day being Sunday, I considered how this day was eight-six [1590] years and then Friday about seven o'clock in the evening was my blessed mother with very hard labour brought to bed of me in her own chamber in Skipton Castle in Craven, where she then lay, my brother Robert, Lord Clifford, then also lying in the castle. But my noble father then lay in Bedford House in the Strand at London, as also my aunt of Warwick and her husband Ambrose, Earl of Warwick, who died the 21st of the month following. And about six years before my birth was my blessed mother in the same place delivered of my eldest brother, Francis, Lord Clifford, but he died before I was born. Proverbs 20.24; Ecclesiastes 3; 8.6; Job 7.1; Psalm 121.

And this day was twenty-seven years [1649] our then King Charles (who was born in Scotland) was beheaded on a scaffold in the open air near the Banqueting House at Whitehall and his dead body afterwards buried in the chapel at Windsor in Berkshire. And when this tragedy was performed did I lie in Baynard's Castle in London and my second Lord was in his lodgings by the Cockpit at Whitehall where he died about a year after. Job 7.1; Psalm 23.4, 5; Proverbs 20.24; Ecclesiastes 3; 8.6.

And though it was Sunday yet I went not to church nor out of my chamber today, but my two gentlewomen and most of my menservants went and three of my laundry maids to the church of Ninekirks where Mr Grasty the parson preached a good sermon to them and the rest of the congregation. And today there dined without in the Painted Room with my folks, Mr Grasty and my two farmers here, namely William Spedding and his wife and Jeffrey Blamire and his son and John Webster. So after dinner I had them into my chamber and kissed the woman and took the men by the hand. And afterwards Mr Grasty

---

50 Or Sewell. There were several families of this name in the area.

said prayers and sung a Psalm as usual upon Sundays, to me and them and my family, and when prayers was done they all went away.

And today I had two or three stools downwards which I thought did me good. Psalm [blank]. I went not out of the house nor out of my chamber today, though it were Sunday. Psalm 121.

The 31st day, remembered how this day was fifty-nine years [1617] when my first and then only child the Lady Margaret and I then lay in Knole House in Kent, did she grow extremely sick and ill of several fits of her long ague, so as she was in great danger of death in all folk's opinion, but it pleased God to recover her miraculously. Psalm 23.4,5; Ecclesiastes 3; 8.6.

And this day did my family keep as a fast for the Martyrdom of King Charles the 1st,[51] though he was beheaded the day before. The day being commanded to be kept by Act of Parliament.

And this day, about three o'clock in the afternoon did John Twentyman,[52] gardener to the Lord Bishop of Carlisle, come from Rose Castle in Cumberland hither to this Brougham Castle to look after and order my garden here. So he lay in the Bannister Room five nights together during which time he worked in my garden here. Upon Saturday the 5th of February in the morning he went home again, and I sent by him a bottle of the pulp of pomcitron[53] to the Bishop of Carlisle. I went not out of the house nor out of my chamber today. Psalm 121.

February 1676

The 1st day. I remembered how this day was forty-seven years [1629] died in her own chamber at the Court at Whitehall the Lady Susan Vere, Countess of Montgomery, she who was first wife to him that was afterwards my second Lord. And when she died did I and my two daughters then lie in the Priory House in St Bartholomew in London. And her dead body was buried soon after

---

51 Charles I is still considered an Anglican martyr for his refusal to accede to Parliamentary demands to accept their religious reforms, including a denunciation of the Book of Common Prayer and the episcopal hierarchy. Anne was steadfast in her use of the Book of Common Prayer (1559) and supported bishops in exile during the Interregnum, so the celebration of this day would be for her more about constancy in religion than the celebration of Charles I as a political figure. In the Anglican church calendar 30 January is still celebrated as the festival of Charles, King and Martyr, 1649.
52 John Twentyman was a landscape gardener employed by Edward Rainbow, Bishop of Carlisle. He had previously done work for Anne in April 1675 to September 1675, see accounts 1669–1675.
53 Anne's accounts 1669–1675 reveal that Francis Pate and Arthur Swindon often made lemon preserves. A pomcitron resembles a large lemon with less acidic flesh and a thick fragrant peel.

in the Cathedral Church of Westminster by her grandmother and her mother the Countess of Oxford and the Lady Burghley.[54] And I was first told the news of her death by Sir George Manners, afterwards Earl of Rutland. And I was married (a second wife) to her husband about a year and four months after her death. Job 7.1; Ecclesiastes 3; 8.6; Proverbs 20.24.

And this morning did William Johnson my housekeeper at Appleby Castle and Henry Benson my herdsman at Southfield come hither, so I see them both paid their board wages in my chamber, and they dined here below in the Hall and then they went away.

And this morning I also so paid to William Birkbeck of Mallerstang (who lay here the last night) for twelve bushels of malt for beer for my house and then he went away. And I also saw paid for loading of wood from Whinfell to this Brougham Castle for firing for my house, and then they went away. And Robert Harrison my housekeeper of Brough Castle this morning came hither and he brought along with him workmen, whom I saw paid for making a new garden and walling of it and for mending the glass windows there, and after they had dined here they went away. And this forenoon did John Webster come hither to me, so I had him into my chamber and took him by the hand and talked with him, and he dined without with my folks in the Painted Room, and a little after dinner he went away. I went not out of the house nor out of my chamber all this day. Psalm 121.

The 2nd day, I remembered how this day was fifty-six years [1620], about twelve of the clock in the day time, I was delivered of my little son Thomas, Lord Buckhurst, in my own chamber in Knole House in Kent, where I and my eldest daughter the Lady Margaret then lay. And the same day John Conniston rid on horseback from thence to my first Lord to Great Dorset House in London town to carry him the news of the birth of that son of his, who died in that house the 26th of July following.[55] Ecclesiastes 3; 8.6; Proverbs 20.24; Job 7.1.

And today there dined here with my folks Mr Grasty our parson. So after dinner he came into my chamber and I talked with him and took him by the hand. And afterwards he said Common Prayers as usual upon Wednesdays to me and my family, and a little after he went away. I went not out of the house, nor out of my chamber all this day. Psalm [blank]

The 3rd day, and this morning I set my hand to four good letters of Hasell's writing for me, one to my daughter Thanet, one to my Lord Northampton, one to my grandchild the Lady Alethea Compton and one to Mr William Edge; all

---

54 St Nicholas chapel where Mildred Cecil, Lady Burghley, and Anne Cecil, Countess of Oxford's large monument stands.
55 He was buried in the Sackville chapel at St Michael's and All Angels church, Withyham, Sussex.

in answer of letters I received from them by the last post. I went not out of the house nor out of my chamber all this day. Psalm 121.

The 4th day, I remembered how this day was fifty-six years [1620] my first Lord Richard, Earl of Dorset, came from Great Dorset House in London town down to Knole House in Kent to me and my eldest daughter the Lady Margaret and his young son the Lord Buckhurst, who was born but two days before that, being the first time he ever saw that young son of his who died there the 26th of July following. Ecclesiastes 3; 8.6; Proverbs 20.24; Job 7.1

And the 4th day of this month, about seven o'clock at night, did Robert Goodgion and Thomas Kitching my tenants at Skipton come hither, but I did not see them till the next day, that I then had them into my chamber and took them by the hand and talked with them, and they lay in the Baron's Chamber for three nights together, and when they were past they went away back towards Skipton again.

And today there dined without with my folks in the Painted Room Mr Phillip Nanson, who is Fellow of Queen's College in Oxford,[56] so after dinner I had him into my chamber and took him by the hand and talked with him and gave him 5^s and then he went away. And there also dined here with my folks Mr Thomas Langhorne of Penrith the shopkeeper, and so after dinner I had him into my chamber and talked with him a good while and then he went away. And there also dined without John Webster. I went not out of the house nor out of my chamber all this day. Psalm [blank]

The 5th day, I remembered how this day was fifty-nine years [1617] was my first and then only child the Lady Margaret (now Countess Dowager of Thanet) dangerously sick of her long ague in Knole House in Kent where I then lay, but her father, my first Lord, then lay in Great Dorset House in London town. Ecclesiastes 3; 8.6; Proverbs 20.24; Psalm 23.4, 5.[57]

And by a letter I received by the post from my cousin Sir Thomas Wharton dated at Goldesborough the 10th I came to know that, a little before, his son's wife was brought to bed there of a son (which is her first child) who is christened by the name of Thomas.

And today I had a very ill fit of the wind but yet notwithstanding I slept well and soundly in the night, I thank God. Psalm [blank]. I went not out of the house nor out of my chamber all this day. Psalm [blank]

---

56 Philip Nanson, originally of Appleby, rector of Newnham, Hampshire. His daughter Jane married Anne's cousin, Sir Christopher Lowther, 3rd Baronet Lowther, in 1710. Anne had a close connection with Queen's College, where her Tufton nephews and many others she supported matriculated.

57 See p. 51

The 6th day being Shrove Sunday, I considered how this day was eighty-six years [1590] the good news was brought to my father and my aunt of Warwick and her husband, to Bedford House in the Strand, both by letter and word of mouth, that my mother was brought a bed of me the 30th of the month before in Skipton Castle in Craven with very hard labour. Ecclesiastes 3; 8.6; Proverbs 20.24.

And though it was Sunday today yet I went not to church nor out of my chamber all this day. Psalm 23. Nor neither of my gentlewomen, but three of my laundry maids and the two Yorkshire men Robert Goodgion and Thomas Kitching and most of my menservants went to Ninekirks, where Mr Grasty the parson preached to them and the congregation.

And today there dined without with my folks in the Painted Room, besides the two Craven men aforenamed, Mr Grasty the parson, and my two farmers, namely William Spedding and his wife, and Jeffrey Blamire and his son, and John Webster. And after dinner I had them into my chamber and kissed the woman and took the men by the hand. And then Mr Grasty said Common Prayers and read a chapter (as usual upon Wednesdays and Sundays) to me and them and my family and a little after they all went away from me.

And this afternoon about four o'clock did I take my leave of the two Craven men, Robert Goodgion and Thomas Kitching, and took them by the hand and talked with them, and then about eight o'clock after they had laid in the Baron's Chamber three nights, they rode away on horseback out of this Brougham Castle toward their own homes in Craven. I went not out of the house nor out of my chamber all this day. Psalm 121.

The 7th day, being Shrove Monday, and today there dined without, with my folks, Dorothy Wybergh, the deaf woman of my almshouse at Appleby, and after dinner I had her into my chamber and kissed her.[58] And I saw her paid for five dozen yards of Bonlace, but I was very angry with her for bringing so much and told her I would have no more of her.[59] And there also came along with her and dined here Dorothy Winter of Clifton, sister to John Webster, so I

---

58 Dorothy Irton.
59 Bone lace was made generally with linen thread, knitted on a pattern marked by pens with bobbins initially made of bone; thus this lace was also called bone-work lace. According to Anne's accounts Dorothy had been supplying bone lace to her from at least March 1665, for which she was generally paid between 5d and 6d per yard. Anne also notes in her accounts that she buys this lace to give away to her women servants and others. Dorothy generally brought between eight and twelve yards to Anne, but by 1675 was bringing up to twenty-four yards at a time, about four times per year. This sixty yards was clearly extravagant, especially as Anne was buying the lace as an act of charity. It also shows that, while Anne was indulgent, she refused to allow anyone to take advantage of her and was fully able to make this distinction in the last months of her life.

had her into my chamber and kissed her and talked with her awhile, and a little after they both went away.

And by the letters I received by the post from my daughter Thanet and my Lord Northampton dated the 3rd of February I came to know that there was lately a great sea-fight before Messina between the Dutch and Spanish fleet, and the French fleet, and the French were much worsted, many of their ships being taken and sunk.[60] I went not out of the house nor out of my chamber today. Psalm 121.

The 8th day, being Shrove Tuesday, I remembered how this day was seventy-five years [1601] Robert Devereux, Earl of Essex, with others of quality then go into his house called Essex house in the Strand in a rebellious manner against Queen Elizabeth into the city of London, in which rebellion he was taken and beheaded for it at the Tower in London on 25th of that month.[61] Job 7.1; Ecclesiastes 3; 8.6.

And today there dined without with my folks the widow Margaret Spedding, who is sister-in-law to William Spedding, one of my farmers, and after dinner I had her into my chamber and kissed her, and talked with her a good while, and a little after she went away. I went not out of the house nor out of my chamber today. Psalm 121.

The 9th day being Ash Wednesday, I remembered how this day was seventy-two years [1604] died in North Hall house in Hertfordshire, in her own chamber there, my worthy aunt Anne Russell, Countess Dowager of Warwick. And she was buried a while after, unopened, in the vault of Chenies church in Buckinghamshire by her ancestors, my mother, my self, my cousin german the Lady Frances Bourchier, and my uncle the Lord William Russell and his wife and their son, who was afterwards Earl of Bedford, lying in North Hall house at the time of her death and burial. Ecclesiastes 3; 8.6; Proverbs 20.24; Job 7.1.

And I remembered how this day was fifty-two years [1624] my first Lord Richard, Earl of Dorset, came into the tower chamber in Knole House in Kent where I then lay, and there he kissed me and my two daughters, which I had by him, and that was the last time he lay in Knole House, for that day he went up to Great Dorset House in London town and there lay the Parliament then sitting and being very full of business so as he continued to lie there in that Great Dorset House till his death happened the 29th of March following. Ecclesiastes 3; 8.6; Proverbs 20.24; Job 7.1.

---

60 The Battle of Messina in the Franco-Dutch war of 1672–1678. Spain, England, Sweden, Austria and other countries were also involved in this war.
61 Robert Devereux led an unsuccessful armed uprising against Queen Elizabeth on this day in 1601. Anne's parents were close friends of Devereux. Nevertheless, George Clifford sat in judgement and agreed to Devereux's sentence of death.

And this day being Ash Wednesday, about one o'clock did Mr Samuel Grasty our parson read Common Prayers and a chapter as usually upon Wednesdays to me and my family. And afterwards, about four o'clock, he dined here without with my folks. And the following day in the morning did I see Mr Robert Willison of Penrith paid for a rundlet of sack, but I was very angry with him, because I thought it was too dear, and told him I would have no more of him, and then he slipped away from me in a good hour.

And today I had a very sore fit of the wind, but notwithstanding I slept well after it in the night, I thank God. Psalm 121. I went not out of the house nor out of my chamber all this day. Psalm [blank].

The 10th day I remembered how this day was fifty-nine years [1617] did my first and then only child the Lady Margaret (now Countess Dowager of Thanet) remove out of the great chamber at Knole House in Kent, called the Lord Treasurer's Chamber, into the little room within it called the Lord Treasurer's Closet, where she continued to lie that month and the most part of the next, where she was dangerously ill with her long ague, so as everyone thought she would have died. And then did I lie in the same house, but her father then lay in Great Dorset House in London town.

And this morning I set my hand to three good letters of Hasell's writing for me, one to my daughter Thanet, one to my Lord Northampton and one to Mr William Edge, all in answer of letters I received from them by the last post. And this 10th day in the morning did John Webster bring the two maps of Flakebridge that he had drawn for me, so I had him into my chamber and saw him paid for them,[62] and he dined here without with my folks, and a little while after he went away.

And this afternoon about one o'clock did Sir George Fletcher and his lady and her daughter by her first husband,[63] and Mr Fleming and his eldest daughter [also came],[64] so I had them into my chamber and kissed the women and took the men by the hand, and Sir George delivered to me several letters of my ancestors which were sent me by order of my Lord Marshal,[65] and after I had

---

62 In December 1675 Webster had drawn a map of Brougham, and was paid 5s.
63 Mary Johnstone's first husband was Sir George Graham of Netherby. Their daughter is Margaret.
64 Daniel Fleming of Rydal Water and his daughter Catherine. George Fletcher and Daniel Fleming were good friends who attended Queen's College, Oxford, together, and became brothers-in-law when Daniel married George's sister Barbara. Anne gave Daniel and Barbara a piece of silver for their wedding when they visited her at Appleby on 28 August 1655. Their eldest daughter was Catherine.
65 Henry Howard, 6th Duke of Norfolk. Even in these final years of her life Anne continued to pursue her antiquarian interests.

talked with them and given the women each of them enamelled gold rings, they all went away. I went not out of the house nor out of my chamber all this day. Psalm 121.

The 11th day, and this afternoon a little after dinner, about one o'clock, after I had taken my leave of them in my chamber, did Mr Edward Hasell and his man Cuthbert[66] ride on horseback out of this Brougham Castle towards Rose Castle in Cumberland to his uncle and aunt, the Bishop of Carlisle and his Lady,[67] where he and his man lay three nights, and on the 14th day in the evening a little after supper they came back again hither to me and us here into this Brougham Castle. I went not out of the house nor out of my chamber all this day. Psalm [blank]

The 12th day, and today there dined without with my folks in the Painted Chamber Mr Lancelot Machell of Crakenthorp, for he came from his own house here this morning. And after dinner I had him into my chamber and talked with him a good while, and took him by the hand, and he now told me that his eldest son, Mr Hugh Machell, had by a fall from his horse badly broken his leg about a fortnight hence. So that he came now to borrow my horselitter. I went not out of the house nor out of my chamber all this day. Psalm [blank]

The 13th day being Sunday, though it was so I went not to church nor out of my chamber all this day. Psalm 121. But my two gentlewomen and three of my laundry maids behind several of my menservants rode on horseback to Ninekirks, where Mr Grasty the parson preached a good sermon to them and the rest congregated. And today there dined without in the Painted Room with my folks Mr Samuel Grasty our parson and my two farmers, namely William Spedding and his wife and Jeffrey Blamire and his son, and John Webster. So after dinner I had them into my chamber and kissed the woman and took the men by the hand. And a little after Mr Grasty said Common Prayers and read a chapter and sung a Psalm (as usual upon Sundays) to me and them and my family, and after prayers was done they all went away. I went not out of the house nor my chamber all this day though it was Sunday.

The 14th day, I remembered how this day was sixty-three years [1613] our King James's eldest daughter, the Lady Elizabeth, married in the King's Chapel at Whitehall to Prince Frederick, Elector Palatine of the Rhine and Heidelberg, her father and mother and myself and my first Lord and most of the nobility being present at her marriage, Ecclesiastes 3; 8.6; Proverbs 20.24. And I remember

66 Cuthbert Rawling.
67 Edward Rainbow and Elizabeth Smyth. Hasell's mother was Martha Smyth, Elizabeth's sister.

how the 14th day of this month (or about that time) was ten years [1666] died my good servant Mr Gabriel Vincent in the Roman Tower at Brough Castle, I and my family lying then in that castle. Job. 7.1.

And the 14th day, about six o'clock in the morning, did John Hall and Abraham Fittin ride out of this Brougham Castle with my horselitter.[68] And this 14th day, early in the morning, did my black spotted bitch called [Quinne] puppy in my bed and chamber four little puppies, but they were all dead.

And yesternight did Arthur Swindin leave off lying in the music room[69] where he used to lie and began to lie in the housekeeper's chamber, Richard Lowes, that is under the Great Chamber. And this forenoon did John Webster come hither into my chamber, so I took him by the hand and talked with him, and he retreated from me into the Drawing Room and dined with my folks. I went not out of the house nor out of my chamber all this day. Psalm [blank].

The 15th day. And this morning did I see paid for twelve bushels of malt in my chamber to Mr Thomas Wright the Quaker of Mallerstang,[70] who came hither last night and lay here in the Bannister Room, and a little after he went away. And this forenoon about 10 o'clock did Mr Henry Machell (my Steward) ride away on horseback out of this Brougham Castle towards Appleby Castle and lay there one night, next day towards evening he came home.

And there came hither this afternoon about one o'clock, my cousin Mrs Anne Howard, sister to my cousin Mr Francis Howard of Corby, and her cousin Sir Charles Howard's daughter,[71] and two other gentlemen with them (whose names I know not). So I had them into my chamber and kissed the women and took the men by the hand and talked with them a good while, and a little after they rode away on horseback from out of this castle to the said Corby Castle in Cumberland. I went not out of the house nor out of my chamber today. Psalm 121.

The 16th day, and today there dined without with my folks, Mr Samuel Grasty our parson, and after dinner I had him into my chamber and talked with him and took him by the hand. And a little after he said Common Prayers and read

---

68 To take it to Sir Lancelot Machell, see above.
69 Arthur Swindin is ill here and will die on 7 March 1676 as described below. He entered Anne's service as a boy about 1662 and is recorded in the 1665 accounts as a fisher boy. For several years he served Anne as her under-butler, quite a promotion from fisher boy. Anne was clearly fond of him and took great care of him during his illness.
70 Anne bought malt from a number of different sources, Thomas Wright supplied her more regularly than any other supplier in 1675–1676. She also did business with another Quaker, Edward Guy, who is paid in 1675 for binding her mother's Bible and for supplying malt.
71 One of Sir Charles Howard and Dorothy Widdrington's daughters, Elizabeth or Dorothy. They would be double first cousins with Anne Howard, as their mothers were sisters and their fathers were brothers.

a chapter (as usual upon Wednesdays) to me and my family, and after prayers he went away again. I went not out of the house nor out of my chamber all this day. Psalm 121.

The 17th day, I remembered how this day fifty-nine years [1617] was my first and then only child the Lady Margaret desperately sick and in great danger of death in Knole House in Kent, by a fit of her long ague, where she and I then lay. And then was I first told there the sad news from Ancona in Italy which did at the time much trouble me.[72] Ecclesiastes 3; 8.6; Proverbs 20.24.

And I remember how this day was sixty years [1616] when I and my first Lord the Earl of Dorset lay in Little Dorset House in London town and in the afternoon in the best gallery of Great Dorset House did George Abbott, Archbishop of Canterbury, and many others come to my first Lord and me, and did earnestly persuade me both by fair words and threatenings to stand to the award the four chief judges would then make betwixt my first Lord and me of the one part and my uncle of Cumberland and his son on the other part, concerning the lands of mine Inheritance. And thereupon it was agreed that I should go to my blessed mother into Westmorland and begin my journey the 21st of that month, which I did accordingly. Ecclesiastes 3; 8.6; Proverbs 20.24.

And the 17th day towards evening did Mr Johnson (who is brother to Mrs Anne Johnson who formerly served me) and his man come from his own house near Skipton into this Brougham Castle, and he lay this night in the Baron's Chamber, and the next morning I had him into my chamber and took him by the hand and talked with him a good while and gave him three pairs of buckskin gloves, and a little after (after he had eaten something in the Painted Room) he and his man rode away on horseback out of this Brougham Castle.

And this morning I set my hand to four good letters of Hasell's writing for me, one to my daughter Thanet, one to my Lord Northampton, one to my cousin Sir Thomas Wharton and one to Mr William Edge, all in answer of letters I received from them by the last post.

And this 17th day in the afternoon, about three o'clock, did my cousin Mr Richard Musgrave, eldest son to my cousin Sir Philip Musgrave, and his Lady, and their daughter,[73] who is their only child Mary, come in their coach hither from Edenhall, so I had them into my chamber and kissed my cousin and his wife and the child and also their gentlewoman, and I gave to my cousin's wife and daughter each of them a gold ring, and after they had stayed awhile they went away.

72 The imprisonment of Henry Bertie by the Inquisition in Acona, see above.
73 Margaret Harrison and Mary Musgrave.

And this 17th day did my servant Mr Thomas Strickland and his man, Lancelot Machell, ride from his own house near Kendal, called Garnet House, towards Appleby (whither they came that night) to gather my Candlemas rents. And he lay in the Baron's Chamber there, and his man in the Musty Chamber. And today I had one or two ill fits of the wind, but yet I slept well in the night, I thank God. Psalm 12[1]. I went not out of the house nor out of my chamber all this day. Psalm 23.

The 19th day I remembered how this day was fifty-nine years [1617] my first and then only child the Lady Margaret was desperately sick and ill of a fit of her long ague in Knole House in Kent where she and I lay, but her father, my first Lord, then lay at Great Dorset House in London town. Ecclesiastes 3; 8.6; Proverbs 20.24; Psalm 23.4, 5.

And this morning I saw Robert Dennison, the deaf woman's son, paid for leading forty cartloads of ling[74] out of Whinfell Park to this Brougham Castle for brewing and baking with, and then he went away.

And this evening did my servant Thomas Strickland and his man Lancelot Machell come about eight o'clock into this Brougham Castle to us here, but I saw them not until the next morning and then I talked with them and took him by the hand, and they now lay as usual in the Tower of League for six nights which, being expired upon the 25th day, the said Mr Thomas Strickland and his man Lancelot Machell rid out of this Brougham Castle to Appleby, there to receive the rest of my Candlemas rents. I went not out of the house nor out of my chamber today. Psalm 121.

The 20th day, being Sunday, I remembered how this day was fifty-nine years [1617] had my first and then only child the Lady Margaret a desperate fit of her long ague in Knole House in Kent, where she then lay. But her father, my first Lord, then lay in Great Dorset House in London town. Ecclesiastes 3; 8.6; Proverbs 20.24; Psalm 23.4, 5.

And though today was Sunday yet I went not to church nor out of my chamber all this day. But my two gentlewomen and three of my laundry maids with most of my chief menservants went to this church called Ninekirks, where he preached a good sermon (Mr Grasty our parson) to them and the rest of the congregation (though one part thereof seemed to reflect upon the writer so that I thought he spoke to none but me).[75] And today there dined here as usual Mr Grasty the parson, and my two farmers here, namely William Spedding and his

---

74 Heather, which in the north of England was called ling.
75 Anne did not attend this sermon, so did he allow her to see a written script? Or was it reported to her? It may be this was her usual practice as she could not attend the sermon. Taking sermon notes was not unusual in the period.

wife, and Jeffrey Blamire and his son, and John Webster. So after dinner I had them into my chamber, and kissed her, and took the men by the hands. And then Mr Grasty said Common Prayers and read a chapter and likewise sung a Psalm (as usual upon Sundays) to me and them and my family, and prayers being done they went away.

And today I had one or two ill fits of the wind, but I slept indifferent well in the night notwithstanding. Psalm 23.4, 5. I thank God, but that wind put me in great danger of death. I went not out of the house nor out of my chamber all this day. Psalm 121.

The 21st day, I remembered how this day was sixty years [1616] my first Lord and I did go out of Little Dorset House in London Town onwards on our journey northwards, so as that night we lay together in the inn at Dunstable in Bedfordshire, as we were in our journey towards Brougham Castle in Westmorland, to my blessed mother, and he to set me as far on my way as Lichfield in Staffordshire. Ecclesiastes 3; 8.6; Proverbs 20.24.[76]

And I considered how this day was eight-six years [1590] died Ambrose, Earl of Warwick, who was husband to my blessed mother's eldest sister Anne Russell, Countess of Warwick, in Bedford House in the Strand in London town, where my noble father, George, Earl of Cumberland, then lay, but my blessed mother then lay in of me in Skipton Castle in Craven. Ecclesiastes 3; 8.6; Proverbs 20.24; Job 7.1.

And this morning did John Webster come hither, so he came into my chamber and I took him by the hand and talked with him. And he dined here without in the Painted Room with my folks and after dinner I had him again into my chamber and spoke to him awhile and a little after he went away.

And this day there likewise dined without Mr Samuel Grasty, our parson, who came hither this forenoon to see Arthur Swindin, who is now in a very weak condition, and so after dinner I had him into my chamber and talked with him and inquired of Arthur Swindin, whether he was better, but he told me that he was no better at all, and then he went away from me. And today my gentlewoman Mrs Frances Pate preserved for me four pots and two bottles of syrup of lemons.[77] I went not out of the house nor out of my chamber today. Psalm 121.

The 22nd day, I remembered how this day was sixty years [1616] my first Lord and I went out of the inn at Dunstable in Bedfordshire, and so through

---

76 Many more details are provided in these remembrances of 1616 than are included in the diary for this year above. This suggests that both the diary and the reminiscences were taken from a third text, a daybook of 1616.
77 In the accounts for 1675 Arthur Swindin often assisted France Pate when she preserved fruit, but by this point he is clearly too ill to do so.

Stony Stratford hard by Grafton House in Northamptonshire, into the inn at Towcester in that county, as we were in our journey Northwards, I towards Brougham Castle in Westmorland to my blessed mother, and he to set me as far on my way as Lichfield in Staffordshire. Ecclesiastes 3; 8.6; Proverbs 20.24; Job 7.1.

And I considered how this day was eighty-six years [1590] was I christened in the parish church of Skipton in Craven by the name of Anne. Philip, Lord Wharton, my Aunt's husband, being my godfather, my noble father then lying in Bedford House in the Strand in London town, as he also did when my blessed mother was brought to bed of me the 30th day of the month before in Skipton Castle in Craven.[78]

And this 22nd day in the morning, before I was out of my bed, did I pare off the tops of the nails of all my fingers and toes, and when I was up out of bed I burnt them in the fire in the chimney in my chamber in Brougham Castle.

And a little after in that same chamber of mine did George Goodgion clip off all the hairs of my head,[79] which I likewise burnt in the fire. And after supper I washed and bathed my feet and legs in warm water, wherein beef had beenn boiled and some bran. And I had done none of this for myself, nor had George Goodgion cut my hair for me since the 18th of December last that he did the like in this chamber of mine in Brougham Castle.[80] God grant that good may betide me and mine after it. Psalm 23.4, 5.

And this 22nd day there came several letters by the post from London, which I heard read to me next morning; and amongst the post, one from my daughter of Thanet dated the 17th of this month, whereby she desired me that if there be another Parliament, I would make her son John one of the burgesses for Appleby, to which I returned an answer.[81] I went not out of the house nor out of my chamber all this day. Psalm 121.

The 23rd day I remembered how this day was sixty years [1616] my first Lord

---

78 See *Great Books*, ed. Malay, p. 734 for details of the christening.
79 George Goodgion had cut Anne's hair from at least 1668. He appears both here and in the accounts to be a particularly trusted and versatile employee providing a wide variety of services.
80 In the accounts for 1675 she generally had her hair cut monthly.
81 The phrase first read 'I would give my vote'. However 'give my vote' is scored out and replaced with 'make'. Anne's influence in the region was such that she was able to dictate the choice of burgess (Member of Parliament) to the electors of Appleby. She 'made' John's brother, Thomas Tufton, burgess of Appleby in 1668 despite opposition by powerful men in the realm. See Malay, 'The Transmission of Political Power' (2017). The next parliament was held in 1679. By this time John Tufton had inherited Anne's lands and sheriffwick. He used the influence in the region he inherited from Anne to 'make' his brother Richard burgess for Appleby.

and I went out of the inn at Stony Stratford into my cousin Thomas Elmes's house at Lilford in Northamptonshire for a while, so that day into the inn at Warwick in Warwickshire where we lay that night as we were in our journey, I towards Brougham Castle in Westmorland to my blessed mother, and he to set me as far on my way as Lichfield in Staffordshire. Ecclesiastes 3; 8.6; Proverbs 20.24.

And today there dined with my folks in the Painted Room Mr Samuel Grasty our parson, and after dinner I had him into my chamber and took him by the hand. And afterward he said Common Prayers and read a chapter (as usual upon Wednesdays) to me and my family, and after prayers was done they went away.

And there also dined without with my folks Mr Thomas Ubank of Ormside, the doctor (that married the widow Mrs Hilton), so after dinner I had him into my chamber and took him by the hand and I gave him 6^s and I caused him to go into Arthur Swindin's chamber to see him, and he came up and stayed [for] prayers, and then he went away.[82] I went not out of the house nor out of my chamber today. Psalm 121.

The 24th day, I remembered how this day was sixty years [1616] my first Lord and I, after I had been to see Warwick Castle and church, went out of the inn there and so out of that town into Guy's Cliffe in that county to see it, and onwards to Killingworth [Kenilworth] Castle for a while to see it, and from thence that night we went into the inn at Lichfield in Staffordshire where we lay two nights together because the next day was Sunday, as I was in my journey to Brougham Castle in Westmorland to my blessed mother. Ecclesiastes 3; 8.6; Proverbs 20.24.

And this 24th day in the morning I had a most extreme fit of the wind, and so as it had like to have been a swooning fit, though it did not prove so![83] God be thanked.

And this morning I set my hand to four good letters of Hasell's writing for me, one to my daughter Thanet, one to my Lord Northampton, one to Mr William Edge and one to Dr Johnstone,[84] this last being in answer of one from him with which he sent by my Lord Marshal's directions several of my ancestors' letters. And the other three first are in answer of letters I received from them by the last post.

---

82 Throughout 1675 Anne regularly paid Ubank to attend her servants and he may have treated her as well.
83 This is one of the rare times Anne uses an exclamation mark in any of her work.
84 Johnstone may be related to Mary Johnstone, Lady Fletcher, as she and her husband brought the previous set of ancestral letters from the Lord Marshal.

And this morning John Webster came hither and I had him into my chamber and talked with him and took him by the hand, and he dined here with my folks, and after dinner he went away. And there also dined without with my folks young Mr Blenkinsop[85] of Brough, so after dinner I had him into my chamber and talked with him and gave him 10^s and he now told me that his youngest sister who was lame was lately deceased,[86] and then he went away. And Henry Ram, my tenant of Flakebridge, also dined here and after dinner he came into my chamber and I took him by the hand and talked with him a while after he went away. I went not out of the house nor out of my chamber all this day. Psalm 121.

The 25th day, I remembered how this day was sixty-seven years [1609], and then Saturday, I was married to my first Lord Richard Sackville, then but Lord Buckhurst, in my mother's chamber in Austin Friars in London, where she and I then lay. But that Lord of mine came to be Earl of Dorset within two days after by the death of his father, Robert Sackville, Earl of Dorset. Ecclesiastes 3, 8.6; Proverbs 20.24.

And I remembered how this day was sixty years [1616], and then Sunday, my first Lord and I went forenoon and afternoon into the church at Lichfield[87] to the sermon and service there, and afterwards into other of the most remarkable places in that town and that night we lay again in the inn there, from whence I continued my journey the next day towards Brougham Castle in Westmorland to my blessed mother. Ecclesiastes 3, 8.6; Proverbs 20.24.

And today [blank].

And this 25th day in the forenoon, about nine o'clock, after I had taken my leave of him, did Mr Thomas Strickland, one of my chief officers, and his man, Lancelot Machell, ride on horseback out of this Brougham Castle towards Appleby Castle to receive there the rest of my Candlemas rents, and they lay there for three nights, and upon the 28th day, being Monday, a little after supper they came back hither to me and us here. I went not out of the house nor out of my chamber all this day. Psalm [blank].

The 26th day, I remembered how this day was sixty years [1616] I and my Lord went out of the inn at Lichfield, where we had lain two nights together, into Sir George Curzon's house at Croxall in Derbyshire and that was the first and last time that I was ever in that house, from whence we went to Burton upon Trent in Derbyshire where my first Lord and I then parted, he returning back to

---

85 Francis Blenkinsop.
86 Katherine Blenkinsop.
87 Lichfield Cathedral.

Lichfield where he was to make stay for four or five days there, about a great foot race that was then there. But I proceeded on my journey towards Brougham Castle in Westmorland to my blessed mother and came that night to Derby and lay in the inn there that night, which was the first and last time that I ever lay in that town. Ecclesiastes 3; 8.6; Proverbs 20.24. I went not out of the house nor out of my chamber today. Psalm 121.

The 27th day, I remembered how this day was sixty years [1616] did I go out of the inn at Derby into two houses at Hardwick,[88] now both belonging to the Earl of Devonshire, and so from thence into the inn at Chesterfield in that county where I lay there that one night as I was in my journey towards Brougham Castle in Westmorland to see my blessed mother.

And though today was Sunday yet I went not to the church nor out of my chamber all this day. Psalm 23. But my two gentlewomen went and two of my laundry maids and most of my menservants rode on horseback to Ninekirks, where Mr Grasty the parson preached a very good sermon to them and the congregation.

And today in the forenoon I was much troubled with wind so I had very ill fits but God be thanked I recovered of it soon after, so that I slept well in the night notwithstanding. I went not out of the house nor out of my chamber all this day, though it be Sunday. Psalm 121.

The 28th day, I remembered how this day was sixty years [1616] I went out of the inn at Chesterfield in Derbyshire into the Earl of Shrewsbury's house called Sheffield[89] in Yorkshire for a while to see it, and that evening I went into the inn at Rotherham in that county where I lay that one night as I was in my journey towards Brougham Castle in Westmorland to see my blessed mother. And that was the first time I came into Yorkshire after I was married and [became] Countess of Dorset. Ecclesiastes 3; 8.6; Proverbs 20.24.

And today here in the Painted Room with my folks there dined Mr Christopher Dalston of Acorn Bank, eldest son to my cousin Mr John Dalston, and his wife.[90] So after dinner I had them into my chamber and kissed his wife and took him by the hand, and likewise I talked with them a good while, and I gave his wife a pair of buckskin gloves, and then they went away.

---

88 Hardwick Old Hall and Hardwick New Hall, both built by Elizabeth Hardwick, Countess of Shrewsbury, best known as 'Bess of Hardwick'. The Old Hall is a ruin, but the New Hall remains with the exterior much as Bess built it and was innovative in its time. The interior, while somewhat altered, continues to house textiles, paintings and furniture from Bess's time, which Anne would have seen.
89 Sheffield Castle.
90 Bridget Fletcher.

And there also dined here with my folks John Webster, who came hither this morning, at which time I had him into my chamber and talked with him and took him by the hand, and after dinner he went away. And this evening about five o'clock did John Twentyman (who is gardener to the Lord Bishop of Carlisle) come hither and he lay in the Bannister Room. I went not out of the house nor out of my chamber today. Psalm 121.

The 29th day, I remembered how this day was sixty years [1616] I went out of the inn at Rotherham in Yorkshire into a poor parson's house at Penistone in that county, where I lay there that one night, as I was in my journey towards Brougham Castle in Westmorland to see my blessed mother. Ecclesiastes 3; 8.6; Proverbs 20.24.

And today there dined here with my folks Margaret Waugh of Appleby,[91] that formerly served me, so I had her into my chamber after dinner and kissed her and talked with her a good while, this being the first time I saw her since I came to Brougham Castle, and a little while after she went away. And there also dined without with my folks young William Middleton, Roger Middleton's brother, that once served me, and after dinner I had him into my chamber and took him by the hand, but I gave him nothing, and then he went away. He came hither yesternight and lay in the Bannister Room.

And this afternoon did Thomas Strickland pay to Mr Edward Hasell for my use £305 5ˢ of my Westmorland rents due at Candlemas last, for which I now gave Strickland an acquittance under my hand and saw the money put up in the trunk in my chamber. And this forenoon about nine o'clock after I had taken my leave of Mr Thomas Strickland in my chamber did he and Lancelot Machell after they had lain here in the Tower of League eight nights, ride out of this Brougham Castle on horseback towards his own house near Kendal. I went not out of the house nor out of my chamber today. Psalm 121.

March 1676

The 1st day I remembered how this day was sixty years [1616] I went out of the poor parson's house at Penistone in Yorkshire, over Penistone Moor (where never any coach went before mine), into the inn at Manchester in Lancashire where I lay that one night as I was on my journey towards Brougham Castle in Westmorland to see my blessed mother. Ecclesiastes 3; 8.6; Proverbs 20.24.

And today there dined here with my folks John Webster, who came into my

---

91 She likely served Anne in the 1650s. She was the mother of John Waugh, Bishop of Carlisle, who was born in 1661.

chamber before dinner. And I took him by the hand and talked with him, and after dinner he came again into my chamber and stayed till Mr Grasty had said prayers, and then he went away. And there also dined here Mr John Gilmore who lives at Julian Bower, and his man William Labourne dined below in the Hall, and after dinner I had them both into my chamber and talked with them and took them by the hand, and after prayers they went away. And today there dined here also Mr Samuel Grasty our parson. And after dinner he came into my chamber and said Common Prayers (as usual upon Wednesdays) and read a chapter to me and them and my family, and when prayers was ended he went away. I went not out of the house nor out of my chamber today. Psalm 121.

The 2nd day I remembered how this day was sixty years [1616] I went out of the inn at Manchester in Lancashire into the poor cottage at Chorley where I lay in a poor ale-house there that one night, which was within three miles of Lathom House,[92] but I did not see it by reason of the mist, as I was in my journey towards Brougham Castle in Westmorland to see my blessed mother. Ecclesiastes 3; 8.6; Proverbs 20.24.

And this morning I set my hand to three good letters of Hasell's writing for me, one to my daughter Thanet, one to my Lord Northampton and one to Mr William Edge, all in answer of letters I received from them by the last post. And today there dined without with my folks in the Painted Room Mrs Willison of Penrith (whose husband is gone into Scotland), and after dinner I had her into my chamber and kissed her and took her by the hand, but I told her I would have no more wine off her husband because he used me so badly, and then she went away.

I had a very ill fit of the wind today, and yet nevertheless I slept well in the night notwithstanding, I thank God. Psalm 23. 4, 5. I went not out of the house nor out of my chamber all this day. Psalm [blank].

The 3rd day I remembered how this day was sixty years [1616] I went out of the poor cottage at Chorley (though it was Sunday, by reason the lodgings were so bad) into the inn at Preston in Andersey in Lancashire where I lay that one night as I was in my journey towards Brougham Castle in Westmorland to see my blessed mother.

And this day, both in the forenoon and afternoon did Mrs Frances Pate preserve for me in her own chamber a good many of apples and lemons. And today I had a very ill fit of the wind, but yet nevertheless I slept well in the night,

---

92 A stone castle built in 1496 by the Stanleys, Anne's first cousins. It was surrounded by a thick wall and moat, and had a defensive gateway tower.

I thank God. Psalm 23.4,5. I went not out of the house nor out of my chamber all this day. Psalm [blank].

The 4th day I remembered how this day was sixty years [1616] I went out of the inn at Preston in Lancashire into Lancaster town in that county, where I lay in a poor inn there that one night and where I went up upon the leads of the remaining part of that old castle, as I was in my journey towards Brougham Castle in Westmorland to see my blessed mother. Ecclesiastes 3; 8.6; Proverbs 20.24.

And this morning I saw paid several persons for graving[93] and working in my garden here at Brougham Castle. And afterwards I saw Mr Willison of Penrith paid for a rundlet of sack and white wine, and he dined here with my folks in the Painted Room, and then he went away.[94] And today there also dined without with my folks in the Painted Room Mr Robert Hilton of Murton, and after dinner I had him into my chamber and took him by the hand and gave him 3 yards of ducape[95] and a pot of alchermy[96] to carry to his wife, and then he went away.

And though I had a very ill fit of the wind today yet I slept well at night, I thank God. Psalm 23. I went not out of the house nor out of my chamber today. Psalm 23.

The 5th day, being Sunday, I remembered how this night was fifty-two years [1624] was the last night that ever I lay in Great Dorset House in London town, for the next day I went from thence from my first Lord down to Knole House in Kent to my two daughters, and I never lay in Great Dorset House after, for my first Lord died the 28th day of that month in the Lead Chamber in Great Dorset House. Job 7.2; Ecclesiastes 3; 8.6; Proverbs 20.24.

And I remembered how this day was sixty years [1616] I went out of the poor inn in Lancaster town and so out of that county into the inn at Kendal in Westmorland, where I lay that one night, as I was in my journey to Brougham Castle to see my blessed mother. Ecclesiastes 3; 8.6; Proverbs 20.24. And I remembered how this 5th day of March is just five months since I and my family removed out of Appleby Castle hither to Brougham Castle, Revelations 9. 5, 10.[97]

---

93 Digging, or formed by digging.
94 Anne must have decided to give his wine another chance, see 2 March entry.
95 A strong and soft silk fabric.
96 A medicinal preparation made of the dried bodies of Mediterranean insects found on kermes oaks.
97 Revelations 9.5: 'And to them it was given that they should not kill them, but that they should be tormented five months: and their torment was as the torment of a scorpion, when he striketh a man'; 9.10: 'And they had tails like unto scorpions, and there were stings in their tails: and their power was to hurt men five months.'

And today there dined without with my folks in the Painted Room Mr Samuel Grasty our parson, and my two farmers here, namely William Spedding and his wife, and Jeffrey Blamire and his son, and John Webster. So after dinner I had them all into my chamber and kissed the woman and took them by the hand, and Mr Grasty was paid his 20^s for saying prayers to me and my family for a month last past, and after he said Common Prayer and read a chapter and sung a Psalm (as usual upon Sundays) to me and them aforesaid, and when prayers was done they all went away. I went not out of the house nor out of my chamber for all this Sunday, though it was so!⁹⁸ Psalm [blank]

The 6th day I remembered how this day was sixty-seven years [1609] my blessed mother with many in our company brought me from her house in Austin Friars to the court of Little Dorset House in Salisbury Court in London town to lie there with my first Lord, which was the first time I ever lay in that new-built house, I being but married to my first Lord the 25th of the month before. Ecclesiastes 3; 8.6; Proverbs 20.24.

And I remembered how this day was sixty years [1616] I went out of the inn at Kendal to Brougham Castle in Westmorland to my blessed mother to see her, and that was the first time that I was in Brougham Castle after I was Countess of Dorset, or in a good while before.

And this morning I saw John Pattison of Moorhouse paid for a stack of hay for my stables, and then he went away. And today there dined here with my folks John Webster, so after dinner I had him into my chamber and took him by the hand and talked with him, and a little after he went away from me.

And this evening, about four o'clock, did Thomas Wright the Quaker of Mallerstang come hither, so he lay in the Bannister Room, and the next morning I had him into my chamber and took him by the hand and saw him paid for twelve bushels of malt for my house, and then he went away. I went not out of the house nor out of my chamber all this day. Psalm [blank].

The 7th day, and this 7th day in the morning, about nine of the clock, died Arthur Swindin, my under-butler, in the chamber under the Great Chamber at this Brougham Castle, who has served me about fourteen or fifteen years. And the next day, about two of the clock in the afternoon, his dead body was buried in Ninekirks Church (this parish church), where Parson Grasty preached his funeral sermon, and most of my servants and others attended the corpse at the funeral.

> This biblical reference suggests Anne suffered more in these last months than the daybook would suggest and that she understood she was in her final days.
> 98 Again the infrequently used exclamation point expresses impatience with her inability to leave her chamber, and suggests her health is deteriorating.

And today there dined without with my folks in the Painted Room Mr Thomas Gabetis, my sheriff, and Mr John Thwaite of Appleby,[99] and after dinner I had them both into my chamber and took them by the hand and talked with them a good while, and afterward they both went away. And there also dined here in the Painted Chamber with my folks John Webster, so I had him into my chamber after dinner and before dinner and took him by the hand and talked with him, and then he went away. I went not out of the house nor out of my chamber all this day. Psalm [blank].

The 8th day, and today I had a very ill fit of wind after dinner, but nevertheless I did sleep indifferent well in the night, I thank God. Psalm 23.4,5. I went not out of the house nor out of my chamber all this day. Psalm [blank]

The 9th day, and this morning I set my hand to four good letters of Hasell's writing for me, one to my daughter Thanet, one to my Lord Northampton, one to Mr William Edge and one to Mrs Elizabeth Gilmore,[100] all in answer of letters I received from them by the last post.

And today there dined with my folks in the Painted Room my cousin Mr John Dalston of Acorn Bank. So after dinner I had him into my chamber and took him by the hand and talked with him, and then he went away. And there also dined with my folks Mr John Gilmore, my keeper of Whinfell Park, and his man William Labourne dined below in the Hall, and after dinner (after my cousin was gone from me) I had them both into my chamber and took them by the hand and talked with them, and then they went away.

And though today I had an extreme ill fit of the wind, yet, notwithstanding, I slept pretty well in the night, I thank God. Psalm 23.4, 5. I went not out of the house nor out of my chamber all this day.

The 10th day, and this morning I saw not only Allan Strickland paid for the week book in my chamber, but I also saw George Goodgion paid for 249 yards of linen cloth that he bought for me at Penrith, designed for twenty pairs of sheets and some pillowberes[101] for the use of my house. And after dinner I gave away several old sheets which were divided amongst my servants.

And this afternoon did Margaret Montgomery of Penrith, the seamstress, come hither so I had her into my chamber and kissed her and talked with her, and she came to make up the twenty pairs of sheets and pillowberes. I went not out of the house nor out of my chamber all this day. Psalm [blank].

---

99 A townsman who served as mayor of Appleby at times, most recently in 1674.
100 Elizabeth Nicholls, whose husband, John Gilmore was Anne's keeper of Whinfell forest. Elizabeth returned to the South to live with her daughter in April 1671.
101 Pillowcases. The world pillowbere comes from pillover, an archaic form that continued to be used in the North.

The 11th day, and this morning did Henry Benson, my [shep]herd at Southfield, and two other men with him, come hither from Appleby, so I had them into my chamber and saw them paid for mending the fences, scaling the molehills and dressing the meadows at Southfield and Rampkin Close, and they dined below in the Hall, and after dinner they went away.

And today I had a very extreme fit of the wind, but yet I slept well in the night, I thank God, notwithstanding. Psalm 23. I went not out of the house nor out of my chamber today. Psalm 121.

The 12th day, being Sunday, and though it was so, yet I went not to church nor out of my chamber all this day, but one of my gentlewomen and one of my laundry maids and most of my chief menservants went to Ninekirks, where Mr Grasty the parson preached a good sermon to them and the congregation. And today there dined without my folks in the Painted Room Mr Samuel Grasty our parson, and my two farmers here, namely William Spedding and his wife, and Jeffrey Blamire and his son, and John Webster. So after dinner I had them into my chamber and kissed the woman and took them by the hand. And a little after Mr Grasty said Common Prayers and read a chapter and sung a Psalm in my chamber to me and my family (as usually is done upon Sundays), and after prayers they all went away.

And though this day I had an extreme ill fit of the wind in the afternoon, so that I was in great danger (and yet in no danger) of death, but yet I slept well in the night I thank God, notwithstanding. Psalm 23.4. I went not out of the house nor out of my chamber all this day, though it was Sunday. Psalm 121.

The 13th day, I remembered how this day was sixty years [1616] I went from my blessed mother out of Brougham Castle in Westmorland to Naworth Castle in Cumberland where I lay there in it for two nights with the Lord William Howard (my first Lord's uncle) and his wife the Lady Elizabeth Dacre (my father's cousin german) and with many of their sons and their sons' wives, and their daughters and their children and grandchildren, which was the first time I came into Cumberland since I was first married and Countess of Dorset. Ecclesiastes 3; 8.6; Proverbs 20.24.

And today there dined without with my folks in the Painted Room Sir Christopher Clapham. And after dinner I had him into my chamber and discoursed with him a good while, and then he went away, and I had not seen him a long time before. And the said Sir Christopher brought me a letter from my grandchild, Lady Alethea, to which I returned an answer. And there also came along with him and dined here Mr James Buchanan, the parson of Appleby, so after dinner I had him into my chamber and took him by the hand and talked with him, and then he went away. And there also dined without with my folks

John Webster and his mother, Isabell Webster, and after dinner I had them both into my chamber and kissed her and took him by the hand, and a little after they went away. I went not out of the house nor out of my chamber today. Psalm 121.

The 14th day I remembered how this day was fifteen years [1661] my youngest daughter, Isabella, Countess of Northampton, since deceased, was delivered of her youngest and only surviving child of six, and was her third daughter, in her Lord's house in Lincoln Inn Fields, which child was afterwards christened by the name of Alethea, I then lying in Appleby Castle in Westmorland, whose life and fortune God preserved. Ecclesiastes 3; 8.6; Proverbs 20.24.

And this morning I set my hand to a good letter of Hasell's writing for me to my dear grandchild, the Lady Alethea Compton, in answer to a letter Sir Christopher Clapham brought me yesterday from her.

And this forenoon about ten o'clock did John Webster come hither, so I had him into my chamber and talked with him and took him by the hand, and he dined without with my folks in the Painted Room, and a little after he went away. I went not out of the house nor out of my chamber today. Psalm 121.

The 15th day I remembered how this day was sixty years [1616] in the morning I went out of Naworth Castle in Cumberland from the Lord William Howard and his wife into the city of Carlisle in the same county, where I went into the castle there and into the chamber in that castle wherein was born into the world the Lady Anne Dacre, she that was afterwards Countess Dowager of Arundel, and I went into the Cathedral church there wherein was buried my great-grandfather, William, Lord Dacre. And from thence I went the same day into Brougham Castle in Westmorland, where I continued to lie with my blessed mother till the 2nd of the month following, that I went away from her, and never saw her after. Ecclesiastes 3; 8.6; Proverbs 20.24.

And today there dined without with my folks in the Painted Room Mr Samuel Grasty our parson, so after dinner I had him into my chamber and talked with him, and afterward he said Common Prayer and read a chapter to me and my family (as usual upon Wednesdays), and when prayers was ended he went away. And today I had a very ill fit of the wind. Psalm 23.4. I went not out of the house nor out of my chamber all this day. Psalm [blank].

The 16th day, and today there dined without with my folks in the Painted Room Mr Richard Jackson, the schoolmaster of Appleby, so after dinner I had him into my chamber and took him by the hand and talked with him a good while, and then he went away. And there also dined here Mr Leonard Smith of Appleby, and likewise John Atkinson, the tailor.[102] So after dinner I had them

---

102 Both were Appleby aldermen and served as mayor for the town.

into my chamber and talked with them a good while and took them by the hand, and a little after they went away. And John Webster also dined without with them and my folks, and after dinner he came into my chamber and I took him by the hand and spoke to him, and then he went away.

And this afternoon, a little after dinner, did Mr James Bird, the attorney, come hither, he being but lately come from his journey from London, so I had him into my chamber and took him by the hand and talked with him, and I gave him 10^s as I used to do, and then he went away. I went not out of the house nor out of my chamber today. Psalm [blank].

The 17th day, and today no body dined here but my own folks, so that there is none to be superadded. And today I had a very ill fit of the wind, but yet I slept in the night indifferently well, I thank God. Psalm 23. I went not out of the house nor out of my chamber all this day. Psalm [blank].

The 18th day, and yesternight did Thomas Wright the Quaker that was at Mallerstang come hither, and he lay this night in the Bannister Room, and this morning I had him into my chamber and took him by the hand and saw him paid for twelve bushels of malt for a brewing of beer for my house at this Brougham Castle. And a little after he went from me and us here towards his own home. I went not out of this house nor out of my chamber today.

The 19th day, being Sunday, Palm Sunday. And this Sunday morning I had a very violent fit of the wind, so that it caused me to fall into a swooning fit for about half an hour together, so as I thought I should have died, but it pleased God I recovered and was better afterward.

And today there dined without with my folks in the Painted Room Mr Grasty our parson, and my two farmers here, namely William Spedding and his wife, and Jeffrey Blamire and his son, and John Webster. So after dinner they came into my chamber and I kissed the woman and took the men by the hand. And a little after Mr Grasty said Common Prayer and read a chapter and sung a psalm as usual upon Sundays to me and them and my family, and after prayers they all went away. I went not out of the house nor out of my chamber today. Psalm [blank].

The 20th day, I remembered how this day was sixty years [1616] I and my blessed mother in Brougham Castle in Westmorland, where we then lay, give in our answer in writing that we would not stand to the award the then four chief judges meant to make concerning the lands of mine inheritance, which did spin out a great deal of trouble to us, yet God turned it for the best, Deuteronomy 23.5.[103]

---

103 Deuteronomy 23.5: 'Nevertheless the Lord thy God would not hearken unto Balaam; but the Lord thy God turned the curse into a blessing unto thee, because the Lord thy God loved thee.'

And this morning John Webster came hither, so I had him into my chamber and took him by the hand and spoke to him, and he dined without with my folks and then he went away. I went not out of the house nor out of my chamber today. Psalm [blank].

The 21st day, I went not out of the house nor out of my chamber all this day. Psalm 121.

The 22nd day:[104] [No entry]

Thus far of this book and a great many more of the same kind, answerable to as many several years last past successively as containing a continued thankful commemoration (as my Honorable Lady hath often said), of God's great mercies and blessings to her and hers, were written altogether by her Ladyship or her directions (except where there be any errors). But she proceeded no further therein then to this 22nd day of March. For on Sunday last, being the 19th instant, it pleased the Almighty to visit her with sickness, which wrought so sharply upon her all that day (being Wednesday) about six o'clock in the afternoon, after she had endured her pains with a most Christian fortitude always answering those that asked her how she did with 'I thank God I am very well',[105] which were her last words directed to mortals. She with much cheerfulness yielded up her precious soul into the hands of her merciful Redeemer to whom with the Father and the Holy Ghost, be ascribed all Glory, Honour and Praise, world without end. Amen.[106]

Not long after her death, her dead body (according to her will) was wrapped in cere cloth and lead with an inscription in brass upon the breast showing whose body it was, and the 14th day of April following, it was carried in a hearse drawn with six horses to Appleby church, and was buried about midday in the vault there which her ladyship had caused to be made in her lifetime for that purpose,[107] having been attended thither by her grandchild Mr John Tufton, and all or most of her own servants in mourning as also by the Lord Bishop of Carlisle[108] who preached her funeral sermon. Sir Philip Musgrave and Mr John Dalston and some of their sons, and others of the gentry of this county being there present at her funeral.

---

104 This date and the date for the 23rd were pre-entered. The heading 'The 23rd day' is scored out, and Hasell writes the following paragraph after the heading, 'The 22nd day'.
105 This is written in bold print, unlike the cursive script of the rest of the entry.
106 From Revelations 5.18. Anne died in the chamber where her father was born and her mother died.
107 Her monument survives and her body remains in the vault below it wrapped in lead as she directed.
108 Edward Rainbow. See *A Sermon Preached at the Funeral of the Right Honorable Anne, Countess of Pembroke, Dorset, and Montgomery* (1677).

11 Anne Clifford's Monument, St Lawrence's church, Appleby, Westmorland (now Cumbria)

APPENDIX

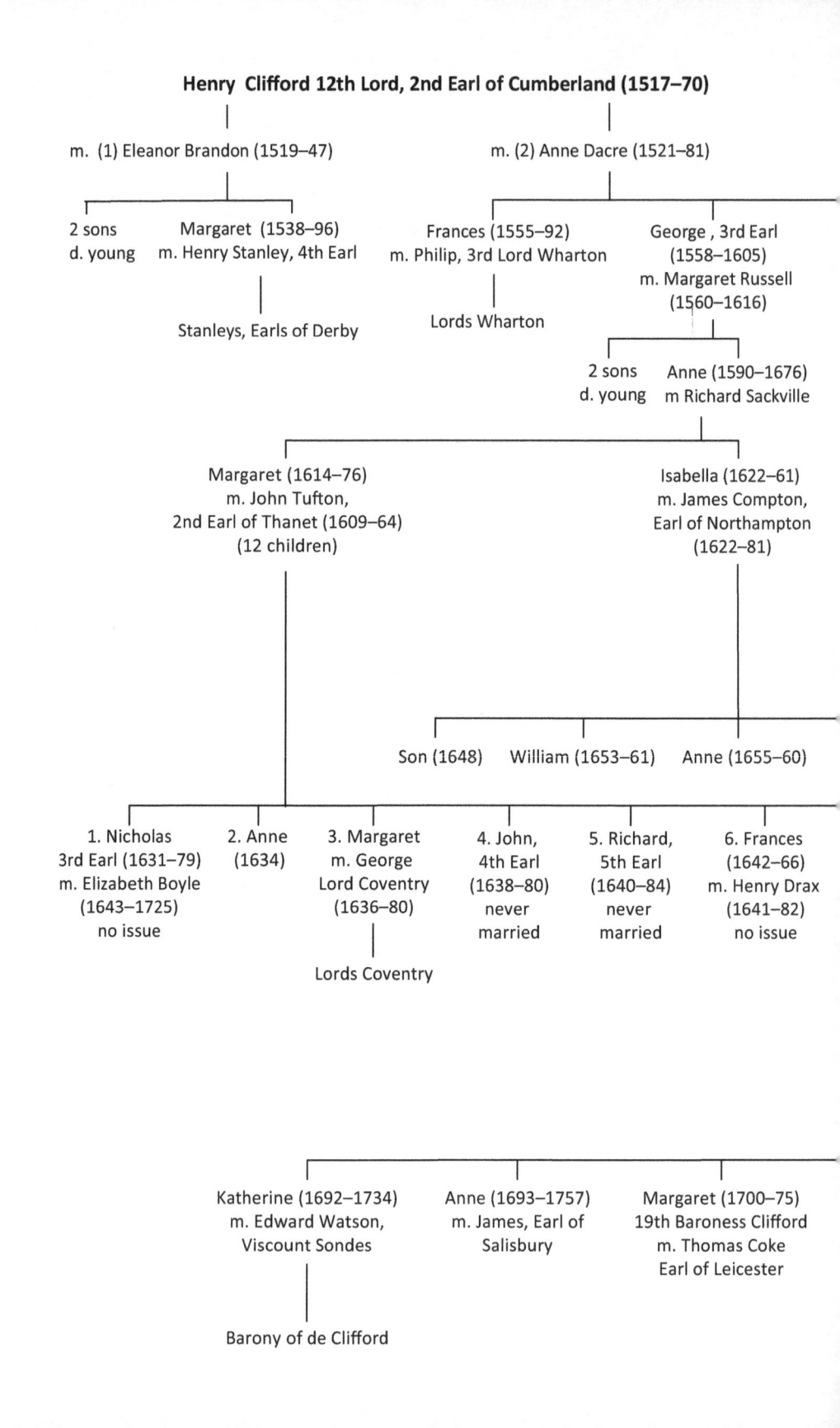

Henry Clifford 12th Lord, 2nd Earl of Cumberland (1517–70)

m. (1) Eleanor Brandon (1519–47) m. (2) Anne Dacre (1521–81)

- 2 sons d. young
- Margaret (1538–96) m. Henry Stanley, 4th Earl
  - Stanleys, Earls of Derby
- Frances (1555–92) m. Philip, 3rd Lord Wharton
  - Lords Wharton
- George, 3rd Earl (1558–1605) m. Margaret Russell (1560–1616)
  - 2 sons d. young
  - Anne (1590–1676) m Richard Sackville
    - Margaret (1614–76) m. John Tufton, 2nd Earl of Thanet (1609–64) (12 children)
    - Isabella (1622–61) m. James Compton, Earl of Northampton (1622–81)
      - Son (1648)
      - William (1653–61)
      - Anne (1655–60)

Children of Margaret and John Tufton:

1. Nicholas 3rd Earl (1631–79) m. Elizabeth Boyle (1643–1725) no issue
2. Anne (1634)
3. Margaret m. George Lord Coventry (1636–80)
   - Lords Coventry
4. John, 4th Earl (1638–80) never married
5. Richard, 5th Earl (1640–84) never married
6. Frances (1642–66) m. Henry Drax (1641–82) no issue

- Katherine (1692–1734) m. Edward Watson, Viscount Sondes
  - Barony of de Clifford
- Anne (1693–1757) m. James, Earl of Salisbury
- Margaret (1700–75) 19th Baroness Clifford m. Thomas Coke Earl of Leicester

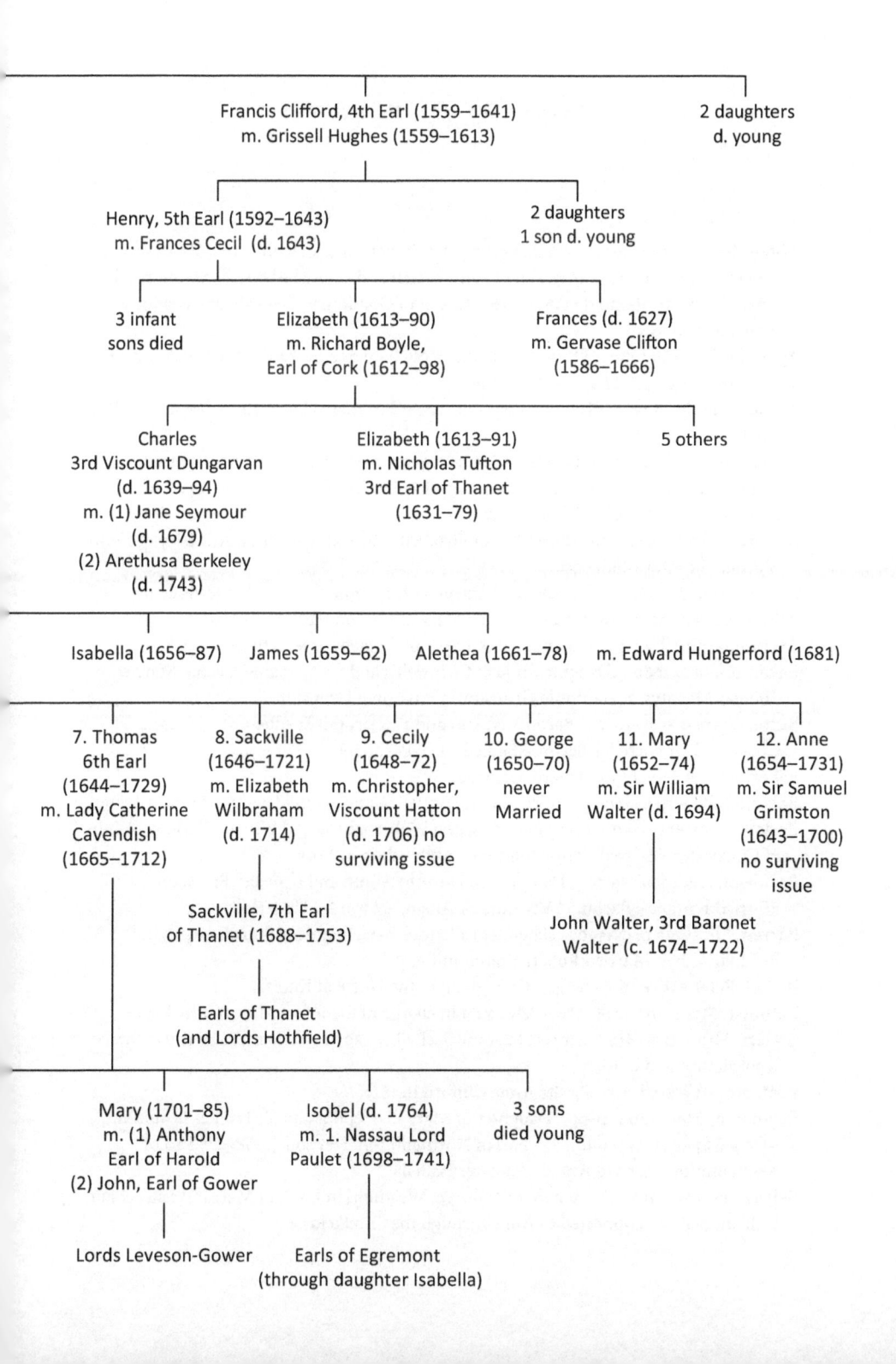

```
                    Francis Clifford, 4th Earl (1559–1641)                    2 daughters
                    m. Grissell Hughes (1559–1613)                            d. young

        Henry, 5th Earl (1592–1643)           2 daughters
        m. Frances Cecil (d. 1643)            1 son d. young

  3 infant          Elizabeth (1613–90)           Frances (d. 1627)
  sons died         m. Richard Boyle,             m. Gervase Clifton
                    Earl of Cork (1612–98)        (1586–1666)

        Charles                    Elizabeth (1613–91)        5 others
        3rd Viscount Dungarvan     m. Nicholas Tufton
        (d. 1639–94)               3rd Earl of Thanet
        m. (1) Jane Seymour        (1631–79)
            (d. 1679)
        (2) Arethusa Berkeley
            (d. 1743)
```

Isabella (1656–87)   James (1659–62)   Alethea (1661–78)   m. Edward Hungerford (1681)

7. Thomas	8. Sackville	9. Cecily	10. George	11. Mary	12. Anne
6th Earl	(1646–1721)	(1648–72)	(1650–70)	(1652–74)	(1654–1731)
(1644–1729)	m. Elizabeth	m. Christopher,	never	m. Sir William	m. Sir Samuel
m. Lady Catherine	Wilbraham	Viscount Hatton	Married	Walter (d. 1694)	Grimston
Cavendish	(d. 1714)	(d. 1706) no			(1643–1700)
(1665–1712)		surviving issue			no surviving
					issue

Sackville, 7th Earl of Thanet (1688–1753)

John Walter, 3rd Baronet Walter (c. 1674–1722)

Earls of Thanet
(and Lords Hothfield)

Mary (1701–85)	Isobel (d. 1764)	3 sons
m. (1) Anthony	m. 1. Nassau Lord	died young
Earl of Harold	Paulet (1698–1741)	
(2) John, Earl of Gower		

Lords Leveson-Gower   Earls of Egremont
                       (through daughter Isabella)

GLOSSARY OF PERSONS

Abbot, George 1562–1633   4th Chancellor of Trinity College, Dublin, and Archbishop of Canterbury from 1611 to 1633, son of Alice Marsh and George Abbot. Never married.

Acuña, Diego Sarmiento de 1567–1526   Count of Gondomar, Spanish ambassador to England 1613–1622.

Aglionby, Mary d. 1680   Daughter of Jane Brougham and Edward Aglionby. Married 1: John Sandford of Askham, 2: Mr Winch.

Amherst, Richard 1565–1632   Lawyer and steward to Sackvilles, Earls of Dorset, until his death.

Anna Maria of Austria 1601–1666   Queen consort of France and Navarre, Queen Regent for Louis XIV of France. Daughter of Philip III of Spain and Margaret of Austria. Married Louis XIII of France.

Annesley, Grace b. c. 1570   Daughter of Elizabeth More and Sir Brian Annesley of Kent. Married Sir John Wildgoose.

Askew, Mr active 1616   Gentleman, Anne gives him money to travel to Jerusalem.

Atkins, Edward active 1653–1666   Judge of the Common Pleas and assizes.

Atkinson, John d. 1733   Alderman and mayor of Appleby several times.

Bacon, Anne d. 1680   Daughter of Jane Cornwallis and Sir Nathaniel Bacon. Married 1: Thomas Meautys, 2: Harbottle Grimston, 2nd Baronet Grimston.

Bacon, Francis 1561–1626   Baron Verulam and 1st Viscount St Alban, son of Anne Cooke and Sir Nicholas Bacon. Married Alice Barnham.

Baker, Mr   A servant to Richard Sackville.

Baker, Sibilla active 1660   Gentlewoman servant to Anne's granddaughter, Frances Tufton.

Barlow, Frances c. 1550   Daughter of Agatha Wellesbourne and William Barlow, Bishop of Chichester. Married Tobias Matthew, Archbishop of York.

Barnham, Alice 1592–1650   Daughter of Dorothy Smith and Benedict Barnham. Married 1: Francis Bacon, 1st Viscount St Alban, 2: Sir John Underhill.

Barrett, Elizabeth b. c. 1590   Daughter of Lettice Barrett and Sir Francis Knollys of Reading Abbey. Married Robert Hammond.

Basket, Peter active 1616–1624.   Gentleman of the Horse at Knole.

Bathurst, Mrs active 1616   Gentlewoman in charge of the infant Margaret Sackville.

Batters, Mrs active 1619   Servant to Anne Sackville, Lady Beauchamp. She enters the Knole household in 1619.

Beat, Mr   A traveller who visits Anne Clifford in 1619.

Beaumont, Mary 1604–1654   Daughter of Mary Pierrepont and Sir Francis Beaumont. Married Spencer Compton, 2nd Earl of Northampton. Her son, James, 3rd Earl of Northampton, married Anne's daughter Isabella.

Bellasis, James b. 1562   A tenant of Hallrigg, Westmorland, son of Margaret Fairfax and William Bellasis, connected to Anne through the Threlkelds.

Benn, Annabel 1606–1698 Countess of Kent, daughter of Jane Evelyn and Anthony Benn. Married 1: Anthony Fane, 2: Henry Grey, 10th Earl of Kent. Nicholas Tufton, Anne's eldest grandson, hoped to marry her but she never consented.

Benson, Henry active 1670–1676 Called both herdsman and steward of Southfield near Brougham.

Bernard, Robert 1601–1666 1st Baronet, lawyer, son of Mary Woodhouse and Francis Bernard. Married 1: Elizabeth Tallakerne, 2: Elizabeth Altham. Part of Anne's legal team in her disputes with her tenants. Connected to Anne through the marriage of his daughter to a St John.

Bertie, Henry d. 1655 Of Lound, son of Mary De Vere and Peregrine Bertie, 13th Baron Willoughby. Married Dorothy Corbet.

Bertie, Robert 1582–1642 14th Baron Willoughby and 1st Earl of Lindsey, son of Mary De Vere and Peregrine Bertie, 13th Baron Willoughby. Married Elizabeth Montagu (d. 1654), daughter of Elizabeth Harrington and Sir Edward Montagu.

Billingsley, Bridgett active 1666 Gentlewoman servant to Mary Tufton, Anne's granddaughter, likely daughter or granddaughter of Thomas Billingsley, gentleman servant to Richard Sackville at Knole, and later governor of two of Anne Clifford's Tufton grandsons.

Billingsley, Thomas c. 1600 – after 1666 Knight, gentleman servant at Knole. He accompanied Anne's Tufton grandsons to Europe.

Billingsley, Tobias active 1616–1624 Richard Sackville's gentleman servant, likely connected to Sir Thomas Billingsley.

Bird, James active 1660 and 1676 Of Brougham Hall, lawyer for Anne, also steward for John Lowther. He had nine sons. He was also active in the politics of Westmorland.

Birkbeck, Thomas d. 1676 Of Hornby Hall, Penrith, son of Eleanor Poole and Henry Birkbeck. Married Margaret Catterick. Hornby Hall was given to the Birkbecks by Henry Clifford, 2nd Earl of Cumberland, in 1552.

Birkbeck, William d. 1698 Of Deep Gill, Mallerstang, son of Isabel and Geoffrey Birkbeck. Married Isabel Bell.

Blamire, Jeffrey d. 1678 Anne's tenant farmer who dined weekly at Brougham in the last months of Anne's life.

Blenkinsop, Francis b. c. 1630 Son of Anne Osbaldston and Thomas Blenkinsop.

Blenkinsop, Katherine d. 1675 Daughter of Anne Osbaldston and Thomas Blenkinsop. Never married.

Blenkinsop, Thomas c. 1595 – c. 1675 Gentleman of Helbeck Hall, son of Margery Wykeliffe and Henry Blenkinsop and ward of Margaret Russell, Anne's mother. Married Anne Osbaldston, daughter of Sir Edward Osbaldston. He was a Catholic and his sister was a nun in Lisbon, Portugal.

Blount, Charles 1563–1606 8th Baron Mountjoy and later 1st Earl of Devonshire, son of Catherine Leigh and James Blount, 6th Baron Mountjoy. Married Christiana Bruce.

Bonham, Dorothy d. 1641 Daughter of Charles Bonham. Married William Selby.

Bosville (Boswell), Ralph d. 1682 Knight of Brabourne House, Sevenoaks, Kent.

Bourchier, Francis 1587–1612 Daughter to Elizabeth Russell and William Bourchier. Never married. First cousin to Anne, who erected a monument for her in the Bedford Chapel at Chenies, Buckinghamshire.

Bourchier, William 1557–1623 3rd Earl of Bath, son of Frances Kitson and John Bourchier, Lord Fitzwarren. Married Anne's aunt Elizabeth Russell.

Bourchier, Richard b. c. 1585   Lord Fitzwarren, son of William Bourchier and Elizabeth Russell. Never married.

Boyle, Charles 1639–1694   3rd Baron Clifford of Londesborough, 3rd Viscount Dungarvan, son of Elizabeth Clifford and Richard Boyle. Married 1: Jane Seymour, daughter to William Seymour, 2nd Duke of Somerset; 2: Arethusa Vernon.

Boyle, Charles c. 1669–1704   4th Viscount Dungarvan, 3rd Earl of Cork, 2nd Earl of Burlington, son of Jane Seymour and Charles Boyle, 3rd Viscount of Dungarvan. Married Juliana Noel.

Boyle, Elizabeth 1662–1703   Countess of Barrymore, daughter of Jane Seymour and Charles Boyle, 3rd Viscount Dungarvan. Married James Barry, 4th Earl of Barrymore.

Boyle, Elizabeth d. 1725   Daughter of Elizabeth Clifford and Richard Boyle. Married Nicholas Tufton, 3rd Earl of Thanet, son of Margaret Sackville and Anne's grandson.

Boyle, Frances b. c. 1640   Daughter of Elizabeth Clifford and Richard Boyle. Married 1: Colonel Francis Courtenay, 2: Wentworth Dillon, 4th Earl of Roscommon.

Boyle, Henrietta 1646–1687   Daughter of Elizabeth Clifford and Richard Boyle. Married Lawrence Hyde, 1st Earl of Rochester.

Boyle, Henry 1669–1725   1st Baron Carleton, son of Jane Seymour and Charles Boyle, 3rd Viscount of Dungarvan. Never married.

Boyle, Mary Anne d. 1671   Daughter of Elizabeth Clifford and Richard Boyle. Married Edward Montagu, 2nd Earl of Sandwich.

Boyle, Richard c. 1641–1665   Son of Elizabeth Clifford and Richard Boyle. He died at the Battle of Lowestoft.

Boyle, Richard 1612–1698   1st Earl of Burlington and 2nd Earl of Cork, Lord Clifford of Londesborough. Married Elizabeth Clifford and heir of Henry Clifford, 5th Earl of Cumberland.

Bracken, John active 1665–1719.   Painter, of London. He produced portraits (and often copies of portraits) for a number of north-eastern families including Anne Clifford, the Flemings, the Fletchers and others.

Bradford Adam active 1617–1624   A servant (barber) at Knole.

Braganza, Catherine 1638–1705   Infanta of Portugal, Queen consort of England, Scotland and Ireland, daughter of Luisa de Guzmán and John, 8th Duke of Braganza. Married Charles II, King of England.

Bricknell, Jane d. c. 1670   Anne's elderly servant who lodged in a room at Brougham.

Bromedish, Mrs active 1619   Gentlewoman servant to Anne at Knole.

Bromley, Edward 1563–1626   Knight and Baron of the Exchequer, son of Joan Waverton and Sir George Bromley of Hallon, Shropshire. Married Margaret Lowe, heiress of Nicholas Lowe of Tymore.

Brooke, Henry 1564–1619   11th Baron Cobham, son of Frances Newton and William Brooke, 10th Baron Cobham. Married Frances Howard, Countess of Kildare and daughter of Charles Howard, 1st Earl of Nottingham.

Browne, Elizabeth d. 1616   Daughter of Jane Radcliffe and Anthony Browne, 1st Viscount Montagu. Married Robert Dormer, 1st Baron.

Bruce, Christiana 1595–1674   Daughter of Magdalene Clark and Edward Bruce, 1st Lord Kinloss. Married William Cavendish, 2nd Earl of Devonshire.

Bruce, Janet b. c. 1596   Daughter of Magdalene Clark and Edward Bruce, 1st Lord Kinloss. Married Thomas Dalyell of The Binns.

Bruce, Thomas 1599–1663   3rd Lord Kinloss and 1st Earl of Elgin, son of Magdalene Clark and Edward Bruce, 1st Lord Kinloss. Married 1: Anne Chichester, 2: Diana Cecil.

Brydges, Elizabeth c. 1578–1617   Maid of Honour to Elizabeth I, daughter of Frances Clinton and Giles Brydges, 3rd Baron Chandos. Married Sir John Kennedy.

Brydges, Frances 1580–1663   Daughter of Mary Hopton and William Brydges 4th Baron Chandos. Married 1: Thomas Smith, 2: Thomas Cecil, 1st Earl of Exeter.

Brydges, Katherine 1580–1657   Daughter of Frances Clinton and Giles Brydges, 3rd Baron Chandos. Married Francis Russell, 4th Earl of Bedford, Anne's first cousin.

Buchanan, Charles b. 1661   Son of Emma Burton and James Buchanan. Ordained Deacon, 1681.

Buchanan, James, d. 1680   Vicar of St Lawrence's, Appleby and Rector of Dufton, son of George Buchanan, Vicar of Kirkby Lonsdale. Married Emma Burton.

Buckle, William active 1675–1676   Anne's scullery boy.

Burke, Richard 1572–1635   4th Earl of Clanricarde, son of Honora Burke (daughter of John Burke) and Ulrick Burke, 3rd Earl of Clanricarde. Married Frances Walsingham.

Burton, Edward 1566–1638   Knight, Rector of Broadwater, Sussex. Married Mary Perrin.

Burton, Katherine 1599–1660   Anne's gentlewoman servant at Knole, daughter of Mary Perrin and Sir Edward Burton.

Butler, Thomas 1634–1680   6th Earl of Ossory, son of Elizabeth Preston and James Butler, 1st Duke of Ormonde. Married Emilia van Nassau-Beverweerd, a Dutch aristocrat.

Byfield, Rev. active 1664   Chaplain to the Richard Boyle, Earl of Cork.

Caldicott, Matthew active 1616–1624   One of Richard's Sackville closest gentleman servants who vied with Anne for authority in the family at Knole. He was one of the witnesses of Richard's Sackville's will.

Calvert, George 1579–1631   1st Baron Baltimore, son of Alice Crossland and Leonard Calvert, a tenant of Whartons. Married Anne Mynne. Became Secretary of State in 1619.

Care, Mistress active 1619   Likely the wife of Richard Sackville's servant and tenant Robert Care.

Care, Robert active 1616–1624   Richard Sackville's servant and tenant.

Carew, George 1555–1629   Baron Carew of Clopton, 1st Earl of Totnes, son of Catherine Huddesfield and Dr George Carew, Dean of Windsor. Married Joyce Clopton.

Carey, Frances b. 1571   Daughter of Katherine Knyvet (daughter of Sir Henry Knyvet) and Sir Edward Cary. Married George Manners, 7th Earl of Rutland.

Carey, Henry 1580–1666   4th Baron Hunsdon, after 1621 Viscount Rochford, and after 1628 1st Earl of Dover, son of Mary Hyde and Sir John Carey, 3rd Baron Hunsdon. Married Mary Morris.

Carey, Mary 1615–1672   Daughter of Judith Pelham and Henry Carey, 1st Earl of Dover. Married Sir Thomas Wharton.

Carey, Philadelphia d. 1655   Daughter of Elizabeth Trevannion and Robert Carey, 1st Earl of Monmouth. Married Sir Thomas Wharton.

Carey, Robert 1560–1639   1st Earl of Monmouth, son of Anne Morgan and Henry Carey, 1st Baron Hunsdon. Married Elizabeth Trevannion.

Carlton, Jane d. after 1676.   Daughter of Nichola Elliot and Gerald Carleton.

Carlton, Robert d. after 1676   Son of Barbara Delaval and William Carleton.

Carlton, William 1607–1665 Knight, of Penrith, son of Nichola Elliot and Gerald Carleton. Married 1: Dorothy Dalston, 2: Barbara Delaval.

Carlton, Thomas active 1657 One of Anne Clifford's officers in Westmorland.

Carniston, Mrs active 1603 Anne Clifford's gentlewoman servant and governess in 1603.

Carr, Anne 1615–1654 Daughter of Frances Howard, Countess of Somerset, and Robert Carr, Earl of Somerset. Married William Russell, 1st Duke of Bedford.

Carr, Colonel active 1670 A retired military man who lived in Skipton. He may be the Scottish colonel who was proposed as Governor of Plymouth.

Carter, Dr active 1617 A minister who visits Knole in 1617.

Cary, Mary 1581–1654 Daughter of George Cary and Catherine Russell. Married John Arundell of Trerice, Cornwall.

Catterick, John d. after 1676 Of Carlton Hall, Westmorland. Married Margaret [maiden name unknown].

Catterick, Margaret d. 1685 Daughter of Margaret and John Catterick of Carleton Hall. Married Thomas Birkbeck.

Cavendish, Mary 1556–1632 Daughter of William Cavendish and Elizabeth Hardwick (Bess of Hardwick). Married her step-brother Gilbert Talbot, 7th Earl of Shrewsbury.

Cavendish, William 1590–1628 2nd Earl of Devonshire, son of Anne Keighley and William Cavendish 1st Earl of Devonshire. Married Christiana Bruce, daughter of Edward Bruce, 1st Lord Kinloss.

Cecil, Elizabeth 1578–1646 Daughter of Dorothy Neville and Thomas Cecil, 1st Earl of Exeter. Married 1: Sir William Hatton, 2: Sir Edward Coke.

Cecil, Elizabeth 1595–1672 Daughter of Elizabeth Drury and William Cecil, 2nd Earl of Exeter. Married Thomas Howard, 1st Earl of Berkshire.

Cecil, Frances d. 1643 Daughter of Elizabeth Brooke and Robert Cecil, Earl of Salisbury. Married Henry Clifford, 5th Earl of Cumberland.

Cecil, Frances d. 1653 Daughter of Dorothy Neville and Thomas Cecil, 1st Earl of Exeter. Married Nicholas Tufton, 1st Earl of Thanet.

Cecil, John 1628–1678 4th Earl of Exeter, son of Elizabeth Edgerton and David Cecil, 3rd Earl of Exeter. Married Frances Manners.

Cecil, Robert 1563–1612 1st Earl of Salisbury, son of Mildred Cooke and William Cecil, 1st Baron Burghley. Married Elizabeth Brooke.

Cecil, Thomas 1542–1623 1st Earl of Exeter, son of Mary Cheke and William Cecil, 1st Baron Burghley. Married 1: Dorothy Neville, 2: Frances Brydges.

Cecil, William 1590–1618 Lord de Ros, son of Elizabeth Manners, 16th Baroness de Ros of Helmsley *suo jure* and William Cecil, 2nd Earl of Exeter. Married Anne Lake.

Cecil, William 1591–1668 2nd Earl of Salisbury, son of Elizabeth Brooke and Robert Cecil, 1st Earl of Salisbury. Married Catherine Howard, daughter of Thomas Howard, 2nd Earl of Suffolk.

Chaloner, Robert d. 1621 Doctor of Divinity, and Rector of Amersham, Canon of Windsor, maintained close ties to Christ Church, Oxford.

Chaloner, Thomas 1521–1565 Knight, son of Margaret Middleton and Roger Chaloner. Married 1: Joan Cotton, 2: Audrey (or Ethelreda) Frodsham.

Chambers, Simon active 1603 Steward to Anne Russell, Countess of Warwick.

Chantler, Nicholas d. 1620 A clergyman and schoolmaster of Lewes and Vicar of Udimore, Sussex, until 1614.

Cheyney, Mr active 1616–1624   Gentleman servant at Knole.

Chichester, Arthur 1663–1625   1st Baron Chichester of Belfast, son of Gertrude Courtenay and Sir John Chichester, both of Devon. Married Lettice Perrot.

Chippindale, Anne active 1675–1676   Anne's gentlewoman, daughter of Peter Chippendale, Anne's bailiff at Skipton.

Cholmley, Henry 1609–1666   Knight and MP for Appleby, 1660 Convention, son of Susan Ledgard and Sir Richard Cholmley of Whitby. Married Katherine Stapleton.

Clapham, Christopher d. 1686   Knight and MP for Appleby, 1660 Convention Parliament, son of Martha Heber and George Clapham of Beamsley. Married 1: Mary Lowden, 2: Margaret Oldfield, 3: Mary Needham.

Clapham, Richard b. c. 1610, d. after 1666.   Son of Martha Heber and George Clapham of Beamsley, brother to Sir Christopher Clapham. Served Anne in a variety of capacities both locally and in the South.

Clapham, Sheffield d. 1676   Son of Mary Lowden and Sir Christopher Clapham of Beamsely. Married Elizabeth Thornbury.

Clement X 1590–1676   Pope (1670–1676) born Emelio Bonaventura Altieri, son of Victoria Delfin and Lorenzo Altieri.

Clifford, Elizabeth 1613–1690   Lady Clifford of Londesborough *suo jure*, daughter of Frances Cecil and Henry Clifford, 5th Earl of Cumberland. Married Richard Boyle, 2nd Earl of Cork and 1st Earl of Burlington.

Clifford, Francis 1559–1641.   4th Earl of Cumberland, son of Anne Dacre and Henry, 2nd Lord Clifford. Married Grisold Hughes.

Clifford, George 1561–1626.   3rd Earl of Cumberland, son of Anne Dacre and Henry Clifford, 2nd Earl of Cumberland. Married: Margaret Russell.

Clifford, Henry 1493–1542   1st Earl of Cumberland, son of Anne St John and Henry, 10th Lord Clifford. Married 1: Margaret Talbot, 2: Margaret Percy.

Clifford, Henry 1517–1570   2nd Earl of Cumberland, son of Margaret Percy and Henry Clifford, 1st Earl of Cumberland. Married 1: Eleanor Brandon, daughter to Mary Tudor, youngest sister of Henry VIII, 2: Anne Dacre.

Clifford, Henry 1591–1643   5th Earl of Cumberland, son of Grisold Hughes and Francis Clifford. Married Frances Cecil.

Clifton, Anne b. c. 1625   Daughter of Frances Clifford and Gervase Clifton. Married Sir Francis Rodes of Barlborough.

Coke, Edward 1552–1634   Knight, Attorney General and Chief Justice of the King's Bench, son of Winifred Knightley and Edward Coke. Married 1. Bridget Paston, 2. Elizabeth Hatton.

Coleby, John active 1655–1665   Of Coleby Hall, Askrigg, Yorkshire, son of Mary and John Coleby. Married and had at least a daughter, Anne, who married Sir James Metcalfe of Nappa.

Compton, Alethea 1661–1678   Daughter of Isabella Sackville and James Compton, 3rd Earl of Northampton, and Anne's granddaughter. Married Sir Edward Hungerford.

Compton, Anne d. 1675   Marchioness of Clanricarde, daughter of Elizabeth Spencer and William Compton, 1st Earl of Northampton. Married Ulrick Burke, 1st Marquess of Clanricarde.

Compton, Henry c. 1584 – c. 1659   MP for East Grinstead, son of Anne Spencer and Sir Henry Compton, 1st Baron Compton. Married his step-sister, Cecily Sackville.

274 GLOSSARY OF PERSONS

Compton, Henry 1632–1713   Bishop of Oxford and later Bishop of London, son of Mary Beaumont and Spencer Compton, 2nd Earl of Northampton. Never married.

Compton, James 1622–1681   3rd Earl of Northampton, son of Mary Beaumont and Spencer Compton, 2nd Earl of Northampton. Married 1: Isabella Sackville, Anne's daughter, 2: Mary Noel.

Concini, Concini 1575–1617   Marquis d'Ancre. A Florentine who went to France with Marie de Medici upon her marriage to Henri IV of France. Married Lenora Dori. He was murdered apparently with the consent of Louis XIII. Lenora was executed for sorcery.

Conniston, John active 1620   Servant in the Knole household.

Conniston, Ralph active 1612–1616   Gentleman servant to Margaret Russell in Westmorland. Likely related to Walter 'Wat' Conniston.

Conniston, Walter, 'Wat' active 1616   Gentleman servant of Anne's at Knole, likely related to Ralph Conniston.

Cook, John active 1617   A servant at Knole.

Cooling, Peter active 1619   Anne intercedes on his behalf for a post as gunner at Carlisle.

Cope, Isabel 1590–1638   Daughter of Dorothy Grenville and Sir Walter Cope. Married Henry Rich, 1st Earl of Holland.

Corbet, Elizabeth d. 1623   Daughter and heir of Robert Corbet of Moreton Corbet. Married Sir Henry Wallop.

Cornwallis, Frances 1573–1625   Daughter of Lucy Neville and Sir William Cornwallis. Married Sir Edmund Withypole.

Cornwallis, Thomas d. 1618   Knight, groom-porter 1597–1618, son of Margaret Lowthe and Richard Cornwallis. Married Elizabeth Molineux.

Cotton, John b. 1613   A Roman Catholic, imprisoned (1613–1619) falsely as the author of the seditious pamphlet *Balaam's Ass*.

Cotton, Mary d. 1580   Daughter of Mary Olney and Sir George Cotton. Married Henry Grey, 6th Earl of Kent.

Coventry, George 1628–1680   3rd Baron Coventry, son of Mary Craven and Thomas Coventry, 2nd Baron Coventry. Married Margaret Tufton.

Coventry, Henry 1619–1686   Secretary of State, son of Elizabeth Aldersley and Thomas Coventry, 1st Baron Coventry. Never married.

Coventry, John 1654–1687   4th Lord Coventry, son of Margaret Tufton and George Coventry. Never married.

Coventry, Thomas 1578–1640   1st Baron Coventry, Lord Keeper of the Great Seal, son of Margaret Jeffreys and Sir Thomas Coventry. Married 1: Sarah Sebright, 2: Elizabeth Aldersley.

Coventry, Thomas 1606–1661   2nd Baron Coventry, son of Sarah Sebright and Thomas Coventry, 1st Baron Coventry. Married Mary Craven.

Crawley, Mrs active 1619   Anne's gentlewoman servant at Knole.

Crew, Ranulph 1558–1646   Chief Justice of the King's Bench, son of Alice Mainwaring and John Crew of Nantwich. Married 1: Julia Clipsby, 2: Julian Fasey.

Croke, Unton 1596–1671   Serjeant at Law, assize judge and MP, son of Katherine Blount and Sir John Croke. Married Anne Hore.

Crow, Charles 1630–1682   Vicar of Warcop, son of Edward Crow. His son Charles Crow became Bishop of Cloyne.

GLOSSARY OF PERSONS 275

Curvett, Acton active 1616–1624 Chief footman at Knole.
Curzon, George d. 1623 Knight, of Croxall Hall, son of Katherine Babington and George Curzon. Married Mary Leveson.
Curzon, Mary 1585–1645 Governess to the royal children, including Prince Charles and Prince James. Daughter of Mary Leveson and Sir George Curzon. Married Edward Sackville, 4th Earl of Dorset.
Dacre, Anne 1557–1630 Poet, daughter of Elizabeth Leyburne and Thomas Dacre, 4th Baron Dacre. Married her stepbrother Philip Howard, Earl of Arundel.
Dacre, William 1493–1563 Son of Elizabeth Greystoke and Thomas Dacre, 2nd Baron. Married Elizabeth Talbot.
Dallison, Maximillian 1577–1631 Knight and High Sheriff of Kent, son of Silvestra Dene and William Dallison, stepson to William Lambarde the antiquarian. Married 1: Paulina Sondes, 2: Mary Spencer.
Dalston, Bridget d. after 1668 Daughter of Sir George Dalston. Married Thomas Sandford, 1st Baronet.
Dalston, Christopher 1638–1697 Son of Lucy Fallowfield and Sir John Dalston. Married Bridget Fletcher.
Dalston, John 1611–1692 Knight, MP for Appleby, son of Anne Hutton and Christopher Dalston of Acorn Bank. Married Lucy Fallowfield.
Dalton, John d. c. 1676 Vicar of Shap 1668–1671.
Darby, John active 1657 Anne's officer in Westmorland.
Darcy, Elizabeth d. 1617 Daughter of Frances Rich and John Darcy, 2nd Baron of Chiche. Married John Lumley, 1st Baron.
Dargue, Margaret active 1669–1676 Anne's laundry maid, maybe daughter of Jane Dargue, a resident of Anne's almshouse in Appleby.
Dargue, William active 1669–1676 Anne's kitchen servant or scullery man, maybe son of Jane Dargue, a resident of Anne's almshouse in Appleby.
Davis, Mr active 1619–1624 Gentleman, possibly one of the Inner Temple lawyers – Charles or John Davis – mentioned in Richard Sackville's will.
Davis, Mrs active 1619 Gentlewoman servant of Anne Clifford's at Knole in 1619, possibly the wife of one of Inner Temple lawyers – Charles or John Davis – mentioned in Richard Sackville's will.
Dawson, Richard active 1616–1617 A servant of Margaret Russell. The Dawson family had served the Cliffords in the North since the time of Henry, 10th Lord Clifford.
De Vere, Bridget 1584–1631 Daughter of Anne Cecil and Edward De Vere, 17th Earl of Oxford. Married Francis Norris, 1st Earl of Berkshire.
De Vere, Elizabeth 1575–1627 Daughter of Anne Cecil and Edward de Vere, 17th Earl of Oxford. Married William Stanley, 6th Earl of Derby.
De Vere, Susan 1587–1629 Daughter of Anne Cecil and Edward De Vere, 17th Earl of Oxford. Married Philip Herbert, Earl of Montgomery later Earl of Pembroke as his first wife.
Delaval, Barbara d. after 1676 Daughter of Barbara Selby and Robert Delaval. Married William Carlton.
Demaine, Dorothy, the younger active 1668–1676 Anne's laundry (household) maid, from the Demaine family of Barden, Yorkshire, daughter of Dorothy Demaine and George Demaine, both of whom served as Anne's housekeepers at Barden Tower.
Demaine, George active 1668–1676 Housekeeper of Barden Tower. Married likely

Dorothy. His eldest son is William who lives in Barden Forest, had son John also, and likely several daughters who served Anne as laundry (or household) maids.

Dennison, Robert active 1670–1676 A labourer of Brougham, son according to Anne of a deaf woman.

Devereux, Dorothy 1564–1619 Countess of Northumberland, daughter of Lettice Knollys and Walter Devereux, 1st Earl of Essex. Married 1: Sir Thomas Perrot, 2: Henry Percy, 9th Earl of Northumberland.

Devereux, Frances 1599–1674 Countess of Somerset, daughter of Frances Walsingham and Robert Devereux 2nd Earl of Essex. Married William Seymour, 2nd Duke of Somerset.

Devereux, Penelope 1562–1607 Daughter of Lettice Knollys and Walter Devereux, 1st Earl of Essex. Married 1: Sir Robert Rich, 2: her lover Charles Blount.

Devereux, Robert 1591–1646 3rd Earl of Essex, son of Frances Walsingham and Robert Devereux, 2nd Earl of Essex. Married 1: Frances Howard, later Countess of Somerset, marriage annulled, 2: Elizabeth Paulet.

Dick, Grey active 1616 A servant of Richard Sackville at Knole

Digby, Anne d. 1612 Daughter of Anne Cope and Kenelm Digby of Stoke Dry (d. 1590). Married Sir Edward Watson of Rockingham Castle.

Digby, John 1580–1653 1st Earl of Bristol, son of Abigail Heveningham and Sir George Digby. Married Beatrice Walcott.

Domville, Robert b. c. 1590 Clergyman, B.A. from Trinity College, Cambridge, curate at Bolton, Rector of Waldron, Sussex, in 1617.

Dorothy Bonham 1572–1641 Daughter and heir of Charles Bonham of Malling, Kent. Married Sir William Selby III.

Douglas-Hamilton William 1634–1694 1st Marquess of Douglas and Duke of Hamilton, son of Mary Gorden and William Douglas. Married Anne Hamilton, 3rd Duchess Hamilton *suo jure*. Duke of Hamilton through his wife, and took her surname, as did their children.

Drax, Henry 1641–1682 Son of Meliora Horton and Sir James Drax. Married 1: Frances Tufton, 2: Dorothy Lovelace.

Drummond, Jane c. 1585–1643 Mistress of the Robes to Queen Anne, daughter of Elizabeth Lindsay and Patrick Drummond, 3rd Lord Drummond. Married Robert Ker, Earl of Roxburgh.

Drury, Elizabeth c. 1578–1654 Daughter of Elizabeth Stafford and Sir William Drury of Hawstead. Married William Cecil, 3rd Lord Burghley and 2nd Earl of Exeter.

Duck, Mr active 1616–1624. A page at Knole.

Dudley, John b. c. 1600 Son of Edward Sutton, 5th Baron Dudley, with Elizabeth Tomlinson.

Dunn, William active 1616–1619 A servant to Richard Sackville. He is listed as one of the James Town Adventurers in 1620.

Duton, Henry active 1593 Knight, MP in 1593.

Earle, Erasmus 1590–1667 Serjeant at Law, son of Anne Fountaine and Thomas Earle. Married Frances Fontaine, daughter of James Fountaine.

Edge, William d. after 1676 Receiver of Anne's rents in Sussex and Kent.

Edmonds, Thomas 1563–1639 Knight, Treasurer of the Royal Household to King James, son of Joan Delbere and Thomas Edmonds. Married Magdalen Wood, co-heir of Sir John Wood.

Edwards, Evan b. c. 1600 d. after 1650   Of Rhual in Wales, gentleman servant of Richard and Edward Sackville.

Egerton, Thomas 1540–1617   1st Viscount Brackley, Lord Keeper and Lord, son of Alice Sparks and Sir Richard Egerton. Married 1: Elizabeth Ravenscroft, 2: Elizabeth More, 3: Alice Spencer.

Elisabeth of France 1602–1644   Queen consort of Spain and Portugal. Daughter of Henry IV of France and Marie de Medici. Married Philip IV of Spain.

Ellis, William 1609–1680   Knight, King's Serjeant of Law, assize judge, son of Jane Armstrong and Sir Thomas Ellis. Never married.

Elmes, Edmund b. c. 1520   Son of Edith Mordaunt and John Elmes. Married Alice St John.

Elmes, Thomas d. 1602   Knight, son of Alice St John and Edmund Elmes. Married Christian Hickling of Greens Norton.

Erskine, Thomas 1566–1639   1st Earl of Kellie, son of Margaret Home and Sir Alexander Erskine. Married 1: Anne Ogilvie, 2: Elizabeth Pierrepont, 3: Elizabeth Norreys.

Etheldreda 'Audrey' Shelton 1561–1631.   Lady Walsingham, Keeper of the Queen's Wardrobe, daughter of Mary Wodehouse and Sir Ralph Shelton of Norfolk. Married Sir Thomas Walsingham of Scadbury.

Eure (or Evers), Samson b. c. 1592, d. by 1659   Serjeant at law, son of Elizabeth Lennard and Sir Francis Eure. Married Martha Cage.

Evans, Dr active 1667   Chaplain to Anne Hyde, Duchess of York. He performed the marriage of Anne Clifford's granddaughter Cecily Tufton and Christopher Hatton.

Fairer, Elizabeth d. after 1676   Daughter of William Fairer of Shap Grange. Elizabeth Married 1: Richard Crackenthorp, 2: John Atkinson.

Fanshawe, Thomas 1632–1674   2nd Viscount Fanshawe, son of Elizabeth Cockayne and Thomas Fanshawe. Married 1: Katherine Ferrers, 2: Sarah Evelyn.

Fermor, Hatton d. 1640   Of Easton Neston, Sheriff of Northamptonshire, son of Sir John Fermor.

Fettiplace, Edmund 1554–1613   Knight, of Bessels Leigh, son of Elizabeth Ashfield and William Fettiplace. Married Anne Alford.

Fielding, William 1567–1643   1st Earl of Denbigh, son of Elizabeth Aston and Basil Fielding. Married Susan Villiers.

Finch, Catherine d. 1639   Daughter of Elizabeth Heneage, 1st Countess of Winchilsea *suo jure*, and Sir Moyle Finch. Married Sir John Wentworth, 1st Baronet of Gostfield.

Finch, Moyle 1550–1614   1st Baronet, son of Catherine Moyle and Sir Thomas Finch. Married Elizabeth Heneage, 1st Countess of Winchilsea.

Fittin, Abraham active 1665–1676   Anne's coachman in Westmorland.

Fleming, Catherine b. c. 1657, d. after 1676   Daughter of Barbara Fletcher and Daniel Fleming. Married 1: Roger Moore, Recorder of Kendal, 2: Edward Wilson of Dallam Tower.

Fleming, Daniel 1633–1701   Of Rydal Hall, antiquarian, son of Alice Kirkby and William Fleming. Married Barbara Fletcher.

Fletcher, Barbara b. c. 1633, d. after 1676   Daughter of Catherine Dalston and Henry Fletcher, 1st Baronet. Married Daniel Fleming of Rydall Hall.

Fletcher, Bridget b. c. 1644, d. after 1698   Daughter of Catherine Dalston and Henry Fletcher, 1st Baronet. Married Christopher Dalston.

Fletcher, George 1633–1700   2nd Baronet, son of Catherine Dalston and Henry Fletcher,

1st Baronet, Vice Chamberlain to Queen Catherine of Braganza. Married 1: Alice Hare, 2: Mary Johnstone.

Flocknell, Mr active 1603   Gentleman servant to Anne Russell, Countess of Warwick.

Gabetis, Anne active 1650–1676   Wife of Thomas Gabetis, Anne's deputy sheriff of Westmorland.

Gabetis, Thomas 1595–1691   Anne's Deputy Sheriff of Westmorland. Married Anne (maiden name unknown).

Gamage, Barbara 1562–1621   Countess of Leicester, daughter and heir of Gwenllian Powell and John Gamage of Coity Castle. Married Robert Sidney, Lord de L'Isle and Earl of Leicester.

Gently, John active 1663   Gentleman servant to John Tufton, grandson to Anne Clifford.

Gifford, Mr active 1616–1619   A servant of Richard Sackville at Knole.

Gilmore, John active 1668–1676   Gentleman, of Ramsbury, Anne's under-keeper of Whinfell forest. Married Elizabeth Nicholls.

Glemham, Thomas b. c. 1589   Knight, son of Anne Sackville, Richard Sackville's aunt, and Henry Glemham. Married Catherine Vavasour.

Golding, Humphrey   An associate of Anne's, possibly a servant or tenant of Margaret Russell's in Westmorland.

Goodgion, George active 1662–1676   One of Anne Clifford's chief servants, likely the son of George Goodgion, gentleman, officer of the Crimple mining works in Brougham and later clerk and overseer at Brougham.

Goodgion, Robert active 1676   Anne's tenant at Skipton, likely related to George Goodgion.

Goodwin, Jane d. 1658   Daughter and heir to Jane Wenman and Arthur Goodwin of Buckinghamshire. Married Philip, 4th Baron Wharton.

Goodwin, Mistress active 1603   Gentlewoman servant to Anne Clifford in 1603.

Gorges, Edward c. 1582 – c. 1650   1st Baron Gorges of Dundalk, son of Sir Thomas Gorges and Helena von Snakenborg, cousin to Anne. Married Katherine Osborne.

Gorges, Elizabeth 1578–1658   Daughter of Sir Thomas Gorges and Helena von Snakenborg. Married 1: Sir Hugh Smyth of Long Ashton, 2: Ferdinando Gorges.

Graham, Margaret d. after 1676   Daughter of Mary Johnstone and Sir George Graham.

Grasty, Samuel b. c. 1630, d. 1683   Vicar of Brougham (including Ninekirks), son of Thomas Grasty. B.A. Brasenose College, Oxford. Married Margaret Sharshall.

Grey, Henry 1583–1639   8th Earl of Kent, son of Susan Cotton and Charles Grey, 7th Earl of Kent. Married Elizabeth Talbot.

Grey, Mary d. 1702   Baroness Lucas of Crudwell *suo jure*, daughter and heir of Anne Neville and John Lucas, 1st Baron Lucas. Married Anthony Grey, 11th Earl of Kent.

Grey, Susan d. 1620   Daughter of Susan Cotton and Charles Grey, 7th Earl of Kent. Married Sir Michael Longueville.

Griffin, Edward d. 1621   Knight, son of Lucy Palmer and Sir Edward Griffin. Married 1: Lucy Coniers, 2: Anne Smith, 3: Elizabeth Chambers. Married his stepsister Lucy Coniers.

Grimston, Harbottle 1603–1685   2nd Baronet, son of Elizabeth Coppenger and Sir Harbottle Grimston, 1st Baronet. Married 1: Mary Croke, 2: Anne Bacon.

Grimston, Samuel 1643–1700   3rd Baronet, son of Mary Croke and Harbottle Grimston, 2nd Baronet. Married Anne Tufton.

Grosvenor, Richard 1585–1645   1st Baronet, son of Christian Brooke and Richard Grosvenor of Eaton. Married 1. Lettice Cholmley, 2: Elizabeth Wilbraham, 3: Elizabeth Warburton.

Guy, Edward active 1671–1676   A Quaker and merchant of both foodstuffs and high-quality items like silver and paper. Married a Garth.

Hale, Matthew 1609–1676   Baron of the Exchequer, son of Joan Poyntz and Robert Hale. Married 1: Anne Moore, 2: Anne Bishop. One of Anne's lawyers.

Hall, John active 1665–1676   Chief groom of Anne's stables in Westmorland.

Hall, Margaret active 1619   Cousin to Anne, from Guildford.

Hammond, Robert c. 1594–1627   Son of Mary Harrison and John Hammond. Married Elizabeth Knollys.

Harington, Theodosia d. 1650   Daughter of Lucy Sidney of Penshurst and John Harington. Married Edward Sutton, 5th Baron Dudley.

Harington, Lucy 1581–1627   Lady of the Privy Chamber to Queen Anne, daughter of Anne Kelway and John Harington, 1st Baron Harington. Married Edward Russell, 3rd Earl of Bedford.

Harmon, Thomas active 1616–1624   Gentleman servant at Knole.

Harrison, Christopher active 1670s   Vicar of Brough. Married to a Farrand

Harrison, Margaret b. c. 1635, d. 1677   Daughter of Margaret Darcy and Sir Thomas Harrison. Married Sir Richard Musgrave, 3rd Baronet of Hartley Castle.

Harrison, Mistress   Anne's gentlewoman servant in 1603.

Harrison, Robert, active 1668–1676   Anne's housekeeper of Brough Castle, also does tailoring work for her.

Harrison, Thomas 1616–1660   A Parliamentarian army officer and regicide, son of Mary and Richard Harrison, mayor of Lyme, Staffordshire. Married his cousin Catherine Harrison.

Hart, Percival 1559–1642   Knight of Lullingstone Castle, son of Elizabeth Bowes and Sir George Hart. Married 1: Mary Harrison, 2: Anne Manwood, 3: Jane Stanhope.

Hasell, Edward 1642–1707   Knight, son of Rev. Edward Hasell and Martha Smyth. Married 1: Jane Fetherstonhaugh, 2: Dorothy Williams.

Hastings, Elizabeth 1556–1621   Countess of Worcester, daughter of Francis Hastings, 2nd Earl of Huntingdon, and Catherine Pole. Married Edward Somerset, 4th Earl of Worcester.

Hatfield, Henry active 1660   Gentleman servant to Anne's grandson, John Tufton.

Hatton, Christopher 1605–1670   1st Baron Hatton, son of Sir Christopher Hatton and Alice Fanshawe. Married Elizabeth Montagu. He was a collector of books and antiquities and contributed material to Anne Clifford's *Great Books of Record*.

Hatton, Christopher 1632–1706   1st Viscount Hatton and Governor of Guernsey, son of Elizabeth Montagu and Christopher Hatton, 1st Baron Hatton. Married 1: Cecily Tufton, 2: Frances Yelverton, 3: Elizabeth Haslewood.

Hatton, Frances 1590–1623   Daughter and heiress of Elizabeth Gawdy and Sir William Hatton. Married Sir Robert Rich, 2nd Earl of Warwick.

Hawkridge, Mrs   Gentlewoman servant to Anne Clifford in 1603.

Hay, James 1580–1636   1st Earl of Carlisle, favourite of James I and gentleman of the bedchamber, son of Margaret Murray and George Hay, 1st Earl of Kinnoull. Married 1: Honoria Denny, 2: Lucy Percy.

Herbert, James 1623–1677 MP, son of Susan De Vere and Philip Herbert, 4th Earl of Pembroke. Married Jane Spiller.

Heneage, Elizabeth 1556–1634 1st Countess of Winchilsea *suo jure*, daughter and heir Anne Poyntz and Sir Thomas Heneage. Married Sir Moyle Finch.

Henrietta Maria of France 1609–1669 Queen Consort of England, daughter of Marie de Medici and Henry IV of France. Married Charles I of England, mother of Charles II and James II, Kings of England.

Henrietta of England 1644–1670 Duchess of Orléans, youngest daughter of Henrietta Maria of France and Charles I, King of England. Married Philippe of France, brother of Louis XIV, King of France.

Herbert, Henry c. 1538–1601 2nd Earl of Pembroke, son of Anne Parr (sister to Queen Catherine Parr) and Henry Herbert, 1st Earl of Pembroke. Married Mary Sidney, poet and sister to Sir Philip Sidney.

Herbert, John Companion of Richard Sackville in 1616.

Herbert, Philip 1584–1650 4th Earl of Pembroke and 1st Earl of Montgomery, son of Mary Sidney and Henry Herbert 2nd Earl of Pembroke. Married 1: Susan De Vere, 2: Anne Clifford

Herbert, Philip 1621–1669 5th Earl of Pembroke, 2nd Earl of Montgomery, son of Susan De Vere and Philip Herbert, 4th Earl of Pembroke.

Herbert, William c. 1572–1655 1st Baron Powis, son of Mary Stanley and Edward Herbert. Married Eleanor Percy.

Herbert, William 1580–1630 3rd Earl of Pembroke, son of Mary Sidney and Henry Herbert, 2nd Earl of Pembroke. Married Mary Talbot.

Herbert, William 1641–1674 6th Earl of Pembroke, son of Penelope Naunton and Philip Herbert, 5th Earl of Pembroke. Never married.

Herdson, John d. 1622 Gentleman, owner of Brome Park, Kent. His monument is in St Michael's church, Hawkinge, Kent.

Hickling, Christian d. 1635 Daughter of Frances Goodwin and William Hickling of Greens Norton. Married Thomas Elmes.

Hickling, William d. after 1606 Of Greens Norton, Northamptonshire. Married Frances Goodwin and had a daughter, Christian who married Thomas Elmes.

Hilton, Alice active 1675 Daughter of Robert Hilton of Murton.

Hilton, George active 1644–1675 Gentleman of Westmorland, served as an agent for Anne in the North in the 1640s.

Hilton, Robert 1616–1683 Of Murton, the younger. Married Mary Hilton (her maiden name) of Hylton Castle. He was entrusted by Anne with keeping her father's tomb in good repair.

Hilton, Robert active 1675 Son of Mary and Robert Hilton of Murton.

Hilton, Thomas active 1675 Godson of Anne Clifford. Of Hilton, near Appleby. Brother of Robert Hilton the younger.

Hinde, Samuel active 1640–1670 Reverend, chaplain to Charles II, also chaplain to Margaret Sackville, son of William Hinde incumbent of Bunbury in Cheshire. Vicar of St Mary's church, Dover.

Hitchen, Mary active 1614–1619 Margaret Sackville's nursemaid at Knole.

Hobart, Henry 1554–1625 Knight and King's attorney, judge, son of Audrey Hare and Thomas Hobart of Plumstead, Norfolk. Married Dorothy Bell.

Hodgson, Mr Westmorland manservant serving Margaret Russell. His family were tenants on the Clifford estates in Westmorland.

Hogan (or Huggins), William c. 1524 – after 1603 Held the office of Keeper of the Gardens, Hampton Court, from 1561 to 1588.

Holles, Denzil 1599–1680 1st Baron, son of Anne Stanhope and John Holles, 1st Earl of Clare. Married 1: Dorothy Ashley, 2: Jane Covert, 3: Esther Le Lou.

Home, Alexander c. 1566–1619 1st Earl of Home, a Scottish nobleman, son of Agnes Gray and Alexander Home, 5th Lord Home. Married 1: Christian Douglas, 2: Mary Sutton.

Home, Elizabeth d. 1633 Daughter of Catherine Gordon and George Home, 1st Earl of Dunbar. Married Theophilus Howard, 2nd Earl of Suffolk.

Hookfield, Mr active 1616 A servant to Richard Sackville.

Howard, Anne 1629–1703 Daughter of Mary Butler and Edward Howard, 1st Baron Howard of Escrick. Married Charles Howard, 1st Earl of Carlisle.

Howard, Anne d. 1683 Daughter of Mary Widdrington and Sir Francis Howard (1588–1660). Never married.

Howard, Charles 1579–1642 2nd Earl of Nottingham, son of Catherine Carey, Lady of the chamber to Queen Elizabeth, and Charles Howard, 1st Earl of Nottingham. Married 1: Charity White, 2: Mary Cokayne.

Howard, Charles 1583 – c. 1655 Son of Elizabeth Dacre and Lord Howard of Naworth Castle. Married Dorothy Widdrington.

Howard, Charles 1629–1685 1st Earl of Carlisle, son of Mary Eure and Sir William Howard of Naworth. Married Anne Howard, daughter of Mary Butler and Edward Howard, 1st Baron Howard of Escrick.

Howard, Edward 1646–1692 2nd Earl of Carlisle, son of Anne Howard (daughter of Edward Howard, 1st Baron Howard of Escrick) and Charles Howard, 1st Earl of Carlisle. Married Elizabeth Uvedale.

Howard, Elizabeth c. 1586–1658 Daughter of Catherine Rich and Thomas Howard, 1st Earl of Suffolk. Married 1: William Knollys, 1st Earl of Banbury, 2: her lover Edward Vaux, 4th Baron Vaux of Harrowden.

Howard, Frances 1572 – c. 1628 Countess of Kildare, maid of honour to Queen Elizabeth I, daughter of Katherine Carey and Charles Howard, 1st Earl of Nottingham. Married 1: Henry FitzGerald, 12th Earl of Kildare, 2: Henry Brooke, Lord Cobham.

Howard, Frances 1578–1639 Countess of Hertford and Duchess of Lennox, daughter of Thomas Howard, 1st Viscount Howard of Bindon and Mable Burton. Married 1: Edward Seymour, 1st Earl of Hertford, 2: Lodovic Stuart, Duke of Lennox.

Howard, Frances 1590–1632 Daughter of Catherine Knyvet and Thomas Howard, 1st Earl of Suffolk. Married 1: Robert Devereux, 3rd Earl of Essex (marriage annulled), 2: Robert Carr, later Earl of Somerset. Convicted of murder of Thomas Overbury.

Howard, Francis 1588–1660 Knight, of Corby Castle, son of Elizabeth Dacre and Lord Howard of Naworth Castle. Married 1: Margaret Preston, 2: Mary Widdrington.

Howard, Francis b. 1635 Captain, of Corby Castle, son of Mary Widdrington and Sir Francis Howard (1588–1660).

Howard, Henry 1628–1684 6th Duke of Norfolk, son of Elizabeth Stuart and Henry Howard, Earl of Arundel. Married Anne Somerset.

Howard, Henry 1655–1701 7th Duke of Norfolk, son of Anne Somerset and Henry Howard, 6th Duke of Norfolk. Married Mary Mordaunt from whom he was later divorced.

Howard, Henry Frederick 1608–1652 Earl of Arundel, son of Alethea Talbot and Thomas Howard, Earl of Arundel. Married Elizabeth Stuart.

Howard, Theophilus 1584–1640 2nd Earl of Suffolk, son of Catherine Knyvet and Thomas Howard, 1st Earl of Suffolk. Married Elizabeth Home, daughter of the 1st Earl of Dunbar.

Howard, Thomas 1536–1572 4th Duke of Norfolk, son of Frances De Vere and poet Henry Howard Earl of Surrey. Married 1: Mary FitzAlan, heiress of Henry FitzAlan, 19th Earl of Arundel, 2: Margaret Audley, 3: Elizabeth Leyburne. Executed in 1572 for treason.

Howard, Thomas 1561–1656 1st Earl of Suffolk, son of Margaret Audley and Thomas Howard, 4th Duke of Norfolk. Married to Catherine Knyvet.

Howard, Thomas 1585–1646 1st Earl of Norfolk, son of Anne Dacre daughter and co-heir of Thomas, Lord Dacre and Philip Howard, 13th Earl of Arundel. Married Alethea Talbot.

Howard, Thomas 1587–1669 1st Earl of Berkshire, son of Catherine Knyvet and Thomas Howard, 1st Earl of Suffolk. Married Elizabeth Cecil.

Howard, William 1563–1640 Lord Howard of Naworth Castle, son of Margaret Audley and Thomas Howard, 4th Duke of Norfolk. Married Elizabeth Dacre.

Howard, William 1577–1615 3rd Baron Howard of Effingham, son of Catherine Carey, Lady of the chamber to Queen Elizabeth, and Charles Howard, 1st Earl of Nottingham. Married Anne St John.

Howard, William 1589–1644 Son of Elizabeth Dacre and Lord Howard of Naworth Castle. Married Mary Hungate.

Humfrey, Justina c. 1557–1627 Daughter of Joane Inkforbie and Laurence Humfrey. Married to Gaspar Dormer.

Hutchins, Mary active 1619 Nursemaid to Margaret Sackville at Knole.

Hutton, Julia b. c. 1620, d. after 1676 Daughter of Anne Briggs and Sir Richard Hutton. Married Sir Philip Musgrave, 2nd Baronet.

Hutton, William b. c. 1550, d. 1637 Knight, of Penrith, son of Elizabeth Romney and Anthony Hutton of Hutton Hall.

Hyde, Anne 1637–1671 Daughter of Frances Aylesbury and Henry Hyde, made 1st Earl of Clarendon. Married James, Duke of York, later James II, King of England. Mother of Mary I and Anne I, Queens of England.

Hyde, Mary d. 1627 Daughter of Leonard Hyde of Hyde Hall, Hertfordshire. Married 1: Richard Peyton, 2: John Carey, 3rd Baron Hunsdon.

Inkforbie, Joan d. 1611. Daughter of Andrew Inkforbie of Ipswich. Married Laurence Humfrey.

Ireland, Thomas 1560–1625 Knight, son of Margaret Fox and Robert Ireland and served the Earl of Derby, represented Anne Clifford during her interview with King James about Clifford lands. Married 1: Margaret Pope, 2: Margaret Aston, 3: Susan Macwilliam, 4: Margaret Lloyd.

Irton, Dorothy active 1608–1697 A deaf woman living in Anne's almshouse at Appleby, a prodigious weaver of bone lace. Married Thomas Wybergh.

Irwin, Marianna 1603–1676 Countess of Musgrave, daughter of Sir William Irwin. Married Edmund Sheffield, 1st Earl of Musgrave.

Jackson, Richard active 1671–1681 Schoolmaster of Appleby, previously schoolmaster at Kendal and Bampton.

Jenkins, Jack active 1603 Musician in the service of Anne Russell, teaches Anne Clifford the bass viol.

Johnson, Thomas fl 1657 One of Anne's officers in Westmorland. May be the husband of Anne Johnson, Anne's gentlewoman servant.

Johnson, William active 1668–1676 Housekeeper at Appleby.

Johnstone, Mary 1627–1676 Daughter of Mary Douglas and James Johnstone, Earl of Hartfell. Married 1: Sir George Graham, 2: Sir George Fletcher.

Jones, Richard active 1616 Servant to Richard Sackville at Knole.

Jordan, Isabell active 1669–1676 Anne's washerwoman in Westmorland.

Juvenal, François active 1619 Ambassador from France to England, 1619.

Kellaway, Mr d. before 1663 Of Wicks, Wiltshire. Married Elizabeth Turner.

Kendal, Mr active 1616 Servant of Margaret Russell in Westmorland.

Kidd, Mr active 1616 Servant of Margaret Russell and later Anne Clifford in Westmorland.

King, John d. 1621 Bishop of London, son of Elizabeth Conquest and Philip King. Married Joan Freeman.

Kingston, Thomas active 1668 Servant to John Gilmore in Westmorland.

Kirkhoven, Dorothea Helena d. 1564 Daughter of Katherine Stanhope and Jehan, Lord of Heenvliet. Married Charles Stanley, 8th Earl of Derby.

Kitching, Thomas active 1670–1676 Anne's tenant and also servant at Skipton.

Knightley, Richard 1533–1615 Of Fawsley Hall, son of Anne Ferrers and Valentine Knightley. Married 1: Mary Fermor, 2: Elizabeth Seymour, the daughter of Edward Seymour, 1st Duke of Somerset.

Kniveton, St Loe 1560–1625 Antiquarian from Mercaston, Derbyshire, son of John Kniveton and Jane Leche. Worked for Margaret Russell on Clifford lawsuits.

Knollys, Lettice 1583–1655 Daughter of Margaret Cave and Sir Henry Knollys. Married William Paget, 5th Baron Paget.

Knollys, William 1545–1632 1st Earl of Banbury, son of Katherine Carey and Sir Francis Knollys. Married 1: Dorothy Braye, 2: Elizabeth Howard, daughter of Thomas Howard, 1st Earl of Suffolk.

Knyvet, Catherine, 1564 –c. 1638 Countess of Suffolk, daughter of Elizabeth Stumpe and Sir Henry Knyvet. Married 1: Richard Rich, 1st Baron Rich, 2: Thomas Howard, 1st Earl of Suffolk.

Knyvet, Elizabeth 1574–1630 Author of *The Countess of Lincoln's Nursery* (1622), daughter and heir of Elizabeth Stumpe and Sir Henry Knyvet. Married Thomas Clinton, 3rd Earl of Lincoln.

Labourne, William active 1669–1676 Servant to John Gilmore, Keeper of Whinfell Park, may be connected to George Labourne, Sir John Lowther's servant.

Lafuente, Diego de, active 1618–1623 'Padre Maestro', confessor and informant to the Spanish Ambassador Diego Sarmiento de Acuña, Count of Gondomar. He was active in negotiations for the Spanish marriage of Charles I.

Lake, Anne c. 1604–1630. Daughter of Mary Rider and Thomas Lake. Married 1: William Cecil, 16th Baron Ros of Helmsley, which led to Lake/Ros scandal, 2: George Romney.

Lake, Arthur 1598–1633 Knight, son of Mary Rider and Thomas Lake. Married Lettice Rich, daughter of Penelope Devereux and Robert Rich.

Lake, Thomas 1561–1630 Knight, Secretary of State, son of Emery or Almeric Lake. Married Mary Rider.

Lane, Edward active 1617 A gentleman neighbour living near Knole.

Langhorne, Thomas d. 1693 Of Dockray Hall, Penrith, wealthy merchant, son of Thomas Langhorne.

Langworth family Of Broyle, Sussex with property in Little Horsted. Rose Durant and Arthur Langworth had five sons: John, Adam, Richard, Arthur and Nicholas.

Layfield, John c. 1563–1617 Doctor of Divinity, Fellow of Trinity College, Cambridge; Rector of St Clement Danes, London; translator for the King James Bible, son of Elizabeth and Edward Layfield. Married Bridget Robinson.

Legg, Edward active 1590–1624 Gentleman retainer and steward at Knole, long employed by the Sackvilles.

Leighton, Robert 1611–1684 Bishop of Glasgow and Principal of the University of Edinburgh, son of Alexander Leighton and a Mrs Mears. Never married.

Lennard, Pembroke c. 1576–1632 Daughter of Chrysogona Baker and Henry Lennard, 12th Lord Dacre. Married William Brooke, 12th Baron Cobham.

Lewis or Lewes, John active 1616 A companion of Richard Sackville in 1616.

Ligne, Charles de 1550–1616 2nd Prince of Arenberg, ambassador to England, son of Margaretha von der Mark, *suo jure* Countess of Arenberg and Jean de Ligne. Married Anne de Croy of Aarschot.

Lindsey, Edward active 1620–1624 Receiver general of Richard Sackville's revenue.

Lindsey, Mrs active 1620–1624 Wife of Edward Lindsey, a household officer of Richard Sackville's at Knole.

Littleton, Charles 1629–1716 3rd Baron Littleton, son of Catherine Crompton and Sir Thomas Littleton, 1st Baron Littleton of Hagley Hall. Married 1: Catherine Fairfax, 2: Anne Temple.

Littleton, Timothy 1608–1679 Knight, Baron of the Exchequer, son of Mary Walter and Sir Edward Littleton of Henley, Shropshire. Married 1: Elizabeth (maiden name not known), 2: Elizabeth Ayliffe.

Lloyd, Mary active 1671 Daughter of a Mr Lloyd. Married Cecil Tufton.

Long, Elizabeth b. 1569 Daughter and heir of Dorothy Clarke and Henry Long of Shingay, Cambridgeshire. Married William Russell, Baron Russell of Thornhaugh.

Longueville, Michael b. 1585 Knight. Married Susan Grey, daughter of Susan Cotton and Charles Grey, 7th Earl of Kent.

Lough, George active 1676 Clerk of Brougham.

Louis XIII, King of France 1601–1643 King of France and King of Navarre, son of Henry IV, King of France and Marie de Medici. Married Anna Maria of Austria, the Infanta of Spain and Portugal.

Lowes, Richard active 1676 Anne's housekeeper at Brougham.

Lowther, John 1605–1675 1st Baronet Lowther, Anne's administrator in the North (1643–1649), son of Eleanor Fleming and Sir John Lowther of Lowther Hall. Married 1: Mary Fletcher, 2: Elizabeth Hare.

Lowther, John 1628–1668 Son of Mary Fletcher and Sir John Lowther, 1st Baronet Lowther. Married 1: Elizabeth Bellingham, 2: Mary Withins.

Lowther, John 1655–1700 2nd Baronet, and later 1st Viscount Lonsdale, son of Elizabeth Bellingham and John Lowther. Married Katherine Thynne.

GLOSSARY OF PERSONS   285

Machell, Henry 1635–1678   Steward of Anne's house and gentleman of her horse, son of Margaret Beck and Hugh Machell.

Machell, Hugh 1635–1719   Anne's receiver of rents for Temple Sowerby, son of Lancelot Machell of Crackenthorpe and Elizabeth Sleddall. Married Anne Nevinson.

Machell, Lancelot b. c. 1617, d. 1681   Of Crackenthorpe. Receiver General for Westmorland, governor of Appleby School, son of Margaret Beck and Hugh Machell. Married Elizabeth Sleddall.

Machell, Lancelot d. after 1700   Gentleman servant to Thomas Strickland and later warden for Thomas Tufton, son of Elizabeth Sleddall and Lancelot Machell. Married Elizabeth Walker.

Machell, Susanna d. after 1681   Gentlewoman to Anne Clifford, daughter of Elizabeth Sleddall and Lancelot Machell. Unmarried before 1681.

Machell, Thomas 1647–1698   Clergyman and antiquarian, son of Elizabeth Sleddall and Lancelot Machell. Married Elizabeth Godson. His sister was gentlewoman to Anne Clifford.

Mainwaring, Henry 1587–1653   Knight, Gentleman of the bedchamber to James I, son of Anne More and Sir George Mainwaring. Married Fortune Gardiner.

Manners, Francis 1578–1632   6th Earl of Rutland, son of Elizabeth Charlton and John Manners, 4th Earl of Rutland. Married 1: Frances Knyvet, 2: Cecily Tufton.

Manners, George 1580–1641   7th Earl of Rutland, son of Elizabeth Charleton and John Manners, 4th Earl of Rutland. Married Frances Cary.

Manners, Katherine c. 1603–1649   Daughter of Frances Knyvet and Francis Manners, 6th Earl of Rutland. Married George Villiers, 1st Duke of Buckingham and James I's favourite.

Marsh, Christopher d. 1656   Gentleman servant first for the Sackvilles, and later Anne Clifford's agent and friend.

Marshall, Mr d. 1616   Richard Sackville's auditor and surveyor at Knole.

Martinozzi, Laura 1639–1687   Regent of Modena, daughter of Laura Mazarin and Count Girolamo Martinozzi. Married Alfonso IV d'Este, Duke of Modena.

Mary of Modena 1658–1718   Maria Beatrice Anna Margherita Isabella d'Este, Queen Consort of England and later called Queen over the Water. Daughter of Laura Martinozzi and Alfonso IV, Duke of Modena. Married James II, King of England.

Massey, Francis active 1675   Married the daughter of George's Hilton's wife (from a previous marriage).

Matthew, Tobias 1546–1628   Archbishop of York, son of Eleanor Croft and Sir John Matthew. Married Frances, the daughter of William Barlow, Bishop of Chichester.

Maynard, John 1604–1690   Knight, Serjeant at Law, son of Honora Arscott and Alexander Maynard. Married 1: Elizabeth Henley, 2: Jane Selhurst, 3: Margaret Gorges, 4: Mary Unton.

Medici, Cosimo III de 1642–1723   Grand Duke of Tuscany, son of Vittoria della Rovere of Urbino and Ferdinando III de Medici. Married Marguerite Louise d'Orléans, cousin to King Louis XIV of France. He travelled to England in 1669.

Metcalfe, Thomas 1579–1665   Knight, of Nappa Hall, Yorkshire, son of Elizabeth Slingsby and James Metcalfe. Married Joan Savile.

Middleton, Roger active 1668–1676   Clerk of Anne's kitchen at Appleby Castle.

Milbourne, Richard d. 1624   Chaplain to Prince Henry and Prince Charles, Bishop of Carlisle. Rector of Sevenoaks near Knole.

Molineux, Alice d. 1643 Daughter of Frances Gerard and Sir Richard Molineux. Married Sir William Dormer.

Molineux, Roger b. 1615, d. after 1669 Colonel, son of Anne Harrington and Sir John Molineux. Married Jane Monson.

Monck, George 1608–1670 1st Duke of Albemarle, son of Elizabeth Smyth and Sir Thomas Monck. Married Anne Leaver. He was instrumental in the restoration of the English monarchy.

Montagu, Elizabeth 1586–1654 Daughter of Elizabeth Harrington and Sir Edward Montagu of Boughton. Married Robert Bertie, 14th Baron Willoughby and 1st Earl of Lindsey.

Montagu, Elizabeth 1611–1672 Daughter of Mary Whitmore and Sir Charles Montagu of Boughton. Married Christopher Hatton, 1st Baron Hatton.

Montagu, Henry 1564–1642 1st Earl of Manchester, son of Elizabeth Harington and Sir Edward Montagu of Boughton. Married 1: Catherine Spenser, 2: Anne Wincot, 3: Margaret Crouch.

Montagu, Ralph 1638–1709 Ambassador to France, Duke of Montagu, son of Anne Winwood and Edward Montagu, 2nd Baron Montagu of Boughton. Married 1: Elizabeth Wriothesley, co-heir of Thomas, 4th Earl of Southampton, 2: Elizabeth Cavendish.

Montgomery, Margaret active 1676 Seamstress of Penrith, may be related to Fabian Montgomery, a Lowther servant.

Mordaunt, Henry 1657–1609 4th Baron Mordaunt, son of Elizabeth Darcy and Lewis Mordaunt. Married Margaret Compton.

Mordaunt, James c. 1588, d. after 1651 Son of Margaret Compton and Henry Mordaunt, 4th Baron Mordaunt. Married Mary Tyringham.

Mordaunt, John b. c. 1595, d. 1642. 1st Earl of Peterborough, favourite of James I, son of Margaret Compton and Henry Mordaunt, 4th Baron Mordaunt. Married Elizabeth Howard, daughter of William Howard, 3rd Baron Howard of Effingham.

Mordaunt, John b. c. 1637 Son of Mary Tyringham and James Mordaunt.

Morgan, Elizabeth b. c. 1590 Daughter and co-heir (with her brother Christopher) of Christopher Morgan of Mattperton, Dorset. Married 1: John Molford, 2: Sir Thomas Trenchard of Wolveton, Dorset.

Morison, Bridget d. 1623 Daughter of Dorothy Clerke and Charles Morison. Married Robert Radclyffe, 5th Earl of Sussex.

Murgatroyd, Jacob active 1676 May be connected to Thomas Murgatroyd, vicar of and schoolmaster of Kendal.

Murray, George d. 1606 Knight, Groom of the Bedchamber, son of Sir Charles Murray of Cockpool and Margaret Somerville. He was a cousin of the Tullibardine Murrays.

Murray, William c. 1574 – c. 1627 2nd Earl of Tullibardine, son of John Murray, 1st Earl Tullibardine and Catherine Drummond. Married 1: Cecilia Wemyss, 2: Dorothea Stewart. Possibly married Euphame Littlejohn in 1593.

Musgrave, Frances b. c. 1635 Daughter of Julia Hutton and Sir Philip Musgrave, 2nd Baronet. Married Edward Hutchinson.

Musgrave, Mary b. 1661 Daughter of Margaret Harrison and Sir Richard Musgrave, 3rd Baronet. Married John Davison.

Musgrave, Philip 1607–1678 2nd Baronet, son of Frances Wharton and Sir Richard Musgrave. Married Julia Hutton of Goldsborough Hall.

Musgrave, Richard 1635–1687   3rd Baronet, son of Julian Hutton and Sir Philip Musgrave, 2nd Baronet. Married Margaret Harrison.

Musgrave, William active 1676   Of Musgrave Hall, Justice of the Peace in Penrith, likely son of Felicia Tilliol and William Musgrave.

Nanson, Philip b. 1647, d. c. 1718   Originally from Appleby, son of Robert Nanson, elected Fellow of Queen's College, Oxford, in 1674, rector of Newnham and Dogmersfield in 1680. Married Hannah Duncombe.

Naunton, Robert 1563–1635   Knight and secretary of state, son of Elizabeth Ashby and Henry Naunton of Letheringham. Married Penelope Perrot.

Needham, John d. 1619   Knight, of Litchborough. Married Elizabeth Watson.

Neville, Cecily c. 1589–1625   Daughter of Mary Sackville and Henry Neville, 7th Baron of Abergavenny. Married Fitzwilliam Coningsby.

Neville, Edward 1560–1622   6th Baron Abergavenny, son of Katherine Brome and Edward Neville. Married Rachel Lennard of Knole.

Neville, Elizabeth b. c. 1590   Daughter of Mary Sackville and Henry Neville, 7th Baron of Abergavenny.

Neville, Henry c. 1580–1644   7th Baron of Abergavenny, son of Rachel Lennard and Edward Neville, 6th Baron of Abergavenny. Married 1: Mary Sackville, daughter of Cecily Baker and Thomas Sackville, 1st Earl of Dorset, 2: Catherine Vaux.

Neville, Mary 'Moll' b. c. 1590   Daughter of Mary Sackville and Henry Neville, 7th Baron of Abergavenny, niece and god-daughter of Richard Sackville, part of the household at Knole.

Newdigate, Richard 1602–1678   1st Baron Newdigate, Common Pleas and assize judge, son of Anne Fitton and Sir John Newdigate. Married Julianna Leigh.

Nicholls, Augustine 1586–1647   Of Faxton in Northampton, keeper of the Great Seal for Prince Charles.

Nicholls, Elizabeth b. c. 1617, d. after 1676   Gentlewoman servant to Anne, entered her service as a child in 1626. Married 1: John Turner, receiver of Anne's rents in Skipton, Westmorland and later Kent, 2: John Gilmore, whom Anne appointed Keeper of Whinfell forest after the marriage.

Noel, Mary b. c. 1643, d. 1719   Daughter of Elizabeth Bertie and Baptist Noel, 3rd Viscount Campden. Married James Compton, 3rd Earl of Northampton.

North, Dudley 1582–1666   3rd Baron North, son of Dorothy Dale and Sir John North. Married Frances Brocket.

North, John c. 1583 – after 1619   Knight, son of Dorothy Dale and Sir John North, brother to Dudley North, 3rd Baron North, and Roger North.

North, Roger 1585–1652   Captain, deputy governor of Guyana, son of Dorothy Dale and Sir John North. A merchant explorer who led an expedition to Guyana.

Ogle, Mary d. before 1657   Daughter of Thomas Ogle of Dressington, Northumberland. Married Thomas Savage, 2nd Earl Rivers.

Oldenbarnevelt, Johan van 1547–1619   A Netherlands statesman, ambassador to England. Married to Maria van Utrecht.

Oldsworth, Arnold 1561 – c. 1633   Antiquarian, Clerk of the Hanaper, one of the executors of Anne Russell, Countess of Warwick's will, son of Tacy Porter and Edward Oldsworth. Married Lucy Barty of Antwerp.

Orfeur, Cuthbert d. 1688   Of Pryor Hall, agent for Anne Clifford in the North. Married Mary Richmond.

Orfeur, Elizabeth b. c. 1630, d. 1705 Of Plumland Hall, daughter of Bridget Musgrave and William Orfeur. Married Thomas Sandford of Askham.

Osberton, Mr active 1617 Possibly an attorney who was later employed by James, Duke of Ormond.

Osborne, Katherine b. c. 1580, d. after 1619 Daughter and heir of Sir Robert Osborne of Kelmarsh. Married 1: Edward Haselwood, 2: Edward Gorges, 1st Baron Gorges of Dundalk.

Otway, John 1620–1693 Knight, of Ingmire Hall, King's attorney, son of Anne Mayer and Roger Otway. Married 1: Mary Riggs, 2: Elizabeth Braithwaite. Close family connections with Cliffords.

Palmer, James 1585–1659 Vicar of St Bride's, London. He baptized Samuel Pepys at St Bride's. He founded an almshouse and free school.

Palmes, Francis, 1554–1613 Knight, of Lindley, Yorkshire, and later Lancelevy, Hampshire. Served as Sheriff of Hampshire 1600–1601.

Parker, John active 1648–1659 Serjeant at Law, one of the assize judges on the Northern circuit.

Parker, Thomas 1595–1663 Baron of Ratton, lawyer and judge, son of Katherine Temple and Sir Nicholas Parker. Married Philadelphia Lennard of Herstmonceaux Castle.

Paston, Catherine d. 1605 A lady of the Privy Chamber to Elizabeth I, daughter of Agnes Leigh and Sir Thomas Paston. Married Sir Henry Newton.

Pate, Frances active 1668–1676 Anne's chief gentlewoman. Married Edmund Pate of Burton upon Trent. Mother of Marmaduke Pate who received his B.A. from Oxford 1673.

Pattison, John active 1670–1676 Yeoman of Moorhouse. Married to Elizabeth Pattison.

Paulet, Jane active 1666 Gentlewoman servant to Cecily Tufton.

Paulet, William c. 1560–1628 4th Marquess of Winchester, son of Agnes Howard and William Paulet, 3rd Marquess of Winchester. Married Lucy Cecil, daughter of Thomas Cecil, 1st Earl of Exeter and Dorothy Neville.

Penn, Mrs active 1619 A nursery maid at Knole.

Penyston, Thomas 1591–1644 1st Baronet Penyston, one of Richard Sackville's retinue, son of Mary Sommer and Thomas Penyston. Married 1: Martha Temple, 2: Elizabeth Watson, 3: Anne Stonhouse. His wife Martha was one of R. Sackville's mistresses.

Percy, Dorothy 1598–1659 Daughter of Dorothy Devereux and Henry Percy, 9th Earl of Northumberland. Married Robert Sidney, 2nd Earl of Leicester.

Percy, Henry 1564–1632 9th Earl of Northumberland, called the Wizard Earl, son of Katherine Neville and Henry Percy, 8th Earl of Northumberland. Married Dorothy Devereux.

Percy, Lucy 1598–1659 Daughter of Dorothy Devereux and Henry Percy, 9th Earl of Northumberland. Married James Hay, 1st Earl of Carlisle.

Perrot, Penelope d. 1655 Daughter and co-heir of Anne Cheyne and Sir Thomas Perrot. Married 1: Sir William Lower, 2: Sir Robert Naunton.

Petley, Thomas active 1617 Brewer at Knole.

Petley, William active 1617 Footman at Knole.

Petty, Thomas active 1616 Margaret Russell's footman at Brougham Castle, Westmorland.

Philip IV of Spain 1605–1665 King of Spain and Portugal, son of Philip III, King of Spain, and Margaret of Austria. Married 1: Elisabeth of France, daughter of Henry IV,

King of France, and Marie de Medici, 2: Marianna of Austria daughter of Ferdinand III, Holy Roman Emperor, and Maria Anna of Spain.

Philippe I, Duke of Orléans 1640–1701   Duke of Anjou and after 1660 Duke of Orléans, son of Anne of Austria and Louis XIII, King of France, brother to Louis XIV, King of France. Married Henrietta, daughter of Charles I, King of England.

Pickering, Christopher 1544–1621   Knight of Threlkeld, son of Winifred Threlkeld and Christopher Pickering.

Pigott, Frances d. 1615   Daughter of Thomas Pigott of Doddershall and Mary Lane. Married Sir Thomas Pope Blount.

Pond, William active 1603   Servant of Margaret Russell.

Preston, John active 1675–1676   Servant to Thomas Gabetis, Anne's under-sheriff.

Preston, Katherine active 1666   Gentlewoman servant to Anne Tufton.

Puckering, Frances d. 1619.   Daughter of Jane Chowne and John Puckering. Married Sir Thomas Grantham.

Puckering, Katherine b. before 1596   Daughter of Jane Chowne and John Puckering. Married Sir Adam Newton.

Puleston, John 1583–1659   Justice of the Common Pleas, assize judge, son of Alice Lewis and Richard Puleston.

Pursglove, Dorothy d. 1691   Married Allan Smallwood, Rector of Greystoke.

Rainsford, Richard 1602–1680   Knight, Chief Justice of the Kings Bench, assize judge, son of Mary Kirton and Robert Rainsford. Married Catherine Clerke.

Raivy, John active 1616–1617   A servant of Margaret Russell.

Raleigh, Walter 1554–1618   Knight, poet, courtier and explorer, son of Catherine Champernowne and Walter Raleigh. Married Elizabeth Throckmorton.

Raleigh, Walter d. 1618   Son of Elizabeth Throckmorton and Sir Walter Raleigh. Never married, died during attack on San Thomé de Guyana.

Ram, Henry active 1676   Of Flakebridge, Anne's tenant.

Rands, Richard   Rector of St Mary the Virgin, Hartfield, East Sussex, a living in the Sackville gift.

Rawling, Cuthbert active 1675–1676   Edward Hasell's servant. May have married Bridget Fetherstonhaugh in 1699.

Reynoldson, Richard active 1675–1676   Anne's baker, brewer and porter.

Rich, Charles d. 1627   Knight, son of Penelope Devereux and Robert Rich, 1st Earl of Warwick. Never married.

Rich, Lettice d. 1619   Daughter of Penelope Devereux and Robert Rich, 1st Earl of Warwick. Married 1: Sir George Carey, 2: Arthur Lake.

Rich, Margaret c. 1580–1635   Daughter of Jane Machell (or Mitchell) and Richard Rich of Leighs, illegitimate son of Richard, Baron Rich. Married Sir Thomas Wroth.

Rich, Nathanial 1585–1636   Knight, son of Jane Machell (or Mitchell) and Richard Rich of Leighs, illegitimate son of Richard, Baron Rich. Never married.

Rich, Robert c. 1559–1619   1st Earl of Warwick, son of Elizabeth Baldry and Robert Rich, 2nd Baron Rich. Married 1: Penelope Devereux (separated), 2: Frances Wray.

Rich, Robert 1587–1658   2nd Earl of Warwick, son of Penelope Devereux and Robert Rich, 1st Earl of Warwick. Married 1: Frances Hatton, 2: Susan Rowe, 3: Eleanor Wortley.

Rider, Mary 1575–1642   Daughter of Elizabeth Stone and William Rider. Married Sir Thomas Lake.

Rivers, George b. c. 1580   George Rivers, second son of Frances Bower and Sir George Rivers, close friend of Sackville family, executor for both Robert, 2nd Earl of Dorset, and Richard, 3rd Earl of Dorset.

Robbins, Tom active 1618–1619   Servant of Richard Sackville's who left after a quarrel.

Rodes, Francis 1648–1675   3rd Baronet, son of Anne Clifton and Francis Rodes, 2nd Baronet of Barlborough. Married Martha Thornton.

Rodes, Jane b. c. 1649   Daughter of Anne Clifton and Francis Rodes, 2nd Baronet of Barlborough. Married Captain William Hussey.

Roydon, Joan d. 1631   Daughter and heiress of John Roydon of Battersea. Married 1: Sir William Holcroft, 2: Oliver St John.

Rupert of the Rhine, Prince 1619–1682   Count Palatine of the Rhine, Duke of Bavaria, son of Elizabeth Stuart, daughter of James I, King of England, and Frederick V, Elector Palatine. Never married.

Russell, Anne 1549–1604   Longest-serving Gentlewoman of the Privy Chamber to Elizabeth I, daughter of Margaret St John and Francis Russell, 2nd Earl of Bedford. Married Ambrose Dudley, Earl of Warwick.

Russell, Anne d. 1639   Daughter of Elizabeth Cook and John Russell, Anne Clifford's uncle. Married Henry Somerset, 5th Earl of Worcester.

Russell, Edward 1572–1627   3rd Earl of Bedford, son of Eleanor Forster and Sir Francis Russell, Lord Russell, grandson to Francis Russell, 2nd Earl of Bedford. Married Lucy Harington.

Russell, Edward c. 1642–1714   English politician, son of Anne Carr and William Russell, 1st Duke of Bedford. Married Frances Williams.

Russell, Elizabeth 1555–1604   Daughter of Margaret St John and Francis Russell, 2nd Earl of Bedford. Married William Bourchier, 3rd Earl of Bath.

Russell, Francis 1593–1641   4th Earl of Bedford, son of Elizabeth Long and William Russell, 1st Baron Russell of Thornhaugh. Married Catherine Brydges.

Russell, Margaret 1560–1616   Daughter of Margaret St John and Francis Russell, 2nd Earl of Bedford. Married George Clifford, 3rd Earl of Cumberland.

Russell, William c. 1553–1613   1st Baron Russell of Thornhaugh, son of Margaret St John and Francis Russell, 2nd Earl of Bedford. Married Elizabeth Long.

Russell, William 1616–1700   1st Duke of Bedford, son of Catherine Brydges and Francis Russell, 4th Earl of Bedford. Married Anne Carr.

Russell, William 1639–1683   Lord Russell, son of Anne Carr and William Russell, 1st Duke of Bedford. Married Rachel Wriothesley. Executed for treason in Rye House Plot.

Ruthven, Barbara c. 1580–1625   Lady of Queen Anne of Denmark's bedchamber, daughter of Dorothea Stewart and William Ruthven, 1st Earl of Gowrie. Never married.

Ryder, Mr active 1616   A man who comes to Knole and share information about the death of Lady Sheffield.

Sackville, Anne 1564 – c. 1619   Daughter of Cicely Baker and Thomas Sackville, 1st Earl of Dorset. Aunt to Richard Sackville. Married Sir Henry Glemham.

Sackville, Anne 1586–1664   Daughter of Margaret Howard and Robert Sackville, 2nd Earl of Dorset. Married 1: Edward Seymour, Lord Beauchamp, 2: Sir Edward Lewis.

Sackville, Anne 1650–1722   Daughter of Frances Cranfield and Richard Sackville, 5th Earl of Dorset. Married Alexander Home, 4th Earl of Home.

Sackville, Cecily c. 1589–1624   Daughter of Margaret Howard and Robert Sackville, 2nd Earl of Dorset. Married Henry Compton, her stepbrother.

Sackville, Edward 1591–1652   4th Earl of Dorset, son of Margaret Howard and Robert Sackville, 2nd Earl of Dorset. Married Mary Curzon.

Sackville, Edward 1624–1646   Son of Mary Curzon and Edward Sackville. Died in the custody of Parliamentary army. Never married.

Sackville, Isabella 1622–1661   Daughter of Anne Clifford and Richard Sackville. Married James Compton, 3rd Earl of Northampton.

Sackville, John active 1616–1624   Gentleman servant to Richard Sackville, may be the grandson of Christopher Sackville, uncle of Thomas Sackville, 2nd Earl of Dorset. He witnessed Richard Sackville's will.

Sackville, Margaret 1614–1676   Baroness Clifford *suo jure*, daughter of Anne Clifford and Richard Sackville. Married to John Tufton, 2nd Earl of Thanet.

Sackville, Mary 1584–1613   Daughter of Cicely Baker and Thomas Sackville, 1st Earl of Dorset and aunt to Richard Sackville. Married Henry Neville, 7th Baron of Abergavenny.

Sackville, Richard 1568–1624   3rd Earl of Dorset, son of Margaret Howard and Robert Sackville, 2nd Earl of Dorset. Married Anne Clifford.

Sackville, Richard 1622–1677   5th Earl of Dorset, son of Mary Curzon and Edward Sackville, 4th Earl of Dorset. Married Frances Cranfield.

Sackville, Richard 1649–1712   Son of Frances Cranfield and Richard Sackville, 5th Earl of Dorset.

Sackville, Thomas 1536–1608   1st Earl of Dorset, Lord Treasurer to Queen Elizabeth, son of Winifred Bruges and Sir Richard Sackville. Married Cicely Baker. Grandfather of Richard Sackville.

Salkeld, John Fl 1657   Anne's tenant in Nether Brough, assumed the tenancy of James Walker. The Salkelds were an established Westmorland family.

Salvetti, Amerigo, also Allesandro Antelminelli c. 1572 – 1657   Tuscan ambassador and agent in England from 1616 to 1657. He was a friend of Sir Henry Wotton. Married Frances Colbrand.

Sandford, John 1653–1717   Of Askham, son of Elizabeth Orfeur and Thomas Sandford. Married Mary Emersen.

Sandford, Richard d. 1675   2nd Baronet Sandford of Howgill Castle, son of Bridget Dalston and Thomas Sandford, 1st Baron Sandford. Married Mary Bowes. He served as Anne's deputy sheriff in 1647.

Sandford, Thomas 1628–1677   Of Askham, son of John Sandford and Mary Aglionby. Married Elizabeth Orfeur.

Sandys, George 1578–1644   Writer and traveller, son of Cicely Wilford and Edwin Sandys, Archbishop of York. Married his father's ward, Elizabeth Norton.

Sandys, Hester d. 1656   Daughter of Miles Sandys. Married Sir Thomas Temple, 1st Baron Stowe. Mother of fifteen children including Martha Temple, mistress of Richard Sackville.

Saunders, Thomas 1626–1670   MP, son of Margaret Evelyn and John Saunders of Woolstone Berkshire. Married 1: Anne Morris, 2: Anne Allen.

Scott, James 1649–1685   1st Duke of Monmouth, 1st Duke of Buccleuch, son of Charles II of England and his mistress Lucy Walter. Married Anne Scott. Mistresses: 1. Eleanor Needham, 2 Henrietta Maria Wentworth, 6th Baroness Wentworth.

Sedgewick, George 1618–1685   Of Collingfield, son of George Sedgewick of Killington, Anne's secretary and gentleman servant.

Selby, William 1556–1638 Knight, of Ightham Mote, son of Margaret and Sir John Selby. Married Dorothy Bonham.

Seymour, Edward 1539–1621 1st Earl of Hertford, son of Anne Stanhope and Edward Seymour, 1st Duke of Somerset, the brother of Queen Jane Seymour. Married 1: Catherine Grey, 2: Frances Howard, daughter of Lord William Howard of Effingham (d. 1598), 3: Frances Howard (Duchess of Lennox and Richmond, d. 1639).

Seymour, Edward 1561–1612 Lord Beauchamp, son of Catherine Grey and Edward Seymour, 1st Earl of Hertford. Married Honora Rogers.

Seymour, Edward 1586–1618 Lord Beauchamp, son of Honora Rogers and Edward Seymour, 1st Earl of Hertford. Married Anne Sackville, Richard Sackville's sister.

Seymour, Elizabeth d. 1603 Daughter of Anne Stanhope and Edward Seymour, 1st Duke of Somerset. Married Richard Knightley of Fawsley Hall in Northamptonshire.

Seymour, Jane 1637–1679 Lady Dungarvan, daughter of Frances Devereux (d. 1674) and William Seymour, 2nd Duke of Somerset. Married Charles Boyle, 3rd Viscount Dungarvan.

Seymour, Mary 1637–1673 Countess of Winchilsea, daughter of Frances Devereux (1599–1674) and William Seymour, 2nd Duke of Somerset. Married Heneage Finch, 3rd Earl of Winchilsea.

Seymour, William 1588–1660 2nd Duke of Somerset, son of Honora Rogers and Edward Seymour, Lord Beauchamp. Married 1: Arbella Stuart, 2: Frances Devereux, daughter of Frances Walsingham and Robert Devereux, 2nd Earl of Essex.

Sharshall, Margaret b. 1631 Wife of Samuel Grasty, mother of John Grasty.

Sheffield, Edmund 1564–1646 1st Earl of Mulgrave, son of Douglas Howard and John Sheffield, 2nd Baron Sheffield. Married 1: Ursula Tyrwhitt, 2: Mariana Irwin.

Sherburne, Edwin 1578–1641 Served Dudley Carlton as a financial agent, later in the service of Francis Bacon, 1st Viscount St Alban. Married Mary Turner.

Sidney, Barbara 'Babs' 1599–1643 Daughter of Barbara Gamage and Robert Sidney, Viscount De L'Isle and 1st Earl of Leicester. Married 1: Thomas Smythe, Viscount Strangeford, 2: Sir Thomas Culpeper.

Sidney, Mary 1561–1521 Poet, literary patron, daughter of Mary Dudley and Sir Henry Sidney. Married Henry Herbert, 2nd Earl of Pembroke. Anne married her son, Philip.

Sidney [Wroth], Mary 1587–1651 Poet, wrote *The Countess of Montgomery's Urania*, the sonnet sequence *Pamphilia to Amphilanthus* and the play *Love's Victory*, daughter of Barbara Gamage and Robert Sidney, 1st Earl of Leicester. Married Sir Robert Wroth of Loughton Hall. Long-term liaison with William Herbert, 3rd Earl of Pembroke.

Sidney, Robert 1563–1626 Viscount de L'Isle and 1st Earl of Leicester, son of Mary Dudley and Sir Henry Sidney. Married Barbara Gamage.

Sidney, Robert 'Robin' 1595–1677 2nd Earl of Leicester, son of Barbara Gamage and Robert Sidney, 1st Earl of Leicester. Married Dorothy Percy.

Simpton, Judith active 1616–1624 Anne's maid at Knole.

Sisley, Jane active 1616–1624 Nursery maid at Knole.

Skinne, Mr active 1619 Likely servant at Knole. Married Sarah (maiden name unknown) in St Bride's church, London, 1 May 1619.

Skinne, Sarah Likely servant at Knole. Married in St Bride's church, London, 1 May 1619.

Sleddall, Jane active 1675–1676 Anne's laundry maid.

Slingsby, Francis active 1568–1619 Knight of Scriven, Yorkshire. Captain on George Clifford's Puerto Rico expedition, son of Mary Percy and Francis Slingsby.

Smallwood, Alan 1608–1686 Rector of Greystoke, Cumberland, son of Jane Garnett and Thomas Smallwood. Married Dorothy Pursglove.

Smith, Leonard active 1667–1676 Alderman and mayor of Appleby, a governor of Appleby Grammar School. Married Dulcibel Smith.

Smith, William active 1616–1624 Yeoman of the Buttery at Knole.

Smyth, Elizabeth d. 1702 Daughter of Dr Henry Smyth, master of Magdalene College, Cambridge. Married Edward Rainbow, also master of Magdalene College and later Bishop of Carlisle. Aunt of Edward Hasell, one of Anne's gentlemen officers.

Somerset, Edward 1553–1628 4th Earl of Worcester, son of Christian North and William Somerset, 3rd Earl of Worcester. Married Elizabeth Hastings.

Somerset, Elizabeth 1618–1684 Daughter of Anne Russell and Henry Somerset, 1st Marquess of Worcester. Married Francis Browne, 3rd Viscount Montagu.

Somerset, Henry 1577–1646 1st Marquess of Worcester, son of Elizabeth Hastings and Edward Somerset, 4th Earl of Worcester. Married Anne Russell.

Somerset, Katherine 1585–1654 Daughter of Elizabeth Hastings and Edward Somerset, 4th Earl of Worcester. Married Sir Thomas Windsor, 6th Baron Windsor.

Sort, Edmund active 1676 Anne's household servant in Westmorland.

Spedding, Margaret active 1676 Perhaps wife to John Spedding of Kirkbarrow, Westmorland, brother of Anne's tenant William Spedding,

Spedding, William active 1670–1676 Anne's tenant, and substantial farmer in Brougham.

Spencer, Alice 1559–1637 Daughter of Catherine Kitson and Sir John Spencer. Married 1: Ferdinando Stanley, 5th Earl of Derby, 2: Thomas Egerton, 1st Viscount Brackley.

Spencer, Anne d. 1618 Daughter of Catherine Kitson and Sir John Spencer of Althorp. Married 1: William Stanley, 3rd Baron Monteagle, 2: Henry Compton, 1st Baron Compton, 3: Robert Sackville, 2nd Earl of Dorset.

Spencer, Mary c. 1586–1631 Daughter of Margaret Bower and Sir William Spencer. Married Maximillian Dallison of Halling, Kent.

Spencer, Robert 1570–1627 1st Baron Spencer of Wormleighton, owner of Althorp, Northamptonshire, son of Mary Catlyn and Sir John Spencer. Married Margaret Willoughby.

St John, Alice b. c. 1622 Daughter of Margaret Waldegrave and John St John. Married Edmund Elmes. Raised Margaret Russell during her childhood.

St John, Anne c. 1580–1638 Daughter of Catherine Dormer and John St John, 2nd Baron. Married William Howard, 3rd Baron Howard of Effingham.

St John, Oliver 1559–1630 1st Viscount Grandison, Lord Deputy of Ireland, son of Elizabeth Blount and Nicholas St John.

St John, Oliver 1598–1673 Judge, son of Sarah Buckley and Oliver St John. Married 1: Joanna Altham, 2: Elizabeth Cromwell.

St Leger, Thomas 1581–1631 Son of Sir Anthony St Leger and Mary Scott.

Stanley, Charles 1628–1672 8th Earl of Derby, son of Charlotte de La Trémouille and James Stanley, 7th Earl of Derby. Married Dorothea Helena Kirkhoven.

Stanley, Ferdinando 1559–1594 5th Earl of Derby, son of Margaret Clifford and Henry Stanley, 4th Earl of Derby. Married Alice Spencer.

Stanley, Frances 1583–1636 Daughter of Alice Spencer and Ferdinando Stanley, 5th Earl of Derby. Married John Egerton, 1st Earl of Bridgewater.

Stanley, Robert d. after 1673 Son of Dorothea Helena Kirkhoven and Charles Stanley, 8th Earl of Derby. Never married.

Stanley, William 1561–1642 6th Earl of Derby, son of Margaret Clifford and Henry Stanley, 4th Earl Derby. Married Elizabeth de Vere.

Stanley, William 1655–1702 9th Earl of Derby, son of Dorothea Helena Kirkhoven and Charles Stanley, 8th Earl of Derby. Married Elizabeth Butler.

Steele, William 1610–1680 Baron of the Exchequer and Lord Chancellor of Ireland, son of Cecily Shaw and Richard Steele. Married 1: Elizabeth Godfrey, 2: Mary Mellish.

Stewart, Patrick c. 1566–1615 2nd Earl of Orkney, son of Jean Kennedy and Robert, 1st Earl of Orkney. Married Margaret Livingston. Executed for treason in 1615.

Stidolph, Francis Of Norbury, Surrey, son of Thomas Stidolph and Elizabeth Hussey. Married Mary Altham.

Strickland, Allan active 1669–1676 Anne Clifford's steward in Westmorland.

Strickland, Thomas active 1663–1676 Gentleman officer for Anne Clifford and receiver of her rents in Westmorland. Married Dorothy, had two daughters Anne and Ursula and one son James.

Stuart, Arbella 1575–1615 Daughter of Charles Stuart, Earl of Lennox, and Elizabeth Cavendish, granddaughter to Elizabeth Hardwick, Countess of Shrewsbury (Bess of Hardwick), first cousin to James I, and claimant to the crown of England. Married William Seymour and died in the Tower of London in 1615.

Stuart, Elizabeth 1596–1662 Princess Royal, daughter of Anne of Denmark and James I. Married Frederick V, Elector Palatine, King of Bohemia.

Stuart, Elizabeth 1610–1673 Daughter of Katherine Clifton, 2nd Baroness Clifton *suo jure* and Esmé Stewart, 3rd Duke of Lennox. Married Henry Frederick Howard, Earl of Arundel.

Stuart, Henry 1594–1612 Prince of Wales, son of Anne of Denmark and James I.

Stuart, Henry 1640–1660 Duke of Gloucester, son of Henrietta Maria of France and Charles I of England.

Stuart, James 1633–1701 King James II of England, son of Henrietta Maria of France and Charles I of England. Married 1: Anne Hyde, 2: Mary of Modena.

Stuart, Ludovick 1574–1624 2nd Duke of Lennox and Duke of Richmond, son of Catherine de Balsac and Esmé Stuart, 1st Duke of Lennox. Married Sophia Ruthven.

Stuart, Mary 1631–1660 Princess Royal, daughter of Henrietta Maria of France and Charles I, King of England. Married William II of Orange.

Suckling, John (the elder) 1569–1627 Knight, son of Elizabeth Barwick and Robert Suckling, one-time Mayor of Norwich. Married Martha Cranfield. His son was the poet Sir John Suckling (the younger).

Sutton, Margaret b. c. 1590 Daughter of Theodosia Harington and Edward Sutton, 5th Baron Dudley. Married Sir Miles Hobart.

Sutton, Mary 1586–1645 Daughter of Theodosia Harington and Edward Sutton, 5th Baron Dudley. Married Alexander Home, 1st Earl of Home.

Sutton, Mrs d. 1676 The mother or superintendent of Anne's almshouse at Beamsley, Yorkshire.

Swarton, Sarah active 1617–1619 Servant of Anne Lake, participated in the libellous activities directed at William Cecil, Lord Ros and Frances Brydges, Countess of Exeter, in Lake/Ros scandal.

Swindin, Arthur d. 1676 Son of John Swindin, began in Anne's service as her fisher boy at least by 1665. In 1675 listed as a kitchen servant.

Symondson, John active 1667 Of Old Hall, Starbotton, Yorkshire, gentleman servant of Richard Boyle, 2nd Earl of Cork. Possibly son of Lister Symondson, Keeper of the Deer at Buckden.

Talbot, Alethea 1585–1564 Art collector and literary patron, daughter of Mary Cavendish and Gilbert Talbot, 7th Earl of Shrewsbury. Married Thomas Howard, Earl of Arundel, 4th Earl of Surrey and 1st Earl of Norfolk.

Talbot, Elizabeth 1582–1651 Countess of Kent, daughter of Mary Cavendish and Gilbert Talbot, 7th Earl of Shrewsbury. Married 1: Henry Grey, 8th Earl of Kent, 2: possibly the antiquarian John Selden.

Talbot, Gilbert 1562–1616 7th Earl of Shrewsbury, son of Gertrude Manners and George Talbot, 6th Earl of Shrewsbury. Married Mary Cavendish.

Talbot, Mary c. 1594–1650 Daughter of Mary Cavendish and Gilbert Talbot, 7th Earl of Shrewsbury. Married William Herbert, 3rd Earl of Pembroke.

Tassis, Juan de d. 1607 2nd Count of Villamediana, leader of the delegation that brokered the 1604 peace treaty between England and Spain.

Taylor, Ann active 1595–1603 Anne's childhood governess, daughter of Mr Cholmley (a relation of Anne's). She married William Taylor and had a number of children by him who did not survive into adulthood.

Taylor, John active 1606–1619 Gentleman servant to George Clifford and Francis Clifford.

Taylor, Thomas active 1606–1619 Gentleman servant to George Clifford, Anne's father, and Francis Clifford.

Temple, Anne b. 1630 Maid of honour to Catherine of Braganza, Queen consort of England, daughter and co-heir of Rebecca Carew and Thomas Temple of Frankton, Warwickshire. Married Sir Charles Littleton.

Temple, Martha d. 1620 Daughter of Hester Sandys and Sir Thomas Temple, 1st Baron Stowe. Married Sir Thomas Penyston. Richard Sackville's mistress.

Thatcher (or Thacker), Mr active 1619 Possibly Gilbert Thacker of Repton, Derbyshire, or Godfrey Thacker of Repton, high sheriff of Derbyshire (appt. 1619).

Thorpe, Francis 1595–1665 Baron of the Exchequer, assize judge, son of Elizabeth Danyell of Beswick and Roger Thorpe of Birdsall, North Yorkshire.

Throckmorton, Elizabeth 'Bess' 1565–1647 A maid of honour to Elizabeth I, daughter of Anne Vaux and Sir Nicholas Throckmorton. Married Sir Walter Raleigh.

Thwaites, John, the younger d. 1698 An alderman and mayor of Appleby.

Todd, Thomas active 1616 Of Westmorland, servant to Margaret Russell.

Trenchard, Thomas 1582–1657 Knight, son of Anne Speke and Sir George Trenchard. Married Elizabeth Morgan.

Tufton, Anne b. and d. 1634 Infant daughter of Margaret Sackville and John Tufton, 2nd Earl of Thanet.

Tufton, Anne 1654–1713 Daughter of Margaret Sackville and John Tufton, 2nd Earl of Thanet. Married Sir Samuel Grimston.

Tufton, Cecil 1519–1682 Son of Frances Cecil and Sir Nicholas Tufton, 1st Earl of Thanet. Married Mary Lloyd.

Tufton, Cecily 1648–1672 Daughter of Margaret Sackville and John Tufton, 2nd Earl of Thanet. Married Christopher, 1st Viscount Hatton.

Tufton, Cecily d. 1653 Daughter of Christian Browne and Sir John Tufton, 1st Baronet Tufton. Married Francis Manners, 6th Earl of Rutland.

Tufton, Charles b. c. 1645 Knight, son of Mary Lloyd and Cecil Tufton.

Tufton, Diana b. c. 1610, d. after 1671 Daughter of Frances Cecil and Sir Nicholas Tufton, 1st Earl of Thanet. Married Sir Robert Curson of Witer-Prye, Oxford.

Tufton, Frances 1642–1666 Daughter of Margaret Sackville and John Tufton, 2nd Earl of Thanet. Married Henry Drax and died in childbirth with her first child.

Tufton, George 1650–1670 Son of Margaret Sackville and John Tufton, 2nd Earl of Thanet and Anne's grandson. Never married.

Tufton, John 1608–1664 2nd Earl of Thanet, son of Frances Cecil and Nicholas Tufton, 1st Earl of Thanet. Married Margaret Sackville.

Tufton, John 1638–1680 4th Earl of Thanet, son of Margaret Sackville and John Tufton, 2nd Earl of Thanet. Inherited the Clifford hereditary lands. Never married.

Tufton, Margaret 1636 – after 1676 Daughter of Margaret Sackville and John Tufton, 2nd Earl of Thanet. Married George, 3rd Baron Coventry.

Tufton, Mary 1651–1674 Daughter of Margaret Sackville and John Tufton, 2nd Earl of Thanet. Married Sir William Walter.

Tufton, Nicholas 1578–1631 1st Earl of Thanet, son of Christian Browne and Sir John Tufton, 1st Baronet Tufton. Married Frances Cecil.

Tufton, Nicholas 1631–1639 3rd Earl of Thanet, son of Margaret Sackville and John Tufton, 2nd Earl of Thanet. Married Elizabeth Boyle, his second cousin. Inherited the Clifford hereditary lands.

Tufton, Richard 1640–1684 5th Earl of Thanet, son of Margaret Sackville and John Tufton, 2nd Earl of Thanet. Inherited the Clifford hereditary lands.

Tufton, Sackville 1646–1721 Son of Margaret Sackville and John Tufton, 2nd Earl of Thanet. Married Elizabeth Wilbraham. Their son Sackville became 7th Lord Tufton and inherited the Clifford hereditary lands.

Tufton, Thomas 1644–1729 6th Earl of Thanet and Baron Clifford, son of Margaret Sackville and John Tufton, 2nd Earl of Thanet. Inherited the Clifford hereditary lands. Married Catherine Cavendish.

Turner, Elizabeth c. 1635 – after 1663. Daughter of Elizabeth Nicholls and John Turner. Married 1: Mr Kellaway, 2: Mr Green.

Turner, John d. 1663 One of Anne's gentlemen officers, receiver of her jointure rents in Kent. Married Elizabeth Nicholls, Anne's former gentlewoman servant.

Turnor, Christopher 1607–1675 Knight, assize judge, son of Ellen Samm and Christopher Turnor. Married Joyce Warwick.

Twentyman, John active 1670s Gardener for the Bishop of Carlisle, Edward Rainbow, at Rose Castle near Carlisle. Works on Anne's gardens in 1670s.

Twisden, Thomas 1602–1683 1st Baronet, son of Anne Finch and Sir William Twysden. Married Jane Thomlinson of Whitby, Yorkshire.

Tyrwhitt, Ursula c. 1565–1617 Daughter of Elizabeth Oxenbridge and Sir Robert Tyrwhitt of Kettelby. Married Sir Edmund Sheffield, 1st Earl of Musgrave.

Ubank, Thomas active 1675–1676 Physician. He served the Clifford household from at least 1675. Married the widow Mrs Hilton.

Uvedale, Elizabeth 1646–1696 Daughter and co-heir of Victoria Cary (daughter of

Elizabeth Tanfield, writer and playwright) and Sir William Uvedale. Married 1: Sir William Berkeley, 2: Edward Howard, 2nd Earl of Carlisle.

Vane, Henry 1589–1655 Knight, son of Margaret Twysden and Henry Vane of Hadlow, Kent. Married Frances Darcy, daughter of Thomas Darcy of Tolleshurst Darcy, Essex.

Vaux, Edward 1591–1661 4th Baron of Harrowden, son of Elizabeth Roper and George Vaux. Married Elizabeth Howard (daughter of Thomas Howard, 1st Earl of Suffolk).

Vavasour, Anne active 1601–1603 Gentlewoman of the privy chamber during Elizabeth I. Married Sir Richard Warburton.

Vavasour, Catherine b. c. 1595 Daughter of Katherine Coupe and Sir Peter Vavasour. Married Sir Thomas Glemham.

Vernon, Elizabeth 1572–1655 Maid of Honour to Elizabeth I, daughter of Elizabeth Devereux and John Vernon. Married Henry Wriothesley, 3rd Earl of Southampton.

Veteripont, Idonea c. 1261–1333 Lady of Pendragon and Brough castles *suo jure*, daughter and co-heir of Isabella FitzGeoffrey and Robert, 3rd Lord Veteripont. Married 1: Roger de Leyburne, 2: John de Cromwell.

Veteripont, Isabella 1254–1291 Sheriff of Westmorland and Lady of Appleby and Brougham castles *suo jure*, daughter and co-heir to Isabella FitzGeoffrey and Robert, 3rd Lord Veteripont. Married Roger de Clifford III.

Villiers, George 1592–1628 1st Duke of Buckingham and favourite of James I, son of Mary Beaumont and George Villiers. Married Katherine Manners, Baroness de Ros *suo jure*. Assassinated in 1628.

Villiers, Susan d. 1655 Daughter of Mary Beaumont and Sir George Villiers, Sister of George Villiers, 1st Duke of Buckingham. Married William Fielding 1st Earl of Denbigh.

Vincent, Gabriel d. 1665 Anne's steward and chief gentleman officer. He managed her building works in the north.

Wade, Cuthbert 1619 – after 1666 Captain of Horse in the army of Charles I, son of Christopher Cuthbert of Kinsley Old Hall. Married 1: Agnes Bracken, 2: Dorothy Malham, 3: Frances Beilby.

Walker, Isaac active 1665–1676 Groom of Anne's stables in Westmorland.

Walker, James active 1655–1657 Likely of Sharrow Bay, near Penrith, Anne's tenant in Nether Brough. Anne ejected him from his tenancy after a legal dispute.

Waller, Thomas active 1669 Serjeant at law and assize judge, son of Thomas Waller of Gregories, Buckinghamshire.

Wallop, Henry, 1568–1642 Knight, of Farleigh Wallop in Hampshire, Sheriff of Hampshire. Married Elizabeth Corbet.

Walter, David c. 1610 – c. 1678 Son of Margaret Offlet and Sir John Walter. Married Elizabeth Bayning, Countess of Sheppey *suo jure*.

Walter, John 1566–1630 Lawyer, Chief Baron of the Exchequer, worked for Richard Sackville, son of Edmund Walter, Chief Baron of the Exchequer.

Walter, John active 1668 Servant to John Gilmore, Anne's Keeper of Whinfell forest.

Walter, John 1674–1722 3rd Baronet, MP for Appleby, son of Mary Tufton and Sir William Walter, 2nd Baronet. Married Elizabeth Vernon.

Walter, Mr active 1616 Lawyer, worked for Richard Sackville.

Walter, William 1604–1675 1st Baronet, Chief Baron of the Exchequer, son of Margaret Offlet and Sir John Walter. Married Elizabeth Lucas.

Walter, William d. 1694 2nd Baronet, son of Elizabeth Lucas and Sir William Walter, 1st Baronet. Married Mary Tufton.

Warburton, Peter 1588–1666 Lawyer, assize judge, son of Magdalen Moulton and Peter Warburton of Hefferston Grange, Cheshire. Married (likely as second wife) Alice Gardiner.

Warburton, Richard d. 1610 Knight, Constable of Lancaster Castle, son of Alice Cooper and Peter Warburton of Hefferston Grange, Cheshire. Married Anne Vavasour.

Waste, Thomas active 1619 A servant of Richard Sackville.

Watson, Edward 1549–1617 Knight of Rockingham Castle, Leicestershire, son of Dorothy Montagu and Edward Watson of Rockingham. Married Anne Digby.

Watson, Elizabeth b. c. 1570 Gentlewoman servant to Anne Russell, Countess of Warwick, daughter of Anne Digby and Edward Watson of Rockingham Castle. Married 1: Sir John Needham, 2: Sir Edward Tyrrell, 1st Baronet of Thornton.

Watson, Lewis 1584–1653 1st Baron Rockingham, son of Anne Digby and Sir Edward Watson of Rockingham Castle. Married 1: Catherine Bertie, 2: Eleanor Manners.

Watson, Mrs active 1617 Likely related to the Watson family of Rockingham Castle.

Waugh, Margaret c. 1635 – after 1676 Anne's gentlewoman servant in Westmorland. Married John Waugh, a yeoman farmer in Appleby. Her son John Waugh became Bishop of Carlisle in 1723.

Webb, Gregoryactive 1603 Of Wantage, Oxfordshire, town bailiff and tenant of William Boucher, 3rd Earl of Bath.

Webster, Dorothy d. after 1676 Daughter of Isabel Webster, sister to John Webster. Married John Winter, Rector of Clifton,

Webster, John active 1670–1676 Anne's tenant farmer in Brougham, son of Isabel Webster. May also be Anne's woodward of Whinfell and Flakebridge forest, builder who oversees work for her.

Wells, John active 1666–1719 Appointed curate of St Botolph without Aldersgate, 1666, later Rector of Hanwell, and of Hanworth, St Paul's Cathedral, Prebend of Harleston.

Wenman, Richard 1573–1640 1st Viscount Wenman, son of Jane West and Sir Thomas Burke. Married 1: Agnes Fermor (writer and translator), 2: Alice Chamberlain, 3: Elizabeth (maiden name unknown), 4: Mary Keble.

Wentworth, John c. 1583–1631 1st Baronet, of Gosfield, Essex, son of Cecelia Unton and John Wentworth. Married Catherine Wentworth.

Whalley, Thomas active 1671–1676 Servant to George Sedgewick.

Wharton, Anne 1640–1689 Daughter of Jane Goodwin and Philip 4th Baron Wharton. She was goddaughter to Anne. Married William Carr.

Wharton, Elizabeth d. 1669 Daughter of Elizabeth Wandesford and Philip Wharton, 4th Baron Wharton. Married Robert Bertie, 3rd Earl of Lindsey.

Wharton, George 1583–1609 Son of Frances Clifford and Philip 3rd Baron Wharton. Killed in a duel with Sir James Stewart, Master of Blantyre.

Wharton, Goodwin 1653–1704 Son of Jane Goodwin and Philip, 4th Baron Wharton. Never married. Mistress, the medium Mary Parish.

Wharton, Hugh active 1676–1681 Steward of Philip, 4th Baron Wharton.

Wharton, Margaret 1581–1659 Daughter of Frances Clifford and Philip, 3rd Baron Wharton. Married Sir Edward Wotton.

Wharton, Margaret c. 1643 – after 1695 Daughter of Jane Goodwin and Philip, 4th Baron Wharton. Married 1: a Major Dunch, 2: Sir Thomas Sulyarde, 3: William Ross, 12th Lord Ross.

Wharton, Mary 1655–1701 Daughter of Jane Goodwin and Philip, 4th Baron Wharton. Married Sir Charles Kemys, 4th Baronet Kemys.

Wharton, Philip 1613–1696 4th Baron Wharton, son of Philadelphia Carey and Sir Thomas Wharton of Aske Hall. Married 1: Elizabeth Wandesford, 2: Jane Goodwin, 3: Anne Carr.

Wharton, Thomas c. 1615–1684 Son of Philadelphia Carey and Sir Thomas Wharton of Aske Hall. Married 1: Mary Carey, 2: Jane Robinson. He was brother to Philip, 4th Baron Wharton.

Wharton, Thomas 1648–1715 5th Baron Wharton, 1st Marquis Wharton, son of Jane Goodwin and Philip, 4th Baron Wharton. Married Anne Lee, a poet, 2: Lucy Loftus.

Whitchard, Alexander d. 1659 Gentleman servant to John Tufton, 4th Earl of Tufton, during Tufton's youth and during his European tour.

Whittington, Timothy active 1616 A knight and a lawyer.

Wilde, William 1611–1679 1st Baronet, assize judge, son of William Wilde, a vintner of Bread Street, London. Married 1: Hannah Terry, 2: Jane Wilson, 3: Frances Barcroft.

William II, Prince of Orange 1626–1650 Son of Frederick Henry, Prince of Orange and Amalia of Solms-Braunfels. Married Princess Royal, Mary Stuart, daughter of Charles I.

William III 1650–1702 Prince of Orange and King of England, son of Mary Princess Royal of England, daughter of Henrietta Maria and Charles I, and William II of Orange. Married his first cousin, Mary Stuart, later Mary II of England, who was the daughter of Anne Hyde and James, Duke of York, later James II of England.

Williams, John d. 1619 Lawyer, author of *Balaam's Ass* (1613), executed for sedition in 1619. Married Anne Weston of the Westons of Roxwell.

Willison, Robert active 1676 Of Penrith, Wine merchant and Postmaster.

Willoughby, Mistress active 1616–1624 Anne's gentlewoman servant at Knole.

Windham, Hugh 1603–1684. Knight, Baron of the Exchequer, Common Pleas and assize judge, son of Joan Portman and Orchard Wyndham. Married 1: Jane Wodehouse, 2: Elizabeth Mynne, 3: Katherine Fleming.

Woodgate, Thomas d. 1647 Yeoman of East Grinstead, Sussex, Yeoman of the Great Chamber at Knole (upper household servant).

Woolrich, William active 1617 Gentleman of Sussex. Married Anne Wharton, daughter of Thomas Wharton, 2nd Baron Wharton.

Worleigh, Mr active 1616–1617 Gentleman servant of Margaret Russell, and tenant of the Cliffords in Westmorland.

Wray, Frances d. 1634 Daughter of Anne Girlington and Christopher Wray. Married: 1. George St Poll, 2. Robert Rich, 1st Earl of Warwick.

Wray, James active 1590–1619 Likely son of Anne Girlington and Christopher Wray, or a near relation.

Wright, Rowland d. 1671 Clergyman appointed to Mallerstang chapel in 1660 by Anne Clifford.

Wright, Thomas d. 1678 A Quaker of Castlethwaite, Westmorland. Married Dorothy (maiden name unknown). Anne purchased malt from him.

Wriothesley, Henry 1573–1624 3rd Earl of Southampton, son of Mary Browne and Henry Wriothesley, 2nd Earl of Southampton. Married Elizabeth Vernon.

Wriothesley, Rachel c. 1636–1723 Lady Russell, the daughter of Rachel de Massue and Thomas Wriothesley, 4th Earl of Southampton. Married 1: Francis, Lord Vaughan; 2:

William, Lord Russell, who was executed for alleged involvement in the Rye House Plot of 1683.

Wroth, Thomas 1584–1672 Knight, lawyer, active in the Virginia Company, son of Joan Bulmer and Thomas Wroth. Married Margaret Rich.

Yaxley, Robert 1560–1629 Knight, under command at Berwick under George and/or Francis Clifford, son of Rose Langton and William Yaxley. Never married.

Yelverton, Francis d. 1684 Daughter of Susan Longueville, *suo jure* Baroness Grey of Ruthin, and Henry Yelverton, 2nd Baronet. Married Christopher Hatton.

Yelverton, Henry 1566–1630 Knight, lawyer, son of Margaret Catesby and Sir Christopher Yelverton. Married Mary Beale.

Zouche, Edward d. 1634 Knight Marshal of the Royal Household, son of Sir William Zouche. Married Dorothea Silking of Denmark, a lady of Queen Anne's bedchamber.

Zouche, Edward la 1556–1625 11th Baron Zouche, son of Margaret Welby and George la Zouche, 10th Baron Zouche. Married 1: his cousin Eleanor, daughter of Sir John Zouche, 2: Sarah Harrington.

BIBLIOGRAPHY

MANUSCRIPT SOURCES

Bibliothèque Nationale, Paris
MSS. 4112, 15988, Instructions April 1619.

Bodleian Library, Oxford
MS. Eng. misc. d. 133, Anne Clifford, 1613 memoir, 1616, 1617 and 1719 Diary.

British Library, London
Additional MS 21425, Letters from Anne Clifford to Adam Baynes, 1659, fols 127, 148.
Additional MS 29551, Letter Anne Clifford to Cecily Tufton, 1668, fol. 453.
Additional MS 75351, Cumberland Papers, vol. 51.
Additional MS 75352, Cumberland Papers, vol. 52.
Additional MS 75384, 1603 Memoir, transcribed by Rachel Lloyd.
Harley MS 6177, Lives of the Cliffords.
Harley MS 7001, Letter from Anne Clifford to Frances Russell, Earl of Bedford, 1638, fol. 143.
Harley MS 7001, Letter from Anne Clifford to Elizabeth Talbot, Countess of Kent, 1650, fol. 212.
MS 558, Process in the Arches for proving the marriage of Richard Earle of Dorsett with the Lady Anne Clifford, 1609.

Chatsworth House, Derbyshire
Cork MSS, misc. 5, Diary of Elizabeth Clifford.

Cumbria Archives Service, Carlisle
D/CHA/11/4/1, Manuscripts of Thomas Machell, 1676–1692.
DLONS/L1/1/28/8, Letter from Anne Clifford to John Lowther, 23 November 1647.
DLONS/L12/2/16, Life of George Sedgewick.
DLONS/L13/1/3 The Substance of the King's Award.
D MUS 5/5/6/3 Execution of Captain Robert Atkinson, 1664.

Cumbria Archives Service, Kendal
JAC 495–497, Anne Clifford's accounts, 1669–1675 (microfilm).
WDCAT/16, Anne Clifford's Great Books of Record.
WDHOTH 1/5, Margaret Russell, Book of Physik and Alchemye
WDHOTH 1/7, A Brief Relation of the Severall Voyages.
WDHOTH 1/17, Anne Clifford's Account Books, 1665–1668.
WDHOTH/44, Letters to and from Anne Clifford.
WDHOTH10 Anne Clifford's Great Books of Record (2 sets – Hothfield set and Skipton set).

WDHOTH 1/13, The Claim and Title of Lady Anne Clifford to the Baronies of Clifford, Westmorland and Vescy.
WDHOTH 1/18, The Barony of Clifford: Thomas Earl of Thanet's claim to title of Lord Clifford, 1690–1691.
WDHOTH 1/21, *The Praise of Private Life* (The Harington MS).
WDHOTH 3/33, Will of Margaret Russell, Countess of Cumberland.

Dalmain House, Cumbria
Anne Clifford's Day-Book, 1676.
Edward Hasell's Notebook.

Flintshire Archives, Hawarden, Wales
D/HE/732, Letter book of Richard Sackville, 3rd Earl of Dorset, 1614–1624.
D/HE/477 Letter from Anne Clifford to Evan Edwards, 1657.

Folger Library, Washington DC, USA
MS H.b.1, *The Old Arcadia*, fols 2r–216r.

Hertfordshire Archives, Hertford
DE/Lw/F74, The Earl of Cumberland's Voyages, 1598.

Kent History Centre, Maidstone
U269/A2/2, Accounts of George Wood for Richard, 3rd Earl of Dorset, 1611–1612.
U269/A3, Accounts of Richard, 3rd Earl of Dorset 1621–1623.
U269/E67, The Substance of his Majesties Award, 1617.
U269/3/3/5, Anne Clifford, 1613 memoir, 1616, 1617 and 1719 Diary.
U269/Q18/1, Archiepiscopal letters of absolution, 1609.

Lambeth Palace, London
MS 250, Voyages of George Clifford, fols 256r–268v.

Lincoln's Inn Library, London
MS 104, The Title of the Lady Anne Clifford.
MS 205, Augustus Vincent, On Baronyes by Writt.

Lincolnshire Archives, Lincoln
8ANC8/16, Henry Bertie to Robert Bertie, Lord Willoughby, 1620.

Longleat Archives, Wiltshire
Portland MS 23, Anne Clifford, Memoir of 1603, 1616, 1617, and 1619 diary.

National Archives, Kew, London
ASSI 45/6/3, Northern Circuit: Criminal Depositions and Case Papers, 1663.
PROB/11/108/59, Will of George Clifford, 1606.
PROB /11/103/291, Will of Anne Russell, 1604.
PROB /11/143/239, Will of Richard Sackville,1624.
PROB/11/350/488, Will of Anne Clifford, 1676.

STAC 8/89/11, Countess of Cumberland v Skayfe, 1611.
SP 14/90, James I pronouncement against duelling, 1617.

Northamptonshire Archive Service, Northampton
FH 4412 Letter, Elizabeth Boyle to Cecily Tufton, 1666.

Public Record Office Northern Ireland, Belfast
D3044/G/5, Anne Clifford, Memoir of 1603, 1616, 1617, and 1619 diary.

Surrey History Centre, Woking
LM/COR/4/22, Letter from Thomas Sackville to George More, 28 April 1607.

Yorkshire Archaeological Society Archives, University of Leeds, Leeds
YAS, DD121/109, George Clifford's Tomb.

PRINT AND SECONDARY SOURCES

Aikins, Lucy, *Memoirs of the Court of Queen Elizabeth* (London, 1818).
Anon., *Leycester's Commonwealth* (Paris, 1584).
Ayres ... played at Brougham Castle (London, 1618).
Bayer, Penny, 'Margaret Clifford's Alchemical Receipt Book and the John Dee Circle', *Ambix* 52.3 (2005), 271–284.
Bedford, Ronald and Philippa Kelly, *Early Modern English Lives: Autobiography and Self-Representation 1500–1660* (Burlington, Vermont: Ashgate, 2007).
Bellamy, Elizabeth Jane, 'Afterward: Intention Redux: Early Modern Life Writing and its Discontents', *Textual Practice* 23.2 (2009), 307–309.
Bradshaw, William, *A Direction for the Weaker sort of Christians ... Receiving of the Sacrament* (London, 1615).
Breay, John, *Light in the Dales: Studies in Religious Dissent and Land Tenure* (Norwich: Canterbury Press, 1996).
Brooker, Joseph, 'Around 2000: Memoir as Literature', in *A History of English Autobiography*, ed. Adam Smyth (Cambridge: Cambridge University Press, 2016), pp. 374–387.
Buck, Samuel and Nathanial, *A Collection of Engravings of Castles, and Abbeys in England* (London, 1726–39).Bunny, Edmund, *A Booke of Christian Exercise ... by R.P. Perused by Edmund Bunny* (London, 1615).
Burkett, M.E., *John Bracken* (Kendal: Abbot Hall Art Gallery and Museum, 1976).
Calendar of the Manuscripts of the Most Hon. the Marquis of Salisbury, G. Dyfnallt Owen, vol. 22: 1612–1668 (London: Her Majesty's Stationery Office, 1971).
Chamberlain, John, *The Letters of John Chamberlain*, 2 vols, ed., Norman Egbert McClure (Philadelphia: American Philosophical Society, 1939).
Churchill, Wendy, *Female Patients in Early Modern Britain: Gender, Diagnosis, and Treatment* (Burlington, Vermont: Ashgate, 2012).
Clifford, Anne, *The Diary of Anne Clifford*, ed. Katherine O. Acheson (New York: Garland, 1995).
——, *The Diaries of Lady Anne Clifford: 1616–1619*, ed. D.J.H. Clifford (Stroud: Sutton, 1990).

——, *The Diary of the Lady Anne Clifford*, ed. Vita Sackville-West (London: William Heinemann, 1923).
——, *Great Books of Record*, ed. Jessica L. Malay (Manchester: Manchester University Press, 2015).
——, *Lives of Lady Anne Clifford*, ed. J.P. Gilson (London: Roxburghe Club, 1916).
——, *The Memoir of 1603 and the Diary of 1616–1619*, ed. Katherine O. Acheson (Peterborough, Ontario: Broadview, 2007).
Clinton, Elizabeth, *The Countesse of Lincolnes Nurserie* (Oxford: 1622).
Coleridge, Hartley, *Biographia Borealis: Lives of Distinguished Northerns* (London, 1833).
Craik, George Lillie, *The Romance of the Peerage*, vol. 4 (London, 1850).
Cummings, Brian, ed., *The Book of Common Prayer: The Texts of 1549, 1559, and 1662* (Oxford: Oxford University Press, 2011).
Dee, John, *The Private Diary of John Dee*, ed. James Orchard Halliwell, Camden Society, vol. 19 (London, 1842).
Delaney, Peter, *British Autobiography in the Seventeenth Century* (1969; London: Routledge, 2016).
Dicey, Thomas, *Historical Account of Guernsey* (London, 1751).
Dowd, Michelle M. and Julie A. Eckerle, *Genre and Women's Life Writing in Early Modern England* (Burlington, Vermont: Ashgate, 2007).
Foster, Sandys B., *Birkbeck of Mallerstang and Settle, Braithwaite of Kendal, Benson of Stang End* (London, 1890).
Foyster, Elizabeth, 'At the Limits of Liberty: Married Women and Confinement in Eighteenth Century England', *Continuity and Change* 17.1 (2002), 39–62.
Halder, Janine, Laurent Decrouy and Torsten W. Vennemann, 'Mixing of Rhône River water in Lake Geneva (Switzerland–France) Inferred from Stable Hydrogen and Oxygen Isotope Profiles', *Journal of Hydrology* 477 (2013), 152–164.
Hasted, Edward, *The History and Topographical Survey of the County of Kent*, vol. 2 (Canterbury, 1797).
Heninger, S.K., *A Handbook of Renaissance Meteorology* (Durham, South Carolina: Duke University Press, 1960).
Heywood, Thomas, *The Four Prentises of London, Godfrey of Bouillon and the Conquest of Jerusalem* (London, 1615).
Illick, Joseph E. 'Child-Rearing in Seventeenth-Century England and America', in *The History of Childhood*, ed. Lloyd de Mause (Lanham, Maryland: Rowman & Littlefield, 1974), 303–350.
Jackson, William, *Papers and Pedigrees Mainly Relating to Cumberland and Westmorland* (London, 1892).
James I, *A Meditation upon the Lords Prayer* (London, 1619).
Knight, Leah, 'Reading Across Borders: The Case of Anne Clifford's "Popish" Books', *Journal of the Canadian Historical Association* 25.2 (2014), 27–56.
Lee, Maurice ed., *Dudley Carleton to John Chamberlain 1603–1624: Jacobean Letters*. (New Brunswick, New Jersey: Rutgers University Press, 1972).
Lejeune, Philippe, *On Autobiography*, trans., Katherine Leary (1973; Minneapolis: University of Minnesota Press, 1989).
Leland, John, *Leland's Itinerary*, ed. Lucy Toulmin Smith, part 1 (London, 1908).
Lodge, Thomas, trans., *The Famous and Memorable Workes of Josephus* (London, 1602).
Lowther Family Estate Books, Surtees Society 191 (1976–1977), 185.

Malay, Jessica L. 'Anne Clifford: Appropriating the Rhetoric of Queens to Become the Lady of the North', in *The Rituals and Rhetoric of Queenship: Medieval to Early Modern*, eds Liz Oakley-Brown and Louise J. Wilkinson (Dublin: Four Courts, 2009), 157–170.

——, 'Beyond the Palace: The Transmission of Political Power in the Clifford Circle', in *Family Politics in Early Modern Literature*, eds Hannah Crawforth and Sarah Lewis (London: Palgrave Macmillan, 2017), 153–169.

——, 'Constructing Narrative of Time and Place: Anne Clifford's Great Books of Record', *Review of English Studies* 66.277 (2015), 859–875.

——, 'The Marrying of Anne Clifford: Marriage Strategy in the Clifford Inheritance Dispute', *Northern History* 159.2 (2012), 251–264.

——, 'Positioning Patronage: Lanyer's Salve Deus Rex Judæorum and the Countess of Cumberland in Time and Place', *Seventeenth Century* 28.3 (2013), 251–274.

Matchinske, Megan, *Writing, Gender and State in Early Modern England: Identity Formation and the Female Subject* (Cambridge: Cambridge University Press, 1998).

Montaigne, Michel de, *Essayes or Morall, ... of Lord Michaell de Montaigne*, trans. John Florio (London, 1603).

Moote, A. Lloyd and Dorothy C. Moote, *The Great Plague* (Baltimore: Johns Hopkins University Press, 2004).

Morrissey, Mary, *Politics and Paul's Cross Sermons, 1558–1642* (Oxford: Oxford University Press, 2011).

Myers, Anne M., 'Construction Sites: The Architecture of Anne Clifford's Diaries', *English Literary History* 73.3 (2006), 581–600.

——, *Literature and Architecture in Early Modern England* (Baltimore: Johns Hopkins University Press, 2013).

Nichols, John, *The Progresses, Processions, and Magnificent Festivities, of King James the First*, vol. 1 (London, 1828).

Nicholson, J. and Burn, R., ed., *The History and Antiquities of the Counties of Westmorland and Cumberland*, vol. 1 (London, 1777).

Nussbaum, Felicity, *The Autobiographical Subject: Gender and Ideology in Eighteenth Century England* (Baltimore: Johns Hopkins University Press, 1989).

Pennant, Thomas, *A Tour in Scotland and Voyage to the Hebrides, 1772* (London, 1776).

Petit, Jean François Le, *A Generall Historie of the Netherlands*, trans. Edward Grimston (London, 1608).

Phillips, C.B., ed., *Lowther Family Estate Books*, Publications of the Surtees Society, vol. 191 (1979).

Pocock, Robert, *Memorials of the Family of Tufton, Earls of Thanet* (London, 1800).

Proclamation for the Suppression of Coffee-Houses (London, 1675).

Rainbow, Edward, *A Sermon Preached at the Funeral of the Right Honorable Anne, Countess of Pembroke, Dorset, and Montgomery* (London, 1677).

Raine, James, 'Anne Countess of Pembroke, Dorset, and Montgomery', *Archaeologia Aeliana* 1 (1857), 1–22.

Rich Storehouse or Treasury for the Diseased (London, 1596).

Salzman, Paul, 'Anne Clifford's Annotated Copy of Sidney's Arcadia', *Notes and Queries* 56.4 (2009), 554–5.

Sandys, George, *A Relation of a Journey ... Containing a description of the Turkish Empire* (London, 1615).

Sedgewick, George, 'A Summary or Memorial of My own life', eds Joseph Nicholson and Richard Burn, in *The History and Antiquities of the Counties of Westmorland and Cumberland*, vol 1 (London 1777), 294–304.

Seward, William, 'Anne, Countess of Dorset, Pembroke and Montgomery [including 1603 memoir]' *Anecdotes* (London, 1795), 302–317.

Sharpe, Kevin and Steven N. Zwicker, eds, *Writing Lives: Biography and Textuality, Identity and Representations in Early Modern England* (Oxford: Oxford University Press, 2008).

Sidney, Philip, *The Countess of Pembroke's Arcadia* (London, 1605).

Skura, Meredith Anne, *Tudor Autobiography: Listening for Inwardness* (Chicago: University of Chicago Press, 2008).

Smyth, Adam, ed., *A History of English Autobiography* (Cambridge: Cambridge University Press, 2016).

Smyth, Adam, *Autobiography in Early Modern England* (Cambridge, Cambridge University Press, 2010),

Sorocold, Thomas, *Supplications of Saints* (London, 1612).

Southey, Robert, *Southey's Commonplace Books: Analytical Readings*, 3rd series, ed. John Wood Warter (London, 1859).

Spedding, John Carlisle D., *Spedding Family* (Dublin, 1909).

Spence, Richard, *The Lady Anne Clifford* (Stroud: Sutton, 1997).

——, *The Privateering Earl: George Clifford, 3rd Earl of Cumberland 1558–1605* (Stroud: Alan Sutton, 1995).

——, *Skipton Castle in the Great Civil War 1642–1645* (Skipton: Skipton Castle, 1991).

Strong, Roy, *Henry Prince of Wales and England's Lost Renaissance*. (London: Thames and Hudson, 1986).

Suzuki, Mihoko, 'Anne Clifford and the Gendering of History', *Clio* 30.2 (2001), 195–229.

——, ed., *Anne Clifford and Lucy Hutchinson* (Burlington, Vermont: Ashgate, 2009).

Whitaker, Thomas D., *The History and Antiquities of the Deanery of Craven in the County of York* (1805; London, 1878).

White, Adam. 'Lady Anne Clifford's Church Monuments', in *Lady Anne Clifford: Culture, Patronage and Gender in 17th Century Britain*, eds Karen Hearn and Lynn Hulse. Yorkshire Archaeological Society Occasional Paper, YAS 7 (2009), 43–72.

Williamson, George, *Lady Anne Clifford* (Kendal: Titus Wilson, 1922).

Wood, Anthony, *Athenæ Oxonienses* (London, 1691).

Wright, Edward, *Certaine Errors in Navigation* (London, 1599).

INDEX

Abbot, George, Archbishop of Canterbury 28, 29, 248, 268
Acheson, Katherine O. 8n.29
Aglionby, Mary 226, 268
Aikins, Lucy 8n.27
Alexander, Walter 20
Alexander, William 20
Alteiri, Paulus Emelius *see* Clement X
Amherst, Geoffrey, Rector of Horsmonden 50
Amherst, Richard 35, 37–38, 50, 54, 94, 268
Ancre, Cocino Marechall, d' 57, 274
Anna Maria of Austria 39, 268
Anne of Denmark 3, 18–28, 39–40, 46–49, 51, 54, 60, 63, 67, 69, 72, 77–78, 82–86, 98, 100, 234
Annesley, Grace 91, 268
Appleby town and castle 1n.3, 38–42, 60, 101, 105, 115, 122, 117–263 *passim*
Arundel House, London 26, 46, 82, 219
Askew, Mr 52, 90n.528, 268
Atkins, Edward 131, 138, 141, 143, 268
Atkinson, John 261, 268
Atkinson, Robert 173n.181, 177, 228n.16, 301
Augustine, Saint 76, 78
autobiography 4–6
Ayres ... played at Brougham Castle, The (1618) 66n.346

Bacon, Anne 216, 268
Bacon, Francis 55, 57, 60, 64, 84, 86, 217n.261, 268
Bacon, Nicholas 217n.261
Baker, Cecily, Countess of Dorset 34, 66, 104, 106
Baker, Sibilla 149, 268
Balaam's Ass 83, 299
Balliol, Edward, King of Scotland 147, 226n.4
Barden Tower 115–202 *passim*

barley break, a game 59, 62
Barlow, Frances 45, 268
Barnham, Alice 74, 268
Baron de la Tour 51
Barrett, Elizabeth 83, 268
Barton Court, Berkshire 24
Basket, Peter 32, 38, 45, 53–55, 92, 269
Bathurst, Mrs 32, 35, 40, 80, 268
Batters, Mrs 88, 268
Battle of Lowestoft (1665) 196n.200
Battle of Messina (1676) 244
Battle of Newbury (1643) 236n.44
Battle of Worcester 123n.30
Baynard's Castle, London 72, 112–113, 115, 139, 145, 185, 197, 239
Baynes, Adam 123n.33, 151n.133, 301
Beamsley Hospital, Bolton, Yorkshire 10, 133, 184, 202, 224
Beaumont, Mary Countess of Northampton 132, 268
Bedford House, London 39, 81, 96, 113, 239, 250, 251
Bedford, Ronald 5, 5n.16, 18
Belcamp, van Jan 118
Bellamy, Elizabeth Jane 5n.15
Bellasis, James 33, 268
Benn, Annabel, Countess of Kent 173
Bennet, Henry 1st Earl of Arlington 189
Benningholme Grange, Yorkshire 191
Benson, Henry 241, 260, 269
Bentinck, Margaret Cavendish, Duchess of Portland 7
Berkshire House, London 186
Bernard, Robert 138, 155, 158, 269
Bertie, Henry 52, 58, 65, 248n.72, 269, 302
Bertie, Robert 14th Baron Willoughby and 1st Earl of Lindsey 28, 34, 52, 269, 302
Billingsley, Bridget 184, 269
Billingsley, Thomas 29, 177, 182, 184, 269
Bird, James 235, 262, 269

Birkbeck, William 241, 269
Blamire, Jeffrey 227-262 *passim*, 269
Blenkinsop, Francis 253, 269
Blenkinsop, Katherine 253, 269
Blenkinsop, Thomas 44n.182, 269
Blount, Charles, 1st Earl of Devonshire 7, 269, 276
Boetius, Ancius 61n.312
Bolebroke Castle, Sussex 32, 106, 109, 112, 180-181, 193, 195, 200-201, 209, 214, 215
Bolton Abbey, Yorkshire 121, 133, 155, 167, 175, 191
Bonham, Dorothy 36, 74, 87, 91, 269
Book of Common Prayer 32, 124, 227, 227n.14, 231-262 *passim*, 304
Booke of Christian Exercise ... by R.P. Perused by Edmund Bunny (1615) 88
Booth's Uprising (1659) 150
Bosville, Ralph 74, 93, 269
Boughton House, Northamptonshire 60
Bourchier, Anne 107
Bourchier, Dorothy 107
Bourchier, Edward, 4th Earl of Bath 107, 111
Bourchier, Elizabeth 107
Bourchier, Frances 18, 22, 24-25, 104, 111, 244, 269
Bourchier, Richard, Lord Fitzwarren 18, 270
Bourchier, William, 3rd Earl of Bath 18, 107, 111, 269-270
Boyle, Charles, 3rd Baron Clifford of Londesborough, 3rd Viscount Dungarvan 120-121, 127, 141, 155, 166, 186
Boyle, Charles, 3rd Earl of Cork 186n.200, 270
Boyle, Elizabeth, Countess of Thanet 120-121, 127, 166-167, 173, 175, 178n.189, 180-181, 186, 189, 191, 266, 270
Boyle, Frances, Countess of Roscommon 120-121, 127, 166, 270
Boyle, Henrietta, Countess of Rochester 120-121, 127, 166, 270
Boyle, Henry, 1st Baron Carleton 186n.200, 270
Boyle, Mary Anne, Countess of Sandwich 120-121, 127, 166, 270
Boyle, Richard, 1st Earl Burlington and 2nd Earl of Cork 120-121, 127, 166, 173n.183, 186, 267, 270
Boyle, Richard, 120-121, 127, 141, 155, 166, 173n.183, 186n.200
Bracken, John 118, 228, 270, 303
Bradford, Adam 55, 63, 270
Bradford, John 238-239
Bradshaw, William 59
Brandon, Eleanor 122n.25
Breay, John 3n.12, 82n.459, 132n.79, 303
Bricknell, Jane 209, 217, 270
Bromedish, Mrs 94, 270
Bromflete, Margaret, Baroness Vesey 95, 121n.20
Bromley, Edward 41, 270
Brooke, Henry, 11th Baron Cobham 74, 270
Brooker, Joseph 6, 303
Brough Castle, Westmorland 1n.3, 116, 153, 150-253 *passim*
Brougham Castle, Westmorland 1n.3, 6, 28n.39, 30n.54, 31, 39-66 *passim*, 101, 105-106, 115, 125, 122-263 *passim*
Brougham Hall, Westmorland 235
Browne, Christian 110
Browne, Elizabeth 74, 270
Bruce, Christina, Countess of Devonshire 37, 74, 81, 89, 270
Bruce, Edward, 1st Lord Kinloss 2, 270-272
Bruce, Edward, 2nd Lord Kinloss 37n.113, 270
Bruce, Janet 74, 270
Bruce, Thomas, 1st Earl of Elgin 74, 270
Brunskall, Michael 93
Brydges, Catherine 75
Brydges, Elizabeth 17, 271
Brydges, Frances, Countess of Exeter 42, 58, 76, 271
Buchanan, Charles 229, 271
Buchanan, James 229, 260, 271
Buckhurst, Sussex 36-37, 53-56, 60, 66, 69-70, 75, 78-79, 80, 108
Buckle, William 237, 271
Bunney, Edmund 88
Burke, Richard, 4th Earl of Clanricarde 59, 82n.457, 271
Burridge, Mr 38
Burton, Edward 89-91, 271

Burton, Katherine 38–39, 59, 65, 89–92, 271
Butler, Thomas 207, 271
Byfield, Rev. 173, 271

Caldicott, Matthew 34–35, 42, 56, 59, 62–63, 66, 70, 271
Calvert, George, Secretary of State 76, 271
Capel, Sarah, Countess of Essex 8–9
Capel-Coningsby, George, 5th Earl of Essex 8
Care, Robert 94, 271
Carew, George, 1st Earl of Totnes 81, 86, 271
Carew, Thomas 19n.32
Carey, Frances, Lady Manners and Couness of Rutland 46, 67, 271
Carey, Henry, 1st Earl of Dover 80–81, 271
Carey, John, 3rd Baron Hunsdon 67
Carey, Mary 130, 271
Carey, Philadelphia 130, 271
Carey, Robert, 1st Earl of Monmouth 47
Carlisle Cathedral 261
Carlton, Jane 232, 271
Carlton, Robert 234, 271
Carlton, Thomas 142, 272
Carlton, William 232, 272
Carniston, Mrs 22, 272
Carr, Anne 40n.139, 194, 272, 290
Carr, Colonel 202, 272
Cary, Mary 18, 22, 24, 64n.331, 272
Cary, Victoria 200, 296–297
Catherine of Braganza, Queen consort of England 163, 165, 179, 188n.205, 193, 202
Catterick, John 234, 272
Catterick, Margaret 234, 272
Cavendish, Mary, Countess of Shrewsbury 26, 69, 82, 272
Cavendish, William, 2nd Earl of Devonshire 74, 272
Cecil, Anne, Countess of Oxford 241n.54
Cecil, Elizabeth, Countess of Berkshire 26, 272
Cecil, Elizabeth, Lady Hatton and Lady Coke 20, 64, 88, 272
Cecil, Frances, Countess of Cumberland 89, 103, 113, 267, 273
Cecil, Frances, Countess of Thanet 129, 272
Cecil, John, 4th Earl of Exeter 155, 272
Cecil, Mildred, Lady Burghley 241n.54

Cecil, Robert, 1st Earl of Salisbury 17, 19, 103, 272
Cecil, William, 1st Earl of Exeter 18, 76n.413, 129, 271–272
Cecil, William, 2nd Earl of Salisbury 40, 272
Cecil, William, Lord de Ros 27–28, 58–59, 64, 272
Certaine Errors in Navigation (1599) 96
Chaloner, Robert 21, 272
Chaloner, Thomas 82, 272
Chambers, Simon 24, 272
Chantler, Nicholas 89, 272
Charles I, King of England 43, 47, 53–54, 58, 63, 72, 77, 119, 163, 198, 239–240
Charles II, King of England 123, 152, 154, 156–159, 162–163, 165, 173, 177, 179, 180, 188, 193, 198, 201–202, 206–207, 222, 228
Chaucer, Geoffrey 60
Chaworth, George 50
Chenies Manor, Buckinghamshire 90, 104, 109–111, 142, 244, 269
Cheyney, Mr 44, 273
Chippendale, Anne 227n.9, 237
Cholmley, Henry 152, 273
Christmas, His Mask 47, 49
City of God 76, 78
Clapham, Christopher 152, 260–261, 273
Clapham, George 101, 273
Clapham, Richard 139, 273
Clapham, Sheffield 184, 273
Clement I 201
Clerk, Magdalene, Lady Kinloss 81
Cliborne, Mr 45
Clifford Castle, Herefordshire 1
Clifford, Anne, Countess of Pembroke
  arrival in North after inheriting the Clifford lands 115
  birth and childhood 95–102
  death 224–225, 263
  first marriage to Richard Sackville 26–94 *passim*, 103–105
  second marriage to Philip Herbert 110–111
Clifford, D.J.H. 8, 10n.38, 12, 37n.105, 303
Clifford, Elizabeth, Countess of Cork 3n.12, 103, 103n.46, 110n.68, 113, 120, 121, 121n.20, 127, 141, 166–167, 173, 173n.83, 175, 186, 267, 270, 273

310   INDEX

Clifford, Elizabeth, Lady Metcalfe 171
Clifford, Frances, Lady Clifton (daughter of Francis, 4th Earl of Cumberland) 197n.220, 237
Clifford, Frances, Lady Wharton (daughter of Henry Clifford, 5th Earl of Cumberland) 37n.107, 116n.85, 140n.109, 251, 298
Clifford, Francis (brother of Anne Clifford) 95–96, 239
Clifford, Francis, 4th Earl of Cumberland 1–3, 27–29, 34–121 *passim*, 132n.79, 143, 151, 173n.182, 197, 234, 248, 267, 273, 295, 300
Clifford, George, 3rd Earl of Cumberland 1, 2, 17–23, 35, 67n.349, 69n.367, 70, 85, 95–105, 114, 120, 131–138 *passim*, 151, 155, 161, 168, 173n.182, 176–263 *passim*, 266, 273, 290, 295
  death 98
  marital difficulties 18–22
  sea voyages 71, 93, 96, 301–302
Clifford, Henry (son of Henry Clifford, 5th Earl of Cumberland) 3
Clifford, Henry, 1st Earl of Cumberland 159, 186
Clifford, Henry, 2nd Earl of Cumberland 122n.25, 130, 186n.199
Clifford, Henry, 5th Earl of Cumberland 3, 4, 20, 29, 40–87 *passim*, 99, 103, 112–114, 115, 120, 121n.20, 151, 272, 273
Clifford, Henry 10th Lord Clifford 152, 159, 181
Clifford, Margaret, Countess of Derby 96, 139
Clifford, Robert (brother of Anne Clifford) 1, 92, 95–97, 111, 168, 239
Clifford, Robert, 1st Lord Clifford 99, 226n.4
Clifford, Roger, 2nd Lord Clifford 189n.208
Clifford, Robert 3rd Lord Clifford 147, 160
Clifford, Thomas, 9th Lord Clifford 221
Clifton, Anne 196–197, 197n.220, 198, 237, 273, 290
Cocke, Reynald 172
Coke, Edward 43–44, 64n.329, 273
Coke, Frances 64n.329
Colbrand, Francis 27

Coleby Hall (Bowbridge Hall), Yorkshire 183–184, 187, 273
Coleby, John 183, 187, 273
Colt, Maximilian 86
Compton, Alethea 157, 160, 163–164, 198, 202–203, 223, 229n.24, 241, 260, 267, 273
Compton, Anne, Marchioness of Clanricarde 199, 273
Compton, Charles 133
Compton, Henry (1584–c.1559) 35, 52, 65–66, 74, 81, 88, 89n.511, 274
Compton, Henry (1632–16317) Bishop of London 144, 233
Compton, Henry, 1st Baron Compton 106, 293
Compton, James, 3rd Earl of Northampton 114–115, 128–129, 132–164 *passim*, 198–261 *passim*, 266, 273
Compton, William, 1st Earl of Northampton 199n.226, 273
Compton, William, 2nd Baron Compton 36
Compton, William, Lord (child) 133, 134
Conniston, John 241, 274
Conniston, Ralph 37–38, 40, 76, 94, 274
Conniston, Walter 76, 78–79, 93–94, 274
Constable, John, 2nd Viscount Dunbar 191
Convention Parliament (1660) 152n.135
Cook, John 55, 274
Cooke, Elizabeth 28n.36
Cookham, Berkshire 24
Cooling, Peter 86, 274
Cope, Isabel 80, 274
Corbet, Elizabeth 23, 274
Cornet Castle, Guernsey, explosion at (1672) 215–217, 229n.22
Cornwallis, Francis, Lady Withypole 45, 274
Cornwallis, Thomas 70, 274
Cosimo III de Medici 193
Cotton, John 83, 274
Council of State 125, 136, 140, 150n.130
Council of the North 38, 43n.163, 44, 75
Countese of Lincolnes Nursery (1622) 85, 135n.90
Countess of Pembroke's Arcadia (1605) 66n.349

INDEX   311

Countess Pillar, Brougham, Westmorland 31, 105n.53, 209, *210*
Coventry, George, 3rd Baron Coventry 129, 131, 135, 150, 153, 161, 164, 188n.203, 190, 197
Coventry, Henry, Secretary of State 188
Coventry, John, 4th Baron Coventry 135, 144, 197
Coventry, Thomas, 1st Baron Coventry 42, 66, 129, 274
Coventry, Thomas , 2nd Baron Coventry 129, 131, 135, 150, 153, 161
Crew, Ranulphe 49, 274
Cromwell, Oliver, Lord Protector 136, 140
Cromwell, Richard, Lord Protector 150n.130
Cromwell, Thomas, 1st Earl of Essex 129n.62
Croome Court, Worcestershire 130–131, 135, 145, 149, 150–151, 153–154, 164, 175, 190, 197–198
Crow, Charles (1630–1682) 237–238, 274
Crow, Charles, Bishop of Cloyne 274
Cruz, Pantoja de la 60
Curvett, Acton 29, 40, 50, 275
Curzon, George 253, 275
Curzon, Mary 26, 27, 44, 55, 64, 69, 74, 81, 91, 92, 114, 275

D'Ewes, Simon 9n.33
Dacre Castle, Cumberland 204
Dacre, Anne, Countess of Arundel 261, 271, 282
Dacre, Elizabeth 68, 87, 260
Dacre, William, 3rd Lord Dacre 122n.25, 261, 275
Dallison, Maximillian 90, 275
Dalston, Bridget 192, 275
Dalston, Christopher 254, 275
Dalston, John 138, 192, 203, 220, 222, 226, 254, 259, 263, 275
Dalton, John 234, 275
Daniel, Samuel 3, 61n.312
Darby, John 142, 275
Darcy, Elizabeth 26, 275
Dargue, Margaret 227n.9, 237, 275
Dargue, William 237
Davis, Mr 35, 58, 64, 70, 76–77, 83–84, 87, 93, 270

Davis, Mrs 94, 275
De Consolatione Philosophia (The Philosophical Comfort) 61n.312, 74n.397
De Vere, Elizabeth, Countess of Derby 19, 47–48, 275
De Vere, Susan, Countess of Montgomery 42, 47, 49, 110, 112, 119, 240, 275
Dee, John 97
Delaval, Barbara 234, 275
Demain, Dorothy 227n.9, 237
Denham, John 97
Dennison, Robert 248, 276
Dent, John 84, 86
Dent, Richard 84, 86
Devereux, Dorothy, Countess of Northumberland 21, 47, 276, 288
Devereux, Frances 82, 276
Devereux, Penelope, Countess of Essex 20, 23, 276, 283, 289
Devereux, Robert, 2nd Earl of Essex 244
Devereux, Robert, 3rd Earl of Essex 18, 21, 28n.29, 29, 34, 67, 276
Dick, Grey 42
Digby, Anne 19, 276
Digby, John, 1st Earl of Bristol 31, 49, 65, 276
Dingley Hall, Northamptonshire 19
Direction for the Weaker Sort of Christians....Receiving of the Sacrament (1615) 59
Dodsworth, Roger 9n.33
Dolman, Thomas 19
Domville, Robert 37, 43, 276
Donne, John 65
Dorset House, London 16–92 *passim*, 104, 106–108, 126, 185, 215, 230–257 *passim*
Douglas, Robert 50
Douglas-Hamilton, William, Duke of Hamilton 204, 276
Drax, Henry 178–182, 266, 276
Drummond, Jane, Countess of Roxburgh 60, 66–67, 276
Drury, Elizabeth, Countess of Exeter 20, 49, 276
Duchy House *see* Savoy Palace
Dudley, Ambrose, 1st Earl of Warwick 96, 250, 290
Dudley, John 30–31, 41, 276
Dudley, Robert, 1st Earl of Leicester 56n.278

Dugdale, William 9n.33
Dunn, William 42, 44–45, 50, 60, 276
Durant, Rose 87n.499
Dutton, Henry 23

Earle, Erasmus 138–140, 276
East Grinstead Hospital, Sussex 108
Edenhall, Cumberland 139, 175, 187, 191–192, 203, 211, 214, 220, 228, 248
Edge, William 169, 205, 229, 232, 235, 238, 241, 245, 248, 252, 256, 259, 276
Edmonds, Thomas 81, 276
Edward II of England 99–100
Edward III of England 99, 147, 153, 160
Edwards, Evan 42, 52, 277
Edwards, Mr (an upholsterer) 91
Egerton, Thomas 43, 53–54, 277
Elisabeth of France, Queen consort of Spain and Portugal 39, 277
Elizabeth I, Queen of England 1, 7, 15–18, 35, 70, 96, 98, 122n.25, 155, 244n.61
Ellis, William 218, 277
Elmes, Edmond 277
Elmes, John 18, 277
Elmes, Thomas 18, 24n.88, 252, 277
Erskine, Thomas 17, 277
Essayes or Morall...of Lord Michael de Montaigne, The (1603) 44, 50, 305
Eton College, Berkshire 125, 128, 134
Eure, Samson 168–169, 277
Evans, Rev. Dr. 188, 277

Fairer, Elizabeth 232, 277
Fairfax, Charles 9n.33
Fairie Queene (1596) 50
Fallowfield, Lucy 138n.101, 254, 275
Fanshawe, Thomas 202, 277
Fener, Robert 151
Fenton, Geoffrey 23
Fenwick, John, 3rd Baron Fenwick 180, 281
Ferdinando III de Medici 193
Fermor, Hatton 20, 277
Fettiplace, Edmund 23, 277
Finch, Heneage 216
Finch, Moyle 22, 24, 277
Fittin, Abraham 237, 247, 277
Fleming, Daniel 245, 277
Fletcher, Barbara 245n.64, 277
Fletcher, Bridget 254, 277
Fletcher, Catherine 245, 277
Fletcher, George 245, 277
Fletcher, John 47
Fletcher, Mary 197, 284
Florio, John (translator) 44n.176, 305
Foster, Edmund 238
Foster, John 36
Foster, Julianna 36
Foyster, Elisabeth 32n.67, 304
Frederick II of Denmark 72
Frederick V, Elector Palatine and Frederick I King of Bohemia 85, 92, 162, 246, 290

Gabetis, Anne 226–230, 278
Gabetis, Thomas 124–125, 142, 209, 226–230, 235, 238, 259, 278
Gamage, Barbara 18n.26, 66–68, 72, 292
Generall Historie of the Netherlands (1608) 43, 305
Gently, John 167, 171, 278
Gifford, Mr 90, 278
Gilmore, John 232, 238–239, 256, 259, 278
gleek (or glecko), card game 28, 46, 54, 66, 92
Glemham, Thomas 29, 31, 42, 56–59, 66, 74, 88, 278
Globe Theatre 27
Golden Age Restored 26
Golding, Humphrey 33, 278
Goodgion, George 189, 230, 231, 237–238, 251, 259, 278
Goodgion, Robert 242–243, 278
Goodwin, Jane, Lady Wharton 130, 147, 171n.175, 278
Goodwin, Mrs 24, 278
Goodyear, Henry 65
Gorges, Edward 29, 61–63, 69, 74, 81, 92, 278
Gorges, Elizabeth 81, 278
Gorhambury, Hertfordshire 217, 223
Grafton Regis, Northamptonshire 20, 98, 251
Graham, Mr (solicitor) 173n.183
Grasty, Samuel, Rev. 227–262 *passim*, 278
Great Books of Record x, 1–2, 6, 9, 10, 14, 52n.247, 64n.328, 67n.349, 71, 78n.420, 99n.25, 111n.73, 117n.3, 188n.204, 301, 304, 315

INDEX 313

Great Fire of London (1666) 4, 185
Great Plague of London (1665–1666) 4, 179
Greene, Robert 61n.312
Greenham, Richard 61n.312
Greenwich Palace 39–40, 60, 63, 88, 98, 168
Greenwood, John 108n.62
Grey, Henry, 8th Earl of Kent 84, 278, 295
Grey, Susan 84, 278
Griffin, Edward 19, 278
Grimston, Edward (editor and author) 43, 305
Grimston, Harbottle, 2nd Baronet Grimston 216–217, 220–223, 278
Grimston, Samuel, 3rd Baronet Grimston 208n.246, 216–217, 220–223, 267, 279
Grosvenor, Richard 34, 42, 229
Guy, Edward 247n.70
Guy's Cliffe, Warwickshire 252
Guzmán, Luisa de, Duchess of Braganza 163

Hale, Matthew 138, 143, 279
Hall, John 189, 237, 247, 279
Hall, Margaret 73, 93, 279
Hamilton, Anne, 3rd Duchess Hamilton 204n.235, 276
Hammond, Robert 81, 83, 279
Hampton Court Palace 21–23, 50, 72, 75, 78, 163, 179
Hanno, Mrs 46
Hardwick Old and New Halls, Derbyshire 6, 254
Hardwick, Elizabeth, Countess of Shrewsbury 23n.72, 254, 254n.88, 272, 295
Harington, Lucy, Countess of Bedford 19, 21, 23, 27, 39, 47, 61, 75, 81, 89, 279
Harington, Theodosia 86, 279
Harmon, Thomas 37, 279
Harrison, Margaret 203, 248, 279
Harrison, Robert 241, 279
Harrison, Thomas 123
Hart, Percival 64–65, 68, 279
Hart's Horn Tree, Whinfell forest, Westmorland 147, 190, 206, 218
Hartley Castle 203–204, 279
Hartley, Mrs Hugh 65
Hasell, Edward 11–12, 14, 226, 227n.7, 229–263 *passim*, 279, 289, 293, 302

Hastings, Elizabeth 50, 279
Hatfield, Henry 149, 279
Hatton, Christopher, 1st Baron Hatton 188, 193, 206n.238, 279
Hatton, Christopher, 1st Viscount Hatton 188, 190, 192, 200–202, 206–207, 215, 217, 221, 228–229, 267, 279
Hatton, Frances, Countess of Warwick 26, 40, 47, 56–57, 64, 65, 69, 72, 74n.394, 79–82, 279
Hawkridge, Mrs 24, 279
Hay, James, 1st Earl of Carlisle 49, 55, 66, 70, 85, 94, 279
Healaugh Park Priory, Yorkshire 171
Helbeck Hall, Cumberland 44, 269
Heneage, Elizabeth, 1st Countess of Winchelsea 17, 22, 155n.143, 277, 280
Heneage, Thomas 155, 280
Henrietta Maria, Queen Consort to Charles I 118, 156, 165, 179, 198, 207n.244, 208, 280
Henrietta of England, Duchess of Orléans 156, 165, 201–202, 280
Henry VII, King of England 100
Henry VIII, King of England 122n.25
Henry's Welcome to Winchester (1603) 25
Herbert, George, 11th Earl of Pembroke 8
Herbert, Henry, 2nd Earl of Pembroke 117, 280
Herbert, James 199, 280
Herbert, John 36, 280
Herbert, Philip, 4th Earl of Pembroke 1–3, 42n.155, 47n.216, 49, 67n.351, 71, 109–119, 236, 275, 280
Herbert, Philip, 5th Earl of Pembroke 193, 280
Herbert, William, 3rd Earl of Pembroke 3, 21, 42n.155, 47, 49, 66, 71, 109, 117, 119, 280
  death 119, 238
  marriage to Anne Clifford 110–119
Herdson, John 62, 88, 280
Hickling, Christian 24, 277, 280
Hickling, William 19, 24, 280
Hilton, Mr 93
Hilton, Robert 238, 280
Hilton, Thomas 33, 45, 93, 280
Hinde, Samuel 178, 280
Hitchen, Mary 87, 91, 298

Hobart, Henry 39, 40, 49, 57, 281
Hodgson, Mr 31, 62, 281
Hogan (or Huggins), William 22, 281
Holles, John 68
Hollis, Denzill, Lord 188
Holy Trinity church, Skipton, Yorkshire 95, 137
Home, Alexander, 1st Earl of Home 80, 281
Home, Anne 82
Home, Elizabeth 46, 281
Horword, William 7n.23, 7n.25
Hothfield House, Kent 111, 114, 120–195 *passim*, 208
Howard, Anne (d. 1683) 247, 281
Howard, Anne (d. 1696) Countess of Carlisle 184
Howard, Charles (1579–1542), 2nd Earl of Nottingham 68, 80, 281
Howard, Charles (1629–1685) 247, 281
Howard, Charles (1629–1685), 1st Earl of Carlisle 180, 184, 200, 223, 281
Howard, Edward, 2nd Earl of Carlisle 200
Howard, Elizabeth, Lady Knollys and Countess of Banbury 40, 281
Howard, Frances, Countess of Hertford and Duchess of Lennox 21, 82, 86, 292,
Howard, Frances, Countess of Kildare 20, 281
Howard, Frances, Countess of Somerset 28, 30, 34, 36, 40, 47, 61, 63, 81–82, 281
Howard, Francis (1588–1660) of Corby Castle 46, 281
Howard, Francis (b. 1635) of Corby Castle 247, 281
Howard, Henry (1628–1684), 1st Earl of Norwich, 6th Duke of Norfolk 223, 245, 252, 281
Howard, Henry (1655–1701), 7th Duke of Norfolk 219, 223, 282
Howard, Margaret, Countess of Dorset 107
Howard, Mary (d.1708) 180
Howard, Thomas, 1st Earl of Norfolk (1586–1646) 47, 49, 51, 73, 282
Howard, Thomas, 1st Earl of Suffolk (1561–1656) 18, 39n.137, 46, 87, 92–93, 281–282
Howard, Thomas, 4th Duke of Norfolk (1473–1554) 107

Howard, William (1589–1644) 30, 41, 282
Howard, William, 3rd Baron of Effingham 45, 293
Howard, William, Lord of Naworth (1563–1640) 28, 30, 33, 40–43, 51, 56, 59, 75, 85, 87, 101n.35, 261, 282
Howgill Castle, Westmorland 192, 291
Hugh Seat, Westmorland 203
Humfrey, Justina 23, 74, 282
Hutchins, Mary 35, 80, 282
Hutton, William 87, 282
Hyde, Anne, Duchess of York, 165, 188, 203, 207–208
Hyde, Mary 67, 282

Ightham Mote, Kent 36, 68, 259, 292
Inkforbie, Joan 23, 282
Ireland, Mr 49
Irton, Dorothy 243, 282
Irwin, Marianna, Countess of Musgrave 78, 282

Jackson, Richard 261, 283
Jackson, William 12, 304
James I 1–3, 7, 15–18, 20–22, 26, 39, 47, 51, 69, 70, 76n.410, 82, 82n.455, 82n.740, 98–109, 113, 119, 132, 229, 233–235
James II, King of England 152, 158, 162, 165, 167, 169, 179–180, 193, 201, 207–208, 218–219, 224, 294
Janine Halder 102n.40
Jenkins, Jack 24, 283
John I, King of England 99–100
Johnson, Anne 248
Johnson, Mr 248
Johnson, Thomas 142, 283
Johnson, William 241, 283
Johnstone, Dr 252
Johnstone, Mary, Lady Fletcher 245, 252, 283
Jones, Henry, 173n.183
Jones, Inigo 3, 26n.4, 46n.206
Jones, Richard 24, 27, 71, 283
Jonson, Ben 3, 26n.4, n.14, 48n.219, 51n.242, 72n.283
Jordan, Isabell 237, 283
Judges' Award (1616) 27n.23, 30, 32, 32n.70, 36n.103, 38n.117, 49, 49n.233, 248, 262
Julian Bower, Whinfell forest 145n.123, 189–190, 192, 197, 204, 218, 256

Julian of the Bower 189n.208
Julian's Bower, Whinfell forest,
    Westmorland 41, 145n.123, 189, 190,
    192, 197, 204, 209, 218, 256
Juvenal, Francois 84, 283

Kaber Rigg plot (1663) 173
Kelly, Philippa 5, 5n.16, 18
Kelway, Anne 20, 279
Kendal, Mr 36, 283
Kidd, Mr 41, 283
Killawaye, Mr 189
Kilnsey Old Hall, Yorkshire 171, 183
King, John, Bishop of London 62, 80
King's Award (1617) 2, 3, 3n.11, 20n.46, 51,
    56n.279, 57n.284, n.285, 64, 64n.328,
    68n.360, 82n.459, 88n.509, 104, 106,
    110, 132n.79, 163n.160, 233–235, 301,
    302
King's Men acting company 47
Kingston, Thomas 189, 283
Kitching, Thomas 242–243, 283
Knight, Leah 93
Knightley, Richard 19, 283, 292
Kniveton, St Loe 78n.429
Knole House, Kent 3, 8, 24–114 *passim*,
    230–257 *passim*
Knollys, Lettice, Lady Paget 67
Knollys, William, 1st Earl of Banbury 43,
    283
Knyvet, Catherine, Countess of Suffolk 19,
    46, 75–76, 87, 92–93, 281–283
Knyvet, Elizabeth, Countess of Lincoln 85,
    135n.90

Labourne, William 232, 239, 256, 259, 283
Lafuente, Diego de 81, 283
Lake, Anne, Lady de Ros 27, 65, 76, 88, 283
Lake, Arthur 76, 83, 283
Lake, Thomas 27, 52, 76, 88, 283
Lambert, John 123n.30
Lancelevy, Hampshire 23
Lane, Edward 59, 284
Langhorne, Thomas 242, 284
Langley, Edmund 64n.328
Langworth, Arthur 87n.499
Langworth, Mr 87, 284
Lanyer, Aemilia 24, 305
Larkin, William 73

Lathom House, Lancashire 256
Layfield, John 38–39, 55, 96n.9, 97n.12, 284
Le Petit, Jean François 43, 305
Lee, Maurice 21, 304
Legg, Edward 32–33, 52–53, 75, 77, 92, 284
Leighton, Robert 204, 284
Lejeune, Philippe 4–5
Leland, John 149n.128
Leland's Itinerary 149
Lennard, Pembroke 91, 284
Leveson-Gower, John 7–8
Lewis (Lewes), John 36, 284
Leycester's Commonwealth (1584) 93
Lichfield Cathedral 253
Lidcot, John 68
*Life of Josephus: The Famous and
    Memorable Workes of Josephus* (1602)
    94
Ligne, Charles de, 2nd Prince of Arenberg
    21, 284
Lindsey, Edward 56, 71n.276, 284
Lindsey, Mrs 71, 284
Little Dorset House, London 3, 31, 103, 106,
    185, 248, 250, 248, 258
Littleton, Charles 188, 284
Littleton, Timothy 205, 209, 211, 214, 220,
    223, 284
Lloyd, Mary 207, 284
Lloyd, Rachel 7n.23
Lodge, Thomas 61n.312, 94n.551
Lok, Henry 61n.312
Londesborough House, Yorkshire 89, 121,
    167, 175, 186, 191
Long, Elizabeth 24, 290
Longueville, Michael 84, 284
Lough, George 237, 284
Louis XIII of France 39, 57n.283, 268, 274,
    284, 289
Lovers Made Men (1617) 51
Lowes, Richard 229, 237, 247, 284
Lowther Hall, Westmorland 139, 175, 197,
    224
Lowther, Christopher 242
Lowther, John (1605–1675), 1st Baronet
    Lowther 115n.82, 152, 180, 187, 189,
    191–192, 196–197, 214, 218, 220, 224
Lowther, John (1628–1668), 188–189, 284
Lowther, John (1655–1700), 2nd Baronet
    Lowther 197, 224, 284

Lucas, Mary, Baroness Lucas 216, 278
Lullingworth Castle, Kent 65n.342, 279
Lynch, Kathleen 5n.15

Machell family 226n.4
Machell, Henry 226, 227n.8, 228, 232, 237–238, 247
Machell, Hugh 246, 285
Machell, Lancelot (servant to Thomas Strickland) 249, 253, 255, 285
Machell, Lancelot, Sir 228, 246–247, 285
Machell, Susan 226n.4, 237, 285
Machell, Thomas 157n.151, 226n.4, 285, 301
Mad Lover, The (1617) 47
Mainwaring, Henry 58, 285
Manners, George, 7th Earl of Rutland 28, 241, 285
Manners, Katherine, Duchess of Buckingham 89, 285
Marsh, Christopher 34–35, 38–39, 42, 44–45, 52, 58, 64, 67, 77, 126, 139, 285
Mary II, Queen of England 208
Mary of Modena, Queen consort of England 218–219
Mary, Queen of Scot 28, 122n.25
Matthews, Tobias, Archibishop of York 45, 285
Maynard, John 138, 285
Mayney, Anthony 19
Meditation Upon the Lord's Prayer (1619) 76n.410
memoir 6
Menerell, Mr 22
Metamorphoses (1612) 88
Middleton, Roger 255, 285
Middleton, William 255
Milbourne, Richard, Bishop of St David's 27, 32, 37, 285
Molineux, Alice 74, 286
Molineux, Roger 197, 286
Monck, George, 1st Duke of Albemarle 152, 286
Montagu, Elizabeth (1611–1654), Countess of Lindsey 28, 33, 286
Montagu, Elizabeth (1611–1672), Lady Hatton 202, 215–217, 286
Montagu, Henry, 1st Earl of Manchester 44, 49, 286
Montaigne, Michel de 44, 50, 305

Montgomery, Margaret 259
Mordaunt, James 162, 286
Mordaunt, John 162, 286
Mordaunt, John, 1st Earl of Peterborough 36, 162, 286
More, William 43n.171
Morgan, Elizabeth 54, 286
Morison, Bridget 55, 286
Morville, Ada de 203n.233
Morville, Hugh de 203n.233
Mother Shipton's well (Dripping Well), Yorkshire 149
Murgatroyd, Jacob 237, 286
Murray, George 22, 286
Murray, Molly 5n.15
Murray, William, Lord Tullibardine 22, 286
Musgrave, Frances 286
Musgrave, Isabel 204n.234
Musgrave, Mary 203, 248, 286
Musgrave, Philip 180, 187, 191, 203, 211, 214, 218, 220, 228, 263, 286
Musgrave, Richard 203, 248, 287
Musgrave, William 229, 287

Nanson, Philip 242, 287
Naunton, Robert 90, 287
Naworth Castle, Cumberland 43n.163, 101, 129, 184, 260–261
Neville, Anne 216
Neville, Cecily 35, 38–39, 40, 44, 287
Neville, Edward, 6th Baron Abergavenny 29–30, 287
Neville, Elizabeth 74, 287
Neville, Henry, 7th Baron Abergavenny 36, 66, 70, 92, 287
Neville, Mary 'Moll' 27, 35, 50, 65, 66, 69, 76, 80, 81, 87–89, 287
Neville, Thomas 36
Newdigate, Richard 134, 134, 138, 146, 287
Nicholls, Augustine 41, 287
Nicholls, Elizabeth 144–145, 168–169, 189–190, 238, 259
Noel, Mary 198, 287
Nonsuch Palace 24, 25
North Hall, Herefordshire 22, 24–25, 97, 115, 155n.143, 244
North, Dudley 80, 84n.481, 90n.523, 287
North, John 80, 287
North, Roger 80, 287

Northampton House, London 39, 75
Northern Rebellion *see* Rising of the North
Nussbaum, Felicity 5, 5n.16

Ogle, Mary 141, 287
Oldenbarnevelt, Johan van 471, 287
Oldsworth, Arnold 90, 287
Orfeur, Cuthbert 82, 287
Orfeur, Elizabeth 231, 291
Osberton, Mr 51, 288
Otway, John 166, 235, 288
Overbury, Thomas 47, 67n.358
Ovid (Publius Ovidius Naso) 88

Palace of Whitehall 17, 26n.4, 43, 47, 48n.218, 49n.225, 60, 72, 82, 106, 110–117 *passim*, 152, 193, 202, 207–208, 219, 229, 234–235, 238–240, 246
Palmer, Thomas 19
Parker, John 126, 130, 135–136, 140, 144, 146, 150, 288
Parker, Thomas 70
Parson, Robert 88
Paston, Catherine 16, 288
Pate, Edmund 227n.7
Pate, Frances 227, 237, 240n.253, 250, 256, 288
Pate, Marmaduke 227n.7
Pattison, John 238, 258, 288
Paulet, William, 4th Marquess of Winchester 21, 288
Paulett, Jane 184, 288
Pendragon castle 1n.3, 116, *161*, 153–223 *passim*
Penn, Mrs 92, 288
Pennant, Thomas 7, 305
Penruddock's uprising (1655)
Penshurst, Kent 65, 92
Penyston, Thomas 86, 90, 93, 288
Percy, Dorothy, Countess of Leicester 30, 67, 72
Percy, Henry, 2nd Earl of Northumberland 221n.266
Percy, Henry, 9th Earl of Northumberland 17, 82, 288
Percy, Lucy, Countess of Carlisle 66, 70, 288
Perkins, William 61n.312
Perrot, Penelope 65, 90, 288

Petley family 53, 288
Petty, Thomas 34, 288
Philippe of France, Duke of Orléans 156
Phillip IV of Spain 39, 288
Pickering, Christopher 37, 289
Pigott, Frances 19, 289
Pinder, Richard 235
Pleasure Reconciled (1618) 72n.383
Pond, William 24, 289
Praise of Private Life, The 78
Preston, John 238, 289
Preston, Katherine 184, 289
Privy Council 15, 17, 31, 52, 55, 80, 83, 92, 125n.39, 233
Puckering, Frances, Lady Grantham 28, 34, 52, 289
Puckering, Katherine 28, 289
Puleston, John 126, 130–131, 289
Purchas's Pilgrims (1625) 38
Pursglove, Dorothy 231, 289

Queen's College, Oxford 69n.369, 127, 134, 137, 141, 242, 245n.64

Rainbow, Edward, Bishop of Carlisle 55n.270, 123n.31, 240, 240n.52, 246, 255, 263, 263n.108, 296, 305
Rainsford, Richard 180, 184–185, 187, 191, 220, 223, 289
Raleigh, Walter 54, 74n.391, 289
Raleigh, Walter 'Wat' 36, 289
Ramsbury Manor, Wiltshire 112, 115, 117, 168–169
Randes, Edward 53–54, 56, 59, 66, 79, 93, 289
Rawling, Cuthbert 237, 246, 289
Relation of a Journey...Containing a description of the Turkish Empire (1615) 48, 60, 301
Renolds, Mr 81
Revolt of the Northern Earls *see* Rising of the North
Reynoldson, Richard 237, 289
Rhône (Rhodanus) river, Geneva 102
Rich, Charles 80–81, 289
Rich, Henry 80–81, 289
Rich, Lettice 76, 82–83, 289
Rich, Robert, 1st Earl of Warwick 79–81, 289
Richmond Palace 15, 17

Rider, Mary 88, 284, 289
Rising of the North (Revolt of the Northern Earls, Northern Rebellion, 1569) 122n.25
Rivers, George 30, 32–33, 37–38, 41, 42–45, 50–51, 290
Rivers, Sir George 63, 290
Robbins, Tom 72, 290
Robinson, Richard 67
Rockingham Castle, Northamptonshire 19
Rodes, Francis 196–197, 290
Rodes, Jane 196–197, 290
Rokeby, Grace, Countess of Holderness 59
Rose Castle, Cumberland 240, 246, 296
Roydon, Joan 46, 48, 49, 61, 69, 81, 290
Rupert, Prince (of the Rhine) 158, 179, 201, 208, 290
Russell, Anne, Countess of Warwick 1, 15, 17–19, 20–24, 61, 90, 96, 98, 111, 239, 243–244, 250, 290
Russell, Anne, Countess of Worcester 61, 63n.317, 74, 290
Russell, Edward (1643-1714) 194–195, 290
Russell, Edward, 3rd Earl of Bedford 18, 19, 29, 74, 92, 111, 290
Russell, Elizabeth 'Bess' 28n.36
Russell, Elizabeth, Countess of Bath 21–24, 104n.47, 111, 269, 290
Russell, Francis, 2nd Earl of Bedford 21, 90, 109, 111
Russell, Francis, 4th Earl of Bedford 18, 24–25, 28–29, 61–63, 69, 74–75, 92, 110, 112, 113, 142, 228, 244, 271, 279, 290
Russell, Francis (son of Francis Russell, 4th Earl of Bedford) 75
Russell, John, 1st Earl of Bedford 90, 109, 111
Russell, John, Lord Russell 28n.36, 61n.317, 290
Russell, Margaret, Countess of Cumberland *passim*
  Anne Clifford's visit to Westmorland 30–31
  death 36–41
  death of sons 95n.7, 96–97, 239
  marital difficulties 18–22
Russell, William, 1st Baron Russell of Thornhaugh 18, 21, 24, 62n.322, 244, 284, 290

Russell, William, 1st Duke of Bedford 184, 194, 272
Ruthven, Barbara 48–49, 63, 69, 290
Ryder, Mr 60–61, 290
Rye House Plot (1683) 184n.196

Sackville, Anne (1650-1722), Countess of Home 214, 290
Sackville, Anne, Lady Beauchamp (1586-1664) 32–33, 35, 45, 47, 53, 55, 62, 64, 71, 74–75, 80–82, 84–85, 89, 92, 268, 290
Sackville, Anne, Lady Glemham 62, 89n.512, 290
Sackville, Cecily 35, 52–53, 55, 62, 74–75, 81, 84, 91, 290
Sackville, Edward (d. 1646) 236, 291
Sackville, Edward 4th Earl of Dorset 3, 42, 55, 57, 63–64, 67–68, 70, 82, 87, 92, 107–109, 114, 126, 172n.180, 236, 275, 291
Sackville, Elizabeth, Countess De La Warr 8
Sackville, Isabella 3, 102, 113–114, 128, 135n.90, 133–157 *passim* 160, 167, 223, 229n.24, 261, 266–268, 273–274, 291
Sackville, John Frederick, 3rd Duke of Dorset 8
Sackville, Margaret 3, 10, 291, 295–296
  childhood 31–45
  Countess of Thanet 60n.302, 74, 80, 110, 120, 125, 131–282 *passim*
Sackville, Mary, Countess of Amherst 8
Sackville, Mary, Lady Abergavenny 70, 291
Sackville, Richard (1649-1712) 214, 291
Sackville, Richard, 3rd Earl of Dorset 1–3, 16, 19n.38, 26–95 *passim*
  death 107, 226–263 *passim*
  marriage to Anne Clifford 2, 102, 103–110, 253
Sackville, Robert, 2nd Earl of Dorset 103, 107–108, 253, 290, 293
Sackville, Thomas, 1st Earl of Dorset 34, 63–64
Sackville, Thomas, Lord Buckhurst (son of Anne Clifford and Richard Sackville) 3, 91n.530, 103, 104n.45, 107, 241–242
Sackville-West, Vita 4, 8
St Anne's Hospital, Appleby, Yorkshire 123, 128, 142n.15, 159, 224

St Augustine's Abbey, Canterbury, Kent 154
St Bride's church, London 39, 69, 288, 292
St John, Anne, Lady Effingham 26, 45, 61, 69, 293
St John, Margaret, Countess of Bedford 109, 290
St John, Oliver 31, 138, 138n.103, 141, 143, 293
St Lawrence's church, Appleby, Westmorland 105, 136, 143, 158, 224–225, 227, 263–264, 271
St Mary's chapel, Mallerstang, Westmorland 171–172, 183, 187, 203, 299
St Michael's church, Bongate 146, 158
St Michael's church, Brough, Westmorland 182n.192
St Ninian's church (Ninekirks), Westmorland 149, 161–163, 227, 230, 233, 236, 239, 243, 246, 254, 258, 260, 278
St Paul's Cathedral 185
St Wilfred's church, Brougham 146, 162–163

Salisbury Cathedral, Wiltshire 117, 119
Salisbury House, London 51, 85
Salkeld, John 142, 291
Salvetti, Amerigo 27, 291
Salzman, Paul 66n.349, 305
Sandford, Frances 192, 291
Sandford, John 231, 291
Sandford, Richard 192, 291
Sandford, Thomas 226, 291
Sandys, George 48, 291
Sandys, Hester 93, 291
Saul (or Sewell) Mrs 239
Saunders, Thomas 199, 291
Savoy Palace 47, 86, 98
Scott, James, 1st Duke of Monmouth 179, 291
Sedgewick, George 11, 126, 136, 138, 189n.206, 143, 204, 226, 231, 291, 301, 304
Sedgewick, Thomas 189
Selby, William 36, 74, 87, 91, 292
Selden, John 28n.28, 60n.301, 295
Sellinger, Thomas 24
Sermon Preached at the Funeral of the Right Honorable Anne, Countess of Pembroke (1676) 123n.31, 263n.108

Seward, William 7, 20n.51, 306
Seymour, Edward, 1st Earl of Hertford (d. 1621) 52, 82, 86
Seymour, Edward, Lord Beauchamp (1586–1618) 35, 52–53, 71, 292
Seymour, Elizabeth, Lady Knightley 19–20, 283, 292
Seymour, Jane, Lady Dungarvan 166–167, 292
Seymour, Jane, Queen consort of England 77
Seymour, Marie, Countess of Winchelsea 167, 292
Sheffield Castle 254
Sheffield, Edmund, 1st Earl of Musgrave 38n.118, 43n.163, 45, 60, 78, 105
Shelton, Ethelreda 'Audrey' 19, 277
Sherburne, Edwin 84, 292
Shrewsbury House, London 26
Sidney, Barbara 'Babs' 67–68, 292
Sidney, Dorothy 67
Sidney, Mary, Countess of Pembroke 85, 117, 292
Sidney, Mary, Lady Wroth 65, 67, 292
Sidney, Philip 18n.26, 66n.349, 117, 292
Sidney, Robert, Viscount de L'Isle, 1st Earl of Leicester 66–67, 292
Sidney, Robert, 2nd Earl of Leicester 30, 16, 72n.384, 292
Simpton, Judith 29, 55, 58, 91, 94, 292
Sisley, Jane 62
Skinne, Mr 84, 292
Skinne, Sarah 84, 292
Skipton town and castle, Westmorland ix, x,1n.3, 2n.9, 11, 27n.23, 33n.71, 37, 86, 95, 96, 99, 101, 101n.37, 107, 112, *120*, 115–251 *passim*
Skura, Meredith Anne 5, 5n.14, 17
Sleddall, Jane 227n.9, 237, 292
Slingsby, Francis 91, 93, 293
Slingsby, Mary 91
Smallwood, Allan 224, 231, 293
Smallwood, Catherine 231
Smallwood, Charles 231
Smith, Leonard 261, 293
Smith, Mr, a doctor 77
Smith, Thomas 189n.206
Smith, William 50, 293
Smyth, Adam 5, 5n.15, 19, 7n.22

Smyth, Elizabeth 246, 293
Snape Castle, Yorkshire 155
Somer, Paul van 60n.302, 89–90
Somerset House, London 46–47, 81, 85, 98n.21, 179
Somerset, Catherine 82
Somerset, Edward, 4th Earl of Worcester 26, 50, 293
Somerset, Henry, 1st Marquess of Worcester 61, 293
Sorocold, Thomas 79
Sort, Edmund 237, 293
Southey, Robert 11, 12, 306
Spedding, Margaret 244, 293
Spedding, William 227–262 *passim*, 293
Speght, Thomas 60n.301
Spence, Richard T. 2, 3, 20n.52, 27n.23, 43n.163, 120n.14, 121n.18, 306
Spencer, Alice, Countess of Derby 54, 55, 293
Spencer, Anne, Countess of Dorset 53, 61, 71, 81, 88–89, 106, 293
Spencer, Elizabeth, Lady Compton and Countess of Northampton 46
Spencer, Mary 90, 293
Spencer, Robert, 1st Baron Spencer of Wormleighton 20, 293
Spenser, Edmund 50
Stanley, Charles, 8th Earl of Derby 139
Stanley, Ferdinando, 5th Earl of Derby 54
Stanley, Frances 74, 294
Stanley, Robert 220–221, 294
Stanley, William, 9th Earl of Derby 221
Stanley, William, Lord Monteagle 106
Starbotton Old Hall, Yorkshire 187
Steele, William 134, 294
Stewart, James, Master of Blantyre 140n.109
Stewart, Patrick, 2nd Earl of Orkney 22, 294
Stidolph, Francis 22, 294
Strickland, Allan 10, 226, 237, 259, 294
Strickland, Thomas 10, 226n.6, 227n.7, 249, 253, 255, 294
Strongy, Roy 20
Stuart, Arbella 23, 74n.391, 292, 294
Stuart, Edgar, Duke of Cambridge 208n.247
Stuart, Elizabeth (1610–1673), Countess of Arundel 219, 294

Stuart, Elizabeth, Queen of Bohemia, the Winter Queen 20, 21, 24–25, 85, 92, 158, 162, 183n.193, 294
Stuart, Henry, Duke of Gloucester 152, 162, 294
Stuart, Henry, Prince of Wales 2, 19, 20, 24, 43, 78n.421, 108, 208, 285, 294
Stuart, Ludovic, 2nd Duke of Lennox 21, 48, 86n.493
Stuart, Mary (1631–1660) Princess of Orange, 152, 207, 294
Stuart, Walter 91
Suckling, John 77, 84, 90, 294
Suffolk House *see* Northampton House,
Supplications of the Saints 79
Sutton Hospital, London 107
Sutton Place, Kent 98, 104, 114
Sutton, Edward, 5th Baron Dudley 30, 80n.437, 276, 279
Sutton, Margaret 86, 294
Sutton, Mary, Countess of Home 39, 80–81, 294
Sutton, Mrs 238, 294
Sutton's Hospital (the Charter House), London 107
Swarton, Sarah 76, 294
Swinden, Arthur 6, 237, 247, 250, 252, 258, 295
Symondson family 187

Talbot, Alethea, Countess of Arundel 26–47, 46–47, 69, 73, 295
Talbot, Elizabeth, Countess of Kent 28, 46, 60n.301, 166, 278, 295
Talbot, Gilbert, 7th Earl of Shrewsbury 33, 117
Talbot, Mary, Countess of Pembroke 48, 112, 117, 295
Tassis, Juan de, 2nd Count of Villamediana 24, 295
Taylor, Anne 22, 295
Taylor, John 70, 84, 88, 295
Temple, Anne 188, 295
Temple, Martha 86, 90, 93, 288
tenants, Westmorland 3n.11
Thacker, Gilbert 81
Thanet House, Aldersgate Street, London 113–222 *passim*
Theobalds, Herefordshire 18, 54, 81, 83

Thorpe, Francis 121, 150, 295
Three Brothers Tree, Whinfell forest, Westmorland 197, 218
Throckmorton, Elizabeth 27, 82, 295
Thwait, John 259
Todd, Thomas 42, 295
Toeni, Margaret de 1
Tom Fool 44
Tower of London 27n.19, 40n.502, 136, 141, 146, 222, 294
Treaty of Breda (1667) 173n.181, 188
Tresnel, Marquis de 84
Trill, Suzanne 5n.15
Tufton, Anne (b. and d. 1634) 129, 266, 295
Tufton, Anne 134, 139–140, 158, 170, 174–175, 180, 183–185, 190, 193, 195, 200–201, 208–209, 211, 213–214, 216, 220–223, 267, 295
Tufton, Cecil 207, 295
Tufton, Cecily (1648–1672), Lady Hatton 85n.485, 139–140, 158, 167, 170, 174–175, 178, 180–181, 183, 185, 190, 193, 200–205, 215, 215n.251, 217, 221, 229n.22, 266, 296
Tufton, Cecily, (d. 1653) 89, 296
Tufton, Cecily, Countess of Rutland 89, 296
Tufton, Charles 207, 296
Tufton, Diana 207, 223, 296
Tufton, Frances 113, 136, 138, 143, 146–150, 167–170, 174, 176, 178–179, 180–184, 182, 208, 266, 296
Tufton, George 120, 139–140, 169–170, 174, 176–177, 182–183, 195–196, 201, 267, 296
Tufton, John (1608–1664) 2nd Earl of Thanet 110, 115, 125,129–130, 136, 140, 172, 174, 176, 266, 296
Tufton, John (1638–1680) 4th Earl of Thanet 113, 125, 127–128, 131, 134–138, 143–150, 157, 167–176, 181, 194–195, 213–214, 216, 251n.81, 263, 267, 296
Tufton, Margaret, Lady Coventry 113, 129,131, 135, 141, 144–145, 149–151, 153, 158, 161, 164, 188, 190, 197, 216, 266, 296
Tufton, Mary 126, 139–140, 158, 170, 174–175, 180, 183, 185, 190, 193, 195, 200–201, 206, 211, 213, 216–217, 219, 222, 267, 296

Tufton, Nicholas (1578–1631) 3rd Earl of Thanet 111–113, 121, 125–127, 129–130, 134n.86, 136, 139–140, 146, 150, 163n.160, 167, 173–175, 180–181, 186, 191, 202n.232, 266–267, 296
Tufton, Nicholas (1631–1639) 1st Earl of Thanet 110, 113, 296
Tufton, Richard 5th Earl of Thanet 113, 140, 147, 157, 169–170, 174, 176, 181, 194–196, 213, 216, 266, 296
Tufton, Sackville 140, 147, 169–170, 174, 176–177, 182, 190, 193, 195–196, 213, 267, 296
Tufton, Thomas 6th Earl of Thanet 10–11, 113, 157, 174, 176, 181, 188–189, 192, 196, 203, 216, 220, 224, 225n.270, 235n.41, 251n.81, 267, 296
Turner, John 142, 144, 168–169, 189, 236, 238, 296
Turnor, Christopher 158–159, 165, 170–171, 173, 184, 187, 191, 196, 205, 296
Twentyman, John 240, 255, 296
Twisden, Thomas 155, 170–171, 173, 177, 296
Tyrwhitt, Ursula, Lady Sheffield 60, 296

Ubank, Thomas 252
Unton, Croke 144, 274
Uvedale, Elizabeth 200, 296–297
Uvedale, William 200

Van Dyck, Anthony 112
Vane, Henry 89, 91, 297
Vaux, Edward 36, 297
Vavasour, Anne 18–20, 23, 297
Vavasour, Catherine 88, 297
Vavasour, Peter 88, 297
Vavasour, Thomas 85n.489
Vernon, Elizabeth, Countess of Southampton 21, 297, 299
Veteripont, Idonea de 153, 160, 297
Veteripont, Isabella 153n.138, 160, 267
Veteripont, Robert de, 1st Lord Veteripont 203n.233
Veteripont, Robert de, 3rd Lord Veteripont 99, 160
Villiers, George, Duke of Buckingham 26, 46n.205, 47–48, 52, 76, 89n.517, 297
Villiers, John 64, 88
Villiers, Susan 46, 297

Vincent, Gabriel 143, 146, 182, 247, 297
Voronstov, Catherine, Countess of Pembroke 8–9

Wade, Cuthbert 171, 183, 297
Walker family 142n.115
Walker, Isaak 237, 297
Walker, James 141–142, 297
Waller, Thomas 196, 297
Wallop, Henry 23, 297
Walter, David 211, 297
Walter, John, 3rd Baronet Walter, 222, 297
Walter, John, a Baron of the Exchequer 39, 58, 70, 206, 297
Walter, John, servant to John Gilmore 189, 297
Walter, William (1604–75) 1st Baronet Walter 206, 216, 219, 222, 297
Walter, William (d. 1694) 2nd Baronet Walter 206, 211, 216–217, 219, 222, 267, 297
Wandesford, Elizabeth, Lady Wharton 130n.68, 298–299
Warburton, Peter 121, 131, 298
Warburton, Richard 23, 298
Warwick Castle, Warwickshire 252
Waste, Thomas 90, 298
Watkinson, William 10
Watson, Catherine 19
Watson, Edward 19, 298
Watson, Elizabeth (Needham) 19, 58, 298
Watson, Elizabeth (Worsopp) 58, 69, 298
Watson, Mary 19
Watson, Mr 37–38
Watson, Temperance 19
Watson, Thomas 88
Waugh, John, Bishop of Carlisle 255n.91
Waugh, Margaret 255, 298
Webb, Gregory 23
Webster, Dorothy 243
Webster, Isabell 261
Webster, John 227–262 *passim*, 298
Wells, John 207, 298
Wenman, William 211, 298
Wentworth, John 67–68
Westminster Abbey 28
Weston, Anne 83n.470, 299
Weston, Richard 67n.358
Whalley, Thomas 231, 298

Wharton Hall, Westmorland 116n.85, 130, 165, 182, 201, 203–204, 211–212, 221
Wharton, Anne 171, 211, 298
Wharton, Elizabeth, Countess of Lindsey 130, 298
Wharton, George (d. 1609) 140, 298
Wharton, Goodwin 211, 221, 298
Wharton, Hugh 230, 298
Wharton, Margaret, Lady Ross 171, 211, 298
Wharton, Margaret, Lady Wotton 28, 64, 74–75, 154, 298
Wharton, Mary 171, 211, 299
Wharton, Philip 3rd Lord Wharton 37n.107, 95–96, 116n.116, 251, 266, 299
Wharton, Philip, 4th Baron Wharton 130, 140, 146–147, 171, 195, 211, 221, 230, 299
Wharton, Thomas (1615–1684) 130, 146–147, 152, 195, 242, 248, 299
Wharton, Thomas (1648–1715) 211, 221, 230, 299
Whinfell forest 30, 41, 43, 66, 115, 131, 140–259 *passim*
Whitaker, Thomas viii, 11, 120, 306
Whitchard, Alexander 138, 143–144, 299
Whittington, Timothy 30, 299
Widdrington, Mary 169n.174
Wildboar Fell, Westmorland 203
Wilde, William 209–211, 214, 218, 299
William II of Orange 152, 207
Williams, John 83, 299
Williamson, George 11–12, 78n.429, 306
Williamson, Joseph 189n.206
Willison, Robert 230, 236, 245, 256–257, 299
Willoughby, Mistress 29, 38, 40, 54–55, 65, 68, 92, 299
Wilton House, Wilshire 102, 112–113, 115, 117, 193
Windham, Hugh 134, 138, 141, 143, 299
Windsor, Berkshire 21
Woburn Abbey, Bedfordshire 109, 157, 184, 194
Woodgate, Thomas 31, 46, 50, 299
Woodstock, Oxfordshire 23, 68
Woolrich, William 37, 61, 63, 299
Worcester House, London 50
Wotton, Edward 154, 298
Wotton, Henry 29n.48, 52n.248, 291
Wray, Frances, Countess of Warwick 74, 79, 80n.442, 299

Wray, James 92, 299
Wrest Park, Bedfordshire 19
Wright, Edward 96
Wright, Rowland 172–173, 299
Wright, Thomas 228, 233, 236, 247, 258, 262, 299
Wriothesley, Henry, 3rd Earl of Southampton 17, 18, 21n.58, 83, 297, 299
Wriothesley, Rachel, Lady Russell 184, 299

Yaxley, Robert 37, 91, 93, 300
Yelverton, Frances 229, 300
Yelverton, Henry 49, 300
York House, London 55

Zouche, Edward 85, 300
Zouche, Edward la, 11th Baron Zouche 65, 300
Zwicker, Steven N. 5n.19